THE CLASSICS OF WESTERN SPIRITUALITY

Catherine of Siena
THE DIALOGUE

TRANSLATION AND INTRODUCTION
BY
SUZANNE NOFFKE, O.P.

PREFACE
BY
GIULIANA CAVALLINI

PAULIST PRESS
NEW YORK • RAMSEY • TORONTO

Cover Art
The artist, JOSEPH TREPICCIONE, studied illustration and advertising at Paier School of Art in New Haven, Connecticut, receiving a post-graduate scholarship for further study there. Mr. Trepiccione has taught graphic design and currently works for Thompson Advertising in Windsor, Connecticut in addition to doing free-lance illustration. This work was inspired by the portrait of Catherine by Andrea Vanni in the Church of St. Dominic in Siena.

Design: Barbini, Pesce & Noble, Inc.

Library of Congress
Catalog Card Number: 79-56755

ISBN: 0-8091-0295-1 (cloth)
       0-8091-2233-2 (paper)

Published by Paulist Press
Editorial office: 1865 Broadway, New York, N.Y. 10023
Business office: 545 Island Road, Ramsey, N.J. 07446

Printed and bound in the
United States of America

Contents

Editor of this Volume

SUZANNE NOFFKE, O.P., is a member of the Sisters of St. Dominic of Racine, Wisconsin. After completing her undergraduate studies and teaching for four years at the elementary and secondary levels, she pursued graduate studies in linguistics at the University of Wisconsin, completed her dissertation research in Israel, Rome, and London under an NDEA-Fulbright-Hays Fellowship in 1966–1967, and received her doctorate from the University of Wisconsin in 1968. She has taught at Dominican College in Racine and Holy Redeemer College in Waterford, Wisconsin, and served as her religious congregation's president from 1970 to 1976. Her previous publications include four adult audiovisual programs: *A Foundation for Dialogue* (Sisters of St. Dominic, 1965), *Churches in the 70's* (Alba House Communications, 1969), *Christians and Jews: A Troubled Brotherhood* (Alba House Communications, 1972), and *Woman, You're Beautiful!* (Leadership Conference of Women Religious, Region IX, 1975), as well as a number of shorter works and articles. She is presently living in Middleton, Wisconsin, and is engaged full time in research, writing, and lecturing on Catherine of Siena and on the question of contemplation in relation to active ministry.

Author of the Preface

Professor GIULIANA CAVALLINI is a member of the Roman congregation of the Missionaries of the Schools. She has taught and lectured not only in Rome but at Fordham University and Middlebury College, and has served as an Italian delegate to UNESCO. Her scholarship has produced critical editions of the *Dialogue* and *Prayers* of Catherine of Siena as well as a number of analytical and interpretive works on the saint in Italian. She is presently director of the National Center of Catherinian Studies in Rome.

Acknowledgments

Many debts of gratitude need expression as this translation of Catherine's *Dialogue* reaches print. First there is Catherine herself, whose presence to this work has been a precious personal gift. So also has the presence of Sister Rose Catherine Moser. Thanks are due to my Racine Dominican community for giving me time and space for what became a full-time occupation, and to my family and friends, too numerous to name, who provided the kind of grandstand encouragement that invigorates the sometime heaviness of research and toil over a manuscript. Professor Giuliana Cavallini has been most gracious in lending me the fruits of her own research and the use of her Italian edition of the *Dialogue* as the basic text for this translation, which she has read and corrected as only she could. Among the libraries I have used, the staffs of the University of Wisconsin, Aquinas Institute of Theology, the Library of Congress, and the New York Public Library have been outstandingly accommodating. Diane Selinske rescued me from deadline panic by transforming my often near-illegible script into type. Finally, there are no thanks adequate to Sister Denise Frohmader, who has lent her critical ear for hours on end, put up with all my ups and downs and comings and goings as the work progressed, given weeks of evenings to the tedium of proofreading, and been friend, support, and consummate sharer along the way.

FOREWORD

Catherine of Siena moved in remarkably wide circles for a woman of fourteenth-century Italy. She was a mystic whose plunge into God plunged her deep into the affairs of society, Church, and the souls of all who came under her influence. Her correspondence was prolific (nearly four hundred of her letters are extant), drawing in popes and politicians as well as the closer circle of her friends and followers. It was with all of these in mind that she composed her *Dialogue* (she called it simply "my book") in 1377–1378, about two years before her death at the age of thirty-three.

The *Dialogue* reflects in its content and even at times in its form some of Catherine's earlier letters and recorded mystical experiences. But here all is drawn together and expanded into a more cohesive whole, in the form of an exchange between God and herself. Its aim is obviously the instruction and encouragement of all those whose spiritual welfare was her concern, for there is reference to all their situations in its pages.

In the opening pages of the *Dialogue* Catherine presents a series of questions or petitions to God the Father, each of which receives a response and amplification. There is the magnificent symbolic portrayal of Christ as the bridge. There are specific discussions of discernment, tears (true and false spiritual emotion), truth, the sacramental heart ("mystic body") of the Church, divine providence, obedience. These headings, however, can be misleading. The whole of the *Dialogue* is more like a great tapestry to which Catherine adds stitch upon stitch until she is satisfied that she has communicated all she can of what she has learned of the way of God. It is not so much a treatise to be read as it is a conversation to be entered into with earnest leisure and leisurely earnest.

PREFACE

To write a few words of introduction to Suzanne Noffke's English translation of St. Catherine of Siena's *Dialogue* is for me to revive emotions long past and never forgotten.

It all happened in Washington, D.C. in January 1965. A letter from Italy suggesting that I should take from the *Dialogue* my subjects for a series of articles on St. Catherine caused me to go over the table of contents in search of inspiring topics. I then noticed the recurrence all through the book of three elements: petition, answer, thanksgiving—the ordinary components of a conversation—and it suddenly occurred to me that the framework of the book must rest on them.

My acquaintance with the *Dialogue* dated many years back, and its fourfold division has always puzzled me. Why were the first eight chapters not accounted for? Why had the first selected part been named *Treatise on Discretion*, if only the first and second of its fifty-six chapters dealt with that virtue? And the same anomaly was even more striking in the next, the so-called *Treatise on Prayer*, where seventy chapters were named after the contents of the first two. It was only in the third and fourth parts that the headings of the "treatises" *on Providence* and *on Obedience* were truly indicative of the matter dealt with.

Modern editors had tried their best to connect the four treatises with the four petitions which Catherine announces at the very beginning of her book: a desperate effort and one doomed to failure, that of trying to find correspondence between a positive statement and the product of fancy. No wonder, then, if all their arguments left me incredulous, and that very incredulity fostered a hope that the matter in the *Dialogue* might find some day a better and truer division. And it probably was that secret hope that, on my noticing the sequence petition-answer-thanksgiving, made me think that the key to a more rational division of the *Dialogue* should be sought there.

The idea was extremely exciting, but the key had to be tested in

PREFACE

order to ascertain whether it would be of use in opening a truer perspective on the genuine structure of the book. This is what I immediately started doing, and as work progressed and something which "made sense" began to take shape, I began to doubt that such a simple and natural idea should not have occurred to anybody before then.

Both a kind of mistrust that the privilege of the discovery, skipping the many learned people who had devoted themselves to the study of Catherine's writings, should have been reserved to my little self, and a sort of jealousy of the treasure that had come within my grasp, caused me, once I was back in Rome, to examine as many editions of the *Dialogue* as I could get hold of, from Azzoguidi's "editio princeps" (Bologna, 1472/75) to the most recent ones, including translations into Latin and modern languages. To my great relief, nothing even vaguely resembling the plan resulting from the use of my key was to be found in any of them.

But the quest had one positive result: it made me aware of the irrational way that absurd fourfold division had started. The older editions, up to that of 1547, have no other cuts but those of the chapters; it was Onorio Farri who, in editing the book (1579), gave undue importance to the word "trattato" which was included in the headings of four chapters, where it just pointed out that the chapter was "dealing" with a particular subject. Farri stressed another meaning of the word, that of "treatise," by printing it in big capitals inserted in a special frame, and putting it at the head of as many chapters as happened to follow until the next heading including the fatal word "trattato."

Farri's behavior is not too surprising if we consider that treatises were the fashion of the sixteenth century—not so surprising at least as the fortune of such a poor contrivance, which was accepted without questioning by subsequent editors until the present day.

It was, then, a discovery, and an important one. The reconstruction of the primitive plan set forth the unity of the work and its long hidden inspiring idea. Catherine's book could no longer be considered a haphazard collection of writings unrelated to one another, a kind of amorphous conglomerate, probably the work of her disciples, as had been asserted more than once. It proved, in fact, an organic work with all its parts strictly linked to a master idea in logical connection, after a continuous guiding thread which is announced at the very beginning of the book, when we are told that "a soul" who has already had a taste of God's love yearns for a better knowledge of truth, that she may love better. This thread running throughout the book is the theme of truth

PREFACE

fostering love, which is fully developed under the image of Christ-the-bridge, whose ascent is a progress to the perfection of love—which is the perfection of human nature—in the light of that truth which alone can attract the heart of man: the supreme truth of God's love for man. It is ever present—as the backbone of the framework—and inspires Catherine's closing prayer that she may be clad with eternal Truth.

This is, as briefly as possible, what the discovery of the "key" amounted to. My "revolutionary" edition of the *Dialogue* (1968) was appreciated both by scholars and literary critics and by humbler readers, who found that Catherine's book was now much easier to understand. This could not but give me joy. But I had realized from the first that the gift of truth with which I had been privileged was not my own: it must be shared with everybody. The new edition made it available to Italian readers, but I was well aware of the fact that beyond the boundaries of my own country and language there were millions and millions of people to whom the *Dialogue* might do a lot of good if translated in their own languages. Opportunities for translation into English appeared every now and then, but sooner or later dissolved, owing to the great difficulty of turning Catherine's language into modern, readable phrasing.

It was quite natural, then, that when I was told that an American woman meant to translate the book in one year, I was rather skeptical. I was not acquainted with the person who was willing to undertake such a desperate job. Suzanne Noffke was still a stranger to me. Then we met. She had brought a copy of the translation she had completed within one year, and we had a wonderful time over it. The elegant fluency of her English which faithfully rendered Catherine's thought without any visible effort filled me with happy wonder. It was as if a long cherished dream had come true, as if a miracle had taken place—a miracle for the benefit of numberless people all over the world.

Today's world is ready to meet Catherine. Men and women eager to realize themselves can find an ideal model to imitate in her singular life, so unlike that of the average woman or man in her time—a model of dedication in courage and humility. Her doctrine is all centered on the fundamental mysteries of the Christian faith—the mystery of the Trinity, and that of the Word of God made flesh for the redemption of man—but her rendering of them is enlivened by their living presence in her life. Faith was no abstraction to her, but a living tie with her Beloved. Her love of truth and her straightforward language aiming at the core of things come to us as a joyful relief from the many compromises and falsehoods weighing on us in our daily life. And above all she presents to us her motherly heart, a heart ever ready to understand and to be compassionate, as well as to encourage and to stimulate.

All this may explain why almost the whole world is now moved by the approaching sixth centenary of Catherine's passage from earth to heaven, and how celebrations are being prepared almost everywhere. Of all such undertakings, those aiming at making St. Catherine's voice audible to the largest possible number of people are, I believe, the most praiseworthy. They will enable Catherine to speak to every single man and woman, and whisper to the secret ear of their souls the words that will make them "better and wiser," as she was wont to do to whoever approached her in her lifetime.

Such is the success I heartily wish this book.

Rome, October 4, 1979   Giuliana Cavallini

INTRODUCTION

The Roman Catholic Church in all its history has granted but two of its women the title of doctor: Teresa of Avila and Catherine of Siena. The date was October 4, 1970; the pontiff, Paul VI. Six centuries lie between the living voice of Catherine and that date, but history bears persistent evidence from then until now of her power to attract an audience. Her own disciples were the first to spread her works, both for the value they saw in them and for the support they would lend to the cause of her canonization. Her *Dialogue* and Raymond of Capua's biography of her were among the first books to see print, not only in her native Italy but in Spain, Germany, and England as well. Century by century new editions and translations have made their appearance and the catalogue of biographical, interpretive, and critical works has continued to grow and will be swelled again in this sixth centenary of Catherine's death. And the interest is not generated by mere historical curiosity but by the perennial relevance of this extraordinary woman.

Catherine lived in a century when Church and society and her own Dominican Order were in chaos. It was also a great century for mysticism. But while her Dominican contemporaries in the north—Meister Eckhart, John Tauler, Henry Suso—were caught up in the speculative, Catherine's impact was inherently practical. She was the center of a group ("*la bella brigata*," she called them) drawn from many levels of society and many religious traditions, and they regarded her as teacher and spiritual guide. And through her influence on Raymond of Capua she was to be a major force in Dominican reform even after her death. Even those who exploited her saw her as a woman to be reckoned with.

1

INTRODUCTION

THE SOURCES

The present-day interpreter of Catherine is faced not with a lack of data but with the critical task of sorting out fact from culturally and pragmatically conditioned myth in the plentiful testimony of the saint's disciples in their efforts to promote her cult and canonization. Vying for first place among these are the works of Raymond of Capua, her spiritual director and close friend from 1374 until her death, and those of Tommaso d'Antonio Nacci da Siena (commonly called Caffarini), a disciple from the earliest days and the prime mover in her cause for canonization. We do not know the academic credentials of Caffarini, but Raymond was a scholar of no mean standing, having studied at Italy's most prestigious university in Bologna, lectured in theology at Siena, and held the degree *magister in Theologia.* Raymond, under pressure from his Dominican brothers (he was by then master general of the order), began writing his life of Catherine, the *Legenda Major,*[1] in 1384 but did not complete it until 1395. And while his work is certainly influenced by the religious mentality of his age, his carefulness about fidelity to his sources is everywhere evident. Caffarini undertook first an ambitious expansion of Raymond's work, his *Libellus de Supplemento,* valuable in many respects, but most significantly in its heavy use of the notes of Catherine's first confessor, Tommaso della Fonte—notes we do not have in any other form. Later, Caffarini saw a need for a more compact presentation and published his *Legenda Minor.*

The *Processus* of Venice, compiled by Caffarini beginning in 1411, affords us testimony from nearly all of Catherine's disciples. Besides this we have the *Miracoli* composed by an anonymous Florentine; the memoirs of another disciple, Cristofano di Gano; letters of her disciples to Catherine and to each other; a few short pieces from the English Augustinian William of Flete, whose hermitage was just outside Siena at Lecceto and who was both teacher and disciple to Catherine for many years; and a number of poems written in her honor by her disciples after her death.

All of this testimony is certainly biased, but hardly merits the extreme suspicion with which Fawtier[2] regards it. Anything at all con-

---

1. For complete data on all sources, see Bibliography.
2. R. Fawtier, *Sainte Catherine de Sienne: essaie de critique des sources* (Paris: E. de Boccard, 1921, 1930). It must, however, be noted that Fawtier made perhaps one of the greatest contributions to Catherinian scholarship in that his sometimes iconoclastic approach roused other students of Catherine to a more careful attention to the data.

temporary with Catherine is bound to be colored by the times that produced it. Yet, while more neutral sources such as chronicles supply but little that reflects directly on Catherine, we do have the internal evidence of her own works: nearly four hundred letters,[3] her *Dialogue*, and some two dozen prayers recorded by her secretaries.[4] It is, in fact, this internal evidence that in the end gives us the clearest picture of Catherine's personality, teaching, and work. All the rest is ultimately merely the setting, necessary for the complete picture but secondary in every sense of the word.

CATHERINE'S LIFE

Caterina di Giacomo di Benincasa was born in 1347[5] in the Fontebranda district of Siena, the twenty-fourth of twenty-five children. Her father was a wool dyer of comfortable means but politically one of the *popolo minuto* in a city-state familiar with family feuds, class conflict, and revolution.

What we know of Catherine's childhood is embedded in pious legend, but it is clear that she was a strikingly pleasant and outgoing youngster, imaginative and idealistic in her devotion. (In light of this it is interesting that in her later years "devotion" as a sham and pretense earned such vivid contempt from her.) The stubborn independence that was to be a hallmark of most of her life showed itself early, as well as the intense emotional struggle she knew when faced with more pleasant alternatives to the austere way she felt herself called to follow. Yet what emerges slowly but steadily and clearly as she approached the age for marriage (the early teens in fourteenth-century Italy) is a passion for the truth of things, a passion that overrode her every other passion.

Dominican influence in Catherine's life was to be expected. Her family lived just down the hill from the church and cloister of San Domenico, a center of Dominican learning and preaching, and Catherine was there often—too often and too long to suit many. Besides, Tommaso della Fonte, brother of Catherine's brother-in-law, had spent his

---

3. Cf. especially the Introduction of E. Dupré-Theseider, *Epistolario di Santa Caterina da Siena*, vol. I (Rome: R. Instituto storico italiano per il Medio Evo, 1940).

4. There is also a short piece, *Il Dialogo Breve*, attributed to Catherine. Her authorship of it has not been established.

5. The data has been questioned by Fawtier (see note 2 above), but his arguments are quite easily refuted.

3

youth in the Benincasa home after being orphaned by the Black Death in 1349 and had joined the Dominicans while Catherine was yet a child. He was to become her first confessor and director. Also very active in Siena were the *Mantellate*, women (the assumption was that they were widows) who were affiliated with the Order of Saint Dominic and wore the habit but lived in their own homes, serving the needs of the poor and the sick under the direction of a prioress and ultimately under the direction of the friars. This was the group to which Catherine sought and finally obtained entrance once her decision not to marry won its hard victory over the opposition of her family.

Raymond tells us she was only seven years old when she vowed her virginity to God;[6] she was fifteen when she cut off her hair in defiance of efforts to make her marry, eighteen when she received the Dominican habit. At this last juncture she began to live in solitude and silence in her room, going out only for Mass at San Domenico. Somewhere, somehow in the silence she learned to read. Her solitude climaxed in 1368 in her "mystical espousal" to Christ. Then, almost brusquely, she sensed the imperative to rejoin her family and give herself to the service of the poor and the sick with her sisters of the *Mantellate*. She was twenty-one.

The tales that have come down to us from these years of "social work" in Siena are full of the warmly human side of Catherine. She served as nurse in homes and hospitals, looked out for the destitute, buried her father. Yet this sudden shift to the outside did not end the silence and contemplation she still found in solitude. Her public activity gained her notoriety, but those who began to gather round her looked for her most of all at home in her room, where in hours of conversation she both learned and taught—learned the subtleties of theological argument and biblical interpretation, and taught what she knew from experience of the way of God.

In 1368 she met the learned Bartolomeo de' Dominici, who was to become her second confessor and lifelong friend. Mystical experiences continued to increase and intensify, with another climactic point in her "mystical death"—four hours during which she experienced ecstatic union with God while her body seemed lifeless to all observers—in 1370. Her austerity was stripped to all-but-total abstinence from food and sleep. Social/political tensions were mounting in Siena and all of

---

6. *Legenda Major* I, iii.

INTRODUCTION

Italy, and Catherine began to find herself drawn to intervene in counsel as well as prayer, at least with individuals, wherever she saw truth being compromised.

She made her first journey to Florence in the spring of 1374,[7] and it seems that at this time she acquired Raymond of Capua as her confessor and spiritual director. He did not nearly measure up to her own stature, but he was intelligent, broadly educated, and sincere. The two were to become tender friends, and she would refer to him in one of her last letters as "the father and son given to me by that gentle mother Mary." It was, in fact, she who urged him and others to share with her the risky mission of tending the sick and dying when the plague burst out again in Siena that summer. She was twenty-seven.

In Pisa, in 1375, she used what influence she had to sway that city and Lucca away from alliance with the anti-papal league whose force was gaining momentum and strength. Convinced that military ambitions could be better used in the Holy Land and that it would be an honor for Christians (including herself) to shed their blood to win unbelievers to salvation in Christ's blood, she also lent her enthusiasm to preaching a crusade. It was in Pisa that she received the stigmata (visible, at her request, only to herself). That same year she began her prolific letter-writing career, and interceded by letter with the English mercenaries who were ravaging the Italian countryside and impoverishing the city-states with their demands for peace money. She traveled back to Siena to assist a young political prisoner, Niccolò di Tuldo, at his execution, and finally returned there toward the end of 1375.

The feud between the city-states and the papacy worsened, and in the spring of 1376 the Signoria of Florence sought the help of Catherine's influence in winning release from the interdict under which they had been placed by Pope Gregory XI, a situation that put them at a severe economic disadvantage. Politically naive yet convinced that every possible measure must be taken to restore peace in the Church, Catherine consented to go to Avignon to plead the cause of Florence, trusting

---

7. Practically all of Catherine's modern biographers have adopted the view that this journey to Florence was motivated by an order to appear before the Dominican General Chapter for examination, presumably of her orthodoxy. But none of the early sources allude to such an order. The confusion may have arisen from a misreading of a passage in the opening paragraph of the *Miracoli*, influenced by a bit of Florentine chauvinism. Cf. T. M. Centi, "Un processo inventato di sana pianta," *Rassegna di Ascetica e Mistica* XXI (1970), pp. 325–42. (Cavallini).

the latter's promise of compliance with whatever would be demanded for reconciliation. Her trust was, as friends had warned her, ill founded: As soon as she had paved the way for them the Florentines disowned her and sent their own ambassadors to negotiate on their own terms. Catherine sent an appropriately scorching letter[8] back to Florence and turned her attention to her larger concerns: the crusade, the reform of the clergy, the return of the papacy to Rome. On the last issue, Gregory XI had already made up his mind, but he was one who placed great store by prophetic voices, and Catherine's insistence that he must return certainly strongly influenced the actual move. Contrary to artistic representations, however, she did not accompany him on the journey, nor was she even present when he entered Rome. Her own way took her slowly back to Siena, where she spent the early months of 1377 founding a women's monastery of strict observance outside the city in the old fortress of Belcaro—a monastery she herself could never be long contained in.

Summer, fall, and most of winter of that year found her at Rocca d'Orcia, about twenty miles from Siena, on a local mission of peacemaking and preaching. It was a period that ended in both loneliness and fullness: loneliness because Raymond was appointed prior of the Church of the Minerva in Rome and never permanently returned to her;[9] fullness because it was during that autumn that she had the experience which led to the writing of her *Dialogue* and actually learned to write herself. (Before this she had always had to dictate.)[10] She was thirty years old.

Late in 1377 or early in 1378 Catherine was again in Florence, this time at the order of Gregory XI, once more to take up the cause of peace between that city-state and Rome. And once again her naiveté was used by the Florentines for their own ends. But she continued to plead for obedience and peace. On March 27 Pope Gregory died and was succeeded by Urban VI. Uprisings and riots continued, during one of which Catherine was almost assassinated as an accomplice of the Guelphs—and in an emotionally charged letter to Raymond she wept over the martyrdom that had escaped her. The olive branch of peace

---

8. Let. 234. (All references to Catherine's letters follow Tommaseo's numbering unless otherwise noted.)

9. Cf. *Leg. Maj.* III, vi, trans. G. Lamb (New York: Kenedy, 1960), p. 377. Raymond says Catherine had sent with him "a number of suggestions which if properly carried out would be to the advantage of the holy Church of God."

10. Let. 272.

came to Florence in July, but Catherine slipped quietly back to Siena, wishing "not to be the cause of new injustice."[11]

Urban had been opposed by many from the time of his election, and now schism was brewing fast. Catherine wrote letters to any and all who were involved, arguing for loyalty and unity. She had ideas of her own as to what was needed to make that possible, and she longed to be in Rome where she might personally promote those ideas. Finally, in late November, Urban VI sent for her. But people in Siena were talking about this woman who was too much on the road, and Catherine pulled back. Only if the pope sent explicit orders would she go, she wrote to Raymond.[12] The written summons came, and Catherine set out for Rome with her "family"—the last journey she was to make.

She set up her household there, a handful of women, a handful of men, all living on alms. She met with pope and cardinals, dictated letters, counseled her disciples. She had her great dream of a "Papal Council" of holy people to bring about—another dream that would splinter in its collision with reality. She basked in the joy of being reunited with Raymond, but hardly for a month, for Urban sent him off on a mission to the king of France. Raymond never completed that mission because he was afraid when he heard that the enemy was lying in wait to kill him as he crossed the border—and Catherine put him in his place for that[13]—but neither did he return to Rome in Catherine's lifetime.

From the beginning of 1380 Catherine could no longer eat or even swallow water. Except for a few more letters, her activity for the Church was now totally in her prayer and the offering of herself. Diabolic visions tormented her as much as ecstasy ravished her. Till late February she still dragged herself the mile to Saint Peter's each morning for Mass and spent the day there in prayer until vespers. On February 26 she lost the use of her legs and was confined to bed. She died on April 29. She was thirty-three years old.

CATHERINE'S MYSTICISM

Looking at a life so short yet so feverishly filled with activity one might legitimately ask, where is the space for the mystical? Yet were it

---

11. Letter published by E. Gardner in *Saint Catherine of Siena* (London: Dent, 1907), pp. 413–414.
12. *Leg. Maj.* III, i, Lamb, p. 304.
13. Let 344.

not for her mystical experience, Catherine's activity as it was would never have been. Grion has rightly said, "To divorce the mystical from the history of a saint like Catherine would be to empty her of her personality."[14] "Being so closely associated with her," says Raymond, "I was able to see at first hand how, as soon as she was freed from the occupations in which she was engaged for the work of souls, at once, one might almost say by a natural process, her mind was raised to the things of heaven."[15]

The balance of contemplation and action in the last twelve years of Catherine's life was not merely a relationship of complementarity. She did not pray simply to "refuel" herself for further activity (the principle behind even the interpretation that her three years of solitude were but a preparation for the years of activity to follow); nor was prayer an oasis of rest from work, a kind of holy self-indulgence. It was precisely what she experienced in contemplation that impelled her into action. And all that she touched or was touched by in her activity was present in her prayer. Indeed, in her later years she was seldom physically alone when she prayed, except in her room at night. And her contemplation, on the other hand, was so present to her active life that she prayed and even burst into ecstasy within the text of many of her letters. This integration is the characteristic that marks Catherine among the mystics more than any striking quality of her mystical experience as such, and makes her writings so very pertinent today, when the interplay between prayer and active ministry is so much at issue.

Inseparable from this integration is the question of Catherine's central motif. There are critics who say it was Truth, others who contend it was Love. Both are in fact right. For Catherine God is *la prima dolce Verità* (gentle first Truth) and God is *pazzo d'amore* (mad with love) and *essa carità* (charity itself). The way to God is the constantly lived dynamic of knowledge and love. The stage is set in the very first paragraph of the *Dialogue* for this dynamic, which is at the heart of her whole teaching as it was of her life:

> A soul rises up, restless with tremendous desire for God's honor and the salvation of souls. She has for some time exercised herself in virtue and has become accustomed to dwelling

---

14. A. Grion, *Santa Caterina da Siena: dottrina e fonti* (Brescia: Morcelliana, 1953), p. 9.
15. *Leg. Maj.* III, i, Lamb, p. 302.

in the cell of self-knowledge in order to know better God's goodness toward her, since upon knowledge follows love. And loving, she seeks to pursue truth and clothe herself in it.

Catherine's love walked always very consciously in the light of truth—so intensely so that one wonders how she has been so facilely idealized as the "social mystic." Her absolute refusal to compromise Truth as she experienced it in God, the urgency she felt to reverse every falsification she saw, made her look the naive fool more than once. It was a tension that, I am convinced, killed her physically but created her triumphant, morally and in the fullest sense humanly. She was indeed a social mystic—but even more properly a mystic activist. Poverty, sickness, the suffering of injustice even to the point of death, were not merely evils or even systemic evils to her: They were that, and as such she fought them—but they were still more pawns in the hand of the will of *both* oppressed and oppressor under God. Political realities were to be reckoned with, but if the ultimate truth in the reckoning played havoc with her human limitations (yes, and her naiveté), if she would be used and abused and to all appearances fail, she would pay that price, along with the price of being judged incircumspect. But the very emotions that were seared in the process and in turn seared her body beyond its capacity emerged ever more whole and healthy. Such an activism is not nearly as pleasant as that in which Catherine has often been cast, but it is the kind of activism her mystical experience demanded and the kind her writings set before us. Some have called it neurotic and pathetic.[16] If it is, then I would suggest it is, like Chesterton's paradox, "truth standing on its head," or in Catherine's own terms, "the madness of love."

CATHERINE'S SOURCES

What, in terms of human inheritance, were the springs of Catherine's knowledge and teaching? She had no formal schooling. Just how extensively she read is not certain, but she was a tireless conversationalist. She never wrote what could be called theology reduced to a system; in fact, it is her lack of an established system that lends her writings their marvelous if sometimes frustrating and tiring style of layer

---

16. E.g., M. B. Ryley, *Queens of the Rennaissance* (Boston: Small, Maynard & Co., 1907), pp. 1–52.

INTRODUCTION

on layer of interwoven development: No thread is ever let go of or left unrelated to every other thread. Yet critics continue to debate her academic pedigree: Her teaching is clearly scholastic and Thomistic (e.g., Cordovani, Taurisano, Paris, Oddasso-Cartotti). Her teaching is clearly *not* Thomistic (e.g., Foster). Her teaching is predominantly Augustinian (e.g., Canet, Hackett). She was most influenced by Ubertino da Casale (Grion). The writings of the Dominicans Jacopo da Voragine and Cavalca exercised the more primary influence on her (D'Urso). This list is certainly not exhaustive. I would lean, however, toward the position of those (e.g., Getto) who are content to recognize multiple influences in Catherine's writings: Augustine, Cassian, Gregory the Great, Bernard, Francis, Thomas, Ubertino, Passavanti, Cavalca, Colombini. Like everything that came her way she absorbed them all and integrated them into her whole knowledge. Theologically there is nothing new or original. Catherine is completely immersed in the main current of Catholic teaching, and she is impeccably orthodox even in subtle distinctions where one might expect her, untrained as she was in formal theology, to have slipped up at least occasionally.

What is original in Catherine is her capacity for fresh and vivid expression of the tradition. The scholars taught and wrote still in Latin. Yet all that she wrote and dictated was in her own Sienese dialect, *nel suo volgare*. True, Passavanti and Cavalca before her had used the vernacular to write of things religious, but they were popularizers. Catherine, though she addressed herself to every imaginable class of people—popes and cardinals; monarchs, princes, and governors; priests, nuns, and pious laity; mercenaries, prisoners, and prostitutes—was not a popularizer. In her own apparently systemless yet close-knit system she developed her arguments and themes in great detail. Her pages are studded with metaphors and compounded metaphors. She repeats, yet always with some new layer of relationship. She explodes into ecstatic prayer. She teaches. Always she teaches.

The Scriptures she heard and read presumably only in Latin are at home in her works, in her own dialect, with a natural sort of familiarity that is strongly reminiscent of the long savoring and fondling of the old Jewish masters. These are no mere recited "proof-texts." They flow in and out of her sentences with such ease and integration that it is more often than not difficult to set them off with quotation marks. She so rearranges and combines passages around a single stream of thought that her own message and that of the Scriptures fuse into one.

Remarkable also, and especially noticeable in the *Dialogue* because of its somewhat secondary nature in relation to some of her earlier letters, is Catherine's handling of her own mystical experiences. What she has "heard" in these encounters with God is not her own to tamper with. She may rephrase stories she repeats from the *Lives of the Fathers* or incidents she has related in other contexts, but whenever she lifts the "words of God" from her own first accounting of them she leaves the original wording intact. If clarification is needed she expands with parenthetical inserts, but seldom touches that original wording. In a way not unlike the Scriptures, these words are hers to use but not to change.[17]

THE DIALOGUE

While Catherine's letters are the better window to her personality, growth, and relationships with others, the *Dialogue* is her crowning work, her bequest of all her teaching to her followers. She called it simply "my book," and in her last letter to Raymond[18] she entrusted its destiny to him: "I ask you also—you and brother Bartolomeo [de' Dominici] and brother Tommaso [della Fonte] and the maestro [Giovanni Tantucci]—to take in hand the book and any of my writings that you find. Together with master Tommaso [Pietra] do with them what you see would be most for the honor of God. I found some recreation in them."

Certain twists in the path by which the tradition has come into English have ended in a rather common belief that Catherine dictated the *Dialogue* entirely in the space of a single five-day ecstasy.[19] The total composite of references to the work by Catherine herself and a number of her contemporaries, however, makes it clear that a much longer time was involved, probably close to a year.

Both Raymond and Caffarini set the beginning and immediate

---

17. Cf. E. Dupré-Theseider, "Sulla composizione del < < Dialogo > > di Santa Caterina da Siena," *Giornale storica della letteratura italiana* 117 (1941): 161–202.

18. Let. 373, written February 15, 1380.

19. Cf. especially J. Hurtaud in the Introduction to his French translation of the *Dialogue* (Paris: Lethellieux, 1931) and J. Jorgensen, *Saint Catherine of Siena* (London: Longmans, Green and Co., 1939), p. 311. The latter, however, takes a broader view in note 8, p. 428.

motive of the work in a particularly significant mystical experience. Raymond writes:

> So about two years before her death, such a clarity of Truth was revealed to her from heaven that Catherine was constrained to spread it abroad by means of writing, asking her secretaries to stand ready to take down whatever came from her mouth as soon as they noticed that she had gone into ecstasy. Thus in a short time was composed a certain book that contains a dialogue between a soul who asks the Lord four questions, and the Lord himself who replies to the soul, enlightening her with many useful truths.[20]

Caffarini further specifies that she "composed her book and set it in order."[21]

The experience referred to is without a doubt the one Catherine elaborates in a long letter to Raymond, written from Rocca d'Orcia in early October 1377, the letter that was to form the framework and basic content of her book. She tells of having offered four petitions to God (for the reform of the Church, for the whole world, for Raymond's spiritual welfare, and for a certain unnamed sinner), to each of which, in her ecstasy, God had responded with specific teachings.[22]

Catherine probably began the work then and there, while still at Rocca d'Orcia. In the same letter to Raymond she relates how she had suddenly learned to write, and in another to Monna Alessa she tells of God's having given her a diversion from her pains in her writing.[23] In any case, the book must have taken some shape by the time she left on her second peacemaking mission to Florence, for in May or June of 1378 she writes to Stefano Maconi back in Siena:

> I sent a request to the countess [Benedetta de' Salimbeni, with whom she had lived at Rocca d'Orcia] for my book. I have waited several days for it and it hasn't come. So if you go

---

20. *Leg. Maj.* III, iii. It is to references such as this that we owe the book's present title. Catherine's early disciples variously called it *The Book of Divine Providence, The Book of Divine Teaching, The Dialogue, The Dialogue of Divine Providence.*

21. *Legenda Minor*, III, iii.

22. Let. 272. For a detailed presentation of parallels between this letter and the *Dialogue*, see Dupré-Theseider, "Sulla composizione. . . . "

23. Let. 119.

there, tell her to send it at once, and tell anyone who might go there to tell her this.[24]

Almost certainly she spent some time on the manuscript between acts during those tumultuous months in Florence. She left it behind at her quick departure, and on her return to Siena wrote to the man who had probably been her host there: "Give the book to Francesco . . . for I want to write something in it."[25] And Raymond records, significantly, that "when the peace [between Florence and the Papacy] had been proclaimed, she returned home and attended *more diligently* to the composition of a certain book, which she dictated in her own dialect, inspired by the supernal Spirit."[26]

The book must have been in a form Catherine considered finished before the schism had fully erupted, for there is no allusion to schism in it, though there is much about corruption in the Church and the need for reform. Also, Caffarini states that she had finished the book before she was called to Rome in November of 1378.[27]

The testimony of Catherine's contemporaries is unanimous that the book involved a great deal of dictation on her part while she was in ecstasy.[28] And Caffarini in his testimony in the *Processus* of Venice adds some fascinating details:

> I say also that I have very often seen the virgin in Siena, especially after her return from Avignon, rapt beyond her senses, except for speech, by which she dictated to various writers in succession sometimes letters and sometimes the book, in different times and in different places, as circumstances allowed. Sometimes she did this with her hands crossed on her breast as she walked about the room; sometimes she was on her knees or in other postures; but always her face was lifted toward heaven. Concerning the composition of her book, then: This among other marvels occurred in

---

24. Let. 365.
25. Addendum to Let. 179, published by R. Fawtier in *Mélanges d'archéologie et d'histoire* 34 (1914): 7.
26. *Leg. Maj.* III, i.
27. *Leg. Min.* III, i.
28. *Leg. Maj.* III, i; Cristofano di Gano Guidini, *Memorie*, ed. Milanesi, p. 37; testimonies of Stefano Maconi, Francesco Malavolti, Bartolomeo de' Dominici, in *Processus*, cited in Grion, *Santa Caterina*, p. 318; Caffarini, *Libellus de Supplemento*, III, vi, 6.

the virgin: When emergencies would cause several days to pass in which she was kept from pursuing her dictation, as soon as she could take it up again she would begin at the point where she had left off as if there had been no interruption or space of time. Moreover, as is evident in the course of her book, sometimes after she had dictated several pages, she would summarize or recapitulate the main content as if the things she had dictated were (and in fact they were) actually present to her mind.[29]

But the style of the *Dialogue* betrays not only such "ecstatic dictation," but also a great deal of painstaking (sometimes awkward) expanding and drawing in of passages written earlier. There is every reason to believe that Catherine herself did this editing. First of all, it is not an editing in the direction of more polished style, which it probably would have been had it been the work of any of her secretaries, for they were men whose own style reflected their learning. And if Raymond's attitude is typical, they considered the saint's writings too sacred to tamper with.[30] Furthermore, besides his reference to Catherine's setting her book in order, Caffarini records having been told by Stefano Maconi that the latter had seen Catherine writing with her own hand "several pages of the book which she herself composed in her own dialect."[31]

It has already been noted how the *Dialogue* owes much of its content and structure to the experience Catherine related to Raymond in her letter of October 1377.[32] Dupré-Theseider, in the article already referred to, elaborates further direct parallels between letter 64/65 and chapters 98 to 104 of the *Dialogue*. Numerous less spectacular instances of carryover must await further study, but no one can read both letters and *Dialogue* without noticing the recurrence of certain themes and images.

---

29. *Processus*, cited in Grion, *Santa Caterina*, p. 318.

30. *Leg. Maj.* III, iii, Lamb, p. 321: "Meanwhile, so that no one will imagine that . . . I have added anything of my own, I call upon first Truth itself to be my judge and witness. . . . On the contrary, I have tried to keep the same order of words, and have made every effort, insofar as is allowed by the Latin syntax, to translate word for word, though strictly speaking this cannot always be done without adding some kind of interpolation, a conjunction or an adverb for instance, that is not in the original. But this does not mean that I have tried to change the meaning or add anything; it simply means that I have tried to achieve a certain elegance and clarity of utterance."

31. *Supp.* I, i, 9.

32. Let. 272.

INTRODUCTION

THE STRUCTURE OF THE DIALOGUE

The *Dialogue* as Catherine left it was almost certainly one continuous narrative, but her own disciples divided it very early into chapters. (These chapter numbers have been retained in this translation as they are indispensable for reference purposes, but they have been set as inconspicuously as possible so as not to interfere with the flow of the text.) The larger division into "tracts" or "treatises," while it may have some foundation in the original progression of composition, was solidified in the late sixteenth century. Neither chapter nor tract divisions correspond exactly with the natural structure of the work, and their perpetuation through the centuries has only further obscured Catherine's already complex logic.

It was Giuliana Cavallini who first dug beneath the discrepancies to reestablish the original structure, which she then followed in her edition of the *Dialogue* in 1968,[33] the edition principally adhered to in the present translation. In her Introduction, Cavallini describes the almost casual manner in which she began to reach her conclusions, noticing first the regular pattern of petition, response, thanksgiving that characterizes the flow of the work. Next she observed that the development of a given theme is almost always followed by a summary, and the thanksgiving expanded in a hymn of praise in harmony with the theme. The validity of the emerging outline was reinforced by her discovery that the divisions she had arrived at solely through the internal structural evidence were in fact marked in the manuscript from which she was working (*Casanatense* 292) by large initial capital letters. (Cavallini retained these large capitals in her edition, and I have done likewise.) The argument was sealed.

Even with this clarification, however, the *Dialogue* makes for no light reading. Catherine's logic follows a relentless pattern of "layering" in which she restates her arguments frequently, but almost always with the addition and integration of new elements. The integration is so intense that even seemingly incompatible metaphors become inextricably joined. Though it is quite possible to isolate striking passages that in terms of their own content can well stand alone, it is impossible to enter fully into the depth of Catherine's thought without slowly absorbing all of the facets that comprise it, layer upon layer.

---

33. *Il Dialogo della Divina Provvidenza* (Rome: Edizioni Cateriniane, 1968). See her Introduction for a complete treatment of the matter.

INTRODUCTION

The outline, as derived by Cavallini,[34] unrolls as follows, and can be useful as a guide for situating any specific part of the *Dialogue* within the context of the whole.

1. PROLOGUE (ch.1–2)
   The fundamental argument of the whole book is capsulized in the opening paragraphs:
   —the intimate interplay of truth and love;
   —the beauty and dignity of the human creature, whose perfection is in union with God.
   The work is placed in its setting within Catherine's life.
   The four petitions she addressed to God are enumerated:
   —for herself (later specified in a plea that she be allowed to suffer in atonement for sin);
   —for the reform of the Church;
   —for the whole world, and especially for peace in relation to rebellious Christians;
   —for divine providence in all things, but specifically in regard to "a certain case that had arisen."

2. THE WAY OF PERFECTION (ch. 3–12)
   God responds briefly to the first petition, instructing her on:
   —the need for infinite desire in relation to finite works;
   —the role of one's neighbors in the economy of charity;
   —the virtues;
   —discernment as the lamp and "seasoning" of all the other virtues.
   (This part lacks a thanksgiving.)

3. DIALOGUE (ch. 13–25)
   Catherine formulates three petitions, corresponding loosely to the second and fourth in the initial listing, to each of which God responds briefly:
   —she asks for mercy for the people of God and the "mystic body"[35] of the Church, to which God responds by telling of the

---

34. *Il Dialogo*, Introduction, pp. xv–xx. This presentation is abridged from Cavallini's. B. Ashley has somewhat adapted her outline in "Guide to Saint Catherine's Dialogue," *Cross and Crown* 29 (1977): 237–249.
35. Cf. note 15, p. 36.

INTRODUCTION

gift of the redemptive blood of Christ and the responsibility that gift imposes;

—she asks for mercy for the world, to which the response is a discussion of selfish love as it poisons the world, and of God's dominion over the wicked as well as the good;

—she asks for grace (specifically for Raymond of Capua) to follow the truth, and God speaks of the way of truth, the bridge of Christ, and of the double vineyard of one's own soul and the Church to be tended by all who would serve him.

The brief "dialogue" is concluded with a hymn of praise to divine love and a request to know more of Christ as the bridge.

4. THE BRIDGE (ch. 26–87)

This is the central and most important part of the whole book, developed in several sections:

—a description of the bridge, the way of truth, with its approach, the three stairs;

—the way of those who cross through the river beneath the bridge;

—the choice between the two ways;

—the way of those who cross the bridge in ordinary charity;

—the way of those who walk in perfect charity.

Because of its proposal of hunger for souls as the crowning point of the whole spiritual journey, The Bridge might be taken as an amplification of the response to the petition for grace to follow the truth, a response that in its brief form begins, "Daughter, this is what I want: that he [Raymond] seek to please me, Truth, by his deep hunger and concern for the salvation of souls." But it is in fact a fuller response in all its points to the petition for mercy to the whole world—a response that continues through the next two sections as well.

After listening to a summary of The Bridge and receiving a renewed promise of mercy, Catherine asks for instruction on tears, because she has seen "that the soul passes through these stages with tears."

5. TEARS (ch. 88–97)

There are five kinds of tears, corresponding to the stages of the soul. This short section ends with a hymn of praise for the gift of love and a triple request for illumination: on judgment, on

17

counseling, and on discerning what comes from God and what from the devil.

6. TRUTH (ch. 98 –109)

There are three lights by which we see—the imperfect, the perfect, and the most perfect—and three things that are necessary if we would not be deceived—refusal to judge others' vices, refusal to judge others' degree of perfection, and refusal to confine everyone to following the same way.

This section is also a further development of The Bridge as well as an amplification of what was said on discernment in chapter 11.

After being encouraged to ask for more and a new promise of mercy, Catherine praises God for his truth and asks for:
—fidelity to the truth for herself, her followers, and her two spiritual fathers (a reflection of her petitions for herself and for Raymond);
—knowledge of the sins of the evil clergy, so that she may intensify her sorrow and desire for mercy (thus leading into a fuller response to her petition for the mystic body of the Church).

Promising a response, God reminds her of the responsibility of knowledge and invites her to pray.

7. THE MYSTIC BODY OF HOLY CHURCH (ch. 110–134)

This section begins with a magnificent eulogy of the priesthood and the eucharistic mystery, after which God treats at length the sins of evil clerics and religious. After all this has been summarized, Catherine praises God as light and fire, as supreme charity and fulfiller of desires, and renews her plea for mercy for the world and for the Church, bringing us once again to her final petition for God's providence, as well as to her general plea for mercy for the whole world.

8. DIVINE PROVIDENCE (ch. 135–153)

God speaks of his general providence in creation and redemption, in the sacraments, in the gift of hope, in the Law; then of his special providence in the events of life and in "a certain case." He provides in a special way for those who espouse voluntary poverty.

After the summary of this theme, Catherine praises divine

charity and asks to be instructed concerning obedience, an amplification of the theme of providence.

9. OBEDIENCE (ch. 154–165)

God speaks of the obedience of the Word as remedy to the sin of Adam, of ordinary obedience, and of the obedience of religious, singing the praises of this virtue that conforms the soul to himself in charity after the example of Christ.

10. CONCLUSION (ch. 166–167)

God summarizes the content of the whole book, and Catherine responds with thanks and a hymn of praise to the Trinity. She closes with a prayer that she may be clothed in truth.

THE TEXT

We do not possess the totally "original" manuscript of the *Dialogue.* Our nearest access is through a comparison of the manuscripts that come from the hands of Catherine's immediate disciples, a critical work that still remains to be done. Giuliana Cavallini has approximated the task in the text used basically for the present translation, her edition of 1968. The text for that edition was MS 292 of the *Biblioteca Casanatense* in Rome, a manuscript traceable to Barduccio Canigiani, one of the three secretaries responsible for the original recording of Catherine's dictation.[36] Its date, therefore, would have to be prior to December 8, 1382, when Barduccio died.

Three factors in particular lead to the judgment that *Casanatense* 292 is closer to the original than other extant manuscripts:

1. In passages where God the Father speaks of the Eucharist as *me, Dio e uomo* (e.g., ch. 110–111), the pronoun *me* has been crossed out. The pronoun does not occur at all in these same passages in other manuscripts.[37]
2. Other manuscripts contain occasional interpolations to clarify obscure passages. These interpolations are missing in *Casanatense* 292.

---

36. The other two were Stefano Maconi and Neri di Landoccio de' Pagliaresi.
37. Cf. B. Motzo, "Per un 'edizione critica delle opere di S. Caterina da Siena," *Annali della Facoltà di Filosofia e Lettere della R. Università di Cagliari,* 1930–31, pp. 111–41.

INTRODUCTION

3. Biblical texts in this manuscript are occasionally freer (i.e., closer to Catherine's memorized rendition?) than in the others.

In her notes, Cavallini has indicated variations with other manuscripts where these are significant from the standpoint of content or syntax. The manuscripts included in the comparison are:

1. T.II.9 of the *Biblioteca Comunale di Siena* (hereafter abbreviated *S*), a manuscript apparently signed by Stefano Maconi; probable date, fourteenth century, though Maconi lived until 1424.
2. T.6.5 of the *Biblioteca Estense* in Modena (abbreviated *E*); Dupré-Theseider dates it early fifteenth century.
3. A manuscript belonging to the family of Senator Pietro Fedele (abbreviated *F*).
4. Gaddiano Pluteo LXXXIX sup. 100 of the *Biblioteca Mediceolaurenziana* in Florence (*L-G*); dated fourteenth century.
5. AD.IX.36 of the *Biblioteca Braidense* in Milan (*B*); dated fourteenth century. (These variants have not affected the English.)

While Cavallini does not consider her work a *punto d'arrivo*, it certainly brings a degree of authenticity worthy of trust and, coupled with other critical literature on Catherine, allows an access to the *Dialogue* that cries for translation.

THE TRANSLATION

The *Dialogue* has been translated into English twice: in the early fifteenth century by an unknown writer who destined the work for the nuns of the monastery of Syon in England and called it *The Orcherd of Syon;* and in 1896 by Algar Thorold.

The fifteenth-century *Orcherd* found its way into print in 1519, and was edited in 1966 by Phyllis Hodgson and Gabriel M. Leigey. It is an all but complete rendition, quite faithful to Catherine's thought but in many senses more a paraphrase than a translation. Its value lies more in its interest for scholars of English mysticism than directly for Catherinian studies. It is, besides, quite incomprehensible to those who do not read Middle English.

Thorold's translation in its first edition included all of the *Dialogue* except chapters 135 to 153 (Divine Providence). But this edition is hard to find in American libraries, and later editions are far more drastically abridged. The translation itself is heavily Victorian in tone, uncomfortable reading for today. Though it is on the whole an extremely slavish rendering of the Italian structures, it is quite frequently inaccurate, and difficult passages are often omitted or broadly paraphrased. It is not, in short, an effective link between Catherine and the present English-speaking world.

The task of translating Catherine is not an easy one. In the torrent of her thought she frequently loses sight of her pronominal antecedents, her tense sequence, even sometimes of the fact that she has left in mid-air the sentence with which she began, while getting lost in a whole series of parentheses. In this realm I have taken the liberty of choosing the most comfortable pronominal reference or tense and staying with it. This choice is in a limited sense a happy necessity, for it makes it possible, at least in the case of pronouns and impersonal references, to avoid the thorny problem of "sexist" language. But there are ways in which Catherine was, in tune with her age, glaringly sexist in her attitudes, and though I have translated, for example, her *virilmente* (legitimately) as "courageously," for her the word definitely carried overtones of "manliness" as such.

Structurally, I have tried to steer the theoretically sound but practically difficult course of translating Catherine's style with *equivalent* English style. This justifies in general a good deal of breaking down of her extremely long sentences. But some of her sentences, as has been mentioned, are not only extremely long but downright obscure. In these cases I have given the passage all the coherence the total context can justify, with the more exact rendering in a note for purposes of reference.

Catherine's style is not only repetitious but often grossly redundant. Since her repetition is seldom without some new layer of meaning, I have to that intent left intact all but the clear redundancies, which I have deleted in translation. Catherine's repetitions are, however, heavily framed in elements such as "as has been said," "as I have told you," and the like. Where these serve only to clutter her flow of thought rather than support it, I have omitted them.

The text I have basically adhered to in translating is Cavallini's 1968 edition, though I have consulted other editions available to me for purposes of comparison. Cavallini's notes have been of tremendous assistance, and I have made liberal use of them. I have, however, felt free to depart from them when my own opinion differed or when the interests of an English-speaking audience versus her Italian readership seemed to warrant it. I believe I have credited her interpretations in the notes wherever due. I have noted manuscript variants only when these have any effect on the sense of the text as transferred into English.

The *Dialogue* is everywhere interlaced with biblical allusions. As often as not these are so integrated with her own thought as to make it awkward if not impossible to isolate them in quotation marks. I have therefore consistently used quotation marks in these instances only when the syntax calls for them. It is important to note that Catherine uses biblical references as she remembers and transposes them from the Latin in which she has heard and read them into her own dialect. It is only reasonable, then, to translate these allusions directly from Catherine's rendition of them (not always literal or even accurate) rather than to lift their equivalents from any given English translation of Scripture. In the notes I have followed the Jerusalem Bible.

There is no fully "lightening" the style of the *Dialogue* without violating it. So I do not apologize for the fact that the style of this translation is, especially in parts, still somewhat tiring if one tries to read it quickly or in great pieces. Catherine herself wrote to Raymond: "Pardon me for writing too much, but my hands and tongue go along with my heart!"[38] And what Bartolomeo de' Dominici testified about her reading and praying holds true a bit paradoxically for her writing: "She was not concerned about reading a lot or saying many prayers. Rather she would chew on every single word, and when she found one she especially liked, she would stop for as long as her mind found pleasure grazing there."[39] If those who can read Catherine only in English find that sort of flavor in her *Dialogue* through this translation, my intention in presenting it will be satisfied.

---

38. Let. 272.
39. *Processus*, in M.-H. Laurent, *Fontes vitae S. Catharinae Senensis historici* 9, p. 303.

Catherine of Siena

THE DIALOGUE

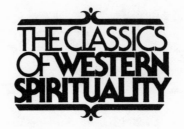

Woodcut from Raymundus de Vinels,
La Vida dela Seraphica Sea Catherina de Sena,
Valencia, Juan Joffre, 1511.

PROLOGUE

In the Name of Christ Crucified and of Gentle Mary

1

A soul rises up, restless with tremendous desire for God's honor and the salvation of souls. She has for some time exercised herself in virtue and has become accustomed to dwelling in the cell of self-knowledge in order to know better God's goodness toward her, since upon knowledge follows love. And loving, she seeks to pursue truth and clothe herself in it.

But there is no way she can so savor and be enlightened by this truth as in continual humble prayer, grounded in the knowledge of herself and of God. For by such prayer the soul is united with God, following in the footsteps of Christ crucified, and through desire and affection and the union of love he makes of her another himself. So Christ seems to have meant when he said, "If you will love me and keep my word, I will show myself to you, and you will be one thing with me and I with you."[1] And we find similar words in other places from which we can see it is the truth that by love's affection the soul becomes another himself.

To make this clearer still, I remember having heard from a certain servant of God[2] that, when she was at prayer, lifted high in spirit, God would not hide from her mind's eye his love for his servants. No, he

---

1. Cf. Jn. 14:21–23.
2. Catherine refers to herself in the third person throughout the *Dialogue*. (Cf. 2 Co. 12:2.) Almost imperceptibly at this point she changes from present to past tense, a perspective she maintains in the narrative passages throughout the rest of the work.

would reveal it, saying among other things, "Open your mind's eye and look within me, and you will see the dignity and beauty of my reasoning creature.[3] But beyond the beauty I have given the soul by creating her in my image and likeness, look at those who are clothed in the wedding garment of charity,[4] adorned with many true[5] virtues: They are united with me through love. So I say, if you should ask me who they are, I would answer," said the gentle loving Word, "that they are another me; for they have lost and drowned their own will and have clothed themselves and united themselves and conformed themselves with mine."

It is true, then, that the soul is united to God through love's affection.

Now this soul's will was to know and follow truth more courageously.[6] So she addressed four petitions to the most high and eternal Father, holding up her desire for herself first of all—for she knew that she could be of no service to her neighbors in teaching or example or prayer without first doing herself the service of attaining and possessing virtue.

Her first petition, therefore, was for herself. The second was for the reform of holy Church. The third was for the whole world in general, and in particular for the peace of Christians who are rebelling against holy Church with great disrespect and persecution.[7] In her fourth petition she asked divine providence to supply in general and in particular for a certain case which had arisen.[8]

---

3. *La mia creatura che à in sé ragione* is one of Catherine's favorite expressions for the human person.

4. In Catherine's writings *carità* and *amore* are often used quite interchangeably. However, I have consistently translated *carità* as "charity" and *amore* as "love" unless otherwise noted, to retain any distinction Catherine did intend.

5. S adds *e reali*. The adjective carries a range of meaning from "real" to "royal." As Catherine's context nowhere gives a clue as to which aspect of meaning she intended, I have consistently chosen the more neutral "solid" where the reference is to *vere e reali virtú*.

6. *Virilmente.* The etymological sense of "manfully" is certainly not alien to Catherine's thought, as she regarded "manliness" as a distinctly positive quality. A frequent admonition of hers was to "act like a man, not like a woman!" (E.g., Let. 344 to Raymond of Capua.) The translation "courageously" is, however, also legitimate, and I have chosen it throughout this translation for its broader connotations.

7. The conflicts, often bloody, between the Italian city-states and the papacy—Catherine had dealt with them firsthand in her journeys to Avignon and Florence—are the hard reality behind these words.

8. There is no clear evidence as to what this "certain case" was. Some have thought that the reference is to Niccolò di Tuldo, the youth Catherine accompanied to execution

THE DIALOGUE

2

This desire of hers was great and continuous. But it grew even more when First Truth[9] showed her the world's need and how storm-tossed and offensive to God it is. And she had on her mind, besides, a letter she had received from her spiritual father,[10] a letter in which he expressed pain and unbearable sadness over the offense against God, the damnation of souls, and persecutions against holy Church. All of ,this stirred up the flame of her holy desire with grief for the offense but with gladness in the hope by which she waited for God to provide against such great evils.

She found herself eager for the next day's Mass—it would be Mary's day[11]—because in communion the soul seems more sweetly bound to God and better knows his truth. For then the soul is in God and God in the soul, just as the fish is in the sea and the sea in the fish. So when it was morning and time for Mass she took her place with eager desire. From her deep knowledge of herself, a holy justice gave birth to hatred and displeasure against herself, ashamed as she was of her imperfection, which seemed to her to be the cause of all the evils in the world. In this knowledge and hatred and justice she washed away the stains of guilt, which it seemed to her were, and which indeed were, in her own soul, saying, "O eternal Father, I accuse myself before you, asking that you punish my sins in this life. And since I by my sins am the cause of the sufferings my neighbors must endure, I beg you in mercy to punish me for them."

(cf. Let. 273 to Raymond). However, there is no reference to the youth's devotion to Mary, which Catherine later mentions in regard to the response to this petition. Others have seen a possible reference to Frate Simone da Cortona, whose despair figures in a number of letters: "*F. S. al Pagliaresi,*" "*Anonimo al Pagliaresi*" (Misciattelli VI, letters VII and VIII); Let. 56, 212, 226. Cf. also Jorgensen, pp. 275–277; note 25, p. 426.

9. *Prima Verità* and *prima dolce Verità* are among Catherine's favorite names for God and Christ.

10. Literally, "the father of her soul," Raymond of Capua, her director from 1374 until her death. The letter from him referred to here is probably the same mentioned by Catherine in her letter to him of October 1377 (272), the letter that contains the basic framework and content of the *Dialogue.*

11. Saturday, the day traditionally dedicated to Mary.

THE WAY OF PERFECTION

T hen eternal *Truth seized her desire and drew it more strongly to himself. Just as in the Old Testament when sacrifice was offered to God a fire came and drew to himself the sacrifice that was acceptable to him,[1] so gentle Truth did to that soul. He sent the fiery mercy of the Holy Spirit and seized the sacrifice of desire she had made of herself to him, saying:*

Do you not know, my daughter, that all the sufferings the soul bears or can bear in this life are not enough to punish one smallest sin? For an offense against me, infinite Good, demands infinite satisfaction. So I want you to know that not all sufferings given in this life are given for punishment, but rather for correction, to chastise the child who offends. However, it is true that a soul's desire, that is, true contrition and sorrow for sin, can make satisfaction. True contrition satisfies for sin and its penalty not by virtue of any finite suffering you may bear, but by virtue of your infinite desire. For God, who is infinite, would have infinite love and infinite sorrow.

The infinite sorrow God wills is twofold: for the offense you yourself have committed against your Creator, and for the offense you see on your neighbors' part. Because those who have such sorrow have infinite desire and are one with me in loving affection (which is why they grieve when they sin or see others sinning), every suffering they bear from any source at all, in spirit or in body, is of infinite worth, and so satisfies for the offense that deserved an infinite penalty. True, these are finite deeds in finite time. But because their virtue is practiced and their suffering borne with infinite desire and contrition and sorrow for sin, it has value.

---

1. 1 Ch. 18:38.

So the glorious apostle Paul taught: "If I had an angelic tongue, knew the future, gave what is mine to the poor, and gave my body to be burned, but did not have charity, it would be worth nothing to me."[2] Finite works are not enough either to punish or to atone unless they are seasoned with loving charity.

4

I have shown you, dearest daughter, that in this life guilt is not atoned for by any suffering simply as suffering, but rather by suffering borne with desire, love, and contrition of heart. The value is not in the suffering but in the soul's desire. Likewise, neither desire nor any other virtue has value or life except through my only-begotten Son, Christ crucified, since the soul has drawn love from him and in virtue follows his footsteps. In this way and in no other is suffering of value. It satisfies for sin, then, with gentle unitive love born from the sweet knowledge of my goodness and from the bitterness and contrition the heart finds in the knowledge of itself and its own sins. Such knowledge gives birth to hatred and contempt for sin and for the soul's selfish sensuality, whence she considers herself worthy of punishment and unworthy of reward. So you see, *said gentle Truth,* those who have heartfelt contrition, love for true patience, and that true humility which considers oneself worthy of punishment and unworthy of reward suffer with patience and so make atonement.

You ask me for suffering to atone for the offenses my creatures commit against me. And you ask for the will to know and love me, supreme Truth. Here is the way, if you would come to perfect knowledge and enjoyment of me, eternal Life: Never leave the knowledge of yourself. Then, put down as you are in the valley of humility you will know me in yourself, and from this knowledge you will draw all that you need.

No virtue can have life in it except from charity, and charity is nursed and mothered by humility. You will find humility in the knowledge of yourself when you see that even your own existence comes not from yourself but from me, for I loved you before you came into being. And in my unspeakable love for you I willed to create you anew in grace. So I washed you and made you a new creation in the blood that my only-begotten Son poured out with such burning love.

---

2. 1 Co. 13:1–3.

This blood gives you knowledge of the truth when knowledge of yourself leads you to shed the cloud of selfish love. There is no other way to know the truth. In so knowing me the soul catches fire with unspeakable love, which in turn brings continual pain. Indeed, because she has known my truth as well as her own sin and her neighbors' ingratitude and blindness, the soul suffers intolerably. Still, this is not a pain that troubles or shrivels up the soul. On the contrary, it makes her grow fat. For she suffers because she loves me, nor would she suffer if she did not love me.

Thus, as soon as you and my other servants come in this way to know my truth you will, for the glory and praise of my name, have to endure great trials, insults, and reproaches in word and in deed, even to the point of death.[3] Behave, then, you and my other servants, with true patience, with sorrow for sin and love of virtue, for the glory and praise of my name. If you do, I shall be appeased for your sins and those of my other servants. The sufferings you endure will, through the power of charity, suffice to win both atonement and reward for you and for others. For you they will win the fruit of life: The stains of your foolishness will be blotted out, and I will no longer remember that you had ever offended me. As for others, because of your loving charity I will pardon them in proportion to their receptiveness.

More particularly, I will pardon both sin and punishment in those who humbly and reverently accept the teaching of my servants. How? They will come in this way to truly know and regret their sins, and so, because of my servants' prayer and desire they will receive (humbly, as I have said) the fruit of grace. And the more willing they are to exercise this grace with virtue, the more they will receive, but if they are less willing, they will receive less. So in general I am saying that through your desires they will receive both forgiveness and its gifts, unless their stubbornness is such that they despair. (Then I would reject them for scorning the blood by which they have so tenderly been bought.)

What fruit do they receive? Pressed by my servants' prayers, I look on them and give them light. I rouse the dog of conscience within them. I make them sensitive to the perfume of virtue and give them delight in the fellowship of my servants. Sometimes I allow the world to show them its true colors, letting them feel all sorts of emotions, so

---

3. *Infino alla morte* is ambiguous. It could be simply "until death" in terms of time or "even unto death" in terms of intensity. I have throughout this translation chosen "even to the point of death" to preserve something of the ambiguity.

that they may know how inconstant it is and be more eager to seek their homeland in eternal life. The eye cannot see, nor the tongue tell, nor can the heart imagine[4] how many paths and methods I have, solely for love and to lead them back to grace so that my truth may be realized in them!

I am constrained to this by the same immeasurable love with which I created them, as well as by prayers and desires and sufferings of my servants. I do not spurn their tears and sweat and humble prayers; no, I accept them, since it is I who make them love and fill them with grief over the damnation of souls.

But ordinarily I grant these others pardon of their sin only, not of its penalty. For they on their part are not disposed to receive my love and that of my servants with perfect love. Nor do they receive my servants' grief with bitterness or perfect contrition for the sin they have committed, but receive it with imperfect love and contrition. For this reason, such as these receive no pardon of the penalty but only of the sin itself. For not only the giver but also the receiver must be rightly disposed. And if these others are imperfect, they receive only imperfectly the perfect desires of those who offer them with pain to me on their behalf.

Why, then, did I tell you that they receive both pardon and its gifts? Such is the truth. Their sin is atoned for in the way I have told you, through the light of conscience and other means of which we have spoken. In other words, in this beginning of awareness they vomit out the filth of their sins, and so they receive the gift of grace. So it is with those who live in ordinary charity. If they accept what comes their way as correction without resisting the Holy Spirit's mercy, they receive the life of grace from him, leaving their sin behind.

But if, like fools, they are ungrateful and heedless of me and of my servants' labors, then what was given in mercy will at once turn to their judgment and ruin—not through any defect in mercy or in those who begged mercy for the ingrates, but only through their own wretchedness and hardness. They have, with the hand of free choice, encrusted their heart in a diamond rock that can never be shattered except by blood.[5] Still, I tell you, in spite of their hardness, let them

---

4. Cf. 1 Co. 2:9.
5. Cf. Vincent of Beauvais, *Speculum Naturale*, L. VIII, c. 39. The fresh warm blood of a goat has power to shatter the diamond, which resists both iron and fire. It is improbable that Catherine was directly familiar with the *Speculum*, but she may have learned the

while they still have time and freedom to choose seek the blood of my Son and with that same hand let them pour it over the hardness of their heart: It will shatter the diamond and they will know the fruit of that blood which was paid out for them. But if they dawdle, time will run out and there will be no remedy at all, because they will have no return to show for the endowment they had from me.[6] For I gave them memory to hold on to my blessings, and understanding to see and know the truth, and will to love me, eternal Truth, once understanding has known me.

This is the endowment I gave to all of you, and I your Father expect a return from it. But if you sell it in barter to the devil, the devil goes off with it and carries away everything you had acquired in this life. Then he fills your memory with delightful recollections of indecency, pride, avarice, selfish love for yourself, and hatred and contempt for your neighbors. (For the devil is a persecutor of my servants.) Your mind is darkened in these wretched things by your disordered will, and so in stench you reap eternal punishment, infinite punishment, for you would not atone for your guilt with contrition and contempt for sin.

So you see, suffering atones for sin not by reason of the finite pain but by reason of perfect contrition of the heart. And in those who have this perfect contrition it atones not only for the sin itself but for the penalty due that sin. But for most, as I have said, their suffering satisfies only for sin itself; for though they are freed from deadly sin and receive grace, if their contrition and love are not strong enough to satisfy for the penalty, they go to the pains of purgatory once they have passed beyond the second and final means.[7]

Atonement is made, then, through the desire of the soul who is united to me, infinite Good, in proportion as love is perfect both in the one who prays with desire and in the one who receives. And my goodness will measure out to you with the very same measure that you give to me and that the other receives.[8] So feed the flame of your desire and let not a moment pass without crying out for these others in my presence with humble voice and constant prayer. Thus I tell you and the

---

notion from the Dominican Friars with whom she associated. The analogy to the human heart may be hers or theirs, but it is already suggested in Heb. 9:13–14.

6. Cf. Mt. 25:14–30.

7. *Passati dal secondo e ultimo mezzo.* The precise sense intended by Catherine is unclear. Perhaps this is the "second reproach" of ch. 37, p. 78.

8. Cf. Lk. 6:38.

spiritual father I have given you on earth: Behave courageously, and die to all your selfish sensuality![9]

5

The willing desire to suffer every pain and hardship even to the point of death for the salvation of souls is very pleasing to me. The more you bear, the more you show your love for me. In loving me you come to know more of my truth, and the more you know, the more intolerable pain and sorrow you will feel when I am offended.

You asked for suffering, and you asked me to punish you for the sins of others. What you were not aware of was that you were, in effect, asking for love and light and knowledge of the truth. For I have already told you that suffering and sorrow increase in proportion to love: When love grows, so does sorrow. So I say to you: Ask and it shall be given to you;[10] I will not say no to anyone who asks in truth. Consider that the soul's love in divine charity is so joined with perfect patience that the one cannot leave without the other. The soul, therefore, who chooses to love me must also choose to suffer for me anything at all that I give her. Patience is not proved except in suffering, and patience is one with charity, as has been said. Endure courageously, then. Otherwise you will not show yourselves to be—nor will you be—faithful spouses and children of my Truth, nor will you show that your delight is in my honor and in the salvation of souls.

6

I would have you know that every virtue of yours and every vice is put into action by means of your neighbors. If you hate me, you harm your neighbors and yourself as well (for you are your chief neighbor), and the harm is both general and particular.

I say general because it is your duty to love your neighbors as your own self.[11] In love you ought to help them spiritually with prayer and counsel, and assist them spiritually and materially in their need—at least with your good will if you have nothing else. If you do not love me you do not love your neighbors, nor will you help those you do not love. But it is yourself you harm most, because you deprive yourself of

---

9. *Sensualità* and the related modifiers invariably carry a pejorative meaning for Catherine, though she speaks positively about the senses as used virtuously.

10. Mk. 11:24.

11. Lv. 19:18; Mk. 12:33.

grace. And you harm your neighbors by depriving them of the prayer and loving desires you should be offering to me on their behalf. Every help you give them ought to come from the affection you bear them for love of me.

In the same way, every evil is done by means of your neighbors, for you cannot love them[12] if you do not love me. This lack of charity for me and for your neighbors is the source of all evils, for if you are not doing good you are necessarily doing evil. And to whom is this evil shown and done? First of all to yourself and then to your neighbors— not to me, for you cannot harm me except insofar as I count whatever you do to them as done to me.[13] You do yourself the harm of sin itself, depriving yourself of grace, and there is nothing worse you can do. You harm your neighbors by not giving them the pleasure of the love and charity you owe them, the love with which you ought to be helping them by offering me your prayer and holy desire on their behalf. Such is the general help that you ought to give to every reasoning creature.

More particular are the services done to those nearest you, under your very eyes. Here you owe each other help in word and teaching and good example, indeed in every need of which you are aware, giving counsel as sincerely as you would to yourself, without selfishness. If you do not do this because you have no love for your neighbors, you do them special harm, and this as persistently as you refuse them the good you could do. How? In this Way:

Sin is both in the mind and in the act. You have already sinned in your mind when you have conceived a liking for sin and hatred for virtue. (This is the fruit of that sensual selfishness which has driven out the loving charity you ought to have for me and your neighbors.) And once you have conceived you give birth to one sin after another against your neighbors, however it pleases your perverse sensual will. Sometimes we see cruelty, general or particular, born. It is a general sort of cruelty to see yourself and others damned and in danger of death for having lost grace. What cruelty, to refuse to help either oneself or others by loving virtue and hating vice! But some actually extend their cruelty even further, not only refusing the good example of virtue but in their wickedness assuming the role of the devil by dragging others as much as they can from virtue and leading them to vice. This is spiri-

---

12. *Non è nella carità sua.*
13. Mt. 25:40.

tual cruelty: to make oneself the instrument for depriving others of life and dealing out death.

Bodily cruelty springs from greed, which not only refuses to share what is one's own but takes what belongs to others, robbing the poor, playing the overlord, cheating, defrauding, putting up one's neighbors' goods—and often their very persons—for ransom.

O wretched cruelty! You will find yourself deprived of my mercy unless you turn to compassion and kindness! At times you give birth to hurtful words, followed often enough by murder. At other times you give birth to indecency toward others, and the sinner becomes a stinking beast, poisoning not only one or two but anyone who might approach in love or fellowship.

And who is hurt by the offspring of pride? Only your neighbors. For you harm them when your exalted opinion of yourself leads you to consider yourself superior and therefore to despise them. And if pride is in a position of authority, it gives birth to injustice and cruelty, and becomes a dealer in human flesh.

O dearest daughter, grieve that I am so offended, and weep over these dead so that your prayer may destroy their death! For you see that everywhere, on every level of society, all are giving birth to sin on their neighbors' heads. For there is no sin that does not touch others, whether secretly by refusing them what is due them, or openly by giving birth to the vices of which I have told you.

It is indeed true, then, that every sin committed against me is done by means of your neighbors.

7

I have told you how every sin is done by means of your neighbors, because it deprives them of your loving charity, and it is charity that gives life to all virtue. So that selfish love which deprives your neighbors of your charity and affection is the principle and foundation of all evil.

Every scandal, hatred, cruelty, and everything unbecoming springs from this root of selfish love.[14] It has poisoned the whole world

---

14. Cf. Ga. 5:22–24: "What the Spirit brings is very different: love, joy, peace, patience, kindness, goodness, trustfulness, gentleness, and self-control. There can be no law against things like that, of course. You cannot belong to Christ Jesus unless you crucify all self-indulgent passions and desires."

and sickened the mystic body[15] of holy Church and the universal body of Christianity. For all virtues are built on charity for your neighbors. So I have told you, and such is the truth: Charity gives life to all the virtues, nor can any virtue exist without charity. In other words, virtue is attained only through love of me.

After the soul has come to know herself she finds humility and hatred for her selfish sensual passion, recognizing the perverse law that is bound up in her members and is always fighting against the spirit.[16] So she rises up with hatred and contempt for that sensuality and crushes it firmly under the foot of reason. And through all the blessings she has received from me she discovers within her very self the breadth of my goodness. She humbly attributes to me her discovery of this self-knowledge, because she knows that my grace has drawn her from darkness and carried her into the light of true knowledge. Having come to know my goodness, the soul loves it both with and without intermediary. I mean she loves it without the intermediary of herself or her own advantage. But she does have as intermediary that virtue which is conceived through love of me, for she sees that she cannot be[17] pleasing or acceptable to me except by conceiving hatred of sin and love of virtue.

Virtue, once conceived, must come to birth. Therefore, as soon as the soul has conceived through loving affection, she gives birth for her neighbors' sake. And just as she loves me in truth, so also she serves her neighbors in truth. Nor could she do otherwise, for love of me and love of neighbor are one and the same thing: Since love of neighbor has its source in me, the more the soul loves me, the more she loves her neighbors.

Such is the means I have given you to practice and prove your virtue. The service you cannot render me you must do for your neighbors. Thus it will be evident that you have me within your soul by grace, when with tender loving desire you are looking out for my hon-

---

15. *Corpo mistico.* The sense is *not* parallel to the present understanding of "Mystical Body." In Catherine, *il corpo mistico* embraces every aspect of the sacramental life at the heart of the Church. She also uses *misterio* in reference to sacrament and things sacramental, i.e., all grace that comes through material things and events. Cf. Grion, who would see *corpo mistico* restricted to "the priests, insofar as they are 'ministers' of the Eucharist or of the Blood" (p. 290). This restriction is not, however, borne out by the total context of the *Dialogue.*

16. Cf. Ga. 5:17.

17. C omits the rest of this sentence and most of the next, but it is an obvious error in copying due to two occurrences of *in altro modo non sarebbe.* S, E, F all have the missing portion.

or and the salvation of your neighbors by bearing fruit for them in many holy prayers.

I showed you earlier how suffering alone, without desire, cannot atone for sin. Just so, the soul in love with my truth never ceases doing service for all the world, universally and in particular, in proportion to her own burning desire and to the disposition of those who receive.[18] Her loving charity benefits herself first of all, as I have told you, when she conceives that virtue from which she draws the life of grace. Blessed with this unitive love she reaches out in loving charity to the whole world's need for salvation. But beyond a general love for all people she sets her eye on the specific needs of her neighbors and comes to the aid of those nearest her according to the graces I have given her for ministry:[19] Some she teaches by word, giving sincere and impartial counsel; others she teaches by her example—as everyone ought to— edifying her neighbors by her good, holy, honorable life.

These are the virtues, with innumerable others, that are brought to birth in love of neighbor. But why have I established such differences? Why do I give this person one virtue and that person another, rather than giving them all to one person? It is true that all the virtues are bound together, and it is impossible to have one without having them all. But I give them in different ways so that one virtue might be, as it were, the source of all the others. So to one person I give charity as the primary virtue, to another justice, to another humility, to another a lively faith or prudence or temperance or patience, and to still another courage.

These and many other virtues I give differently to different souls, and the soul is most at ease with that virtue which has been made primary for her.[20] But through her love of that virtue she attracts all the

---

18. Here begins a long sentence that I have recast for clarity's sake. Literally translated the passage would read: "After she has served through the unitive love she has realized in me, by which she loves him, her affection having been extended to the salvation of the whole world by coming to the aid of its need, she tries, after she has done good to herself by conceiving virtue, whence she had drawn the life of grace, to set her eye on the need of her neighbor in particular, after she has shown it in general to every rational creature through the affection of charity as has been said. Whence she helps those who are nearby, according to the different graces I have given her to minister...."

19. Cf. 1 Co. 12:4–6: "There is a variety of gifts but always the same Spirit; there are all sorts of service to be done, but always to the same Lord; working in all sorts of different ways in different people, it is the same God who is working in all of them."

20. Literally, "These and many others I will give in the soul differently to many persons, although one of these is established as the principal object of virtue in the soul, being disposed more to principal converse with this than with the others."

other virtues to herself, since they are all bound together in loving charity.

The same is true of many of my gifts and graces, virtue and other spiritual gifts, and those things necessary for the body and human life. I have distributed them all in such a way that no one has all of them. Thus have I given you reason—necessity, in fact—to practice mutual charity. For I could well have supplied each of you with all your needs, both spiritual and material. But I wanted to make you dependent on one another so that each of you would be my minister, dispensing the graces and gifts you have received from me. So whether you will it or not, you cannot escape the exercise of charity! Yet, unless you do it for love of me, it is worth nothing to you in the realm of grace.

So you see, I have made you my ministers, setting you in different positions and in different ranks to exercise the virtue of charity. For there are many rooms in my house.[21] All I want is love. In loving me you will realize love for your neighbors, and if you love your neighbors you have kept the law.[22] If you are bound by this love you will do everything you can to be of service wherever you are.

8

I have told you how to serve your neighbors, and how that service proves your love for me. Now I will go further:

You test the virtue of patience in yourself when your neighbors insult you. Your humility is tested by the proud, your faith by the unfaithful, your hope by the person who has no hope. Your justice is tried by the unjust, your compassion by the cruel, and your gentleness and kindness by the wrathful. Your neighbors are the channel through which all your virtues are tested and come to birth, just as the evil give birth to all their vices through their neighbors.

Attend well. When I say that humility is tested by pride, I mean that a proud person cannot harm one who is humble, for the humble person smothers pride. If you are faithful to me your faith cannot be lessened by the infidelity of the wicked who neither love nor trust me. Nor can these lessen your hope once you have conceived it through love of me; rather it will be strengthened and proved in your affectionate love for your neighbors.

Those who do not love me cannot believe or trust me; rather they

---

21. Jn. 14:2.
22. Cf. Mt. 22:37–40.

believe and trust in their selfish sensuality, which they do love. They have no faith or trust in my servants either. But though they do not love me faithfully or with constant hope seek their salvation in me, my faithful servant will not abandon them.[23] You see, in the face of their unfaithfulness and lack of hope you prove your own faith. And whenever it may be necessary to prove your virtue, you prove it both in yourself and through your neighbors.

So your justice is not lessened but proved by the injustices of others. That is, you show you are just through the virtue of patience. Likewise, your kindness and mildness are revealed through gentle patience in the presence of wrath. And in the face of envy, spite, and hatred your loving charity is revealed in hungry desire for the salvation of souls.

I tell you, moreover, when you return good for evil you not only prove your own virtue, but often you send out coals ablaze with charity that will melt hatred and bitterness from the heart and mind of the wrathful, even turning their hatred to benevolence. Such is the power of charity and perfect patience in one who takes up the burden of the sins of the wicked and bears with their anger.[24]

Then consider the virtue of steadfast courage. It is tested when you have to suffer much from people's insults and slanders, which would like to drag you away from the way and teaching of the truth either by abuse or flattery. But if you have conceived the virtue of courage within you, you will always be strong and constant, and you will prove your courage externally through your neighbors. If, on the other hand, your virtue could not give solid proof of itself when tried by all these contrary things, then it could not be grounded in truth.

9

These interior virtues, proved in the way I have explained, are the holy gracious works I ask of my servants. They go far beyond external actions or various bodily penances. These may be instruments of vir-

---

23. Cf. Is. 42:3: "He does not break the crushed reed, nor quench the wavering flame."

24. Cf. Rm. 12:17–21: "Never repay evil with evil but let everyone see that you are interested only in the highest ideals. Do all you can to live at peace with everyone. Never try to get revenge; leave that, my friends, to God's anger. As Scripture says: Vengeance is mine—I will pay them back, the Lord promises. But there is more: If your enemy is hungry, you should give him food, and if he is thirsty, let him drink. Thus you heap redhot coals on his head. Resist evil and conquer it with good."

tue, but they are not virtuous in themselves, and without the interior virtue I have described they would hardly be pleasing to me.

If a soul were to do penance without discernment,[25] that is, if her love were centered mainly on the penance she had undertaken, it would be a hindrance to her perfection. But let her center be in affectionate love, with a holy hatred of herself, with true humility and perfect patience. In hungry desire for my honor and the salvation of souls let her attend to those interior virtues which give proof that her will is dead and her sensuality is continually being slain by the affection of love for virtue. She should be discerning in her penance, with her love fixed more on virtue than on the penance. For penance ought to be undertaken as a means to growth in virtue, according to the measure of one's need as well as one's capability.

Otherwise, if penance becomes the foundation, it becomes a hindrance to perfection. Being done without the discerning light of the knowledge of oneself and of my goodness, it would fall short of my truth. It would be undiscerning, not loving what I most love and not hating what I most hate. For discernment is nothing else but the true knowledge a soul ought to have of herself and of me, and through this knowledge she finds her roots. It is joined to charity like an engrafted shoot.

Charity, it is true, has many offshoots, like a tree with many branches. But what gives life to both the tree and its branches is its root, so long as that root is planted in the soil of humility. For humility is the governess and wet nurse of the charity into which this branch of discernment is engrafted. Now the source of humility, as I have already told you, is the soul's true knowledge of herself and of my goodness. So only when discernment is rooted in humility is it virtuous, producing life-giving fruit and willingly yielding what is due to everyone.

In the first place, the soul gives glory and praise to my name for the graces and gifts she knows she has received from me. And to herself she gives what she sees herself deserving of. She knows that all that she is and every gift she has is from me, not from herself, and to me she attributes all. In fact, she considers herself worthy of punishment for

---

25. Catherine uses *discrezione* and its related forms. I have translated "discernment" in agreement with Meattini (*Il Libro*, pp. 23, 50); Cavallini (in her preface to *Il Messagio di S. Caterina da Siena*, pp. xv–xvi); K. Foster ("Saint Catherine's Teaching on Christ," *Life of the Spirit* 16 (1962): 315; *Dictionnaire de Spiritualité* 3, c. 1258–1260, 1311–1326.

her ingratitude in the face of so many favors, and negligent in her use of the time and graces I have given her. So she repays herself with contempt and regret for her sins. Such is the work of the virtue of discernment, rooted in self-knowledge and true humility.

Without this humility, as I have said, the soul would be without discernment. For lack of discernment is set in pride, just as discernment is set in humility. A soul without discernment would, like a thief, rob me of my honor and bestow it on herself for her own glory. And what was her own doing she would blame on me, grumbling and complaining about my mysterious ways with her and with the rest of my creatures, constantly finding cause for scandal in me and in her neighbors.

Not so those who have the virtue of discernment. These give what is due to me and to themselves. And then they give their neighbors what is due them: first of all, loving charity[26] and constant humble prayer—your mutual debt—and the debt of teaching, and the example of a holy and honorable life, and the counsel and help they need for their salvation.

If you have this virtue, then whatever your state in life may be—whether noble or superior or subject—all that you do for your neighbors will be done with discernment and loving charity. For discernment and charity are engrafted together and planted in the soil of that true humility which is born of self-knowledge.

10

Do you know how these three virtues exist?

Imagine a circle traced on the ground, and in its center a tree sprouting with a shoot grafted into its side. The tree finds its nourishment in the soil within the expanse of the circle, but uprooted from the soil it would die fruitless. So think of the soul as a tree made for love and living only by love. Indeed, without this divine love, which is true and perfect charity, death would be her fruit instead of life. The circle in which this tree's root, the soul's love, must grow is true knowledge of herself, knowledge that is joined to me, who like the circle have neither beginning nor end. You can go round and round within this circle, finding neither end nor beginning, yet never leaving the circle. This knowledge of yourself, and of me within yourself, is grounded in

---

26. Cf. Rm. 13:8: "Avoid getting into debt, except the debt of mutual love."

the soil of true humility, which is as great as the expanse of the circle (which is the knowledge of yourself united with me, as I have said). But if your knowledge of yourself were isolated from me there would be no full circle at all. Instead, there would be a beginning in self-knowledge, but apart from me it would end in confusion.

So the tree of charity is nurtured in humility and branches out in true discernment. The marrow of the tree (that is, loving charity within the soul) is patience, a sure sign that I am in her and that she is united with me.

This tree, so delightfully planted, bears many-fragranced blossoms of virtue. Its fruit is grace for the soul herself and blessing for her neighbors in proportion to the conscientiousness of those who would share my servants' fruits. To me this tree yields the fragrance of glory and praise to my name, and so it does what I created it for and comes at last to its goal, to me, everlasting Life, life that cannot be taken from you against your will.

And every fruit produced by this tree is seasoned with discernment, and this unites them all, as I have told you.[27]

11

S uch are the fruits of action that I ask of the soul: that virtue should prove itself in response to need. This is what I told you long ago, if you remember, when you wanted to do great penance for me. You said, "What can I do to suffer for you?" And in your mind I answered, "I am one who is pleased by few words and many works." I wanted to show you that I am not much pleased with one who simply shouts, "Lord, Lord, I would like to do something for you!"[28] nor with one who wishes to kill the body with great penances without slaying the selfish will. What I want is many works of patient and courageous endurance and of the other virtues I have described to you—interior virtues that are all active in bearing the fruit of grace. ·

Actions based on any other principle I would consider a mere "shouting of words." For these are finite works, and I who am infinite insist upon infinite works, that is, infinitely desirous love. I want works of penance and other bodily practices to be undertaken as

---

27. Cf. also ch. 31, 113, where Catherine contrasts the "tree of love" with the "tree of death" planted on the mountain of pride.
28. Cf. Mt. 7:21.

means, not as your chief goal. By making them your chief goal you would be giving me a finite thing—like a word that comes out of the mouth and then ceases to exist—unless indeed that word comes out of the soul's love, which conceives virtue and brings it to birth in truth. I mean that finite works—which I have likened to words—must be joined with loving charity. Such works, undertaken not as your chief goal but as means, and not by themselves but in the company of true discernment, would please me.

It would not be right to make penance or other bodily works either your motivation or your goal, for, as I have already said, they are only finite. They are done in time that comes to an end, and sometimes one has to abandon them or have them taken away. In fact, it would not only not be meritorious but would offend me if you continued in these works when circumstances or obedience to authority made it impossible to do what you had undertaken. So you see how finite they are. Take them up, then, not as your goal but only as they are useful. For if you take them as a goal and then have to abandon them at some point, your soul will be left empty.

This is what the glorious Paul taught when he said in his letter that you should mortify your body and put to death your selfish will. In other words, learn to keep your body in check by disciplining your flesh when it would war against the spirit.[29] Your selfish will must in everything be slain, drowned, subjected to my will. And the knife that kills and cuts off all selfish love to its foundation in self-will is the virtue of discernment, for when the soul comes to know herself she takes for herself what is her due, hatred and contempt for sin and for her selfish sensuality.

If you act so, you will be my delight, offering me not only words but many works; for, as I have told you, I want few words but many works. I say "many" rather than giving you any number, because when the soul is grounded in charity (which gives life to all the virtues) her desire must reach to the infinite. As for words, I said I want few not because I have no use for them, but to emphasize that any act in itself is finite and can please me only if it is taken as an instrument of virtue and not as virtuous in itself.

Let no one, therefore, make the judgment of considering those great penitents who put much effort into killing their bodies more perfect than those who do less. I have told you that penance is neither vir-

---

29. Cf. Ga. 5:17.

tuous nor meritorious in itself. Were that the case, how unfortunate would be those who for legitimate reasons cannot perform actual works of penance! But the merit of penance rests completely in the power of charity enlightened by true discernment.

I am supreme eternal Truth. So discernment sets neither law nor limit nor condition to the love it gives me. But it rightly sets conditions and priorities of love where other people are concerned. The light of discernment, which is born of charity, gives order to your love for your neighbors. It would not permit you to bring the guilt of sin on yourself to benefit your neighbor. For that love would indeed be disordered and lacking in discernment which would commit even a single sin to redeem the whole world from hell or to achieve one great virtue. No, neither the greatest of virtues nor any service to your neighbor may be bought at the price of sin. The priorities set by holy discernment direct all the soul's powers to serving me courageously and conscientiously. Then she must love her neighbors with such affection that she would bear any pain or torment to win them the life of grace, ready to die a thousand deaths, if that were possible, for their salvation. And all her material possessions are at the service of her neighbors' physical needs. Such is the work of the light of discernment born of charity.

So you see, every soul desirous of grace loves me—as she ought—without limit or condition. And with my own infinite love she loves her neighbors with the measured and ordered charity I have described, never bringing on herself the evil of sin in doing good for others. Saint Paul taught you this when he said that charity cannot fully profit others unless it begins with oneself.[30] For when perfection is not in the soul, whatever she does, whether for herself or for others, is imperfect.

It could never be right to offend me, infinite Good, under the pretext of saving my finite creation. The evil would far outweigh any fruit that might come of it, so never, for any reason, must you sin. True charity knows this, for it always carries the lamp of holy discernment.

Discernment is that light which dissolves all darkness, dissipates ignorance, and seasons every virtue and virtuous deed. It has a prudence that cannot be deceived, a strength that is invincible, a constancy right up to the end, reaching as it does from heaven to earth, that is, from the knowledge of me to the knowledge of oneself, from love of me

---

30. The reference is not directly Pauline.

to love of one's neighbors.[31] Discernment's truly humble prudence evades every devilish and creaturely snare, and with unarmed hand— that is, through suffering—it overcomes the devil and the flesh. By this gentle glorious light the soul sees and rightly despises her own weakness; and by so making a fool of herself she gains mastery of the world, treading it underfoot with her love, scorning it as worthless.

When the soul has thus conceived virtue in the stirring of her love, and through her neighbors proved it and for their sakes brought it to birth, not all the world can rob her of that virtue. Indeed, persecution only serves to prove it and make it grow. But for that very reason, were the soul's virtue not evident and luminous to others in time of trial, it could not have been conceived in truth; for I have already told you clearly that virtue cannot be perfect or bear fruit except by means of your neighbors. If a woman has conceived a child but never brings it to birth for people to see, her husband will consider himself childless. Just so, I am the spouse of the soul, and unless she gives birth to the virtue she has conceived [by showing it] in her charity to her neighbors in their general and individual needs in the ways I have described, then I insist that she has never in truth even conceived virtue within her. And I say the same of vice: Every one of them is committed by means of your neighbors.

12

I who am Truth have taught you now what you need to know to achieve and maintain the highest perfection. I have told you as well how sin and its penalty are atoned for in yourself and in your neighbors, reminding you that the pains you endure while in the mortal body are worth nothing in terms of atonement unless they are joined with loving charity, true contrition, and contempt for sin. But suffering so joined with charity atones not by virtue of any actual pain you may endure but by virtue of charity and sorrow for the sin you have committed. This charity is attained with the light of understanding, with a heart sincere and free gazing into me as its object—for I myself am this charity.

You asked me for a willingness to suffer. So I have shown you all this to teach you and my other servants how you should make this sac-

---

31. *Dalla carità mia alla carità del prossimo.*

rifice of yourselves to me. I am speaking of sacrifice both in act and in spirit joined together as the vessel is joined with the water offered to one's lord. For the water cannot be presented without the vessel, and the lord would not be pleased to be offered the vessel without the water. So I tell you, you must offer me the vessel of all your actual sufferings, however I may send them to you—for the place and the time and the sort of suffering are not yours to choose, but mine. But this vessel of yours must be filled with the loving affection and true patience with which you carry all the burden of your neighbors' guilt even while you hate and reject the sin.

Thus these sufferings (which I set before you as a vessel) are found to be filled with the water of my grace, which gives life to your soul. And I accept this present from my dear spouses, from all who serve me. I accept from you your restless desires, your tears and sighs, your constant humble prayers—all of which, because of my love for you, are a means to placate my anger against my wicked enemies, the wicked ones of the world, who so offend me.

So suffer courageously even to the point of death, and this will be a sign to me that you love me in truth. Nor must you let human respect or troubles make you look back at what you have already plowed.[32] Rather, rejoice in your troubles.[33] The world makes sport of heaping insults upon me, and you will be saddened in the world when you see them insult me.[34] For when they offend me they offend you, and when they offend you they offend me, since I have become one thing with you.[35]

Think of it! I gifted you with my image and likeness.[36] And when you lost the life of grace through sin, to restore it to you I united my nature with you, hiding it in your humanity. I had made you in my image; now I took your image by assuming a human form. So I am one thing with you—except if a soul leaves me through deadly sin. But those who love me live in me and I live in them.[37] This is why the

---

32. Cf. Lk. 9:62. S has *aratro*, "plow," but this is hardly consistent with the biblical reference, for the ancient plower always walked *behind* the plow. Cf. also Let. 126: "Christ said no one should turn back to look at what has already been plowed, that is, to look back at earlier pleasures or at work already done."
33. Cf. Rm. 5:3.
34. Cf. Jn. 16:33.
35. Cf. Jn. 17:21–23.
36. Gn. 1:27.
37. Cf. Jn. 4:16.

world persecutes them. The world has no likeness to me, so it persecuted my only-begotten Son even to the shameful death of the cross, and so it persecutes you. Because it has no love for me, the world persecutes you and will persecute you even to the point of death; for if the world had loved me, it would love you as well.[38] Yet be glad, because in heaven your joy will be complete.[39]

I tell you further: the more the mystic body of holy Church is filled with troubles now, the more it will abound in delight and consolation. And this shall be its delight: the reform of good holy shepherds who are flowers of glory, who praise and glorify my name, offering me the fragrance of virtue rooted in truth. This is the reform of the fragrant blossoming of my ministers and shepherds—not that the fruit of this bride needs to be reformed, because it never spoils or is diminished by the sins of its ministers. So be glad, you and your spiritual father and my other servants, in your bitterness. For I, eternal Truth, promise to refresh you, and after your bitterness I will give you consolation, along with great suffering, in the reform of holy Church.

---

38. Jn. 15:18.
39. Cf. Jn. 17:14; 16:20.

DIALOGUE

13

T hen the soul was restless and aflame with tremendous desire
because of the unspeakable love she had conceived in God's
great goodness when she had come to see and know the expanse of his
charity. How tenderly he had deigned to answer her petition and give
her hope in her bitterness—bitterness over God's being offended and
holy Church's being ravaged, and bitterness over her own wretchedness, which she saw through knowledge of herself! Her bitterness was
softened and at the same time grew, for the supreme eternal Father,
now that he had shown her the way of perfection, was showing her in
a new light how he was being offended and souls were being harmed.

As the soul comes to know herself she also knows God better, for
she sees how good he has been to her. In the gentle mirror of God she
sees her own dignity: that through no merit of hers but by his creation
she is the image of God. And in the mirror of God's goodness she sees
as well her own unworthiness, the work of her own sin. For just as you
can better see the blemish on your face when you look at yourself in a
mirror, so the soul who in true self-knowledge rises up with desire to
look at herself in the gentle mirror of God with the eye of understanding sees all the more clearly her own defects because of the purity she
sees in him.[1]

Now as light and knowledge grew more intense in this soul, a
sweet bitterness was both heightened and mellowed. The hope that
first Truth had given her mellowed it. But as a flame burns higher the
more fuel is fed it, the fire in this soul grew so great that her body
could not have contained it. She could not, in fact, have survived had
she not been encircled by the strength of him who is strength itself.

---

1. Cf. 1 Jn. 3:2 and Jm. 1:24.

Thus cleansed by the fire of divine charity, which she had found in coming to know herself and God, and more hungry than ever in her hope for the salvation of the whole world and the reform of holy Church, she stood up with confidence in the presence of the supreme Father. She showed him the leprosy of holy Church and the wretchedness of the world, speaking to him as with the words of Moses:[2]

My Lord, turn the eye of your mercy on your people and on your mystic body, holy Church. How much greater would be your glory if you would pardon so many and give them the light of knowledge! For then they would surely all praise you, when they see that your infinite goodness has saved them from deadly sin and eternal damnation. How much greater this than to have praise only from my wretched self, who have sinned so much and am the cause and instrument of every evil! So I beg you, divine eternal Love, to take your revenge on me, and be merciful to your people.[3] I will not leave your presence till I see that you have been merciful to them.

For what would it mean to me to have eternal life if death were the lot of your people, or if my faults especially and those of your other creatures should bring darkness upon your bride, who is light itself? It is my will, then, and I beg it as a favor, that you have mercy on your people[4] with the same eternal love that led you to create us in your image and likeness. You said, "Let us make humankind in our image and likeness."[5] And this you did, eternal Trinity, willing that we should share all that you are, high eternal Trinity! You, eternal Father, gave us memory to hold your gifts and share your power. You gave us understanding so that, seeing your goodness, we might share the wisdom of your only-begotten Son. And you gave us free will to love what our understanding sees and knows of your truth, and so share the mercy of your Holy Spirit.

Why did you so dignify us? With unimaginable love you looked upon your creatures within your very self, and you fell in love with us. So it was love that made you create us and give us being just so that we might taste your supreme eternal good.

Then I see how by our sin we lost the dignity you had given us.

---

2. Cf. Ex. 32:11.
3. Cf. Ex. 32:31–32.
4. C omits "that you have mercy on your people." The clause is supplied in Azzoguidi's edition of S.
5. Gn. 1:26.

Rebels that we were, we declared war on your mercy and became your enemies. But stirred by the same fire that made you create us, you decided to give this warring human race a way to reconciliation, bringing great peace out of our war. So you gave us your only-begotten Son, your Word, to be mediator between us and you. He became our justice[6] taking on himself the punishment for our injustices. He offered you the obedience you required of him in clothing him with our humanity, eternal Father, taking on our likeness and our human nature!

O depth of love! What heart could keep from breaking at the sight of your greatness descending to the lowliness of our humanity? We are your image, and now by making yourself one with us you have become our image, veiling your eternal divinity in the wretched cloud and dung heap of Adam. And why? For love! You, God, became human and we have been made divine! In the name of this unspeakable love, then, I beg you—I would force you even!—to have mercy on your creatures.

14

G od let himself be forced by her tears and chained by her holy desire. And turning to her with a glance at once full of mercy and of sadness he said:

Dearest daughter, because your tears are joined to my charity and are shed for love of me, your weeping has power over me and the pain in your desire binds me like a chain. But look how my bride has disfigured her face! She is leprous with impurity and selfishness. Her breasts are swollen because of the pride and avarice of those who feed there: the universal body of Christianity and the mystic body of holy Church. I am speaking of my ministers who feed at her breasts. They ought not only to feed themselves, but hold to those breasts the whole body of Christianity as well as whoever would rise from the darkness of unbelief and be bound into the body of my Church.

Do you see how ignorantly and blindly they serve out the marvelous milk and blood of this bride—how thanklessly and with what filthy hands? And do you see with what presumption and lack of reverence it is received? And so the precious life-giving blood of my only-begotten Son, which dispelled death and darkness, confounded falsehood,

---

6. 1 Co. 1:30.

and brought the gift of light and truth, all too often, because of their sinfulness,[7] brings them death instead.

For those who are receptive this blood bestowed and accomplished all that they need to be saved and made perfect. But since its gift of life and grace is in proportion to the soul's readiness and desire, it deals death to the wicked. So it gives death rather than life to those who receive it unworthily, in the darkness of deadly sin. The fault for this is not in the blood. Nor does it lie in the ministers. The latter may be just as evil or worse, but their sin cannot spoil or contaminate the blood or lessen its grace and power, nor can it harm those they serve. They are, however, bringing on themselves the evil of sin, which will certainly be punished unless they set themselves right through true contrition and contempt for sin.

Those who receive the blood unworthily then, I repeat, are harmed not through any fault in the blood nor because of any fault on the ministers' part, but because of their own evil disposition and their own sin. For they have defiled their minds and bodies with such wretched filth, and have been so cruel to themselves and to their neighbors. They have cruelly deprived themselves of grace, willfully trampling underfoot the fruit of the blood, since it was by virtue of the blood that they were freed in holy baptism from the taint of original sin, which they had contracted when they were conceived by their father and mother.

This is why I gave the Word, my only-begotten Son. The clay of humankind was spoiled by the sin of the first man, Adam, and so all of you, as vessels made from that clay, were spoiled and unfit to hold eternal life. So to undo the corruption and death of humankind and to bring you back to the grace you had lost through sin, I, exaltedness, united myself with the baseness of your humanity.[8] For my divine justice demanded suffering in atonement for sin. But I cannot suffer. And you, being only human, cannot make adequate atonement.[9] Even if you did atone for some particular thing, you still could make atonement only for yourself and not for others. But for this sin you could not make full atonement either for yourself or for others since it was committed against me, and I am infinite Goodness.

---

7. C omits "all too often, because of their sinfulness," supplied in S (LG).

8. Cf. Ga. 4:4–5; 1 Jn. 4:9.

9. Cf. Dante, *Paradiso*, 7, 96: "Never could man, in human bounds confined, have paid his debt" (trans. G. L. Bickersteth, Oxford, 1965).

51

Yet I really wanted to restore you, incapable as you were of making atonement for yourself. And because you were so utterly handicapped, I sent the Word, my Son; I clothed him with the same nature as yours—the spoiled clay of Adam—so that he could suffer in that same nature which had sinned, and by suffering in his body even to the extent of the shameful death of the cross he would placate my anger.

And so I satisfied both my justice and my divine mercy. For my mercy wanted to atone for your sin and make you fit to receive the good for which I had created you. Humanity, when united with divinity, was able to make atonement for the whole human race—not simply through suffering in its finite nature, that is, in the clay of Adam, but by virtue of the eternal divinity, the infinite divine nature. In the union of those two natures I received and accepted the sacrifice of my only-begotten Son's blood, steeped and kneaded with his divinity into the one bread, which the heat of my divine love held nailed to the cross. Thus was human nature enabled to atone for its sin only by virtue of the divine nature.

So the pus was drained out of Adam's sin, leaving only its scar, that is, the inclination to sin and every sort of physical weakness—like the scar that remains after a wound has healed. Now Adam's sin oozed with a deadly pus, but you were too weakened to drain it yourself. But when the great doctor came (my only-begotten Son) he tended that wound, drinking himself the bitter medicine you could not swallow. And he did as the wet nurse who herself drinks the medicine the baby needs, because she is big and strong and the baby is too weak to stand the bitterness. My son was your wet nurse, and he joined the bigness and strength of his divinity with your nature to drink the bitter medicine of his painful death on the cross so that he might heal and give life to you who were babies weakened by sin.

Only the scar remains of that original sin as you contract it from your father and mother when you are conceived by them. And even this scar is lifted from the soul—though not completely—in holy baptism, for baptism has power to communicate the life of grace in virtue of this glorious and precious blood. As soon as the soul has received holy baptism, original sin is taken from her and grace is poured in. The inclination to sin, which is the trace that remains from original sin, is a weakness as I have said, but the soul can keep it in check if she will.

Then the soul is as a vessel ready to receive grace and to make it grow within her as much as she chooses to fit herself, through affection and desire, to love and serve me. Or she can fit herself for evil instead, even though she has received grace in holy baptism. And when she is old enough to discern the one from the other, in her freedom she can choose good or evil as it pleases her.

But such is the freedom of your humanity, and so strong have you been made by the power of this glorious blood, that neither the devil nor any other creature can force you to the least sin unless you want it. You were freed from slavery so that you might be in control of your own powers and reach the end you were created for. How wretched you would be, then, to wallow in the mud like an animal, ignoring the great gift I had given you! A miserable creature full of such foolishness could not receive more.

15

I want you to understand this, my daughter: I created humankind anew in the blood of my only-begotten Son and reestablished them in grace, but they have so scorned the graces I gave them and still give them! They go from bad to worse, from sin to sin, constantly repaying me with insults. And they not only fail to recognize my graces for what they are, but sometimes even think I am abusing them—I who want nothing but their sanctification! I tell you it will go harder for them in view of the grace they have received, and they will be deserving of greater punishment. They will be more severely punished now that they have been redeemed by my Son's blood than they would have been before that redemption, before the scar of Adam's sin was removed.[10]

It is only reasonable that those who receive more should give more in return, and the greater the gift, the greater the bond of indebtedness.[11] How greatly were they indebted to me, then, since I had given them their very existence, creating them in my image and likeness! They owed me glory, but they stole it from me and took it to themselves instead. They violated the obedience I had laid on them and so became my enemies. But with humility I destroyed their pride: I stooped to take on their humanity, rescued them from their slavery to the devil, and made them free. And more than this—can you see?—through this union of the divine nature with the human, God was made human and humanity was made God.

---

10. Cf. Jn. 15:22.
11. Cf. Lk. 12:48.

What indebtedness—to have received the treasure of the blood by which they are created anew in grace! So you see how much more they owe me after their redemption than before. For now they are bound by the example of the incarnate Word, my only-begotten Son, to give me glory and praise. And then they will pay their debt of love for me and for their neighbors, as well as true and solid virtue as I described for you earlier.

Because they owe me so much love, if they refuse it their sin is all the greater, and my divine justice punishes them so much more severely in eternal damnation. False Christians fare much worse there than do pagans. The fire of divine justice torments them the more, burning without consuming; and in their torment they feel themselves being eaten by the worm of conscience,[12] which eats away without eating up—for the damned for all their torment cannot cease to exist. Indeed, they beg for death but cannot have it: They cannot cease to exist. By their sin they can lose the life of grace, but not their very being.

So sin is punished far more severely after people have been redeemed by the blood than before. For they have received more, but they seem to ignore it and to take no notice of their evil deeds. Though I once reconciled them to myself through the blood of my Son, they have become my enemies.

But I have one remedy to calm my wrath: my servants who care enough to press me with their tears and bind me with the chain of their desire. You see, you have bound me with that chain—and I myself gave you that chain because I wanted to be merciful to the world. I put into my servants a hunger and longing for my honor and the salvation of souls so that I might be forced by their tears to soften the fury of my divine justice.

Bring, then, your tears and your sweat, you and my other servants. Draw them from the fountain of my divine love and use them to wash the face of my bride. I promise you that thus her beauty will be restored. Not by the sword or by war or by violence will she regain her beauty, but through peace and through the constant and humble prayers and sweat and tears poured out by my servants with eager desire.

And so I will fulfill your desire by giving you much to suffer, and your patience will spread light into the darkness in all the world's evil.

---

12. Cf. Mk. 9:43.

Do not be afraid: Though the world may persecute you, I am at your side and never will my providence fail you.[13]

16

T hen that soul stood before the divine majesty deeply joyful and strengthened in her new knowledge. What hope she had found in the divine mercy! What unspeakable love she had experienced! For she had seen how God, in his love and his desire to be merciful to humankind in spite of their enmity toward him, had given his servants a way to force his goodness and calm his wrath. So she was glad and fearless in the face of the world's persecution, knowing that God was on her side. And the fire of her holy longing grew so strong that she would not rest there, but with holy confidence made her plea for the whole world.

In her second petition she had concerned herself with the good that both Christians and unbelievers would reap from the reform of holy Church. But as if that were not enough, she now stretched out her prayer, like one starved, to the whole world, and as if he himself were making her ask it, she cried out:

Have mercy, eternal God, on your little sheep, good shepherd that you are! Do not delay with your mercy for the world, for already it almost seems they can no longer survive! Everyone seems bereft of any oneness in charity with you, eternal Truth, or even with each other: I mean, whatever love they have for each other has no grounding in you.

17

T hen God, like one drunk with love for our good, found a way to fire up an even greater love and sorrow in that soul. He showed her with what love he had created us (as we have already begun to tell) and he said:

See how they all lash out at me! And I created them with such burning love and gave them grace and gifts without number—all freely, though I owed them nothing! But see, daughter, how they strike back at me with every sort of sin, but most of all with their wretched and hateful selfishness, that breeding ground of every evil, and with

---

13. Cf. Is. 43:1–5; Jn. 16:33.

this selfish love they have poisoned the whole world. I have shown you how love of me bears every good that is brought to birth for others. By the same principle this sensual selfishness (which is born of pride just as my love is born of charity) is the bearer of every evil.

This evil they do by means of other people. For love of me and love of others are inseparable. And those who have not loved me have cut themselves off as well from any love of their neighbors. This is why I said—and I explained it to you—that every good and every evil is done by means of your neighbors.

How many charges I could bring against humankind! For they have received nothing but good from me, and they repay me with every sort of hateful evil. But I have told you that my wrath would be softened by the tears of my servants, and I say it again: You, my servants, come into my presence laden with your prayers, your eager longing, your sorrow over their offense against me as well as their own damnation, and so you will soften my divinely just wrath.

18

Know that no one can escape my hands, for I am who I am,[14] whereas you have no being at all of yourselves. What being you have is my doing; I am the Creator of everything that has any share in being. But sin is not of my making, for sin is nonbeing. Sin is unworthy of any love, then, because it has no part in me. Therefore, my creatures offend me when they love sin, which they should not love, and hate me, to whom they owe love because I am supremely good and gave them being with such burning love. But they cannot escape me: Either I will have them in justice because of their sin, or I will have them in mercy.

Open the eye of your understanding, then, and look at my hand, and you will see that what I have told you is true.

So in obedience to the most high Father, she raised her eyes, and she saw within his closed fist the entire world. And God said:

My daughter, see now and know that no one can be taken away from me.[15] Everyone is here as I said, either in justice or in mercy.[16]

---

14. Ex. 3:14.
15. Cf. Jn. 10:28.
16. Cf. Tb. 13:1–5: "Blessed be God who lives for ever, for his reign endures throughout all ages! By turns he punishes and pardons; ... no one can escape his hand.... Though he punishes you for your iniquities, he will take pity on you all."

They are mine; I created them, and I love them ineffably. And so, in spite of their wickedness, I will be merciful to them because of my servants, and I will grant what you have asked of me with such love and sorrow.

19

T he fire within that soul blazed higher and she was beside herself as if drunk, at once gloriously happy and grief-stricken. She was happy in her union with God, wholly submerged in his mercy and savoring his vast goodness; but to see such goodness offended brought her grief. She knew, though, that God had shown her his creatures' sinfulness to rouse her to intensify her concern and longing. And so she offered thanks to the divine majesty.

As she felt her emotions so renewed in the eternal Godhead, the force of her spirit made her body break into a sweat. (For her union with God was more intimate than was the union between her soul and her body.) The holy fire of love grew so fierce within her that its heat made her sweat water, but it was not enough. She longed to see her body sweat blood, so she said to herself:

Alas, my soul! You have frittered your whole life away, and for this have all these great and small evils come upon the world and holy Church! So I want you to heal them now with a sweat of blood.

Indeed, this soul remembered well what Truth had taught her: that she should always know herself and God's goodness at work in her, and that the medicine by which he willed to heal the whole world and to soothe his wrath and divine justice was humble, constant, holy prayer. So, spurred on by holy desire, she roused herself even more to open the eye of her understanding. She gazed into divine charity and there she saw and tasted how bound we are to love and seek the glory and praise of God's name through the salvation of souls. She saw that God's servants are called to this—and in particular eternal Truth had called and chosen her spiritual father, whom she brought before the divine goodness, asking God to light within him a lamp of grace by which he might in truth pursue this Truth.

20

T hen, in answer to her third petition, which came from her hunger for her father's good, God said:

Daughter, this is what I want: that he seek to please me, Truth, by his deep hunger and concern for the salvation of souls. But neither he[17] nor anyone else can achieve this without accepting whatever sufferings I grant.

As much as you long to see me honored in holy Church, just so much must you conceive the love it takes to suffer willingly and with true patience. By this will I know that he and you and my other servants are seeking my honor in truth. Then will he be my very dear son, and he will rest, along with the others, on the breast of my only-begotten Son. And I will make of my Son a bridge by which you can all reach your goal and there receive the fruit of all the labors you have borne for my love. So carry on courageously!

21

I told you that I have made a bridge of the Word, my only-begotten Son, and such is the truth. I want you to realize, my children, that by Adam's sinful disobedience the road was so broken up that no one could reach everlasting life. Since they had no share in the good for which I had created them, they did not give me the return of glory they owed me, and so my truth was not fulfilled. What is this truth? That I had created them in my image and likeness so that they might have eternal life, sharing in my being and enjoying my supreme eternal tenderness and goodness. But because of their sin they never reached this goal and never fulfilled my truth, for sin closed heaven and the door of my mercy.

This sin sprouted thorns and troublesome vexations. My creatures found rebellion within themselves, for as soon as they rebelled against me, they became rebels against themselves. Their innocence lost, the flesh rebelled against the spirit and they became filthy beasts. All created things rebelled against them, whereas they would have been submissive if all had been kept as I had established it in the beginning. But they stepped outside my obedience and so deserved eternal death in both soul and body.

With sin there came at once the flood of a stormy river that beat against them constantly with its waves, bringing weariness and troubles from themselves as well as from the devil and the world. You were all drowning, because not one of you, for all your righteousness, could reach eternal life.

---

17. S adds "nor you."

But I wanted to undo these great troubles of yours. So I gave you a bridge, my Son, so that you could cross over the river, the stormy sea of this darksome life, without being drowned.

See how indebted to me my creatures are! And how foolish to choose to drown rather than accept the remedy I have given!

22

Open your mind's eye and you will see the blinded and the foolish, the imperfect, and the perfect ones who follow me in truth. Then weep for the damnation of the foolish and be glad for the perfection of my beloved children. Again, you will see the way of those who choose light and the way of those who choose darkness.

But first I want you to look at the bridge of my only-begotten Son, and notice its greatness. Look! It stretches from heaven to earth, joining the earth of your humanity with the greatness of the Godhead. This is what I mean when I say it stretches from heaven to earth—through my union with humanity.

This was necessary if I wanted to remake the road that had been broken up, so that you might pass over the bitterness of the world and reach life. From earth alone I could not have made it great enough to cross the river and bring you to eternal life. The earth of human nature by itself, as I have told you, was incapable of atoning for sin and draining off the pus from Adam's sin, for that stinking pus had infected the whole human race. Your nature had to be joined with the height of mine, the eternal Godhead, before it could make atonement for all of humanity. Then human nature could endure the suffering, and the divine nature, joined with that humanity, would accept my Son's sacrifice on your behalf to release you from death and give you life.

So the height stooped to the earth of your humanity, bridging the chasm between us and rebuilding the road. And why should he have made of himself a roadway? So that you might in truth come to the same joy as the angels. But my Son's having made of himself a bridge for you could not bring you to life unless you make your way along that bridge.

23

Here the eternal Truth was showing that, although he had created us without our help, he will not save us without our help. [18] *He wants*

---

18. C has "he will not save us without our help" in the margin only.

us to set our wills with full freedom to spending our time in true vir-
tue. So he continued:

You must all keep to this bridge, seeking the glory and praise of
my name through the salvation of souls, bearing up under pain and
weariness, following in the footsteps of this gentle loving Word. There
is no other way you can come to me.[19]

You are the workers I have hired for the vineyard of holy
Church.[20] When I gave you the light of holy baptism I sent you by my
grace to work in the universal body of Christianity. You received your
baptism within the mystic body of holy Church by the hands of my
ministers, and these ministers I have sent to work with you. You are to
work in the universal body. They, however, have been placed within
the mystic body to shepherd your souls by administering the blood to
you through the sacraments you receive from them, and by rooting out
from you the thorns of deadly sin and planting grace within you. They
are my workers in the vineyard of your souls, ambassadors for the
vineyard of holy Church.

Each of you has your own vineyard, your soul, in which your free
will is the appointed worker during this life. Once the time of your life
has passed, your will can work neither for good nor for evil; but while
you live it can till the vineyard of your soul where I have placed it.
This tiller of your soul has been given such power that neither the devil nor any other creature can steal it without the will's consent, for in
holy baptism the will was armed with a knife that is love of virtue and
hatred of sin. This love and hatred are to be found in the blood. For my
only-begotten Son gave his blood for you in death out of love for you
and hatred for sin, and through that blood you receive life in holy baptism.

So you have this knife for your free will to use, while you have
time, to uproot the thorns of deadly sin and to plant the virtues. This is
the only way you can receive the fruit of the blood from these workers
I have placed in holy Church. For they are there, as I have told you, to
uproot deadly sin from the vineyard of your soul and to give you grace
by administering the blood to you through the sacraments established
in holy Church.

So if you would receive the fruit of this blood, you must first rouse
yourself to heartfelt contrition, contempt for sin, and love for virtue.

---

19. Cf. Jn. 14:6.
20. Cf. Mt. 20:1–6.

Otherwise you will not have done your part to be fit to be joined as branches to the vine that is my only-begotten Son, who said, "I am the true vine and you are the branches. And my Father is the gardener."[21]

Indeed I am the gardener, for all that exists comes from me. With power and strength beyond imagining I govern the whole world: Not a thing is made or kept in order without me. I am the gardener, then, who planted the vine of my only-begotten Son in the earth of your humanity so that you, the branches, could be joined to the vine and bear fruit.

Therefore, if you do not produce the fruit of good and holy deeds you will be cut off from this vine and you will dry up. For those who are cut off from this vine lose the life of grace and are thrown into the eternal fire, just as a branch that fails to bear fruit is cut off the vine and thrown into the fire, since it is good for nothing else.[22] So those who are cut off because of their offenses, if they die still guilty of deadly sin, will be thrown into the fire that lasts forever, for they are good for nothing else.

Such people have not tilled their vineyards. They have, in fact, destroyed them—yes, and other people's as well. Not only did they fail to set out any good plants of virtue, but they even dug out the seed of grace that they had received with the light of holy baptism, when they had drunk of the blood of my Son—that wine poured out for you by this true vine. They dug out this seed and fed it to beasts, that is, to their countless sins. And they trampled it underfoot with their disordered will, and so offended me and brought harm to their neighbors as well as to themselves.

But that is not how my servants act, and you should be like them, joined and engrafted to this vine. Then you will produce much fruit, because you will share the vital sap of the vine. And being in the Word, my Son, you will be in me, for I am one with him and he with me.[23] If you are in him you will follow his teaching, and if you follow his teaching you will share in the very being of this Word—that is, you will share in the eternal Godhead made one with humanity, whence you will draw that divine love which inebriates the soul. All this I mean when I say that you will share in the very substance of the vine.

---

21. Jn. 15:1, 5.
22. Cf. Jn. 15:6.
23. Jn. 10:30.

24

Do you know what course I follow, once my servants have completely given themselves to the teaching of the gentle loving Word? I prune them, so that they will bear much fruit—cultivated fruit, not wild.[24] Just as the gardener prunes the branch that is joined to the vine so that it will yield more and better wine, but cuts off and throws into the fire the branch that is barren, so do I the true gardener act. When my servants remain united to me I prune them with great suffering so that they will bear more and better fruit, and virtue will be proved in them. But those who bear no fruit are cut off and thrown into the fire.

These are the true workers. They till their souls well, uprooting every selfish love, cultivating the soil of their love in me. They feed and tend the growth of the seed of grace that they received in holy baptism. And as they till their own vineyards, so they till their neighbors' as well, for they cannot do the one without the other. You already know that every evil as well as every good is done by means of your neighbors.

You, then, are my workers. You have come from me, the supreme eternal gardener, and I have engrafted you onto the vine by making myself one with you.

Keep in mind that each of you has your own vineyard. But every one is joined to your neighbors' vineyards without any dividing lines. They are so joined together, in fact, that you cannot do good or evil for yourself without doing the same for your neighbors.

All of you together make up one common vineyard, the whole Christian assembly, and you are all united in the vineyard of the mystic body of holy Church from which you draw your life. In this vineyard is planted the vine, which is my only-begotten Son, into whom you must be engrafted.[25] Unless you are engrafted into him you are rebels against holy Church, like members that are cut off from the body and rot.

It is true that while you have time you can get yourselves out of the stench of sin through true repentance and recourse to my ministers. They are the workers who have the keys to the wine cellar, that is, the blood poured forth from this vine. (And this blood is so perfect in

---

24. Cf. Is. 5:1–4.
25. Cf. Rm. 11:17–24.

itself that you cannot be deprived of its benefits through any fault in the minister.)

It is charity that binds you to true humility—the humility that is found in knowing yourself and me. See, then, that it is as workers that I have sent you all. And now I am calling you again, because the world is failing fast. The thorns have so multiplied and have choked the seed so badly that it will produce no fruit of grace at all.

I want you, therefore, to be true workers. With deep concern help to till the souls in the mystic body of holy Church. I am calling you to this because I want to be merciful to the world as you have so earnestly begged me.

And the soul, restless in her great love, answered:

25

O immeasurably tender love! Who would not be set afire with such love? What heart could keep from breaking? You, deep well of charity, it seems you are so madly in love with your creatures that you could not live without us! Yet you are our God, and have no need of us. Your greatness is no greater for our well-being, nor are you harmed by any harm that comes to us, for you are supreme eternal Goodness. What could move you to such mercy? Neither duty nor any need you have of us (we are sinful and wicked debtors!)—but only love!

If I see clearly at all, supreme eternal Truth, it is I who am the thief, and you have been executed in my place. For I see the Word, your Son, nailed to a cross. And you have made him a bridge for me, as you have shown me, wretched servant that I am! My heart is breaking and yet cannot break for the hungry longing it has conceived for you!

I remember that you wanted to show me who are those who cross over the bridge and those who do not. So, if it would please your goodness to show me, I would gladly see and hear this from you.

THE BRIDGE

26

T*hen God eternal, to stir up even more that soul's love for the salvation of souls, responded to her:*

Before I show you what I want to show you, and what you asked to see, I want to describe the bridge for you.[1] I have told you that it stretches from heaven to earth by reason of my having joined myself with your humanity, which I formed from the earth's clay.

This bridge, my only-begotten Son, has three stairs. Two of them he built on the wood of the most holy cross, and the third even as he tasted the great bitterness of the gall and vinegar they gave him to drink. You will recognize in these three stairs three spiritual stages.

The first stair is the feet, which symbolize the affections. For just as the feet carry the body, the affections carry the soul. My Son's nailed feet are a stair by which you can climb to his side, where you will see revealed his inmost heart.[2] For when the soul has climbed up on the feet of affection and looked with her mind's eye into my Son's opened heart, she begins to feel the love of her own heart in his consummate and unspeakable love. (I say consummate because it is not for his own good that he loves you; you cannot do him any good, since he is one with me.) Then the soul, seeing how tremendously she is loved, is herself filled to overflowing with love. So, having climbed the second stair, she reaches the third. This is his mouth, where she finds peace from the terrible war she has had to wage because of her sins.

---

1. The basic image of the bridge may well be drawn from Gregory the Great, but Catherine builds it up with a wealth of detail apparently original to her. She may have had in mind a bridge such as that she had seen spanning the River Arno in Florence, a walled bridge complete with shops along its sides.

2. Cf. A.M. Walz, "Il segreto del cuore di Criso nella spiritualità cateriniana," *Studii domenicani* (Rome, 1939).

THE DIALOGUE

At the first stair, lifting the feet of her affections from the earth, she stripped herself of sin. At the second she dressed herself in love for virtue. And at the third she tasted peace.

So the bridge has three stairs, and you can reach the last by climbing the first two. The last stair is so high that the flooding waters cannot strike it—for the venom of sin never touched my Son.[3]

But though this bridge has been raised so high, it still is joined to the earth. Do you know when it was raised up? When my Son was lifted up on the wood of the most holy cross he did not cut off his divinity from the lowly earth of your humanity. So though he was raised so high he was not raised off the earth. In fact, his divinity is kneaded into the clay of your humanity like one bread. Nor could anyone walk on that bridge until my Son was raised up. This is why he said, "If I am lifted up high I will draw everything to myself."[4]

When my goodness saw that you could be drawn in no other way, I sent him to be lifted onto the wood of the cross. I made of that cross an anvil where this child of humankind could be hammered into an instrument to release humankind from death and restore it to the life of grace. In this way he drew everything to himself: for he proved his unspeakable love, and the human heart is always drawn by love. He could not have shown you greater love than by giving his life for you.[5] You can hardly resist being drawn by love, then, unless you foolishly refuse to be drawn.

I said that, having been raised up, he would draw everything to himself. This is true in two ways: First, the human heart is drawn by love, as I said, and with all its powers: memory, understanding, and will. If these three powers are harmoniously united in my name, everything else you do, in fact or in intention, will be drawn to union with me in peace through the movement of love, because all will be lifted up in the pursuit of crucified love. So my Truth indeed spoke truly when he said, "If I am lifted up high, I will draw everything to myself." For everything you do will be drawn to him when he draws your heart and its powers.

What he said is true also in the sense that everything was created for your use, to serve your needs. But you who have the gift of reason were made not for youselves but for me, to serve me with all your

---

3. Cf. 1 Jn. 3:5.
4. Jn. 12:32.
5. Jn. 15:13.

heart and all your love. So when you are drawn to me, everything is drawn with you, because everything was made for you.

It was necessary, then, that this bridge be raised high. And it had to have stairs so that you would be able to mount it more easily.

27

This bridge has walls of stone so that travelers will not be hindered when it rains. Do you know what stones these are? They are the stones of true solid virtue. These stones were not, however, built into walls before my Son's passion. So no one could get to the final destination, even though they walked along the pathway of virtue. For heaven had not yet been unlocked with the key of my Son's blood, and the rain of justice kept anyone from crossing over.

But after these stones were hewn on the body of the Word, my gentle Son[6] (I have told you that he is the bridge), he built them into walls, tempering the mortar with his own blood. That is, his blood was mixed into the mortar of his divinity with the strong heat of burning love.

By my power the stones of virtue were built into walls on no less a foundation than himself, for all virtue draws life from him, nor is there any virtue that has not been tested in him. So no one can have any life-giving virtue but from him, that is, by following his example and his teaching. He perfected the virtues and planted them as living stones built into walls with his blood. So now all the faithful can walk without hindrance and with no cringing fear of the rain of divine justice, because they are sheltered by the mercy that came down from heaven through the incarnation of this Son of mine.

And how was heaven opened? With the key of his blood.[7] So, you see, the bridge has walls and a roof of mercy. And the hostelry of holy Church is there to serve the bread of life and the blood, lest the journeying pilgrims, my creatures, grow weary and faint on the way. So has my love ordained that the blood and body of my only-begotten Son, wholly God and wholly human, be administered.

At the end of the bridge is the gate (which is, in fact, one with the bridge), which is the only way you can enter. This is why he said, "I am the Way and Truth and Life; whoever walks with me walks not in darkness but in light."[8] And in another place my Truth said that no

---

6. Cf. Ps. 129:3; 1 Co. 3:11.

7. Cf. G. Anadol, "Le immagine del linguaggio cateriniano e le loro fonti: la chiave," *Rassegna di ascetica e mistica* 22 (1971): 243–254.

8. Jn. 14:6, 8:12.

one could come to me except through him,[9] and such is the truth.

I explained all this to you, you will recall, because I wanted to let you see the way. So when he says that he is the Way he is speaking the truth. And I have already shown you that he is the Way, in the image of a bridge. He says he is Truth, and so he is, and whoever follows him goes the way of truth. And he is Life. If you follow this truth you will have the life of grace and never die of hunger, for the Word has himself become your food. Nor will you ever fall into darkness, for he is the light undimmed by any falsehood. Indeed, with his truth he confounds and destroys the lie with which the devil deceived Eve. That lie broke up the road to heaven, but Truth repaired it and walled it up with his blood.

Those who follow this way are children of the truth because they follow the truth. They pass through the gate of truth and find themselves in me. And I am one with the gate and the way that is my Son, eternal Truth, a sea of peace.

But those who do not keep to this way travel below through the river—a way not of stones but of water. And since there is no restraining the water, no one can cross through it without drowning.

Such are the pleasures and conditions of the world. Those whose love and desire are not grounded on the rock but are set without order on created persons and things apart from me (and these, like water, are continually running on) run on just as they do. Though it seems to them that it is the created things they love that are running on by while they themselves remain firm, they are in fact continually running on to their end in death. They would like to preserve themselves (that is, their lives and the things they love) and not run away to nothingness. But they cannot. Either death makes them leave all behind, or by my decree these created things are taken away from them.

Such as these are following a lie by going the way of falsehood. They are children of the devil, who is the father of lies.[10] And because they pass through the gate of falsehood they are eternally damned.

28

So you see, I have shown you truth and falsehood, that is, my way, which is truth, and the devil's way, which is falsehood. These are the two ways, and both are difficult.

---

9. Jn. 14:6.
10. Jn. 8:44.

How foolish and blind are those who choose to cross through the water when the road has been built for them! This road is such a joy for those who travel on it that it makes every bitterness sweet for them, and every burden light.[11] Though they are in the darkness of the body they find light, and though they are mortal they find life without death. For through love and the light of faith they taste eternal Truth, with the promise of refreshment in return for the weariness they have borne for me. For I am grateful and sensitive. And I am just, giving each of you what you have earned: reward for good and punishment for sin.

Your tongue could never tell, nor your ears hear, nor your eyes see the joy they have who travel on this road,[12] for even in this life they have some foretaste of the good prepared for them in everlasting life.

They are fools indeed who scorn such a good and choose instead to taste even in this life the guarantee[13] of hell by keeping to the way beneath the bridge. For there the going is most wearisome and there is neither refreshment nor any benefit at all, because by their sinfulness they have lost me, the supreme and eternal Good. So there is good reason—and it is my will—that you and my other servants should feel continual distress that I am so offended, as well as compassion for the harm that comes to those who so foolishly offend me.

Now you have heard and seen what this bridge is like. I have told you all this to explain what I meant when I said that my only-begotten Son is a bridge, as you see he is, joining the most high with the most lowly.

29

When my only-begotten Son returned to me forty days after his resurrection, this bridge was raised high above the earth. For he left your company and ascended to heaven by the power of my divine nature to sit at his eternal Father's right hand. On the day of his ascension the disciples were as good as dead, because their hearts had been lifted up to heaven along with my Son, who is Wisdom. So the angel

---

11. Cf. Mt. 11:30.
12. Cf. 1 Co. 2:9.
13. *Arra.* The word has the sense of a down payment, a pledge of future payment in full.

said to them: "Do not stay here, for he is seated at the Father's right hand."[14]

When he had been raised on high and returned to me, his Father, I sent the Teacher, the Holy Spirit. He came with my power and my Son's wisdom and his own mercy. He is one thing with me, the Father, and with my Son. He came to make even more firm the road my Truth had left in the world through his teaching. So though my Son's presence was no longer with you, his teaching—the way of which he made for you this lovely and glorious bridge—remained, as did his virtues, the solid stones grounded in that teaching. First he acted, and from his actions he built the way. He taught you more by example than with words, always doing first what he talked about.[15]

The Holy Spirit's mercy confirmed this teaching by strengthening the disciples' minds to testify to the truth and make known this way, the teaching of Christ crucified. Through them he reproved the world for its injustice and false judgments.[16] But I will tell you more about this injustice and judgment later.

I have told you this so that no darkness should cloud the minds of those who hear it. So if anyone should say, "I can see the truth of this: that the body of Christ has been made a bridge by the union of the divine nature with the human. But this bridge ascended into heaven and left us behind. He *was* a way for us and taught us the truth by the example of his own habits. But what remains for us now? And where can I find the way?"—I will answer any one who is duped by such foolishness.

The way that he taught and about which I have told you has been verified by the apostles and proclaimed in the blood of the martyrs. It has been lighted up by the doctors, attested to by the confessors, and committed to writing by the evangelists. All of these are living witnesses to the truth in the mystic body of holy Church. They are like lamps set on a lampstand[17] to point out the way of truth, perfectly lighted, that leads to life.

And how do they tell you? With proof, for they have proved it in

---

14. Cf. Ac. 1:11. In the margin of C, in the same hand as the entire manuscript, is written: *sic exponit magister in hystoriis quamvis textus non sic habeatur.*

15. Cf. Ac. 1:1.

16. Cf. Jn. 16:8.

17. Cf. Mt. 5:15.

themselves. So every one of you has enough light to know the truth if you but will, that is, if you do not decide to put out the light of your reason by your perverse selfishness. For his teaching is indeed true. And it is still there like a boat ready to rescue souls from the stormy sea and carry them to the port of salvation.

So first I made a bridge of my Son as he lived in your company. And though that living bridge has been taken from your sight, there remains the bridgeway of his teaching, which, as I told you, is held together by my power and my Son's wisdom and the mercy of the Holy Spirit. My power gives the virtue of courage to those who follow this way. Wisdom gives them light to know the truth along the way. And the Holy Spirit gives them a love that uproots all sensual love from the soul and leaves only virtuous love. So now as much as before, through his teaching as much as when he was among you, he is the way and truth and life—the way that is the bridge leading to the very height of heaven.

This is what he meant when he said, "I came from the Father and I am returning to the Father," and "I will come back to you."[18] In other words: My Father sent me to you and made me your bridge so that you might escape from the river and be able to reach life. He said also, "I will come back to you: I will not leave you orphans but will send you the Advocate."[19] It is as if my Truth had said: I am going away to the Father but I will come back; that is, when the Holy Spirit, the Advocate, comes he will strengthen you and let you see more clearly that I am the way of truth (which is what I have taught you!).

He said he would return and he did return. For the Holy Spirit did not come alone, but with power from me the Father and with the wisdom of the Son and with his own mercy. So you see, he returned, not in the flesh but in his power, to firm up the road of his teaching. That roadway cannot be destroyed or stolen from anyone who wants to follow it, because it is solid and immovable and comes from me, the unchangeable one.

So you must follow the way courageously, not in the fog but with the light of faith that I gave you as your most important adornment in holy baptism.

Now I have fully described for you and shown you the living bridge and the teaching that is one with it. I have shown the ignorant

18. Jn. 16:28, 14:8.
19. Jn. 14:18, 26.

where to find those who point out and teach this way that is truth. These are, I said, the apostles and evangelists, the martyrs and confessors and holy doctors, who have been set like lamps in holy Church.

I have shown you how, although he returned to me, my Son came back to you, but in his power rather than in the flesh. The Holy Spirit came upon the disciples. But my Son will not return in the flesh until the final day of judgment, when he will come in my divine majesty and power to judge the world: to reward the good (body and soul together) for their labors and to punish with eternal suffering those who have wickedly spent their earthly lives.

Now I want to show you what I, Truth, promised you; that is, those who travel imperfectly, perfectly, and most perfectly, and how they behave, as well as the wicked who drown in the river because of their sinfulness and so come to excruciating torments.

So I tell you, my dearest children: travel on the bridge, not underneath it. For the way beneath the bridge is not the way of truth but of falsehood. It is the way of wicked sinners, and I beg you to pray to me for them. I ask for your tears and sweat on their behalf so that they may receive mercy from me.

30

T hen that soul stood before God as if intoxicated and, unable to restrain herself, she said:

O eternal Mercy, you who cover over your creatures' faults! It does not surprise me that you say of those who leave deadly sin behind and return to you: "I will not remember that you had ever offended me."[20] O unspeakable mercy! I am not surprised that you speak so to those who forsake sin, when you say of those who persecute you: "I want you to pray to me for them so that I can be merciful to them." What mercy comes forth from your Godhead, eternal Father, to rule the whole world with your power!

By your mercy we were created. And by your mercy we were created anew in your Son's blood. It is your mercy that preserves us. Your mercy made your Son play death against life and life against death on the wood of the cross. In him life confounded the death that is our sin, even while that same death of sin robbed the spotless Lamb of his bodily life. But who was conquered? Death! And how? By your mercy!

---

20. Cf. Ez. 18:21–22.

Your mercy is life-giving. It is the light in which both the upright and sinners discover your goodness. Your mercy shines forth in your saints in the height of heaven. And if I turn to the earth, your mercy is everywhere. Even in the darkness of hell your mercy shines, for you do not punish the damned as much as they deserve.

You temper your justice with mercy. In mercy you cleansed us in the blood; in mercy you kept company with your creatures. O mad lover! It was not enough for you to take on our humanity: You had to die as well! Nor was death enough: You descended to the depths to summon our holy ancestors and fulfill your truth and mercy in them. Your goodness promises good to those who serve you in truth, so you went to call these servants of yours from their suffering to reward them for their labors!

I see your mercy pressing you to give us even more when you leave yourself with us as food to strengthen our weakness, so that we forgetful fools should be forever reminded of your goodness. Every day you give us this food, showing us yourself in the sacrament of the altar within the mystic body of holy Church. And what has done this? Your mercy.

O mercy! My heart is engulfed with the thought of you! For wherever I turn my thoughts I find nothing but mercy! O eternal Father, forgive my foolish presumption in babbling on so before you—but your merciful love is my excuse in the presence of your kindness.

31

A*fter thus expanding her heart a bit in singing the praises of God's mercy, the soul humbly waited for him to keep his promise. And in reply to her God said:*

Dearest daughter, you have been carrying on about my mercy because I let you experience it when I said to you, "I beg you to pray to me on behalf of these people." But know that my mercy toward you is incomparably more than you can see, because your sight is imperfect and limited, and my mercy is perfect and without limit. So there can be no comparison except that of the finite to the infinite.

I wanted you to experience this mercy as well as your own dignity as I showed you before, so that you would better understand the cruelty and baseness of the wicked who travel beneath the bridge. Open your mind's eye and look at those who drown by their own choice, and see how low they have fallen by their sins.

First they became weak, and this is when they conceived deadly sin in their hearts. Then they gave birth to that sin and lost the life of grace. And now these who have drowned in the river of the world's disordered love are dead to grace, and like the senseless dead they cannot make a move except as they are picked up by others. Because they are dead they remember nothing of my mercy. Their minds neither see nor know my truth (for their sensitivity is dead, and they see nothing but themselves, and that with the dead love of selfish sensuality). And so their wills also are dead to my will, for they love nothing but what is dead.

Because these three powers (memory, understanding, and will) are dead, everything they do in intention or in fact is dead so far as grace is concerned. They can no longer defend themselves against their enemies. They are helpless unless I help them. But they do still have their freedom of choice as long as they are in the flesh, and any time these dead will ask for my help they can have it—but that is the limit of what they can do for themselves.

They become unbearable to themselves. They who wanted to rule the world find themselves ruled by nothingness, that is, by sin—for sin is the opposite of being, and they have become servants and slaves of sin.

I made them trees of love through the life of grace, which they received in holy baptism. But they have become trees of death, because they *are* dead.

Do you know where this tree of death is rooted? In the height of pride, which is nourished by their sensual selfishness. Its core is impatience and its offshoot is the lack of any discernment. These are the four chief vices, which together kill the souls of those I have called trees of death, since they have failed to feed on the life of grace.

Within these trees a worm of conscience nibbles. But as long as a person lives in deadly sin the worm is blinded and so is little felt.

The fruits of such trees are full of death, for their juice comes from the root of pride. So their wretched little souls are filled with thanklessness, the source of all evils. Had they been grateful for the blessings they received from me, they would know me. And in knowing me they would know themselves, and so live in my love. But instead they go on groping their way through the river as if they were blind, not seeing how completely undependable the water is.

32

There are as many different death-dealing fruits on these trees of death as there are sins. Some are food for beasts: These are people who live indecently, using their bodies and minds like pigs rolling in the mud, for that is how they roll about in the mud of lust. O brutish souls! What have you done with your dignity? You who were created kin to the angels have made ugly beasts of yourselves! You have stooped so low that even the demons whose friends and servants you have become cannot stand the sight of such indecency—and much less I, who am purity itself.

No other sin is so hateful and so darkens the human mind as this. The philosophers knew this, not by the light of grace (since they did not have it) but by a natural light: that this sin beclouds the mind. So they were continent the better to be able to study. And they cast aside wealth so that the thought of material things would not clutter their hearts. But not so the foolish false Christians who have lost grace through their own fault.

33

Others there are whose fruits are of clay. These are the greedy misers who act like the mole who feeds on nothing but dirt right up to the end. And when death comes where have they to turn? In their avarice they scorn my generosity, selling their time to their neighbors. They are usurers who become cruel robbers who blot my mercy from their memories. For if they did remember my mercy they would not be cruel either to themselves or their neighbors, but would rather be kind and merciful to themselves by living virtuously and to their neighbors by serving them with love.

How many evils come from this cursed sin of avarice! How many murders, thefts, and pillagings; how many unlawful profits and how much hard-heartedness and injustice toward others! It kills the spirit and makes people slaves to wealth who care nothing for God's commandments. Such people love no one except for their own profit.

This vice is born of pride and it feeds pride, because it is always so concerned about its own reputation that it necessarily links up with pride. And so, with wretched self-opinionated pride, it goes from bad to worse. It is a flame that always generates the smoke of vanity and arrogance, taking pride in what is not its own. It is a root with many branches, chief of which is a self-conceit that always wants to be greater than others. Another of its branches is the deceitful heart that is not sincere and generous but double, that says one thing but thinks another, that hides the truth and tells lies for its own profit. And avarice breeds envy, a worm that is always gnawing, letting the avaricious enjoy neither their own nor anyone else's good.

How can these wretched evil people share their possessions with the poor when they are already stealing from them? How can they rescue others from indecency when they are the ones who shoved them into it? For sometimes they are such animals that they have no respect for their own daughters and other relatives, but stoop to the meanest things with them. And yet my mercy holds them up, and I refrain from ordering the earth to swallow them up, giving them a chance to repent.

But if they will not share their possessions, how will they ever give their lives for the salvation of souls? How will they give affection if they are being eaten up by envy?

O miserable vices that tear down the heaven of the soul! I call the soul "heaven" because I make heaven wherever I dwell by grace. I made the soul my hiding place and by my love turned her into a mansion. But now she has left me like an adulteress because she loves herself and other created persons and things more than me. In fact, she has made a god of herself and strikes out at me with all sorts of sins. And she does all this because she gives no thought to the blood shed for her with such burning love.

34

There are others who are so bloated with the power in their hands that the standard they carry is injustice. They inflict their injustice on God and their neighbors and even on themselves.

They are unjust to themselves by not being virtuous as they owe it to themselves to be. They do not give me the honor that is my due, nor praise my name as is their duty, but like thieves they steal what is mine and put it to the service of their own sensuality. So they are being unjust both to me and to themselves, for like blinded fools they do not recognize me in themselves.

And it is all because of selfishness, like those Jews and ministers of the Law who were so blinded by envy and selfishness that they did not recognize the Truth, my only-begotten Son. Therefore they did not, as they should have, recognize eternal Life when he was in their midst. My Truth told them, "The Kingdom of God is within you."[21] But they failed to recognize it. Why? Because they had lost the light of reason and so they did not offer due honor and glory to me or to him who is one with me. And so they blindly committed the injustice of persecuting him shamefully even to death by crucifixion.

Such as these are unjust to themselves and to me and to their neighbors as well. They are unjust dealers in the flesh of their subjects and of anyone else who may fall into their hands.

35

Through this sin and others they fall into false judgment. They are constantly scandalized at my ways, which are always just and truly spring from love and mercy.

This is the false judgment, venomous with envy and pride, with which they calumniated and unjustly judged my Son's works when they said, "He does these things by the power of Beelzebub."[22] These wicked people are set in their way of selfishness, indecency, pride, and avarice, envy that is grounded in their perverse lack of discernment, their impatience, and many other sins. Yet they are forever taking scandal at me and my servants, judging their virtue to be hypocritical. Because they are rotten to the core and have spoiled their sense of taste, good things seem evil to them and evil (that is, disordered living) seems good.

O blind humanity, to have so lost sight of your dignity! You who were so great have become so small! You who were in command have sold yourselves into servitude to the vilest power there is, for you have become the servants and slaves of sin. Yes, you have become a nothing, since you become like what you serve, and sin is nothingness. It has taken life from you and given you death in its place.

Your life and power were given you by the Word, my only-begotten Son, the glorious bridge. You were slaves of the devil and he rescued you from slavery. I made him a servant to free you from servitude. I put him under obedience to dissipate the disobedience of Adam by humbling himself to his shameful death on the cross and thus putting pride to rout. He destroyed every vice by his death so that no one would be able to say, "There is still such and such a vice that has not

---

21. Lk. 17:21.
22. Mt. 12:24.

been punished and hammered out with suffering"—for, as I told you before, his body was made an anvil. Every help is there to save them from everlasting death, but they have spurned the blood and trampled it underfoot with their disordered passions.

This, then, is the injustice and the false judgment for which the world has been reproved and will be reproved on the final day of judgment. And this is what my Son meant when he said, "I will send the Advocate, who will reprove the world for its injustice and false judgment."[23] The world was thus reproved when I sent the Holy Spirit upon the apostles.

36

There are three reproofs.

The first reproof was given when the Holy Spirit came upon the disciples. When they were strengthened by my power and enlightened by my beloved Son, they received everything in the fullness of the Holy Spirit. It was then that the Holy Spirit, who is one with me and with my Son, reproved the world with my Truth's teaching, through the disciples' mouths. These, as well as all their descendents in the following of the truth (which they understand because of the disciples' teaching), continue to reprove the world.

This is the constant reproof I bring to the world through the Holy Scriptures and through my servants. The Holy Spirit is on their tongues to proclaim the truth, just as the devil is in the mouths of his servants who in their wickedness travel through the river. This is the gentle reproof that I still go on giving because of the tremendous love I have for the salvation of souls. They cannot say, "I had no one to correct me," because I have shown them the truth; I have shown them vice and virtue; I have let them see virtue's reward and the harm that comes from vice so as to fill them with love for virtue and holy fear and hatred for vice. I did not show them this teaching and truth through an angel, though, lest they should be able to say, "The angels have the good fortune to be spirits incapable of sinning. They do not feel the vexations of the flesh as we do, nor the burden of a body." I have made it impossible for them to say this because I have given them my teaching through my Truth, the Word made flesh with your own mortal flesh.

And who are these others who have followed this Word? Mortal

---

23. Jn. 16:8.

creatures as subject to suffering as yourselves, whose flesh rebelled against their spirit. So it was with the glorious Paul, my trumpeter,[24] and so also with many other saints, all of whom suffered from one thing or another. But I permitted and continue to permit such troubles to further the growth of grace and virtue in the soul. They were born of sin as you were and nourished on the same food. And I am God now as then: My power is not and cannot be weakened. So I can and want to and will help whoever wants my help. You show that you want my help when you leave the river behind and keep to the bridge by following the teaching of my Truth.

People have no excuse, then, because they are constantly being reproved and shown the truth. Therefore, if they do not change their ways while they have time, they will be condemned when the second reproof comes. This will be at the end point, which is death, when my justice will shout, "Arise, you who are dead, to be judged!" In other words, "You who are dead to grace and now have come to your bodily death, get up and come before the supreme judge with your injustice and false judgment and with your snuffed-out lamp of faith. You received that lamp burning in holy baptism, and you snuffed it out with the wind of your pride and vanity. You turned your sails to winds that blew contrary to your salvation, and you encouraged the wind of self-conceit to fill the sail of your selfish love till of your own will you went racing down the river of worldly pleasures and honors, running after your weak flesh and the vexatious temptings of the devil. Using the sail of your selfish will the devil led you on through the racing riverway beneath the bridge until he brought you to eternal damnation along with himself."

37

They feel this second of my three reproofs, dearest daughter, by the very fact that they have come to the end point where there is no turning back. At this end point of death, when they see that they cannot escape from my hands, the worm of conscience (which, as I told you, had been blinded by their selfish love of themselves) begins to see again. And in the realization that their own sins have brought them to

---

24. Cf. Ga. 5:17; 2 Co. 12:7.

such an evil end, this worm of conscience gnaws away in self-reproach.

If such souls would have light to acknowledge and be sorry for their sins—and not because of the sufferings of hell that are their consequence, but because they have offended me, the supreme and eternal Good—they would still find mercy.

But if they pass the moment of death without that light, with only the worm of conscience and no hope in the blood, or grieving more for their own plight than for having offended me, then they have come to eternal damnation. Then my justice reproves them harshly for their injustice and false judgment. And not simply in general terms for their pervasive habits of injustice and false judgment during their earthly lives, but even more for that particular unjust judgment by which at the very end they had judged their own wretchedness to be greater than my mercy.[25]

This is that sin which is never forgiven, now or ever: the refusal, the scorning, of my mercy.[26] For this offends me more than all the other sins they have committed. So the despair of Judas displeased me more and was a greater insult to my Son than his betrayal had been. Therefore, such as these are reproved for this false judgment of considering their sin to be greater than my mercy, and for this they are punished with the demons and tortured eternally with them.

They are reproved also for their injustice in grieving more for their own plight than for having offended me. They are being unjust in this because they are not giving me what is mine, nor taking for themselves what belongs to them. It is their duty to offer love and bitter heartfelt contrition in my presence for the sins they have committed against me. But they have done the opposite: They have lavished such tender love on themselves and felt so sorry about the punishment they expect for their sins! So you see how unjust they are.

They will be punished, therefore, on both accounts. They have scorned my mercy, so I turn them over to my justice. I condemn them along with their cruel servant, sensuality, and with the devil, that merciless tyrant to whom they bound themselves as slaves through the mediation of that selfish sensuality of theirs. Together they offended me; together they shall be punished and tormented. Tormented, I mean, by

---

25. Cf. Gn. 4:13, and Cain's attitude in the face of God's judgment.
26. Cf. Mt. 12:31–32.

my ministers the demons, whom my justice has commissioned to repay with torments those who have done evil.

38

Daughter, words could never describe the suffering of these wretched little souls. There are three principal vices: The first is selfishness, which in turn gives birth to the second, self-conceit. From this conceit comes the third, pride, with treacherous injustice and cruelty as well as other evil filthy sins generated by these. So also, I tell you, in hell there are four principal torments, and all the others are offspring of these.

The first is that these souls are deprived of seeing me. This is so painful for them that if they could they would choose the sight of me along with the fire and excruciating torments, rather than freedom from their pains without seeing me.

This first suffering revives the worm of conscience, and this is their second torment. For when they see that their sinfulness has deprived them of me and of the company of the angels and made them worthy instead of seeing the demons and sharing their fellowship, conscience gnaws away at them constantly.

The sight of the devil is their third suffering, and it doubles every other torment. At the sight of me the saints are in constant exultation, joyously refreshed in reward for the labors they bore for me with such overflowing love and to their own cost. But it is just the opposite for these wretched little souls. Their only refreshment is the torment of seeing the devil, for in seeing him they know themselves better: that is, they recognize that their sinfulness has made them worthy of him. And so the worm gnaws on and the fire of conscience never stops burning.[27]

Their suffering is even worse because they see the devil as he really is—more horrible than the human heart can imagine. You will recall that when I once let you see him for a tiny while, hardly a moment, as he really is, you said (after coming to your senses again) that you would rather walk on a road of fire even till the final judgment day than see him again. But even with all you have seen you do not really know how horrible he is. For my divine justice makes him look more horri-

---

27. Cf. Is. 66:24; Mk. 9:48.

ble still to those who have lost me, and this in proportion to the depth of their sinfulness.

The fourth torment is fire. This fire burns without consuming, for the soul cannot be consumed, since it is not material (such as fire could consume) but spiritual. But in my divine justice I allow the fire to burn these souls mightily, tormenting them without consuming them. And the tremendous pain of this torturous burning has as many forms as the forms of their sins and is more or less severe in proportion to their sins.

From these four torments come all the others, with cold and heat and gnashing of teeth. They would not change their ways when I first reproved them during their lifetime for their false judgment and injustice. And when I reproved them a second time as they died, they would not hope, nor were they sorry for having offended me but only for their own plight. So now they have reaped eternal death.

39

I have still to tell you about the third reproof at the final day of judgment. I have already told you about the first two. Now, so you will appreciate the extent to which people deceive themselves, I will tell you about the third. At the general judgment there will be an intolerable reproof that will generate confusion and shame, and the suffering of these wretched little souls will be intensified even more by their reunion with their bodies.

Know that on the final judgment day the Word my Son will come in my divine majesty to reprove the world with divine power. It will not be like when he was born in poverty, coming from the Virgin's womb into the stable among the animals, and then dying between two thieves. At that time I had my power in him to allow him to suffer pains and tortures as a man—not that my divine nature was cut off from his human nature, but I let him suffer as a man to atone for your sins.

Not so will he come in this end time. Then he will come in power to reprove these people in person. There will not be a creature who will not tremble, and he will give them all what they deserve.[28]

His glance will be such a torment and terror to the damned that words could not describe it. But for the just it will be a cause for rever-

---

28. Cf. Mt. 24:30.

ent fear and great rejoicing. Not that his face will change—for he is one with my divine nature and therefore unchangeable, and even in his human nature his face is unchangeable since it has taken on the glory of his resurrection. But it will seem so to the eyes of the damned. For they will see him with their terribly darkened vision. A healthy eye looks at the sun and sees light. But a sick eye sees nothing but darkness when it looks into such lightsomeness—and it is no fault of the light that it seems so different to the two; the fault is in the sick eye. So the damned see my Son in darkness, confusion, and hatred, not through any fault of my divine Majesty with which he comes to judge the world, but through their own fault.

40

Their hatred is such that they can neither will nor desire anything good, but are forever cursing me. And do you know why they are incapable of desiring what is good?

When human life comes to an end the will that was free is bound. So for the dead the time of earning is past. If they end in hatred, guilty of deadly sin, by divine justice they are forever bound by that chain of hatred and remain forever obstinate in their evil, which keeps gnawing away within them. And their suffering grows continually, especially at the sight of others whose damnation they have brought about.

This was taught you, for example, in the rich man who when he was damned begged that Lazarus might go to tell his brothers still on earth how he was suffering. His motive was not love or compassion for his brothers (for he had lost charity and was incapable of desiring what was good). Nor was it my honor or their salvation (for I have already told you that the damned can do no good for others and curse me because they ended their lives hating both me and virtue). What then was his motive? He was the eldest, and he had encouraged the same wretchedness in them that he himself had lived. So he had led them toward damnation. And he saw the suffering that would fall on him if they should come like him to this excruciating torment, gnawing away at themselves forever with hate because they had ended their lives in hate.

41

By the same principle, those just souls who end in loving charity and are bound by love can no longer grow in virtue once time has passed. But they can forever love with that same affection with which they came to me, and by that measure will it be measured out to them.[29] They desire me forever, and forever they possess me, so their desire is not in vain. They are hungry and satisfied, satisfied yet hungry—but they are far from bored with satiety or pained in their hunger.

Forever they rejoice in love at the sight of me, sharing in that goodness which I have in myself and which I measure out to them according to the measure of love with which they have come to me. They are established in love for me and for their neighbors. And they are all united in general and special love, both of which come from one and the same charity. They rejoice and exult, sharing each other's goodness with loving affection, besides that universal good which they all possess together. They rejoice and exult with the angels, and they find their places among the saints according to the different virtues in which they excelled in the world.

And though they are all joined in the bond of charity, they know a special kind of sharing with those whom they loved most closely with a special love in the world, a love through which they grew in grace and virtue. They helped each other proclaim the glory and praise of my name in themselves and in their neighbors. So now in everlasting life they have not lost that love; no, they still love and share with each other even more closely and fully, adding their love to the good of all.

For I would not have you think this special good they have is only for themselves. No, it is shared by all their just companions, my beloved children, and by all the angels. For when a soul reaches eternal life, all share in her good and she in theirs. Not that anyone's vessel can get any larger or have need of filling. They are all full and can grow no larger. But they experience a new freshness in their exultation—a mirthfulness, a jubilation, a gladness—in knowing this soul. They see that by my mercy she has been lifted up from the earth in the fullness of grace, and so they are exultant in me over the good that soul has received from my goodness.

And that soul finds joy in me and in all these souls and blessed spirits, seeing and tasting in them the sweetness of my love. Their desires are a continual cry to me for the salvation of others, for they finished their lives loving their neighbors, and they did not leave that love behind but brought it with them when they passed through that gate

---

29. Cf. Mt. 7:2.

which is my only-begotten Son.[30] So you see that in whatever bond of love they finish their lives, that bond is theirs forever and lasts eternally.

They are so conformed to my will that they can will only what I will. When time came to an end for them and they died in grace, their freedom was so bound with the chains of charity that they are no longer capable of sin. Their will is so one with mine that even if a father and mother saw their child in hell, or a child its parent, it would not trouble them: They would even be content to see them punished, since they are my enemies. Nothing puts them at variance with me. All their desires are fulfilled.

What these blessed ones want is to see me honored in you who are still on the way, pilgrims running ever nearer your end in death. Because they seek my honor they desire your salvation, and so they are constantly praying to me for you. I do my part to fulfill their desire provided only that you do not foolishly resist my mercy.

It is also their desire to have once again the gift of their bodies. But it is not a troubled desire, because although they do not have them now they are happy in the certainty that their desire will be fulfilled. They are not troubled, for they experience no pain or lack of happiness in not having them. Do not think either that the body's happiness after the resurrection will add anything to the soul's happiness. If this were the case, it would follow that the soul's happiness would be imperfect until the return of the body. But this cannot be, for these souls lack no perfection. It is not the body that brings happiness to the soul. The soul, though, will give happiness to the body: Her own fullness will overflow when on the final day of judgment she puts on once more the garment of her own flesh, which she had left behind.

Just as the soul was made immortal and firm in me, so in this reunion the body will become immortal, its heaviness cast off and made fine and light. The glorified body could pass through a wall, and neither fire nor water could hurt it. But know that this is not due to its own power but to the soul's—which is really my own power given her by grace through the unspeakable love with which I created her in my image and likeness.

The good of these souls is beyond what your mind's eye can see or your ear hear or your tongue describe or your heart imagine. What joy they have in seeing me who am all good! What joy they will yet have

---

30. Jn. 10:7, 9.

when their bodies are glorified! But while they do not have this latter good until the general judgment, they do not suffer. They lack no happiness, for the soul is filled, and in this fullness the body will share.

I have told you of the good the glorified body will have in the glorified humanity of my only-begotten Son, and this is the guarantee of your own resurrection. What joy there is in his wounds, forever fresh, the scars remaining in his body and continually crying out for mercy to me the high eternal Father, for you! You will all be made like him in joy and gladness; eye for eye, hand for hand, your whole bodies will be made like the body of the Word my Son. You will live in him as you live in me, for he is one with me. But your bodily eyes, as I have told you, will delight in the glorified humanity of the Word my only-begotten Son. Why? Because those who finish their lives delighting in my love will keep that delight forever. Not that they can do any further good now, but they rejoice in the good that they have brought with them. In other words, they cannot do anything deserving of merit, for it is only in this life, by the choice of free will, that one can either merit or sin.

These souls wait for divine judgment with gladness, not fear. And the face of my Son will appear to them neither terrifying nor hateful, because they have finished their lives in charity, delighting in me and filled with good will toward their neighbors. The different appearances of his face when he comes in my majesty for judgment will not be in him but in those who are to be judged by him. To the damned he will appear with just hatred, but to the saved, with mercy and love.

42

I have told you about the honor of the just so that you might better appreciate the wretchedness of the damned. And the sight of the happiness of the just is yet another suffering for the damned. It adds to their pain just as the punishment of the damned makes the just rejoice even more in my goodness. For light is seen better in contrast to darkness, and darkness in contrast to light. So the sight of the just is suffering for the damned, and they suffer in expectation of the final day of judgment because they see it will bring them even more pain. And so it will be.

When that terrifying voice says to them, "Arise, you dead, and come to judgment!" their souls will return with their bodies. The bodies of the just will be glorified. But the bodies of the damned will be

CATHERINE OF SIENA

forever tortured, and the sight of my Truth and of all the blessed will be for them a great shame and reproach. Then will the worm of conscience gnaw away at the whole tree, both the marrow (that is, the soul) and the bark (the body).

They will be reproached by the blood that was paid out for them, and by the spiritual and material works of mercy I did for them through my Son, which they in turn should have done for their neighbors as you are told in the holy Gospel.[31] They will be reproached by their own cruelty toward their neighbors when they see the mercy they had received from me. And their reproach will be the more harsh for all their pride and selfishness and indecency and avarice. At the moment of death the soul bears this reproach alone. But at the general judgment soul and body will endure it together. For the body was the soul's partner and instrument in doing good and evil as the will was pleased to choose.

Every action, whether good or evil, is done by means of the body. So it is just, my daughter, that my chosen ones should be rewarded with endless glory and good in their glorified bodies for the toil they endured for me in body as well as in soul. And the wicked likewise will be eternally punished in their bodies, which were their instruments of evil.

When they are reunited with their bodies their suffering at the sight of my Son will be renewed and increased. What a reproach to their miserable indecent sensuality, to see their own nature, this clay of Adam, exalted above all the choirs of angels in the humanity of Christ joined with the purity of my Godhead! And they will see themselves thrown down to the depths of hell for their sins.

They will see my generosity and mercy shine forth in the blessed as these receive the fruit of the blood of the Lamb. And they will see how all the sufferings the blessed endured remain as adornments on their bodies, like ornamentation imprinted on cloth—not from the body's own excellence, but because the soul from her fullness will imprint on the body the fruit of its labors, to shine outwardly, since it was her partner in virtue. Just as a mirror reflects a person's face, just so, the fruit of their labors will be reflected in their bodies.

When the darksome ones see such honor, and themselves deprived of it, their suffering and confusion will increase. For on their bodies

31. Cf. Jn. 13:15.

86

will appear the mark of their evil deeds, with pain and excruciating torment. And when they hear with terror those words, "Depart, you cursed ones, into the everlasting fire!"[32] soul and body will enter the company of the demons with no hope of return. They will be engulfed in all the filth of the earth, in as many different ways as their evil deeds were different. The misers will be plunged in the filth of avarice, engulfed at once in the burning fire and in the goods of the world that they loved inordinately. The violent will be engulfed in cruelty, the indecent in indecency and wretched lust, the unjust in their own injustice, the envious in envy, and those who were hateful and bitter toward their neighbors will be engulfed in hate. Their disordered love for themselves, out of which grew all their wickedness, will burn and torture them intolerably, for along with pride it is the head and source of all evil. So will they all be differently punished, soul and body together.

Thus will those miserably come to their end who travel by the way beneath the bridge, through the river. They never turn back to admit their sins or to ask for my mercy, so they come to the gate of falsehood because they follow the teaching of the devil, who is the father of lies. And this devil is their gateway through which they come to eternal damnation.

But my chosen children keep to the higher way, the bridge. They follow closely the way of truth, and this truth is their gateway. This is why my Truth said, "No one can come to the Father except through me."[33] He is the gate and the way through whom they pass to enter into me, the sea of peace.

The others, in contrast, hold to falsehood, which gives them the water of death. The demon calls them to this, and they, blind and mad, do not realize it, because they have lost the light of faith. It is as if the devil said to them, "Let all who are thirsty for the water of death come to me, and I will give it to them."[34]

43

My justice has made the devil my executioner to torment the souls who have wretchedly offended me. And I have appointed the demons to tempt and trouble my creatures in this life. Not that I want my crea-

---

32. Mt. 25:41.
33. Jn. 14:6.
34. Cf. Is. 55:1; Rv. 21:6.

tures to be conquered, but I want them to conquer and receive from me the glory of victory when they have proved their virtue. No one need fear any battle or temptation of the devil that may come, for I have made you strong and given your wills power in the blood of my Son. Neither the devil nor any other creature can change this will of yours, for it is yours, given by me with the power of free choice. You, then, can hold or loose it as you please, by your free choice. It is a weapon that, as soon as you put it in the devil's hands, becomes a knife with which he pursues and kills you. But if you refuse to put this weapon, your will, into the devil's hands (that is, if you refuse to consent to his tempting and troubling) you will never be hurt in any temptation by the guilt of sin. Indeed, temptation will strengthen you, provided you open your mind's eye to see my charity, which lets you be tempted only to bring you to virtue and to prove your virtue.

You cannot arrive at virtue except through knowing yourself and knowing me. And this knowledge is more perfectly gained in time of temptation, because then you know that you are nothing, since you have no power to relieve yourself of the sufferings and troubles you would like to escape. And you know me in your will, when I strengthen it in my goodness so that it does not consent to these thoughts. You realize that my love has granted them, for the devil is weak and can do nothing of himself, but only as I permit him. And I give him leave not through hatred but through love, not so that you may be conquered but that you may conquer and come to perfect knowledge of yourself and of me, and to prove your virtue—for virtue can only be tested by its opposite.

You see, then, that the demons are my ministers to torment the damned in hell and to exercise and test your virtue in this life. Not that it is the devil's intention to make you prove your virtue (for he has no charity). He would rather deprive you of virtue! But he cannot, unless you will it so.

How great is the stupidity of those who make themselves weak in spite of my strengthening, and put themselves into the devil's hands! I want you to know, then, that at the moment of death, because they have put themselves during life under the devil's rule (not by force, because they cannot be forced, as I told you; but they put themselves voluntarily into his hands), and because they come to the point of death under this perverse rule, they can expect no other judgment but that of their own conscience. They come without hope to eternal damnation. In hate they grasp at hell in the moment of their death, and even before they possess it, they take hell as their prize along with their lords the demons.

The just, on the other hand, have lived in charity and die in love. If they have lived perfectly in virtue, enlightened by faith, seeing with faith and trusting completely in the blood of the Lamb, when they come to the point of death they see the good I have prepared for them. They embrace it with the arms of love, reaching out with the grasp of love to me, the supreme and eternal Good, at the very edge of death. And so they taste eternal life even before they have left their mortal bodies.

There are others who have passed through life and arrive at the end point of death with only a commonplace love, and were never very perfect. These embrace my mercy with the same light of faith and hope as those who were perfect. But these have this light imperfectly, and because they are imperfect they reach out for mercy, considering my mercy greater than their own guilt.

Wicked sinners, on the other hand, do the opposite. When in despair they see their place, they embrace it in hate.

So no one waits to be judged. All receive their appointed place as they leave this life. They taste it and possess it even before they leave their bodies at the moment of death: the damned in hate and despair; the perfect in love, with the light of faith and trusting in the blood. And the imperfect, in mercy and with the same faith, come to that place called purgatory.

44

I have told you that the devil invites people to the water of death. For that is what he is in himself. He blinds them with the pleasures and honors of the world. He catches them with the hook of pleasure under the guise of good. There is indeed no other way he could catch them, for they would not let themselves be caught unless they found some good or pleasure in it for themselves, because the soul by its very nature always craves what is good.

Still it is true that the soul, if blinded by selfishness, cannot recognize or discern what is truly good and profitable for soul and body. So the devil, evil as he is, when he sees that the soul is blinded by sensual selfish love, proposes all sorts of sins to her. But they are all disguised as something profitable or good. And he makes different propositions to people according to their situations and the vices he sees them most open to. He proposes one thing to the layperson, another to the religious, another to priests, another to those in authority—to all according to their different situations.

I have told you this because now I am about to describe those who drown themselves down below in the river. They have no concern for anyone or anything but themselves. In other words, their love for themselves is sinful. I have told you how such as these end. Now I want to show you how deluded they are: for in their desire to escape suffering they fall into suffering. It seems to them that following me, that is, keeping to the bridge of my Son's Word, would be a great burden. So they draw back, afraid of the thorns. This is because they are blind, and they neither see nor recognize the truth. You know this because I taught it to you early in your life, when you begged me to have mercy on the world and rescue it from deadly sin.

You know that then I showed myself to you under the figure of a tree. You could see neither its bottom nor its top. But you saw that its root was joined to the earth—and this was the divine nature joined to the earth of your humanity. At the foot of the tree, if you recall, there was a sort of thorn bush. All who were in love with their own sensuality backed off from that thorn bush and ran away to a hill of chaff, in which I symbolized for you all the pleasures of the world. The chaff looked like grain but that is not what it was. So, as you saw, many souls died of hunger there. But many, when they recognized the world's deceit, returned to the tree and crossed through the thorn bush, that is, the will's decision. Beforehand, this decision is a thorn bush they seem to encounter when they follow the way of truth. Conscience always pulls in one direction, and sensuality in the other. But as soon as they decide courageously, despising themselves, and say, "I want to follow Christ crucified," the thorn bush is broken and they discover my immeasurable tenderness, as I showed you at that time. Some experience it more, some less, according to their openness and care.

You know that I said to you then, "I am your unchangeable God, and I never change. I will not draw back from any creature who wants to come to me.

"I have shown them the truth by making myself visible to them, although I am invisible. I have shown them what it is to love anything apart from me. But they, blinded as they are by the cloud of disordered love, know neither me nor themselves. You see how deluded they are, when they would rather die of hunger than cross through a bit of a thorn bush.

"They cannot escape suffering by flight, for no one can pass through this life without a cross except those who keep to the bridge. Not that those cross over without suffering, but for them suffering is refreshing. And it was because, through sin, the world sprouted thorns and troubles, and because this river runs like a stormy sea, that I gave you the bridge so you would not drown."

I have shown you how these souls are deceived by their disordered fear, and how I your God am unchanging and that I accept your holy desire, overlooking your creatureliness. All this I showed you under the image of the tree of which I told you.[35]

45

N ow I want to show you those who are hurt by the thorns and troubles brought forth by the earth because of sin, and those who are not. So far I have shown you the damnation [of the wicked] and my goodness, and I have told you how they are deceived by their selfish sensuality. Now I want to tell you why it is only they who are hurt by the thorns.

No one born into this life passes through it without suffering of body or spirit. My servants may suffer physically, but their spirit is free. In other words, suffering does not weary them, because their will is in tune with mine. It is the will that causes [the deeper] pain. Those I have described to you, who taste already in this life the pledge of hell, suffer spiritually as well as physically, while my servants taste the pledge of eternal life.

Do you know what is the most special good the blessed have? It is to have their will filled with what they long for. They long for me and they possess and taste me without any resistance, for they have left behind the body's heaviness—which was a law that fought against the spirit.[36] The body was a barrier to their knowing the truth perfectly. They could not see me face to face without leaving the body behind.

---

35. Here, as in several other places, Catherine inserts personal experiences. This particular instruction in the form of a vision, which dates to the beginning of her spiritual life, must have been recorded by her first confessor, Tommaso della Fonte, in the notebooks on which Raymond and Caffarini drew. Taurisano in his edition of the *Dialogue* (note 9, p. 99) indicates two manuscripts that contain a record of the document: Ms. AD, IX, II, c. 55 v. (Brera, Milan) and Ms. C, V, 25 in Siena. (Cavallini)

36. Cf. Rm. 7:23.

But after the soul has let go of the body's heaviness, her will is filled. She longed to see me and now she sees me, and in that vision is blessedness. Seeing me she knows me. Knowing me she loves me. Loving me she enjoys me, the supreme eternal Good. This enjoyment fills and satisfies her will, her longing to see me and know me. She longs for what she possesses and possesses what she longs for, and, as I have told you, her desire knows no pain, nor her satisfaction any boredom.[37]

So you see, my servants' chief happiness is in seeing and knowing me. This vision and knowledge fills their will: They have what their will longs for and so they are satisfied. This is why I told you that, most especially, the joy of eternal life is in possessing what the will longs for. But know that its satisfaction is in seeing and knowing me.[38] Even in this life they enjoy the pledge of eternal life, since they have a taste of the very thing that satisfies them.

How do they have this pledge in this life? Let me tell you: They see my goodness in themselves and they know my truth when their understanding—which is the soul's eye—is enlightened in me.[39] The pupil of this eye is most holy faith, and this light of faith enables them to discern and know and follow the way and teaching of my Truth, the incarnate Word.[40] Without this pupil, which is faith, they would see no more than a person who has eyes, but with a film covering the pupils that give the eyes sight. It is the same with the eye of understanding. Its pupil is faith, but if selfish love pulls over it the film of infidelity, it cannot see. It may have the appearance of an eye, but it is sightless because infidelity has deprived it of light. So seeing me these souls know me, and knowing me they love me. And in loving me their selfish will is swallowed up and lost.

Having lost their own selfish will they clothe themselves in mine.

---

37. Cf. Rv. 7:16–17: "They will never hunger or thirst again . . . because the Lamb who is at the throne will be their shepherd and will lead them to springs of living water; and God will wipe away all tears from their eyes."

38. Cf. Ps. 17:15: "For me the reward of virtue is to see your face, and, on waking, to gaze my fill on your likeness."

39. Cf. Mt. 6:22–23. (I have translated *occhio dell'intelletto* as "the eye of understanding" or sometimes simply as "the mind's eye" in accordance with the context and flow of language.)

40. Note the medieval understanding that the *pupil* was the element in the eye that actually did the seeing—an understanding necessary for the consistency of Catherine's image.

But I will nothing less than your holiness. So at once they set about turning their backs on the way beneath the bridge and begin to mount the bridge. They cross through the thorns without being hurt, because their feet (that is, their affections) are shod with my will. This is why I told you that they suffer physically but not spiritually, because their sensual will—which afflicts and pains the spirit—is dead. Since they no longer have a selfish will, they no longer have this pain. So they bear everything with reverence, considering it a grace to suffer for me. And they want nothing but what I will.

If I send them suffering at the hand of the demons, allowing them to be much tempted in order to test their virtue, they stand firm. For they have strengthened their will in me by humbling themselves, considering themselves unworthy of spiritual peace and quiet and deserving of suffering. For this reason they pass through life joyfully, knowing themselves and untroubled by suffering.

They may suffer at the hands of others, or from illness or poverty or the instability of the world. They may lose their children or other loved ones. All such things are thorns the earth produced because of sin. They endure them all, considering by the light of reason and holy faith that I am goodness itself and cannot will anything but good. And I send these things out of love, not hatred.

Once they know how I love them, they look at themselves and recognize their sinfulness. By the light of faith they see that good must be rewarded and sin punished. They see that every smallest sin would be deserving of infinite punishment because it is committed against me, infinite Good. So they count it a favor that I should want to punish them in this life, in this finite time. And thus it is that they atone for their sin with heartfelt contrition, at the same time meriting by their perfect patience, and their efforts are rewarded with infinite good.

They learn that all suffering in this life is small with the smallness of time. Time is no more than the point of a needle, and when time is over, so is suffering—so you see how small it is. Therefore they endure it patiently. The thorns they pass through here and now do not touch their heart, for as far as sensual love is concerned their heart has been drawn away from themselves and is firmly joined to me by the impulse of love.

It is indeed the truth then that these souls have a foretaste and guarantee of eternal life even in this life. They do not lose their lives in the water; when they pass through the thorns they are not pricked, because they have known me, Good itself, and they have sought that goodness where it is to be found, in the Word, my only-begotten Son.

46

I have told you this so that you may better appreciate how those whose delusion I told you about taste the pledge of hell. Now I will tell you the source of their delusion and how they receive this guarantee. It is because they have blinded the eye of their understanding with the infidelity they have drawn over it through their selfish love.

Just as all truth is gained by the light of faith, so falsehood and delusion are won through infidelity. When I speak of infidelity I am referring to those who have received holy baptism. At their baptism the pupil of faith was put into the eye of their understanding. When they reached the age of discernment, if they had exercised themselves in virtue they would have kept the light of faith. Then they would have given birth to living virtues, producing fruit for their neighbors. Just as a woman bears a living child and presents it living to her husband, so they would have presented me, the soul's spouse, with living virtues.

But these wretched people do just the opposite. They reach the age of discernment when they ought to use the light of faith and give birth to virtues with the life of grace. Instead they give birth to dead virtues. They are dead because all their actions, being done in deadly sin and bereft of the light of faith, are dead. They have, in fact, the appearance of holy baptism but not its light, because they have blotted it out with the cloud of sin committed in their selfishness. And this cloud has covered over the pupil through which they used to see.

Of these, whose faith is not carried out in actions, it is said that their faith is dead.[41] And just as the dead do not see, so they, with the pupil of their eye covered over as I told you, do not see. They do not know that of themselves they are nothing. They do not recognize the sins they have committed. Nor do they know my goodness to them, that I am the source of their very being and of every grace beyond that.

Because they know neither me nor themselves, they do not hate their selfish sensuality. No, they even love it. And in seeking to satisfy their appetite, they give birth to dead children, that is, to a host of deadly sins. But me they do not love. And because they do not love me they do not love their neighbors, whom I love. They take no pleasure

---

41. Cf. Jm. 2:26.

in doing what pleases me, that is, the practice of true and solid virtue. It is not for my own good that I am pleased when I see such virtue in you. You can be of no profit to me because I am who I am[42] and nothing is done without me except sin. And sin *is* nothing, because it deprives the soul of me who am every good when it robs her of grace. So it is to your own profit to please me, for I have everlasting life to reward you in myself.

But the faith of these souls is dead, you see, because it is not carried out in action. Whatever they do profits them nothing for eternal life, for they do not have the life of grace. Still, good works should not be abandoned either with grace or without, because every good is rewarded and every sin is punished. The good that is done in grace (without deadly sin) is of value for eternal life. But the good that is done with the guilt of deadly sin is worth nothing for eternal life. Nevertheless, it is rewarded in other ways, as I told you earlier. Sometimes I lend them time, or I put them into my servants' hearts and because of their constant prayers they escape from their sin and wretchedness.

Sometimes they are not open to receive either time or prayer as a way to grace. Such as these I reward with material goods, treating them like animals one fattens before leading them to slaughter.[43] Such as these have always resisted every approach of my goodness. They do some good, however—though not in grace, as I said, but in sin. They were unwilling in these actions of theirs to receive either time or prayer or any of the other ways in which I called to them. But my goodness wants to reward them nonetheless for those actions, for this bit of service they have rendered. So while I reproach them for their sins, I reward them with material things. This makes them grow fat; but if they do not change their ways they will end in eternal punishment.

You see, then, that they are deluded. Who has deluded them? None but themselves, for they have thrown away the light of living faith, and they go about as if they were blind, groping and clutching at everything they touch. They do not see except with blind eyes, since their desire is fixed on passing things, and so they are deceived and act like fools who notice only the gold and fail to see its venomous sting.

---

42. Ex. 3:14.
43. One cannot help wondering a bit at Catherine's attributing such a comparison to God unless the fattening is taken as a sort of "compensation" for the inevitable slaughter, an interpretation that fits the broader context of the remark.

Learn from this that the goods of the world, all its delights and pleasures, if they are got and had apart from me with selfish and disordered love, are just like scorpions. I showed you this image in your early days along with the vision of the tree and I told you that these scorpions carry gold in front of them and venom in their tails. The venom does not come without the gold, nor the gold without the venom—but the gold is what one sees first. And only those whose light is the lamp of faith have a defense against the venomous sting.[44]

47

These, I told you, because of their love for me cut off the venomous sting of selfish sensuality with the double-edged knife that is hatred of sin and love of virtue. Those who would possess the gold of this world's goods acquire and possess it by the light of reason. But those who would go the way of great perfection spurn that gold in actuality as well as in spirit. These follow both materially and in spirit the counsel given and bequeathed by my Truth, while those with possessions keep the commandments, but observe the counsels in spirit only.

However, since the counsels are bound up with the commandments, no one can keep the commandments without following the counsels at least in spirit if not materially. Though they may possess the riches of the world, they must own them humbly, not with pride, as things lent to them rather as their own—for in my generosity I give you these things for your use. You have as much as I give you: you keep as much as I allow you to keep; and I give and let you keep as much as I see would be good for you.

This is the spirit in which people should use things, and if they do, they will be keeping the command that you love me above all things and your neighbor as your very self. They will live with their heart emptied of material things, cutting them off from their affection. In other words, they will neither love nor possess them apart from my will. Though they may in fact have possessions, they will be following

---

44. It is not clear what natural phenomenon Catherine could be referring to. Cf., however, Vincent of Beauvais, *Speculum Naturale:* "The scorpion is said to have a pale, almost virginal face, but in its swollen tail it has a poisonous sting with which it strikes and pierces anyone who comes near." Then he enumerates, following Avicenna, the nine colors of the scorpion: "white, yellow, red, gray, green—*but some are gold with black tails*" (L. XX. c. 160–161). Cf. Rv. 9:7, 10: "To look at, these locusts were like horses armored for battle; they had things like gold crowns on their heads. . . . Their tails were like scorpions', with stings . . . " (Cavallini).

the counsel in spirit by cutting off from themselves the venomous sting of disordered love. This is the way of ordinary love.

But those who keep the commandments and counsels actually as well as in spirit go the way of perfect love. They follow in true simplicity the counsel my Truth, the incarnate Word, gave to that young man when he asked, "What can I do, Master, to win eternal life?" He said, "Keep the commandments of the Law." The other answered, "I do keep them." And he said, "Well, if you want to be perfect go and sell what you have and give it to the poor."

Then the young man was sad. He was still too much in love with what wealth he had, and that is why he was sad.[45] But those who are perfect heed what he said. They let go of the world and all its pleasures. They discipline their bodies with penance and vigils, with constant humble prayer.

Those, however, who go the way of ordinary love without actually rising above material things (for they are not obliged to do so) do not thereby forfeit eternal life. But if they wish to have this world's goods they must possess them in the way I told you. To have these things is not sinful. After all, everything is good and perfect, created by me, Goodness itself. But I made these things to serve my rational creatures; I did not intend my creatures to make themselves servants and slaves to the world's pleasures. So if they would not go the way of great perfection, they may keep these things if they choose, but they will be servants, less than lords. They owe their first love to me. Everything else they should love and possess, as I told you, not as if they owned it but as something lent them.

I am not a respecter of persons or status but of holy desires. In whatever situation people may be, let their will be good and holy, and they will be pleasing to me.

Who are they who possess this world's goods in this way? Those who have cut the venomous sting off them by despising their selfish sensuality and loving virtue. Once they have cut off the venom of disorder from their will and set it in order with love and holy fear of me, they can choose and hold whatever situation they will and still be fit to have eternal life. It remains true that it is more perfect and more pleasing to me to rise above all this world's goods in fact as well as in spirit. But those who feel that their weakness will not let them reach such perfection can travel this ordinary way according to their own situa-

---

45. Mt. 19:16–22.

tion. My goodness has ordained it thus, so that no one in any situation whatever should have an excuse for sin.

Indeed they have no excuse. For I have made allowance for their passions and weaknesses in such a way that if they choose to remain in the world they can. They can possess wealth and hold positions of authority. They can be married and care for their children and toil for them. They can remain in any situation whatever, so long as they truly cut off the venomous sting of selfish sensuality that deals eternal death.

And it surely is venomous. For just as venom is painful to the body and ultimately causes death unless a person makes the effort to vomit it out and take some medicine, so it is with this scorpion of the world's pleasure. I am not speaking of material things in themselves. I have already told you that these are good and that they are made by me, the greatest Good, and so you can use them as you please with holy love and truthful fear. What I am speaking of is the venom of a perverted human will, which poisons souls and causes them death, unless they vomit it up through a holy confession, tearing their heart and affection free from it. Such confession is a medicine that heals the effects of this venom even while it tastes bitter to selfish sensuality.

See then how greatly these souls are deluded! They could have me; they could escape sadness and find joy and comfort. Yet they seek evil under the guise of good and set themselves to grasping at the gold with perverted love. But because they are blinded by their great infidelity they do not recognize the venomous sting, and when they see that they have been poisoned they do not reach for a remedy. They are carrying the devil's cross and tasting the guarantee of hell.

48

I have told you that the will alone is the source of suffering. And because my servants are stripped of their own will and clothed in mine, they feel no grief in suffering but feel me in their souls by grace and are satisfied. Without me they could never be satisfied even if they possessed the whole world. For created things are less than the human person. They were made for you, not you for them,[46] and so they can never satisfy you. Only I can satisfy you. These wretched souls, then, caught in such blindness, are forever toiling but never satisfied. They long for what they cannot have because they will not ask it of me though I could satisfy them.

---

46. Cf. Mk. 2:27.

THE DIALOGUE

Do you want me to tell you why they suffer? You know that love always brings suffering if what a person has identified with is lost. These souls in one way or another have identified with the earth in their love, and so they have in fact become earth themselves. Some have identified with their wealth, some with their status, some with their children. Some lose me in their slavery to creatures. Some in their great indecency make brute beasts of their bodies. And so in one way and another they hunger for and feed on earth. They would like to be stable but are not. Indeed they are as passing as the wind, for either they themselves fail through death or my will deprives them of the very things they loved. They suffer unbearable pain in their loss. And the more disordered their love in possessing, the greater is their grief in loss. Had they held these things as lent to them rather than as their own, they could let them go without pain. They suffer because they do not have what they long for. For, as I told you, the world cannot satisfy them, and not being satisfied, they suffer.

How many are the pains of a troubled conscience! How many are the pains of those who hunger for revenge! They gnaw away at themselves constantly, and they have killed themselves even before they kill their enemies: They are themselves the first to die, slain by their own hand with the knife of hatred.

How must the greedy suffer in endlessly stretching their need! What torture must the envious know, forever gnawing away at their own hearts! They are incapable of taking any delight in their neighbors' well-being. All the things they love sensually bring them only suffering loaded with purposeless fears. They have taken up the devil's cross, and taste the pledge of hell even in this life. Unless they reform, they go through life weakened in all sorts of ways, and in the end receive eternal death.

These are the ones who are hurt by the thorns of many troubles. They crucify themselves with their own perverse will. They are crossed soul and body; that is, they suffer pain and torment in soul and body but without any merit, for they bear their burdens not with patience but with outright impatience. They have gained possession of the gold and pleasures of the world but with perverted love. Bereft of the life of grace or any impulse of love, they have become trees of death, and therefore all their actions are dead. In pain they make their way through the river, drowning—only to reach the water of death. They pass in hate through the gate of the devil and receive eternal damnation.

Now you have seen how deluded these souls are, and how painfully they make their way to hell—like martyrs of the devil! You have seen what it is that blinds them: the cloud of selfish love plastered over the pupil that is the light of faith. And you have seen how the troubles of the world, whatever their source, may hurt my servants physically (for the world hounds them), but not spiritually, because they have identified their wills with mine, and so they are happy to endure pain for me. But the world's servants are hounded within and without—but especially within. They are afraid of losing what they have. And love hounds them with longing for what they cannot have. And words could never describe all the other troubles that follow on the heels of these two principal ones. So you see that even in this life the lot of the just is better than that of sinners. Now you have seen quite fully both the journeying and the end of the latter.

49

I send people troubles in this world so that they may know that their goal is not this life, and that these things are imperfect and passing. I am their goal, and I want them to want me, and in this spirit they should accept such things. Now there are some, I tell you, who when they feel the pressure of trouble are prompted to remove the cloud from their eyes by their very suffering and by what they see must be the consequence of their sin. In this slavish fear they begin to make their way out of the river. They vomit out the venom with which the scorpion had stung them under the guise of gold. They had embraced him without any reservation, and so he had stung them. With this knowledge they begin to get up and turn toward the shore to gain access to the bridge.

But to walk merely in slavish fear is not enough. It is not enough for eternal life to sweep the house clean of deadly sin. One must fill it with virtue that is grounded in love, and not merely in fear.[47] Then one must put both feet on the first stair of the bridge. And the two feet that carry the soul into the love of my Truth, of whom I have made a bridge for you, are affection and desire.

This is the first stair I said you have to climb, when I told you that

---

47. Cf. Mt. 12:43–45.

he had made a stairway of his body.[48] However, this is as it were a common step, which the servants of the world ordinarily take when they are first roused through fear of suffering. Because the world's troubles sometimes weary them, they begin to dislike the world. And if they take advantage of this fear enlightened by faith, they will progress to the love of virtue.

But there are some who walk so sluggishly that they easily turn back. For after they get to the shore, the winds rise and they are pounded by the waves of the stormy sea of this darksome life.

If the wind is that of prosperity, and because of their negligence they have not yet climbed the first stair with their desire and love for virtue, then they turn their faces back to pleasure with disordered delight.

And if the wind is that of adversity, they turn back in impatience, because they had hated their sin not for the offense it gave me but for fear of the punishment it seemed must follow it. With that sort of fear they got up out of their vomit.[49] But anything worthwhile calls for perseverance, and because they do not persevere they never find the object of their desire, never reach the goal toward which they had set out. Without perseverance they will never reach it. So perseverance is essential if you want to see your desires realized.

I have told you that these souls turn back on account of different forces that influence them. The force may be in themselves, when their selfish sensuality fights against the spirit. It may come from other people to whom they turn either through a disordered love apart from me or through fear of being hurt by them. Or it may be the demons with all their varied tactics. Sometimes these will use discouragement to confuse them, saying, "This good thing you have begun is worthless because of your sins and shortcomings"—and they do this to make them turn back and let go of even that little bit of effort they had taken on. At other times they will use complacency in the hope these souls have found in my mercy. They will say, "Why should you want to wear yourself out? Enjoy this life; you can admit your faults at the end and obtain mercy." In this way the devil makes them lose the fear that had enabled them to begin.

---

48. Cf. G. Anadol, "Le immagini del linguaggio cateriniano e le loro fonti: la scala," *Rassegna di ascetica e mistica* 23 (1972): 332–343.
49. Cf. 2 P. 2:22.

For these and all sorts of other reasons they turn back and are not constant or persevering. All this happens to them because the root of selfishness has never been dug out of them. This is why they do not persevere. Rather, they accept my mercy and hope not as they ought, but foolishly and with great presumption. And presumptuous as they are, they put their trust in my mercy even while they are continually abusing it.

I have not given nor do I give my mercy for people to abuse, but that they may use it to defend themselves against the devil's malice and inordinate spiritual confusion. But they do precisely the opposite: They use my mercy as a weapon against me. And this happens to them because they fail to act on their first change of heart, when they were roused by fear of punishment and hurting from the thorns of so many troubles, from the wretchedness of deadly sin. So because they fail to change, they never attain love for virtue, and therefore they do not persevere.

The soul cannot but move: If she does not go forward, she turns back. So if these souls do not go forward in virtue, rising from the imperfection of fear to love, then they will necessarily go backward.

50

T hen was that soul's longing stirred up. She considered her own and others' imperfection. She grieved to hear and see such blindness on the part of creatures, for she had seen how great was God's goodness. He had never ordained that anything in this life should be an obstacle to peoples' salvation, no matter what their situation, but that everything should serve the exercise and proving of virtue. But in spite of all this, because of their selfishness and disordered love, people still went the way of the river below, and if they did not reform, they would certainly end in eternal damnation. And many of those who began to reform turned back. She had learned the reason for this when he in his tender goodness had stooped to show himself to her. This made her bitterly sad, and, fixing her mind's eye on the eternal Father, she said:

O immeasurable love! How greatly are your creatures deluded! I wish you would explain to me more clearly—when it pleases your goodness—the three stairs imaged in the body of your only-begotten

Son. Show me what people must do to escape completely from the flood and keep to the way of your Truth, and who are those who climb these stairs.

51

Then divine Goodness looked with the eye of his mercy upon that soul's hungry longing and said:

My dearest daughter, I am not scornful of desire. No, I am the one who answers holy longings. Therefore I want to explain to you what you ask.

You ask me to explain to you the image of the three stairs, and to tell you how people must act to be able to escape from the river and mount the bridge. I did describe for you earlier people's delusion and blindness, and how they taste even in this life the pledge of hell and, like martyrs of the devil, reap eternal damnation. I told you what fruit they harvest from their evil actions. And when I told you these things, I showed you how they ought to behave. Still, to satisfy your longing, I will now explain it to you more fully.

You know that every evil is grounded in selfish love of oneself. This love is a cloud that blots out the light of reason. It is in reason that the light of faith is held, and one cannot lose the one without losing the other.

I made the soul after my own image and likeness, giving her memory, understanding, and will. The understanding is the most noble aspect of the soul. It is moved by affection, and it in turn nourishes affection. Affection is love's hand, and this hand fills the memory with thoughts of me and of the blessings I have given. Such remembrance makes the soul caring instead of indifferent, grateful instead of thankless. So each power lends a hand to the other, thus nourishing the soul in the life of grace.

The soul cannot live without love. She always wants to love something because love is the stuff she is made of, and through love I created her. This is why I said that it is affection that moves the understanding, saying, as it were, "I want to love, because the food I feed on is love." And the understanding, feeling itself awakened by affection, gets up, as it were, and says, "If you want to love, I will give you something good that you can love." And at once it is aroused by the consideration of the soul's dignity and the indignity into which she has fallen through her own fault. In the dignity of her existence she tastes the immeasurable goodness and uncreated love with which I created her. And in the sight of her own wretchedness she discovers and tastes my mercy, for in mercy I have lent her time and drawn her out of darkness.

Affection in turn is nourished by love, opening its mouth, holy desire, and eating hatred and contempt for its selfish sensuality seasoned with the oil of true humility and perfect patience, which it has drawn from this holy hatred. After the virtues have been conceived, they are born either perfect or imperfect, according to how the soul exercises the perfection within her, as I will tell you further on.

So also, on the other hand, if sensual affection wants to love sensual things, the eye of understanding is moved in that direction. It takes for its object only passing things with selfish love, contempt for virtue, and love of vice, drawing from these pride and impatience. And the memory is filled only with what affection holds out to it.

This love so dazzles the eye that it neither discerns nor sees anything but the glitter of these things. Such is their glitter that understanding sees and affection loves them all as if their brightness came from goodness and loveliness. Were it not for this glitter, people would never sin, for the soul by her very nature cannot desire anything but good. But vice is disguised as something good for her, and so the soul sins. Her eyes, though, cannot tell the difference because of her blindness, and she does not know the truth. So she wanders about searching for what is good and lovely where it is not to be found.

I have already told you that the world's pleasures are[50] all venomous thorns. Understanding is deluded at the sight of them, and the will in loving them (for it loves what it should not love), and the memory in holding on to them. Understanding is acting like a thief who robs someone else, and so the memory holds on to the constant thought of things that are apart from me, and in this way the soul is deprived of grace.

Such is the unity of these three powers of the soul that I cannot be offended by one without all three offending me. The one lends a hand to the other, for good or for evil, by free choice. This free choice is bound up with affection. So it moves as it pleases, whether by the light

---

50. S, E, F, add "without me."

of reason or unreasonably. Your reason is bound to me, unless free choice cuts you off through disordered love. And you have that perverse law that is always fighting against the spirit.[51]

There are, then, two aspects to yourself: sensuality and reason. Sensuality is a servant, and it has been appointed to serve the soul, so that your body may be your instrument for proving and exercising virtue. The soul is free, liberated from sin in my Son's blood, and she cannot be dominated unless she consents to it with her will, which is bound up with free choice. Free choice is one with the will, and agrees with it. It is set between sensuality and reason and can turn to whichever one it will.

It is true that when the soul decides to gather her powers with the hand of free choice in my name, all the actions that person does, whether spiritual or temporal, are gathered in. Free choice cuts itself off from sensuality and binds itself to reason. And then I dwell in their midst through grace. This is what my Truth, the Word incarnate, meant when he said: "Whenever two or three are gathered in my name, I will be in their midst,"[52] and this is the truth. I have already told you that no one can come to me except through him. That is why I have made of him a bridge with three stairs, the latter being an image of the three spiritual stages, as I will describe for you later.

52

I have explained the image of the three stairs for you in general in terms of the soul's three powers. These are three stairs, none of which can be climbed without the others if one wishes to go the way of the teaching, the bridge, of my Truth. Nor can the soul persevere without uniting these three powers as one.

I spoke of this perseverance earlier. You asked me to explain more clearly the three stairs, the way these travelers should behave if they would escape from the river. And I told you it is impossible to reach one's goal without perseverance.

There are two goals, vice and virtue, and both require perseverance. If you would reach life, you must persevere in virtue, and if you would reach eternal death, persevere in vice. So it is through persever-

---

51. Rm. 7:23.
52. Mt. 18:20.

ance that one comes to me, who am Life, or to the devil to taste the water of death.

53

All of you, together and individually, were invited by my Truth when in eager longing he cried out in the temple: "Let whoever is thirsty come to me and drink, for I am the fountain of living water."[53] He did not say, "Go to the Father and drink," but "Come to me." Why? Because no suffering can befall me, the Father, but my Son can suffer. And you, as long as you are pilgrim travelers in this mortal life, cannot walk without suffering, for because of sin the earth has produced thorns.

And why did he say, "Come to me and drink"? Because you can follow his teaching and come to him by either of two ways: by living the commandments in the spirit of the counsels (the way of ordinary charity), or by actually living the counsels as well as the commandments. Along either way you will find the fruit of the blood to drink and enjoy, thanks to the union of the divine nature with the human. And when you find yourselves in him you will find that you are in me, the sea of peace, for I am one with him and he is one with me. So are you invited to the fountain of the living water of grace.

You must stay perseveringly with him whom I have made a bridge for you. Let neither thorn nor contrary wind, neither prosperity nor adversity nor any other suffering you might have to bear make you turn back. You must persevere until you find me and I give you living water through the mediation of this gentle loving Word, my only-begotten Son.

But why did he say, "I am the fountain of living water"? Because when the divine nature was joined with the human nature, he became the fountain holding me, the source of living water. Why did he say, "Come to me and drink"? Because you cannot walk without suffering, and while I cannot suffer, he can. And since I made him a bridge for you, no one can come to me except through him. This is what he said: "No one can come to the Father except through me."[54] And my Truth spoke the truth.

Now you have seen what road you must keep to and how, that is,

---

53. Jn. 7:37; 4:7.
54. Jn. 14:6.

with perseverance. Only thus will you drink, for perseverance is the virtue that receives glory and the crown of victory in me, Life everlasting.[55]

54

Let me return now to the three stairs by which you must go if you would escape from the river and not drown, but reach the living water to which you are invited. By these stairs you must go if you would have me with you, for then I will dwell in your souls by grace and be with you on your journey.

If you would make progress, then, you must be thirsty, because only those who are thirsty are called: "Let anyone who is thirsty come to me and drink." Those who are not thirsty will never persevere in their journey. Either weariness or pleasure will make them stop. They cannot be bothered with carrying the vessel that would make it possible for them to draw the water. And though they cannot travel alone, they do not care for the company. So at the first sight of any prick of persecution (which they consider their enemy) they turn back. They are afraid because they are alone. If they were with the company they would not be afraid. And if they had climbed the three stairs they would be secure, because they would not be alone.

You must be thirsty, then, and you must gather together, as he said, either two or three or more. Why did he say "two or three"? Because there are not two without three nor three without two. One alone is excluded from my companionship, since I cannot be "in the midst" of someone who has no companion. Those who are wrapped up in selfish love of themselves are alone, mere nothings, because they are cut off from my grace and from charity for their neighbors. And once deprived of me through their own fault, they turn to nothingness—for I alone am who I am. So those who are alone, those who are wrapped up in selfish love of themselves, are neither taken account of by my Truth nor acceptable to me.

He says, then, "If two or three or more are gathered in my name, I shall be in their midst."[56] I told you that two are not without three, nor three without two, and so it is. You know that all the commandments of the Law are comprised in two—to love me above all things

---

55. Cf. Rv. 2:10.
56. Mt. 18:20.

and· to love your neighbor as your very self—and without these two none of the commandments can be kept. This is the beginning, the middle, and the end of the commandments of the Law.

These two cannot be gathered together in my name without three—that is, without the gathering of the three powers of the soul: memory, understanding, and will. The memory holds on to my blessings and my goodness to the soul. Understanding contemplates the unspeakable love I have shown you though the mediation of my only-begotten Son, whom I have set before your mind's eye for you to contemplate in him the fire of my charity. The will, finally, is joined with them to know and desire me, your final goal.

When these three powers of the soul are gathered together, I am in their midst by grace. And as soon as you are filled with my love and love of your neighbor,[57] you will find yourself in the company of the multitude of solid virtues. Then the soul's appetite is ready to be thirsty—thirsty for virtue and my honor and the salvation of souls. Every other thirst is now exhausted and dead, and you travel securely, without any slavish fear. You have climbed the first step, that of desire. Once desire is stripped of selfish love, you rise above yourself and above passing things. What you decide to keep, you love and hold not apart from me but with me, that is, with true holy fear and love of virtue.

Then you find that you have climbed the second stair. This is the enlightenment of the mind, which sees itself reflected in the warmhearted love I have shown you in Christ crucified, as in a mirror. Then you find peace and quiet, for memory is filled with my love and no longer empty. You know that when something is empty it resounds if you strike it, but not so when it is full. So when the memory is filled with light from understanding and the overflowing love of the will, even though troubles and the pleasures of the world strike it, it will not resound with inordinate gladness or impatience. For it is filled with me, and I am all good.

After you have climbed you find that you are gathered together. For once reason has taken possession of the three stairs, which are the three powers of the soul, they are gathered together in my name. When the two—that is, love for me and love for your neighbor—are gathered together, and the memory for holding and understanding for seeing and the will for loving are gathered together, you find that I am your

---

57. *Pieno della carità mia e del prossimo.*

companion, and I am your strength and your security. You discover the company of the virtues, and because I am in their midst you walk securely and are secure.

Then you are roused with eager longing, thirsty to follow the way of Truth that leads to the fountain of living water. Your thirst for my honor and for your own and your neighbors' salvation makes you long for the way, for without the way you could never reach what you thirst for. So walk on, carrying your heart like a vessel emptied of every desire and every disordered earthly love. But no sooner is your vessel emptied than it is filled. For nothing can remain empty. If it is not full of something material, it will fill up with air. Just so, the heart is a vessel that cannot remain empty. As soon as you have emptied it of all those transitory things you loved inordinately, it is filled with air— that is, with gentle heavenly divine love that brings you to the water of grace. And once you have arrived there you pass through the gate, Christ crucified, to enjoy that living water—for now you find yourself in me, the sea of peace.

55

Now I have shown you how, in general, everyone gifted with reason must behave if they would escape from the world's flood and not drown and come to eternal damnation. I have also shown you the three ordinary stairs, that is, the soul's three powers, and I have shown you that no one can climb any one of them without climbing them all. I have told you also about that word spoken by my Truth: "Whenever two or three or more are gathered in my name"—how this is the gathering of these three stairs, the soul's three powers. When these three powers are in harmony they have with them the two chief commandments of the Law, love of me and love of your neighbor,[58] that is, to love me above all things and your neighbor as your very self.

When you have climbed the staircase, that is, when you are gathered together in my name, you are immediately thirsty for the living water. So you move forward and cross over the bridge, following the teaching of my Truth who is that bridge. You run after his voice that calls out to you. (I told you earlier that he was inviting you when he cried out in the temple, "Let whoever is thirsty come to me and drink, for I am the fountain of living water.")

I have explained what he meant and how he should be understood

---

58. *Carità mia e del prossimo tuo.*

so that you might better know the abundance of my love, and the confusion of those who seem to delight in running along the devil's way that invites them to the deadly water.

Now you have seen and heard what you asked of me, that is, how you should behave if you would not drown. I have told you that this is the way: to climb up onto the bridge. In this climbing up you are all gathered together and united, loving each other, carrying your hearts and wills like vessels to me (who give anyone to drink who asks), keeping to the way of Christ crucified with perseverance even till death.

This is the way you must all keep to no matter what your situation, for there is no situation that rules out either your ability or your obligation to do so. You can and you must, and every person gifted with reason has this obligation. No one can draw back saying, "My position or my children or other earthly obstacles keep me from following this way." Nor can the difficulties you encounter along this way excuse you. You are not to talk that way, because I have already told you that every state of life is pleasing and acceptable to me if it is held to with a good and holy will. For all things are good and perfect, since they were made by me, and I am supreme Goodness. I made them and gave them to you not for you to use them to embrace death, but that you might have life through them.

It is an easy matter, for nothing is as easy and delightful as love. And what I ask of you is nothing other than love and affection for me and for your neighbors. This can be done any time, any place, and in any state of life by loving and keeping all things for the praise and glory of my name.

You know (for I have told you) that some deluded souls clothe themselves in selfish love of themselves rather than walk in the light. They love and possess creatures apart from me, and so they pass through this life tormented, becoming insupportable even to themselves. If these souls do not rouse themselves, they will end in eternal damnation.

Now I have told you how all people in general ought to behave.

56

I have told you how those ought to walk who go the way of ordinary love (that is, those who keep the commandments in the spirit of the counsels). Now I want to tell you about those who have begun to climb the stairway and want to follow the perfect road by actually living out the counsels as well as the commandments. I will show you these in three stages, explaining to you specifically now the three degrees or stages of the soul and the three stairs that I have already set before you more generally in terms of the soul's three powers. The first of these stages is imperfect, the second more perfect, and the third most perfect. The first is a mercenary, the second my faithful servant, and the third my child who loves me with no regard for selfish interests.

These are three stages for which many have the capacity, and all three can be present in one and the same person. This is done when a person[59] runs along the way perfectly careful to make good use of time, and from the mercenary stage reaches the free, and from the free the filial.

Rise up above yourself. Open your mind's eye and watch how these pilgrims travel: some imperfectly, some perfectly in the way of the commandments, and some most perfectly by keeping and practicing the way of the counsels. You will see what is the source of imperfection and what the source of perfection. And you will see how deluded is the soul from whom the root of selfish love has not been dug up. No matter what your state in life, it is essential to kill this selfish love in yourself.

57

T hen that soul, restless with burning desire and gazing into God's gracious mirror, saw how people took different ways for different motives to get to their goal. She saw many who began to climb when they felt the grip of slavish fear, that is, fear of personal suffering. And many by responding to that first call reached the second. But few seemed to reach the greatest perfection.

58

Then God, wishing to satisfy her longing, said:
Take note. These souls have gotten up from the vomit of deadly sin because of slavish fear. But if they do not get up for love of virtue,

---

59. The precise sense of the beginning of this paragraph is somewhat unclear in the original: "Questi sono tre stati che possono essere e sono in molte creature, e sono in una creatura medesima. In una creatura sono e possono essere...." The three stages could be simultaneously present in different aspects of one's life.

their slavish fear is not enough to win them eternal life. Love joined to holy fear, however, is enough, for the Law is built on love and holy fear.

The law of fear was the Old Law that I gave to Moses. It was built on fear alone: Whoever sinned suffered the penalty.

The law of love is the New Law given by the Word, my only-begotten Son. It is built on love. The Old Law was not dissolved by the New, but fulfilled. This is what my Truth said: "I have come not to destroy the Law but to fulfill it."[60] He thus joined the law of fear with that of love. The imperfectness of the fear of suffering was taken away by love, and what remained was the perfectness of holy fear, that is, fear simply of sinning, not because of personal damnation but because sin is an insult to me, supreme Goodness. So the imperfect law was made perfect by the law of love.

The fiery chariot of my only-begotten Son came bringing the fire of my charity to your humanity with such overflowing mercy that the penalty for sins people commit was taken away. I mean the punishment in this life that follows immediately upon the sin—for it was ordained in the Law of Moses that punishment be dealt out as soon as a sin was committed. Not so now: There is no more need for slavish fear. This does not mean that sin goes unpunished. The punishment is rather set aside until the next life, when the soul is separated from the body, except for sinners who make atonement by means of perfect contrition. While you are alive you have a season of mercy, but once you are dead it is your season of justice.

You ought, then, to get up from slavish fear and come to love and holy fear of me. Otherwise you cannot help but fall back into the river. There you will be exposed to the waves of trouble and the thorns of comfort—for all comforts are thorns that sting the soul who loves them inordinately.[61]

59

I told you that no one can cross over the bridge and so escape the river without climbing the three stairs. Such is the truth, and some climb imperfectly, some perfectly, and others with great perfection.

---

60. Mt. 5:17.
61. Cf. Lk. 8:14. "As for the seed that fell into thorns, this is people who have heard, but as they go on their way they are choked by the worries and riches and pleasures of life and do not reach maturity."

Those who are motivated by slavish fear climb and gather their powers together only imperfectly. When they see the penalty that must follow upon their sin, they climb up and gather together their powers: memory to recall their vices, understanding to see the punishment they expect for their sin, and finally the will to hate it.

Since this is the first step upward and the first gathering together, they must act on it. Their mind's eye, through the pupil, which is most holy faith, should consider not only the punishment but the reward of virtue and the love I bear them. Then they will climb in love, with the feet of their affection stripped of slavish fear. In this way they will become faithful rather than faithless servants, serving me out of love rather than fear. And if they set their hatred to the task of digging up the root of their selfish love of themselves, and if they are prudent, constant, and persevering, they will succeed.

But there are many who begin their climb so sluggishly and pay what they owe me in such bits and pieces, so indifferently and ignorantly, that they quickly fall by the way. The smallest wind makes them hoist their sails and turn back. They had climbed only imperfectly to the first stair of Christ crucified, and so they never reach the second, which is that of his heart.

60

There are others who become faithful servants. They serve me with love rather than that slavish fear which serves only for fear of punishment. But their love is imperfect, for they serve me for their own profit or for the delight and pleasure they find in me. Do you know how they show that their love is imperfect? By the way they act when they are deprived of the comfort they find in me. And they love their neighbors with the same imperfect love. This is why their love is not strong enough to last. No, it becomes lax and often fails. It becomes lax toward me when sometimes, to exercise them in virtue and to lift them up out of their imperfection, I take back my spiritual comfort and let them experience struggles and vexations. I do this to bring them to perfect knowledge of themselves, so that they will know that of themselves they have neither existence nor any grace. I want them, in time of conflict, to take refuge in me by seeking me and knowing me as their benefactor, in true humility seeking me alone. This is why I give them these troubles. And though I may take away their comfort, I do not take away grace.

But it makes such as these grow lax, and they turn back with impatient spirit. Sometimes they slack off their exercises in all sorts of ways, often saying to themselves under pretense of virtue: "This activity is not worthwhile," because they feel bereft of their selfish spiritual comfort.

They act like the imperfect who have not even removed the film of spiritual selfishness from their eye's pupil, most holy faith. For if they had in truth removed it they would see that everything comes from me, that not a leaf falls from the tree apart from my providence,[62] and that I give and permit what I do for their sanctification, so that they may have the final good for which I created all of you.

They ought to see and know that I wish only their well-being through the blood of my only-begotten Son, that blood in which they are cleansed of their sin. By this blood they can know my truth, that to give them eternal life I created them in my image and likeness, and in the blood of my own Son I re-created them, my adopted children. But because they are imperfect they serve me only for their own profit and let their love for their neighbors grow lax.

The first souls I spoke of fail because of their fear of suffering. These second grow lax, desisting from the service they were giving their neighbors and pulling back from their charity if it seems they have lost their own profit or some comfort they had formerly found in them. And this comes about because their love was not genuine. They love their neighbors with the same love with which they love me—for their own profit.

Unless their desire for perfection makes them recognize their imperfection, it is impossible for them not to turn back. To have eternal life it is essential to love without regard for one's own interest. Fleeing sin for fear of punishment is not enough to give eternal life, nor is it enough to embrace virtue for one's own profit. No, one must rise from sin because sin displeases me, and love virtue for love of me.

It is true that, in general, every person's first call is this, because the soul is imperfect before she is perfect. From imperfection she must come to perfection—either in this life by living virtuously with a sincere heart free to love me without self-interest, or in death by recogniz-

---

62. Cf. Mt. 6:28, 10:29; Lk. 12:27.

ing her imperfection with the resolution to serve me without self-interest if only she had time.

It was with this imperfect love that Saint Peter loved the good gentle Jesus, my only-begotten Son. He loved him very tenderly when he was enjoying the pleasure of his companionship. But when he was in trouble he fell, turning so far that not only suffering but his very fear of suffering made him deny that he had ever known him.[63]

Souls who climb this first stair with only slavish fear and mercenary love fall into all sorts of troubles. What they need is to get up and be my children and serve me without regard for their own interest. For I am the rewarder of every labor, and I give to all in accordance with their state in life and their effort.

If these souls do not give up the exercise of holy prayer and other good works, but go on strengthening their virtue perseveringly, they will come to filial love. And I will love them as my children, because with whatever love I am loved, with that love I respond.[64] If you love me the way a servant loves a master, I as your master will give you what you have earned, but I will not show myself to you, for secrets are shared only with a friend who has become one with oneself.[65]

Still, servants can grow because of their virtue and the love they bear their master, even to becoming his very dear friend. So it is with these souls. As long as their love remains mercenary I do not show myself to them. But they can, with contempt for their imperfection and with love of virtue, use hatred to dig out the root of their spiritual selfishness. They can sit in judgment on themselves so that motives of slavish fear and mercenary love do not cross their hearts without being corrected in the light of most holy faith. If they act in this way, it will please me so much that for this they will come to the love of friendship.

And then I will show myself to them, just as my Truth said: "Those who love me will be one with me and I with them, and I will show myself to them and we will make our dwelling place together."[66] This is how it is with very dear friends. Their loving affection makes them two bodies with one soul, because love transforms one into what

---

63. Mt. 26:74.
64. Cf. Pr. 8:17. "I love those who love me; those who seek me eagerly shall find me."
65. Cf. Jn. 15:15.
66. Cf. Jn. 14:21, 23.

one loves. And if these souls are made one soul [with me], nothing can be kept hidden from them. This is why my Truth said, "I will come and we will make a dwelling place together." That is the truth.

61

Do you know how I show myself within the soul who loves me in truth and follows the teaching of this gentle loving Word? I show my strength in many ways, according to her desire, but there are three principal ways.

The first is my showing of my love and affection in the person of the Word, my Son, through his blood poured out in such burning love. This love is known in two manners. Ordinary people, those who live in ordinary love, know it when they see and experience my love in all the different blessings they receive from me. But it is known in a special manner by those who have been made my friends. Beyond the knowledge of ordinary love, these taste it and know it and experience it and feel it in their very souls.

Love's second showing is simply in souls themselves, when I show myself to them in loving affection. I do not play favorites but I do respect holy desire, and I show myself in souls in proportion to the perfection with which they seek me. Sometimes I show myself (this is still the second showing) by giving them the spirit of prophecy and letting them see into the future. This can take many forms, depending on what I see to be their need or that of others.

At other times—and this is the third showing—I will make them aware of the presence of my Truth, my only-begotten Son, and this in different ways, according to their hunger and their will. Sometimes they seek me in prayer, wanting to know my power, and I satisfy them by letting them taste and feel my strength. Sometimes they seek me in the wisdom of my Son, and I satisfy them by setting him before their mind's eye. Sometimes they seek me in the mercy of the Holy Spirit, and then my goodness lets them taste the fire of divine charity by which they conceive true and solid virtues grounded in pure charity for their neighbors.

62

So you see, my Truth spoke the truth when he said, "Those who love me will be one thing with me." For when you follow his teaching you are united with him in loving affection. And when you are united with him you are united with me, because he and I are one. And once we are one, I will show myself to you. So my Truth spoke the truth when he said, "I will show myself to you." For when he showed himself he showed me, and when he showed me, he showed himself.

But why did he not say, "I will show you my Father"? For three distinct reasons.

First of all, he wanted to show that I am not separate from him, nor he from me. So when Saint Philip said to him, "Show us the Father and it is enough for us," he said, "Whoever sees me sees the Father, and whoever sees the Father sees me."[67] He said this because he was one with me, and whatever he had, he had from me, not I from him. This is why he told the Jews, "My teaching is not mine, but it comes from my Father who sent me."[68] For my Son proceeds from me, not I from him. Still, I am one with him and he with me, and so he did not say, "I will show you the Father," but, "I will show myself to you," that is, "because I am one with the Father."[69]

The second reason was that in showing himself to you he was holding out to you only what he had got from me the Father. It is as if he wanted to say, "The Father has shown himself to me, for I am one with him. And I, in my person, will show you both him and myself."

The third reason was that I am invisible and cannot be seen by you who are visible until you are separated from your bodies. Then you will see me, God, face to face. And you will see the Word, my Son, with your minds from now until the general resurrection, when your humanity will be absorbed and filled to bursting in the humanity of the Word (as I told you earlier when I was speaking of the resurrection[70]).

For you cannot see me as I am. This is why I covered the divine nature with the veil of your humanity, so that you would be able to see me. I who am invisible made myself, as it were, visible by giving you the Word, my Son, veiled in your humanity. He showed me to you. And this is why he did not say, "I will show you the Father," but, "I will show myself to you." It is as if he had said, "I will show myself to you in accordance with what the Father has given me."

So you see, when he showed me, he showed himself. So now you have heard why he did not say, "I will show you the Father." It was be-

---

67. Jn. 14:8–9.
68. Jn. 7:17.
69. Jn. 14:21, 10:30.
70. Cf. ch. 42.

117

cause it is impossible for you in your mortal body to see me, and because he is one with me.

63

Now you have seen what a superb state they are in who have attained the love of friendship. They have mounted the feet of their affection and climbed as far as the secret of his heart, the second of the three stairs. I have told you the meaning of the soul's three powers, and now I would suggest to you that the stairs symbolize the three stages through which the soul advances.

But before I go on to the third stair I want to show you how a person comes to be my friend, and once my friend, becomes my child by attaining filial love. I want to show you what makes a person my friend and how you will know that you have become my friend.

First I will tell you how a soul comes to be my friend. In the beginning she was imperfect, living in slavish fear. By dint of practice and perseverance she came to the love of pleasure and self-advantage, because in me she found both pleasure and profit. This is the path those must travel who wish to attain perfect love, the love of friendship and filial love.

Filial love, I tell you, is perfect. For with filial love one receives the inheritance from me the eternal Father. But no one attains filial love without the love of friendship, and this is why I told you that one progresses from being my friend to becoming my child. But how does one come to this point? Let me tell you.

Every perfection and every virtue proceeds from charity. Charity is nourished by humility. And humility comes from knowledge and holy hatred of oneself, that is, of one's selfish sensuality. To attain charity you must dwell constantly in the cell of self-knowledge. For in knowing yourself you will come to know my mercy in the blood of my only-begotten Son, thus drawing my divine charity to yourself with your love. And you must exercise yourself in tearing out every perverse desire, whether spiritual or material, while you are hidden away within your house. This is what Peter and the other disciples did. For Peter wept after he had sinned in denying my Son.[71] His weeping was still imperfect, though, and it remained imperfect for forty days, that is, till after the ascension.

After my Truth returned to me in his humanity, Peter and the

---

71. Mt. 26:75; Lk. 22:62.

others hid away at home and waited for the Holy Spirit to come as my Truth had promised he would. They remained locked up because of their fear. For the soul is always afraid until she has attained true love. But they persevered in watching and in constant humble prayer until they were filled with the Holy Spirit. Then they lost all their fear, and they followed and preached Christ crucified.[72]

So it is with the soul who has decided to or wants to attain this perfection. After she has risen from the guilt of deadly sin and recognized herself for what she is, she begins to weep for fear of punishment. But then she rouses herself to ponder my mercy, and in this finds delight and profit for herself. This is imperfect, so to bring her to perfection, after the forty days (the first two stages) have passed, I withdraw from the soul now and again, but in feeling only, not in grace.

My Truth showed you this when he said to the disciples, "I will go away and I will return to you."[73] Everything he said was said especially to the disciples but in a more general way to everyone then and to all those who would come in the future. He said, "I will go and I will return to you," and so it was. For when the Holy Spirit came upon the disciples, he came too. For, as I told you earlier, the Holy Spirit did not come alone: He came with my power and with the wisdom of the Son who is one with me, and with his own (the Holy Spirit's) mercy, proceeding from me the Father and from the Son. So I tell you, it is to make the soul rise from imperfection that I withdraw from her feelings and deprive her of the comfort she had known.

When she was in deadly sin she cut herself off from me, and because of her guilt I withdrew my grace. Because she had closed the door of her desire, the sun of grace did not shine on her. It was not the sun's fault. It was the fault of the one who had closed the door of her desire. But when she recognizes herself for what she is, and her darksomeness, she opens the window and vomits out the rottenness in holy confession, and then I return to her by grace. After that I withdraw from her feelings only, not withdrawing my grace. I do this to humble her and to exercise her in seeking me in truth and to prove her in the light of faith so that she may attain prudence. Then, if her love is without self-interest, she rejoices in her labors with lively faith and con-

---

72. Cf. 1 Jn. 4:18. "In love there can be no fear, but fear is driven out by perfect love."

73. Jn. 14:28.

tempt for herself, for she considers herself unworthy of spiritual peace and quiet. This is the second of the three points I referred to. The first was to show how the soul comes to perfection, and this, what she does once she has arrived.

Here is what she does. Though she feels that I have withdrawn into myself, she does not turn back. Rather, she perseveres in her exercise with humility and remains locked up in the house of self-knowledge. There, with lively faith, she waits for the coming of the Holy Spirit, for me, the flame of love. How does she wait? Not lazily, but in watching and constant humble prayer. And her watching is not only physical but spiritual as well. Her mind's eye never closes, but watches by the light of faith and with contempt tears out her heart's wandering thoughts. She watches in love of my charity, knowing that I want only her sanctification. My Son's blood stands witness to this.[74]

By the very fact that her eye is watching in the knowledge of me and of herself, the soul is praying continuously. This is the prayer of a good and holy will, and this is continuous prayer. But she watches also in acts of prayer—prayer, I mean, that is made at the regular times ordained by holy Church.

This is what the soul does who has left imperfection behind and arrived at perfection. And it was to bring her to that point that I left her feelings, though in grace I never left her.

I left her so that she might see and know her shortcomings. For when she felt bereft of comfort she would feel distressed and weak, incapable of constancy or perseverance. Here she would find the root of her spiritual selfishness and have reason to know it for what it is and to rise above herself and mount the judgment seat of her conscience. She would dig out the root of selfish love with the knife of contempt for such love and with love for virtue, and would not let pass any feeling that had not been corrected by reproof.

64

I would have you know that every [good], whether perfect or imperfect, is acquired and made manifest in me. And it is acquired and made manifest by means of your neighbor. Even simple folk know this, for they often love others with a spiritual love. If you have received my love sincerely without self-interest, you will drink your neighbor's

---

74. Cf. Rm. 5:8. "What proves that God loves us is that Christ died for us while we were still sinners."

love sincerely. It is just like a vessel that you fill at the fountain. If you take it out of the fountain to drink, the vessel is soon empty. But if you hold your vessel in the fountain[75] while you drink, it will not get empty: Indeed, it will always be full. So the love of your neighbor, whether spiritual or temporal, is meant to be drunk in me, without any self-interest.

I ask you to love me with the same love with which I love you. But for me you cannot do this, for I loved you without being loved. Whatever love you have for me you owe me, so you love me not gratuitously but out of duty, while I love you not out of duty but gratuitously. So you cannot give me the kind of love I ask of you. This is why I have put you among your neighbors: so that you can do for them what you cannot do for me—that is, love them without any concern for thanks and without looking for any profit for yourself. And whatever you do for them I will consider done for me.[76]

My Truth demonstrated this when Paul was persecuting me and he said, "Saul, Saul, why are you persecuting me?"[77] For he considered Paul's persecution of my faithful ones as persecution of me.

So your love should be sincere: You should love your neighbors with the same love with which you love me. Do you know how you can tell when your spiritual love is not perfect? If you are distressed when it seems that those you love are not returning your love or not loving you as much as you think you love them. Or if you are distressed when it seems to you that you are being deprived of their company or comfort, or that they love someone else more than you.

From these and from many other things you should be able to tell if your love for me and for your neighbors is still imperfect and that you have been drinking from your vessel outside of the fountain, even though your love was drawn from me. But it is because your love for me is imperfect that you show it so imperfectly to those you love with a spiritual love.

All this comes of the failure to dig out every bit of the root of spiritual selfishness. This is why I often permit you to form such a love, so that you may come through it to know yourself and your imperfection in the way I have described.

And I withdraw my presence from you so that you will shut your-

---

75. S has "while the vessel is in the fountain"; C has "in me."
76. Cf. Mt. 25:40.
77. Ac. 9:4.

self up in the house of self-knowledge, where you will acquire all perfection. But then I return to you with even greater light and knowledge of my truth, so long as you give credit to grace for having been able to kill your selfish will for my sake, and do not leave off cultivating the vineyard of your soul and uprooting the thorn bushes of evil thoughts and laying the stones of virtues that are built up with the blood of Christ. These stones you will have found in your journey across the bridge of Christ crucified, my only-begotten Son. I told you, if you recall, that on the bridge (that is, my Truth's teaching) the stones of the virtues are built up with the strength of his blood, for it is by the strength of that blood that the virtues bring you life.

65

The soul, once on her way, must cross over by way of the teaching of Christ crucified, truly loving virtue and hating vice. If she perseveres to the end she will come to the house of self-knowledge, where she shuts herself up in watching and continuous prayer, completely cut off from worldly company.

Why does she shut herself up? Through fear, because she knows how imperfect she is. And through her longing to attain a genuine and free love. She sees well that there is no other way to attain it, and so she waits with a lively faith for my coming, so that she may grow in grace.

How does one come to know lively faith? By persevering in virtue. You must never turn back for anything at all. You must not break away from holy prayer for any reason except obedience or charity. For often during the time scheduled for prayer the devil comes with all sorts of struggles and annoyances—even more than when you are not at prayer. He does this to make you weary of holy prayer. Often he will say, "This sort of prayer is worthless to you. You should not think about or pay attention to anything except vocal prayer." He makes it seem this way so that you will become weary and confused, and abandon the exercise of prayer. But prayer is a weapon with which you can defend yourself against every enemy. If you hold it with love's hand and the arm of free choice, this weapon, with the light of most holy faith, will be your defense.

66

Know, dearest daughter, that if she truly perseveres, the soul learns every virtue in constant and faithful humble prayer. Therefore she ought to persevere and never abandon it—neither for the devil's illusion, nor through her own weakness (that is, any thought or impulse within her own flesh), nor because of what others say. For often the devil will sit on their tongues and make them say things calculated to hinder her prayer. She must overcome them all with the virtue of perseverance.

Oh, how delightful to the soul and pleasing to me is holy prayer made in the house of self-knowledge and knowledge of me! The soul opens her mind's eye with the light of faith and with her affection steeped in the fullness of my charity made visible in the sight of my only-begotten Son, who showed it with his blood. That blood inebriates the soul. It clothes her in the fire of divine charity. It gives her the food of the sacrament that I have set up for you in the hostel of the mystic body of holy Church, the body and the blood of my Son, wholly God and wholly human, given to holy Church to be ministered by the hands of my vicar, who holds the key to this blood.

This is the hostel I had mentioned to you that stands on the bridge to dispense the food to strengthen the pilgrim travelers who go the way of my Truth's teaching, so that weakness will not cause them to fall.[78]

This food gives more or less strength according to the desire of those who receive it, whether they receive it sacramentally or virtually. "Sacramentally" is when one communicates in the holy Sacrament. "Virtually" is communicating through holy desire, both in longing for communion and in esteem for the blood of Christ crucified. In other words, one is communicating sacramentally in the loving charity one finds and tastes in the blood because one sees that it was shed through love. And so the soul is inebriated and set on fire and sated with holy longing, finding herself filled completely with love of me and of her neighbors.[79]

Where did the soul learn this? In the house of self-knowledge, in holy prayer. There she lost her imperfection, just as the disciples and Peter lost their imperfection and learned perfection by staying inside in watchful prayer. How? Through perseverance seasoned with most holy faith.

But do not think that such ardor and nourishment is to be had from vocal prayer alone, as many souls believe. Their prayer consists more in words than in affection, and they seem to be concerned only to

---

78. Cf. ch. 11.
79. *Piena solo della carità mia e del prossimo suo.*

complete their multitude of psalms and to say a great many Our Fathers. When they have finished the number they have set themselves to say, they seem to think of nothing more. It seems they place the whole purpose of prayer in what is said vocally. But that is not how they should act, for if that is all they do they will draw little fruit from it and will please me little.

But if you ask me whether one should abandon vocal prayer, since it seems not everyone is drawn to mental prayer, the answer is no. A person has to walk step by step. I know well that, because the soul is imperfect before she is perfect, her prayer is imperfect as well. She should certainly, while she is still imperfect, stay with vocal prayer so as not to fall into laziness, but she should not omit mental prayer. In other words, while she says the words she should make an effort to concentrate on my love, pondering at the same time her own sins and the blood of my only-begotten Son. There she will find the expansiveness of my charity and forgiveness for her sins. Thus self-knowledge and the consideration of her sins ought to bring her to know my goodness to her and make her continue her exercise in true humility.

Now I do not want her to think about her sins individually, lest her mind be contaminated by the memory of specific ugly sins. I mean that I do not want her to, nor should she, think about her sins either in general or specifically without calling to mind the blood and the greatness of my mercy. Otherwise she will only be confounded. For if self-knowledge and the thought of sin are not seasoned with remembrance of the blood and hope for mercy, the result is bound to be confusion. And along with this comes the devil, who under the guise of contrition and hatred for sin and sorrow for her guilt leads her to eternal damnation. Because of this—though not this alone—she would end in despair if she did not reach out for the arm of my mercy.

This is one of the subtle deceptions the devil works on my servants. So for your own good, to escape his deceit and to be pleasing to me, you must keep expanding your heart and your affection in the immeasurable greatness of my mercy, with true humility. For know this: The devil's pride cannot tolerate a humble mind, nor can his confounding withstand the greatness of my goodness and mercy when a soul is truly hopeful.

Do you recall when the devil wanted to frighten you with confusion? He tried to show you that your life was a delusion and that you had neither followed nor done my will. But you did what you should have done and what my goodness gave you strength to do—for my goodness is never hidden from anyone who wants to receive it. By my mercy and with humility you stood up and said, "I confess to my Creator that my life has been spent wholly in darkness. But I will hide myself in the wounds of Christ crucified and bathe in his blood, and so my wickedness will be consumed and I will rejoice with desire in my Creator."

You know that at this the devil fled. But he returned with another attack, wanting to exalt you in pride. He said, "You are perfect and pleasing to God. You no longer need to torture yourself or weep over your sins." But I gave you light and you saw the way you should take, that you should humble yourself. And you answered the devil, "How wretched I am! John the Baptist never sinned. He was made holy in his mother's womb, yet he did such great penance. But I have committed so many sins and have not yet even begun to acknowledge it with tears and true contrition, seeing who God is who is offended by me and who I am who offend him!"

Then the devil, unable to bear your humility of spirit and your trust in my goodness, said to you, "Damnable woman! There is no getting at you! If I throw you down in confusion you lift yourself up to mercy. If I exalt you you throw yourself down. You come even to hell in your humility, and even in hell you hound me. So I will not come back to you again, because you beat me with the cudgel of charity!"

The soul, then, should season her self-knowledge with knowledge of my goodness, and her knowledge of me with self-knowledge. In this way vocal prayer will profit the soul who practices it and it will please me. And if she perseveres in its practice, she will advance from imperfect vocal prayer to perfect mental prayer.

But if she looks only to the completion of her tally of prayers, or if she abandons mental prayer for vocal, she will never advance. A soul may set herself to say a certain number of oral prayers. But I may visit her spirit in one way or another, sometimes with a flash of self-knowledge and contrition for her sinfulness, sometimes in the greatness of my love setting before her mind the presence of my Truth in different ways, depending on my pleasure or her longings. And sometimes the soul will be so foolish as to abandon my visitation, which she senses within her spirit, in order to complete her tally.[80] As if it were a matter of conscience to abandon what one has begun!

This is not the way she should act. If she did, she would be a dupe

---

80. Cf. Lk. 19:41–44.

of the devil. No. As soon as she senses her spirit ready for my visitation, she ought to abandon vocal prayer. Then, after the mental prayer, if she has time, she can resume what she had set herself to say. If she does not have time she ought not worry or be annoyed or confounded in spirit. But the Divine Office is an exception to this. Clerics and religious are obliged to say it, and sin if they do not say it. They must say their Office right up to the time of death. If they feel their mind drawn by desire and lifted up at the time appointed for saying the Office, they should arrange to say it either earlier or later so they will not fail in their duty regarding the Office.

As far as concerns any other prayer the soul might begin, she ought to begin vocally as a way to reach mental prayer. When she senses that her spirit is ready she should abandon vocal prayer with this intent. Such prayer, made in the way I have told you, will bring her to perfection. This is why she should not abandon vocal prayer, whatever its form, but should advance step by step. Thus, with practice and perseverance she will experience prayer in truth and that food which is the body and blood of my only-begotten Son. And this is why I told you that some souls communicate in the body and blood of Christ actually, even though not sacramentally, when they communicate in loving charity, which they enjoy in holy prayer, in proportion to their desire.

A soul who walks with scant prudence and not step by step finds little. But one who has much finds much. For the more the soul tries to free her affection and bind it to me by the light of understanding, the more she will come to know. One who knows more loves more, and loving more, enjoys more.

You see, then, perfect prayer is achieved not with many words but with loving desire, when the soul rises up to me with knowledge of herself, each movement seasoned by the other. In this way she will have vocal and mental prayer at the same time, for the two stand together like the active life and the contemplative life. Still, vocal and mental prayer are understood in many different ways. This is why I told you that holy desire, that is, having a good and holy will, is continual prayer. This will and desire rises at the appointed time and place to add actual prayer to the continual prayer of holy desire. So also with vocal prayer. As long as the soul remains firm in holy desire and will, she will make it at the appointed time. But sometimes, beyond the appointed times, she makes this continual prayer, as charity asks of her for her neighbors' good and according to the need she sees and the situation in which I have placed her.

The principle of holy will means that each of you must work for the salvation of souls according to your own situation. Whatever you do in word or deed for the good of your neighbor is a real prayer. (I am assuming that you actually pray as such at the appointed time.) Apart from your prayers of obligation, however, everything you do can be a prayer, whether in itself or in the form of charity to your neighbors, because of the way you use the situation at hand.[81] This is what my glorious trumpeter Paul[82] said: "One who never stops doing good never stops praying." And this is why I told you that actual prayer can be one with mental prayer in many ways. For when actual prayer is done in the way I described, it is done with loving charity, and this loving charity is continual prayer.[83]

Now I have told you how the soul arrives at mental prayer, that is, by practice and perseverance, and by abandoning vocal prayer for mental when I visit her. I have also told you about ordinary prayer, and ordinary vocal prayer apart from appointed times, and the prayer of a good and holy will, and prayer both in itself and in the form of [service to] your neighbors done with good will apart from the scheduled time for prayer.

Courageously, then, should the soul spur herself on with prayer as her mother. And this is what the soul does when she has attained the love of friendship and filial love, and shuts herself up in the house of self-knowledge. But if she does not keep to the paths I have described, she will stay forever lukewarm and imperfect, and will love only to the extent that she experiences profit and pleasure in me or in her neighbors.

67

In regard to this imperfect love I want to tell you—I will not remain silent—about how people can be deluded by thus loving me for their own consolation. And I want you to know that when my servants

---

81. Cf. Col. 3:17.
82. Possibly a reflection of 1 Th. 5:15-16.
83. Cf. Rm. 8:26.

love me imperfectly, they love this consolation more than they love me.

Here is how you can recognize such imperfection: Watch people when they are deprived of either spiritual or material comfort. Take, for example, worldly people who sometimes act virtuously when they are prosperous, but if trouble comes (which I send for their own good) they are disturbed about what little bit of good they had been doing. If you were to ask them, "Why are you disturbed?" they would answer, "I seem to have lost what little bit of good I was doing. I no longer do it with the same heart and soul as I used to. And the reason is this trouble that has come my way. For it seems I did more before, and did it more peacefully, with a more quiet heart, than I do now." But it is their selfish pleasure that is deceiving them.

It is not true that trouble is the culprit, nor that they love less or are doing less. The works they do in time of trouble are worth as much in themselves as they were before in time of consolation. In fact, they could be worth more if these people had patience. But this comes about because their pleasure was in their prosperity. Then they loved me with a little bit of an act of virtue, and they pacified their spirit with that little bit of effort. And now when they are deprived of what they found contentment in, it seems to them that any contentment they had found in their efforts at all has been taken away, but that is not the case.

They are like a man in a garden who, because it gives him pleasure, finds contentment in working the garden. To him it seems his contentment is in the work, but his contentment is really in the pleasure the garden gives him. Here is how you can tell that he takes pleasure more in the garden than in the work: If the garden is taken away he feels bereft of pleasure. Now if his chief pleasure had been in his work, he would not have lost it, because one cannot be deprived of the practice of doing good unless one so chooses, even though prosperity may be taken away as the garden was taken away from this man.

These people, then, are deluded in their works by their own selfish passion. This is why they have the habit of saying, "I know I used to do better and had more consolation before I had this trouble than I do now. It used to be worth doing good, but now there is no profit in it for me, nor the least bit of pleasure." Their perception and their words are both false. If their pleasure in doing good had come from love for the good that virtue is, they would never have lost it. In fact, their pleasure would have increased. But because their doing good was built on their own sensual well-being, pleasure failed them and fled.

This is how ordinary people are deluded in some of their good works. It is their very own selves, their selfish sensual pleasure, that deceives them.

68

But my servants, even though their love is still imperfect, seek and love me for love's sake rather than for the consolation and pleasure they find in me. Now I do reward every good deed—but the measure of the reward is the recipient's love. Thus I give spiritual consolation in prayer, now in one way, now in another. But it is not my intention that the soul should receive this consolation foolishly, paying more attention to my gift than to me. I want her to be more concerned about the loving charity with which I give it to her, and to her unworthiness to receive it, than to the pleasure of her own consolation. If she foolishly takes only the pleasure without considering my love for her, she will reap the sort of harm and delusion of which I am about to tell you.

First of all, because she is deluded by her own consolation, this is what she seeks and this is where she finds her pleasure. And more: When she has experienced my consolation and my visitation within her in one way, and then that way ceases, she goes back along the road by which she had come, hoping to find the same thing again. But I do not always give in the same way, lest it seem as if I had nothing else to give. No, I give in many ways, as it pleases my goodness and according to the soul's need. But in her foolishness she looks for my gift only in that one way, trying as it were to impose rules on the Holy Spirit.

That is not the way to act. Instead, she should cross courageously along the bridge of the teaching of Christ crucified and there receive my gifts when, where, and as my goodness pleases to give them. And if I hold back it is not out of hate but love, so that she may seek me in truth and love me not just for her pleasure, but humbly accept my charity more than any pleasure she may find. For if she does otherwise and runs only after pleasure in her own way rather than mine, she will experience pain and unbearable confusion when the object of her delight, as her mind sees it, seems to be taken away.

Such are those who choose consolation in their own way. Once they find pleasure in me in a given fashion, they want to go on with just that. Sometimes they are so foolish that if I visit them in any other way than that, they resist and do not accept it, still wanting only what they have imagined.

This is the fault of their selfish passion in the spiritual pleasure they found in me. But they are deluded. It would be impossible to be always the same. For the soul cannot stand still; she has either to advance toward virtue or turn back. In the same way the spirit cannot stand still in me in one pleasure without my goodness' giving her more. And I give these gifts very differently: Sometimes I give the pleasure of a spiritual gladness; sometimes contrition and contempt for sin, which will make it seem as if the spirit is inwardly troubled. Sometimes I am in the soul without her sensing my presence. Sometimes I make my Truth, the incarnate Word, take shape before her mind's eye in different ways, and yet it will seem that in her feelings the soul does not sense him with the ardor and delight she thinks ought to follow on such a vision. And sometimes she will see nothing but will feel tremendous pleasure.

All this I do out of love, to support her and make her grow in the virtue of humility and in perseverance, and to teach her that she should not try to lay down rules for me and that her goal is not consolation but only virtue built on me. I want her to accept humbly, in season and out, with loving affection, the affection with which I give to her, and to believe with lively faith that I give as her welfare demands or as is needed to bring her to great perfection.

So she should remain humble. Her beginning and end should be in the love of my charity, and in this charity she should accept pleasure and its absence in terms of my will rather than her own. This is the way to avoid delusion and to receive all things in love from me, for I am their end and they are grounded in my gentle will.

69

I have told you about the delusion of those who want to experience me and receive me into their minds in their own way. Now I want to tell you about a second sort of delusion.

These people find all their pleasure in seeking their own spiritual consolation—so much so that often they see their neighbors in spiritual or temporal need and refuse to help them. Under pretense of virtue they say, "It would make me lose my spiritual peace and quiet, and I would not be able to say my Hours[84] at the proper time." Then if they do not enjoy consolation they think they have offended me. But they are deceived by their own spiritual pleasure, and they offend me more by not coming to the help of their neighbors' need than if they had abandoned all their consolations.[85] For I have ordained every exercise of vocal and mental prayer to bring souls to perfect love for me and their neighbors,[86] and to keep them in this love.

So they offend me more by abandoning charity for their neighbor for a particular exercise or for spiritual quiet than if they had abandoned the exercise for their neighbor. For in charity for their neighbors they find me, but in their own pleasure, where they are seeking me, they will be deprived of me. Why? Because by not helping they are by that very fact diminishing their charity for their neighbors. When their charity for their neighbors is diminished, so is my love for them. And when my love is diminished, so is consolation. So, those who want to gain lose, and those who are willing to lose gain. In other words, those who are willing to lose their own consolation for their neighbors' welfare receive and gain me and their neighbors, if they help and serve them lovingly.[87] And so they enjoy the graciousness of my charity at all times.

But those who do not act this way are always in pain. For sometimes they simply must help, if not for love then of necessity, whether it is a spiritual or bodily ailment their neighbor has. But though they help, their help is painful. Weary in spirit and goaded by conscience, they become insupportable to themselves and others. And if you ask them, "Why do you feel this pain?" they would answer, "Because I seem to have lost my spiritual peace and quiet. I have abandoned many things I was in the habit of doing, and I believe I have offended God by this." But this is not the case. Because their sight is set on their own pleasure they do not know how to discern or know in truth where their offense really lies. Otherwise they would see that the offense lies not in being without spiritual consolation, nor in abandoning an exer-

---

84. The Hours of the Divine Office, which are spaced throughout the day and night.

85. Cf. Mt. 25:45. "I tell you solemnly, insofar as you neglected to do this to one of the least of these, you neglected to do it to me."

86. *Carità perfetta di me e del prossimo.*

87. Cf. Mt. 16:25 (Mk. 8:35; Lk. 9:24). "Those who would save their life will lose it, but those who lose their life for my sake will find it."

cise of prayer in favor of their neighbor's need, but rather in being found without charity for their neighbor, whom they ought to love and serve for love of me. So you see how deluded they are—and only because of their own spiritual self-centeredness.

70

And sometimes this selfishness of theirs harms them even further. If their desire and searching is fixed only on consolations and visions, then they will fall into spiritual bitterness and weariness when they find themselves deprived of these. They think they have lost grace when sometimes I withdraw from their mind. Now I do often grant my servants consolations and visions. But I have told you how I go away from the soul and then return. I go away in feeling only, not in grace, and this to bring the soul to perfection. But this plunges these souls into bitterness, and it seems to them that they are in hell, when they feel themselves cut off from pleasure and they feel the pains and torments of temptation.

They should not be foolish or let themselves be so deceived by that spiritual selfishness which does not know the truth. Rather they should know me in themselves, that I am that supreme Good who supports their good will in time of conflict lest for the sake of pleasure they turn back. So they should humble themselves, counting themselves unworthy of spiritual peace and quiet. And this is precisely why I withdraw from them: to humble them and to make them know my charity toward them when they find it in the good will I support in them in time of conflict. I want them not only to receive the milk of tenderness that I poured out before their souls, but so to attach themselves to the breast of my Truth that they may receive meat as well as milk.[88] In other words, I would have them draw to themselves the milk of my love through the mediation of the flesh of Christ crucified (I mean his teaching), of which I have made a bridge for you to reach me. This is why I withdraw my presence from them.

If they behave foolishly they will receive only milk. But if they behave prudently, I will return to them with even greater delight and strength, light and warmth of charity. But if they accept the absence of the feeling of spiritual tenderness with weariness and sadness and spiritual confusion, they will gain little and will persist in their lukewarmness.

---

88. Cf. Heb. 5:11–14.

71

After this they are often deluded in yet another way by the devil, when he takes on the appearance of light. For the devil gives whatever he sees the mind disposed to desire and receive. So when he sees the mind gluttonous, with its desire set only on spiritual visions and consolations (whereas the soul should set her desire not on these but only on virtue, counting herself unworthy of the other or of receiving my affection in such consolations), then, I say, the devil presents himself to that mind under the appearance of light. He does this in different ways: now as an angel, now under the guise of my Truth, now as one or the other of my saints. And this he does to catch the soul with the hook of that very spiritual pleasure she has sought in visions and spiritual delight. And unless she rouses herself with true humility, scorning all pleasure, she will be caught on this hook in the devil's hands. But let her humbly disdain pleasure and cling to love not for the gift but for me, the giver. For the Devil for all his pride cannot tolerate a humble spirit.

And should you ask me how one can know that the visitation is from the devil and not from me, I would answer you that this is the sign:[89] If it is the devil who has come to visit the mind under the guise of light, the soul experiences gladness at his coming. But the longer he stays, the more gladness gives way to weariness and darkness and pricking as the mind becomes clouded over by his presence within. But when the soul is truly visited by me, eternal Truth, she experiences holy fear at the first encounter. And with this fear comes gladness and security, along with a gentle prudence that does not doubt even while it doubts, but through self-knowledge considers itself unworthy. So the soul says, "I am not worthy to receive your visitation— but how can I be worthy?" Then she turns to the greatness of my charity, knowing and seeing that I can grant it. For I look not to her unworthiness but to my worth, and so make her worthy to receive me. For I do not scorn the longing with which she calls to me. Then she receives my visitation humbly, saying, "Behold your servant: Let your will be done in me."[90] Then she emerges from the course of prayer and

---

89. Cf. *Leg. Maj.* I, ix.
90. Lk. 1:38.

my visitation with spiritual gladness and joy, in humility considering herself unworthy, and in charity acknowledging that it was from me.

This, then, is how the soul can tell whether she is being visited by me or by the devil: In my visitation she will find fear at the beginning; but in the middle and at the end, gladness and a hunger for virtue. When it is the devil, however, the beginning is happy, but then the soul is left in spiritual confusion and darkness. Now I have warned you by giving you the sign, so that the soul, if she chooses to behave humbly and prudently, cannot be deluded. The one deluded will be the soul who chooses to travel only with the imperfect love of her own consolation rather than of my affection.

72

I did not want to be silent about how ordinary people are deluded in their sensual love, in the little bit of good they do (that is, what little virtue they exercise in time of consolation). Nor about the spiritual selfishness that hankers after the consolations my servants experience: how deluded these people are in their selfish love of pleasure that keeps them from knowing the truth of my affection or discerning sin where it exists. Nor about how the devil uses their own sin to delude them unless they keep to the way I have described for you.

I have told you this so that you and my other servants may follow the path of virtue for love of me and for no other reason. Those whose love is imperfect, who love me for my gifts and not for myself the giver, can be and often are deluded in these ways. But the soul who has entered in truth into the house of self-knowledge, practicing perfect prayer and rousing herself from the imperfect love that goes with imperfect prayer (in the way I described for you when I spoke about prayer[91]), receives me in loving affection. She seeks to draw to herself the milk of my tenderness from the breast of the teaching of Christ crucified.

When a soul has reached the third stage, the love of friendship and filial love, her love is no longer mercenary. Rather she does as very close friends do when one receives a gift from the other. The receiver does not look just at the gift, but at the heart and the love of the giver, and accepts and treasures the gift only because of the friend's affectionate love. So the soul, when she has reached the third stage of perfect

---

91. Cf. ch. 66.

love, when she receives my gifts and graces does not look only at the gift but with her mind's eye looks at the affectionate charity of me, the Giver.

And so that you might have no excuse for not looking at my affection, I found a way to unite gift and giver: I joined the divine nature with the human. I gave you the Word, my only-begotten Son, who is one with me and I with him, and because of this union you cannot look at my gift without looking at me, the Giver.

See, then, with what affectionate love you ought to love and desire both the gift and the giver! If you do, your love will be pure and genuine and not mercenary. This is how it is with those who keep themselves always shut up in the house of self-knowledge.

73

U P to now I have shown you in many ways how the soul rises up from imperfection and comes to perfect love, and what she does after she has attained the love of friendship and filial love.

I told you that she came this far by dint of perseverance and shutting herself up in the house of self-knowledge. (But this self-knowledge must be seasoned with knowledge of me, or it would end in confusion.) For through self-knowledge the soul learns contempt for her selfish sensual passion and for pleasure in her own consolation. And from contempt grounded in humility she draws patience, which will make her strong in the face of the devil's attacks and other people's persecutions, and strong in my presence when for her own good I take away her spiritual pleasure. With this power she will endure it all.

And if difficulties make her selfish sensuality want to rise up against reason, her conscience must use [holy] hatred to pronounce judgment and not let any impulse pass uncorrected. Indeed the soul who lives in [holy] hatred finds self-correction and self-reproach in everything—not only in those [movements] which are against reason but often even in those which come from me.[92] This is what my gentle servant Gregory meant when he said that a holy and pure conscience

---

92. The passage is somewhat obscure: "*E se la propria sensualità per malagevolezza volesse alzare il capo contra la ragione, il giudice della coscienzia debba salire sopra di sè, e con odio tenersi ragione, e non lassare passare i movimenti che non sono corretti. Benchè l'anima che sta ne l'odio sempre si corregge e si reprende d'ogni tempo, non tanto di quegli che sono contra la ragione, ma di quelli che spesse volte saranno da me.*"

makes sin where there is no sin. In other words, the soul in the purity of her conscience sees guilt even where there was no guilt.

Now the soul who would rise up from imperfection by awaiting my providence in the house of self-knowledge with the lamp of faith ought to do and does just as the disciples did. They waited in the house and did not move from there, but persevered in watching and in constant humble prayer until the coming of the Holy Spirit.[93]

This, as I have told you, is what the soul does when she has risen from imperfection and shuts herself up at home to attain perfection. She remains watching, gazing with her mind's eye into the teaching of my Truth. She is humbled, for in constant prayer (that is, in holy and true desire) she has come to know herself, and in herself she has come to know my affectionate charity.

74

Now it remains to say how one can tell that a soul has attained perfect love. The sign is the same as that given to the holy disciples after they had received the Holy Spirit. They left the house and fearlessly preached my message by proclaiming the teaching of the Word, my only-begotten Son. They had no fear of suffering. No, they even gloried in suffering.[94] It did not worry them to go before the tyrants of the world to proclaim the truth to them for the glory and praise of my name.

So it is with the soul who has waited for me in self-knowledge: I come back to her with the fire of my charity. In that charity she conceived the virtues through perseverance when she stayed at home, sharing in my power. And in that power and virtue she mastered and conquered her selfish sensual passion.

In that same charity I shared with her the wisdom of my Son, and in that wisdom she saw and came to know, with her mind's eye, my truth and the delusions of spiritual sensuality, that is, the imperfect love of one's own consolation. And she came to know the malice and deceit the devil works on the soul who is bound up in that imperfect love. So she rose up in contempt of that imperfection and in love for perfection.

I gave her a share in this love, which is the Holy Spirit, within her

---

93. Ac. 1:13–14.
94. Ac. 2:4, 5:41.

will by making her will strong to endure suffering and to leave her house in my name to give birth to the virtues for her neighbors. Not that she abandons the house of self-knowledge, but the virtues conceived by the impulse of love come forth from that house. She gives birth to them as her neighbors need them, in many different ways. For the fear she had of not showing herself lest she lose her own consolations is gone. After she has come to perfect, free love, she lets go of herself and comes out, as I have described.[95]

And this brings her to the fourth stage. That is, after the third stage, the stage of perfection in which she both tastes and gives birth to charity in the person of her neighbor, she is graced with a final stage of perfect union with me. These two stages are linked together, for the one is never found without the other any more than charity for me can exist without charity for one's neighbors or the latter without charity for me. The one cannot be separated from the other. Even so, neither of these two stages can exist without the other.

75

I told you that this soul had gone out, and that this is the sign that she has risen from imperfection and attained perfection.

Open your mind's eye and watch her run across the bridge of the teaching of Christ crucified, who was your rule and way and teaching. It was not me, the Father, that she set before her mind's eye.[96] This is what those do whose love is imperfect. They are not willing to suffer, and since no suffering can befall me, they want to pursue only the pleasure they find in me. This is why I say they follow me—not really me, but the pleasure they find in me. But the perfect soul does not act that way. Rather, as if drunk and ablaze with love, this soul has gathered herself together and climbed the three ordinary stairs that I interpreted for you as the soul's three powers, and also the three effectual[97] stairs that I interpreted for you as the body of my only-begotten Son, Christ crucified. Once she had climbed to his feet on the feet of her

---

95. The true reference of this last sentence is unclear from the context: "*Ma poi che sono venuti all'amore perfetto e liberale, escono fuore per lo modo detto abandonando loro medesimi.*" (S omits "*abandonando loro medesimi.*")

96. S, E, F add "but none other than Christ crucified."

97. *Attuali.*

own affection, she reached his side, where she found the secret of his heart and came to know the baptism of water that has within it the power of the blood provided the soul's vessel is ready to receive the grace of being joined and kneaded into the blood.

Where did she come to know this honor of being fused into the blood of the Lamb as she was baptized in the power of that blood? In his open side, where she came to know the fire of divine charity. This is what my Truth showed you, if you recall, when you asked him, "Why, gentle spotless Lamb, since you were dead when your side was opened, did you want your heart to be pierced and parted?"

He answered, "There were plenty of reasons, but I shall tell you one of the chief. My longing for humankind was infinite, but the actual deed of bearing pain and torment was finite and could never show all the love I had. This is why I wanted you to see my inmost heart, so that you would see that I loved you more than finite suffering could show.

"By shedding both blood and water I showed you the holy baptism of water that you receive through the power of my blood. But I was also showing you the baptism of blood, and this in two ways. The first touches those who are baptized in their own blood poured out for me. Though they could not have the other baptism, their own blood has power because of mine. Others are baptized in fire when they lovingly desire baptism but cannot have it. Nor is there any baptism of fire without blood, for blood has been fused with the fire of divine charity, because it was shed for love.[98]

"There is a second way the soul receives this baptism of blood, figuratively speaking. This my divine charity provided because I know how people sin because of their weakness. Not that weakness or anything else can force them to sin if they do not want to, but being weak they do fall into deadly sin and lose the grace they had drawn from the power of the blood in holy baptism. So my divine charity had to leave them an ongoing baptism of blood accessible by heartfelt contrition and a holy confession as soon as they can confess to my ministers who hold the key to the blood. This blood the priest pours over the soul in absolution.

---

98. The essential argument here, made denser by the effort to integrate it with the total significance of the blood of Christ as symbol of redemptive charity, is that the traditional "baptism of blood" (martyrdom) and "baptism of desire" as well as "baptism of water" are but various paths of entry into the one redemption to be found in Christ alone. This initial entry is then extended into the "ongoing baptism" of repentance and reconciliation.

"But if they cannot confess, heartfelt contrition is enough for the hand of my mercy to give them the fruit of this precious blood. Still, if they can, I want them to confess. And anyone who could confess but chooses not to will be deprived of the fruit of the blood. It is true that if at the moment of death a person wanted to confess but could not, that person would still receive this fruit. But do not be so stupid as to use this hope as an excuse for acting on the assumption that you can set your affairs right at the moment of death. For how do you know that I in my divine justice will not, because of your obstinacy, say 'You did not think of me during your lifetime, when you could have; now I have no thought for you in death.' No one, therefore, should dilly-dally, but if some in their sinfulness have, let them not put off to the last moment this baptism through hope in the blood.

"So you see, this baptism is ongoing, and the soul ought to be baptized in it right up to the end, in the way I have told you. In this baptism you experience that though my act of suffering on the cross was finite, the fruit of that suffering which you have received through me is infinite. This is because of the infinite divine nature joined with finite human nature. It was this human nature in which I was clothed that suffered in me, the Word. But because the two natures are fused with each other, the eternal Divinity took to itself the suffering I bore with such burning love.

"For this reason what I did can be called infinite. Not that either the actual bodily suffering or the pain of my longing to accomplish your redemption was infinite, for all of that ended on the cross when my soul left my body. But the fruit was infinite that came from my suffering and from my desire for your salvation, and therefore you receive it without limit. Had it not been infinite, the whole of humankind, past, present, and to come, would not have been restored. Nor could those who sin get up again if this baptism of blood (that is, the fruit of the blood) had not been given to you without limit.

"I showed you this in the opening up of my side. There you find my heart's secret and it shows you, more than any finite suffering could, how I love you. And I show you this without limit. How? Through the baptism of blood poured out in my burning love, and through the common baptism given to Christians, to whoever wants to receive it—the baptism of water that is one with the blood and the fire, where the soul is fused with my blood. It was to show you this that I willed that blood and water should come forth from my side.

"So now I have answered your question."

76

You know that my Truth's response contained everything I have told you. I have repeated it for you in his own words so that you would appreciate how marvelous is the state of the soul who has climbed this second stair. There she experiences and absorbs such a burning love that she runs on to the third stair, that is, to his mouth, where it is clear that she has arrived at perfection.

By what way did she come? By way of his heart, that is, through the remembrance of his blood in which she was baptized once again, abandoning imperfect love for the knowledge of the hearty love she drew from seeing and tasting and experiencing the fire of my charity. Now she has arrived at his mouth, and she shows this by fulfilling the mouth's functions. The mouth speaks with its tongue and tastes flavors. The mouth takes what is offered to the stomach, and the teeth chew it, for in no other way could the stomach digest the food.

So it is with the soul. First she speaks to me with the tongue of holy and constant prayer that is in the mouth of her holy desire. This tongue has an external and an interior language. Interiorly, the soul offers me tender loving desires for the salvation of souls. Externally, she proclaims the teaching of my Truth, admonishing, advising, testifying, without any fear for the pain the world may please to inflict on her. And she adapts her enthusiastic testimony to the situation of each person she confronts.

She eats the food of souls for my honor at the table of the most holy cross.[99] In no other way and at no other table can it be eaten perfectly and in truth. And she chews it (for otherwise she could not digest it) with hatred and love, the two rows of teeth in the mouth of holy desire. There she takes this food and chews it with hatred for herself and love for virtue in herself and in others. Every sort of assault—derision, insult, slander, reproach, endless persecutions, hunger and thirst, cold and heat, pain-filled longing and tears and sweat for the salvation of souls—she chews them all for my honor as she bears with her neighbors and supports them. And after she has chewed them she tastes the flavor, savoring the fruit of her labor and the delight of this food of souls, enjoying its taste in the fire of charity for me and her neighbors. And so this food reaches the stomach (that is, the heart), which has been prepared by desire and hunger for souls to receive it

99. Cf. Jn. 4:34. Catherine speaks often of "eating souls," i.e., winning them to salvation. The expression *cibo de l'anime*, literally "food of souls," recurs again and again in the *Dialogue* with an ambiguity that clearly says, "The food souls feed on IS souls."

willingly, with heartfelt charity and affection for others. She delights in it and chews it over and over in such a way that she lets go of her delicacy about her bodily life in order to be able to eat this food at the table of the cross, the table of the teaching of Christ crucified.

Then the soul grows so fat on true and solid virtues and so big because of the abundance of this food that the garment of selfish sensuality (that is, the body, which covers the soul) splits apart so far as its sensual appetite is concerned. Now anyone who splits apart dies. So the sensual will is left dead. Because the soul's well-ordered will is alive in me, clothed in my eternal will, her sensual will is dead.

Now this is how the soul acts who has in truth reached the third stair. This is the sign that she has reached it: Her selfish will died when she tasted my loving charity, and this is why she found her spiritual peace and quiet in the mouth. You know that peace is given with the mouth.[100] So in this third stage the soul finds such a peace that there is nothing that can disturb her. She has let go of and drowned her own will, and when that will is dead there is peace and quiet.

She brings forth virtue for her neighbors without pain. Not that this is in itself painless, but the dead will feels no pain because it endures pain willingly for my name's sake.

She runs briskly along the way of the teaching of Christ crucified. Nor does she slacken her pace for any assault that may befall her, or any persecution, or any pleasure the world may offer her. All these things she overcomes with true strength and patience, her will clothed in my loving charity and enjoying the food of the salvation of souls in true and perfect patience. Such patience is a sure sign that the soul loves me perfectly and without self-interest, for if she loved me and her neighbors for her own profit she would be impatient and would slacken her pace.

But she loves me for myself, because I am supreme Goodness and deserve to be loved, and she loves herself and her neighbors because of me, to offer glory and praise to my name. And therefore she is patient and strong in suffering, and persevering.

77

These three glorious virtues—patience, courage, and perseverance—are rooted in true charity and have their place at the very top of

---

100. The "kiss of peace," a traditional exchange of the peace of Christ among Christians, ritualized in various ways in the context of the liturgy through the centuries.

that tree of charity which in turn is crowned with the light of most holy faith by which souls run without darkness along the way of truth. They are lifted high by holy desire, so nothing can hurt them—neither the devil with his temptations (for he fears the soul afire in the furnace of love), nor people's slanders and assaults. Indeed, the world fears them even while it persecutes them.

My goodness permits this to strengthen them and make them great in my own sight and the world's, since they have made themselves small in true humility. You can see this clearly in my saints. They made themselves small for me, and I have made them great in myself, everlasting Life, and in the mystic body of holy Church. There they are forever remembered because their names are written in me, the book of life.[101] Thus the world holds them in reverence because they have despised the world.

These souls hide their virtue only through humility, never through fear. If their neighbors have need of their service, they do not hide their virtue for fear of suffering or for fear of losing their own selfish comfort. No, they serve them courageously, with no concern for themselves. In whatever way they use their lifetime for my honor, they are happy and find spiritual peace and quiet.

Why? Because they choose to serve me not in their own way but in mine. So the time of consolation is worth as much to them as the time of trial, prosperity as much as adversity. The one is worth as much as the other because they find my will in everything, and they think of nothing but conforming themselves to that will wherever they find it.

They have seen that nothing is done apart from me or without mystery and divine providence—except sin, which *is* nothing.[102] Therefore, they hate sin and hold all else in reverence. This is why they are so firm and constant in their will to walk along the path of truth, and do not slow down. Faithfully they serve their neighbors, paying no attention to their lack of recognition or gratitude or to the fact that sometimes vicious people insult and reprove them for their good works. Rather, they cry out for them in my sight with holy prayer, grieving more for the offense done to me and for the harm those souls suffer than for any insult to themselves.

With the glorious apostle Paul, my trumpeter, they say, "The

---

101. Cf. Rv. 13:8.
102. *Il peccato che non è.* It is difficult to do justice in English to the simplicity of this statement of the nonbeing of sin.

world curses us and we bless, it persecutes us and we give thanks. It throws us out as if we were the world's filth and refuse, and we bear it patiently."[103]

So you see, most beloved daughter, what are the gentle signs (the most preeminent is the virtue of patience) by which the soul shows that she has in truth risen from imperfect love and come to the perfect, and is following the gentle spotless Lamb, my only-begotten Son. When he was on the cross, held there by nails of love, he did not draw back because the Jews said, "Come down from the cross and we will believe you."[104] Nor did your ingratitude make him pull back from persevering in the obedience I had placed upon him. [No, he suffered] with such patience that not a sound of complaint was heard from him.

This is how these beloved children and faithful servants of mine follow the teaching and example of my Truth. Though the world, with its enticements and threats, would have them draw back, they do not turn their heads to look back at what has been plowed,[105] but keep their eyes only on their goal, my Truth. They have no desire to leave the battlefield and go back home for the cloak they left there,[106] that is, the cloak of pleasing and fearing creatures more than me their Creator. Indeed, they go into battle filled and inebriated with the blood of Christ crucified. My charity sets this blood before you in the hostel of the mystic body of holy Church to give courage to those who would be true knights and fight against their selfish sensuality and weak flesh, against the world and the devil, using the knife of hatred for the enemies they have to fight and love for virtue. This love is a suit of armor that keeps blows from piercing them through if only they do not take off the armor and let go of the knife and give it into the hands of their enemies, with the hand of free choice willingly surrendering to their enemies. Those who are inebriated with the blood do not act that way. No, they persevere courageously even to the point of death, leaving all their enemies routed.

O glorious virtue! How pleasing you are to me! In the world you so shine on the darksome eyes of the foolish that they cannot but share in my servants' light. On their hatred shines my servants' merciful care for their salvation. On their envy shines love's generosity. On their cruelty shines compassion, for while the world is cruel to my servants,

---

103. 1 Co. 4:13.
104. Mt. 27:40–42.
105. S has *l'aratro*, "the plow."
106. Cf. Mt. 24:18.

they are compassionate. On insult shines patience, the queen who reigns over all the virtues because she is the heart of love. She is the sign and signal of the soul's virtues, showing whether or not they are rooted in me, eternal Truth. She conquers and is never conquered. Her companions are courage and perseverance, and she returns home victorious. When she comes from the battlefield she returns to me, the eternal Father and rewarder of every labor, and she receives from me the crown of glory.[107]

78

Now I would not refrain from telling you with what delight these souls enjoy me while still in their mortal bodies. For having arrived at the third stage, as I have told you, they now reach the fourth. Not that they leave the third. The two are joined together, nor can the one exist without the other any more than charity for me without charity for your neighbor. But there is a fruit that comes from this third stage, from the soul's perfect union with me. She receives strength upon strength until she no longer merely suffers with patience, but eagerly longs to suffer for the glory and praise of my name.

Such souls glory in the shame of my only-begotten Son, as my trumpeter the glorious Paul said: "I glory in the hardships and shame of Christ crucified."[108] And in another place he says, "I bear in my body the marks of Christ crucified."[109] So these also run to the table of the most holy cross, in love with my love and hungry for the food of souls. They want to be of service to their neighbors in pain and suffering, and to learn and preserve the virtues while bearing the marks of Christ in their bodies. In other words, their anguished love shines forth in their bodies, evidenced in their contempt for themselves and in their delight in shame as they endure difficulties and suffering however and from whatever source I grant them.

To such very dear children as these, suffering is a delight and pleasure is wearisome, as is every consolation or delight the world may offer them. And not only what the world gives them through my dispensation (for my kindness sometimes constrains the world's servants

---

107. S, E add: "Now I have told you how people show that they have attained the perfection of friendship and filial love."

108. Cf. 2 Co. 12:9–10. S adds: "and elsewhere, 'I do not think that I should glory except in Christ crucified.' "

109. Gal. 6:17.

to hold them in reverence and help them in their physical needs) but even the spiritual consolation they receive from me, the eternal Father—even this they scorn because of their humility and contempt for themselves. It is not, however, the consolation, my gift and grace, that they scorn, but the pleasure their soul's desire finds in that consolation. This is because of the true humility they have learned from holy hatred, which humility is charity's governess and wet nurse, and is learned in truly knowing themselves and me. So you see how virtue and the wounds of Christ crucified shine forth in their bodies and spirits.

To such as these it is granted never to feel my absence. I told you how I go away from others (in feeling only, not in grace) and then return. I do not act thus with these most perfect ones who have attained great perfection and are completely dead to every selfish impulse. No, I am always at rest in their souls both by grace and by feeling. In other words, they can join their spirits with me in loving affection whenever they will. For through loving affection their desire has reached such union that nothing can separate it [from me]. Every time and place is for them a time and place of prayer. For their conversation has been lifted up from the earth and has climbed up to heaven. In other words, they have shed every earthly affection and sensual selfishness and have risen above themselves to the height of heaven by the stairway of virtue, having climbed the three stairs that I symbolized for you in the body of my only-begotten Son.

At the first step they put off love of vice from the feet of their affection. At the second they taste the secret and the love of his heart and there conceive love in virtue. At the third step of spiritual peace and calm they prove their virtue, and rising up from imperfect love they come to great perfection. Thus have these found rest in the teaching of my Truth. They have found table and food and waiter, and they taste this food through the teaching of Christ crucified, my only-begotten Son.

I am their bed and table. This gentle loving Word is their food, because they taste the food of souls in this glorious Word and because he himself is the food I have given you: his flesh and blood, wholly God and wholly human, which you receive in the sacrament of the altar, established and given to you by my kindness while you are pilgrims and travelers, so that you may not slacken your pace because of weakness, nor forget the blessing of the blood poured forth for you with such burning love, but may be constantly strengthened and filled with pleasure as you walk. The Holy Spirit, my loving charity, is the waiter who serves them my gifts and graces.

This gentle waiter carries to me their tender loving desires, and carries back to them the reward for their labors, the sweetness of my charity for their enjoyment and nourishment. So you see, I am their table, my Son is their food, and the Holy Spirit who proceeds from me the Father and from the Son, waits on them.[110]

You see, then, how they feel me constantly present to their spirits. And the more they have scorned pleasure and been willing to suffer, the more they have lost suffering and gained pleasure. Why? Because they are enflamed and on fire in my charity, where their own will is consumed. So the devil is afraid of the club of their charity, and that is why he shoots his arrows from far off and does not dare come near. The world strikes at the husk of their bodies, but though it thinks it is hurting, it is itself hurt, for the arrow that finds nowhere to enter returns to the one who shot it. So it is with the world and its arrows of insult and persecution and grumbling: When it shoots them at my most perfect servants, they find no place at all where they can enter because the soul's orchard is closed to them. So the arrow poisoned with the venom of sin returns to the one who shot it.

You see, they cannot be struck from any side, because what may strike the body cannot strike the soul, which remains at once happy and sad: sad because of her neighbor's sin, happy because of the union [with me] and the loving charity she has received for herself.

These souls follow the spotless Lamb, my only-begotten Son, who was both happy and sad on the cross. He was sad as he carried the cross of his suffering body and the cross of his longing to make satisfaction for the sin of humankind. And he was happy because his divine nature joined with his human nature could not suffer and made his soul always happy by showing itself to him unveiled. This is why he was at once happy and sad, because his flesh bore the pain the Godhead could not suffer—nor even his soul, so far as the superior part of his intellect was concerned.[111]

---

110. Cf. Let. 278 (to Monna Bartolomea di Domenico in Rome): "On her feast day [St. Lucy, December 13, 1377] she let me taste the fruit of her martyrdom. In my longing I was carried to the table of the Lamb, and he said to me . . . , 'I am the table and I am the food upon it.' And the hand of the Holy Spirit fed me."

111. Catherine holds the common assumption of her time that Christ constantly enjoyed the "beatific vision" of the Godhead throughout his life.

So it is with these very dear children. When they have attained the third and fourth stage they are sad as they carry their actual and spiritual cross by actually enduring physical pain as I permit it, and the cross of desire, their crucifying sorrow at the offense done to me and the harm done to their neighbors. They are happy, I say, because the delight of charity that makes them happy can never be taken away from them, and in this they receive gladness and blessedness. Therefore their sadness is called not "distressing sadness" that dries up the soul, but "fattening sadness" that fattens the soul in loving charity, because sufferings increase and strengthen virtue, make it grow and prove it.

So their suffering is fattening, not distressing, because no sadness or pain can drag them out of the fire. They are like the burning coal that no one can put out once it is completely consumed in the furnace, because it has itself been turned into fire. So it is with these souls cast into the furnace of my charity, who keep nothing at all, not a bit of their own will, outside of me, but are completely set afire in me. There is no one who can seize them or drag them out of my grace. They have been made one with me and I with them. I will never withdraw from their feelings. No, their spirits always feel my presence within them, whereas of the others I told you that I come and go, leaving in terms of feeling, not in terms of grace, and I do this to bring them to perfection. When they reach perfection I relieve them of this lover's game of going and coming back. I call it a "lover's game" because I go away for love and I come back for love—no, not really I, for I am your unchanging and unchangeable God; what goes and comes back is the feeling my charity creates in the soul.

79

I said that these souls are given the feeling [of my presence] never to lose it. But I do leave in another fashion. The soul that is chained within the body is incapable of constantly experiencing union with me, and because of her incapacity I withdraw—not my grace nor its feeling, but the union. For once souls have risen up in eager longing, they run in virtue along the bridge of the teaching of Christ crucified and arrive at the gate with their spirits lifted up to me. When they have crossed over and are inebriated with the blood and aflame with the fire of love, they taste in me the eternal Godhead, and I am to them a peaceful sea with which the soul becomes so united that her spirit knows no movement but in me. Though she is mortal she tastes the reward of the immortals, and weighed down still with the body she receives the lightness of the spirit. Often, therefore, the body is lifted up from the ground because of the perfect union of the soul with me, as if the heavy body had become light.

It is not because its heaviness has been taken away, but because the union of the soul with me is more perfect than the union between the soul and the body. And for this reason the strength of the spirit united with me lifts the body's weight off the ground, and the body is, as it were, immobile, so completely bedraggled by the soul's emotion that (as you recall having heard about several persons) it would have been impossible to go on living had not my goodness encircled it with strength.[112]

So I want you to know that it is a greater marvel to see the soul not leaving the body in this union than to see a host of dead bodies resurrected. This is why I withdraw that union for a while and make the soul return to the vessel that is her body, so that the body's feeling, which had been completely lost because of the soul's emotion, returns. For the soul does not really leave the body (this happens only in death), but her powers and emotions are united with me in love. Therefore the memory finds itself filled with nothing but me. The understanding is lifted up as it gazes into my Truth. The will, which always follows the understanding, loves and unites itself with what the eye of understanding sees.

When these powers are gathered and united all together and immersed and set afire in me, the body loses its feeling. For the eye sees without seeing; the ear hears without hearing; the tongue speaks without speaking (except that sometimes, because of the heart's fullness, I will let the tongue speak for the unburdening of the heart and for the glory and praise of my name, so that it speaks without speaking); the hand touches without touching; the feet walk without walking. All the members are bound and busied with the bond and feeling of love. By this bond they are subjected to reason and joined with the soul's emotion so that, as if against their own nature, they all cry out to me the eternal Father with one voice, asking to be separated from the soul, and the soul from the body. And so the soul cries out in my presence with

---

112. Once again Catherine is referring to her own experience. Cf. Let. 371 (to Pope Urban VI): "And he had drawn my heart to himself with such force that unless (not willing to have the vessel of my body broken) he had encircled it with this strength, the life would have left it."

the glorious Paul, "O unfortunate me! Who will free me from my body? For I have a perverse law that is fighting against my spirit!"[113]

Paul was speaking not only of the fight that sensual feeling puts up against the spirit, for he had, as it were, been given a guarantee by my word when he was told, "Paul, my grace is enough for you."[114] Why then did he say it? Because Paul felt himself bound up in the vessel of his body, and this blocked him off for a time from seeing me. In other words, until the hour of his death his eye was bound so that he could not see me, the eternal Trinity, with the vision of the blessed immortals who forever offer glory and praise to my name. Instead he found himself among mortals who are constantly offending me, deprived of seeing me as I really am.[115]

He and my other servants do see me and enjoy me, though not as I really am but in loving charity and in other ways as my goodness pleases to reveal myself to you. Still, every vision the soul receives while in the mortal body is a darkness when compared with the vision the soul has when separated from the body. So it seemed to Paul that his sense of sight was fighting against his spiritual vision. In other words, his human feeling of his body's bulk was a block to the eye of his understanding and was keeping him from seeing me face to face. His will, it seemed to him, was bound so that he could not love as much as he longed to love, for all love in this life is imperfect until it reaches its perfection.

Not that Paul's love (or that of my other true servants) was imperfect in relation to grace and the perfection of love, for he was perfect. But he was at the same time imperfect in that his love lacked its fulfillment, and so he suffered. For if his desire had been filled with what he loved he would not have been suffering. But because love, while in the mortal body, does not perfectly possess what it loves, it suffers.

Once, however, the soul is separated from the body, her longing is fulfilled and so she loves without suffering. She is sated, but her satiety is far removed from boredom. Though sated she is hungry, but her hunger is far removed from pain. For once the soul is separated from the body, her vessel is filled up in me in truth, so steadied and strengthened that she can desire nothing but that she has it. Because she desires to see me, she sees me face to face. Because she desires to see my name

---

113. Rm. 7:24, 23.
114. 2 Co. 12:9.
115. Literally, "of seeing me in my essence."

'glorified and praised in my holy ones, she sees it, both in the angelic nature and in the human. *(80)* And so perfect is her vision that she sees my name glorified and praised not only in those who dwell in eternal life but also in mortal creatures. For, whether the world wills it or no, it offers me glory.

True, the people of the world do not offer me glory in the way they ought, by loving me above all things. But I for my part draw from them glory and praise for my name. For my mercy and the fullness of my charity are reflected in them because I lend them time and do not order the earth to swallow them up for their sins. No, I look on them and order the earth to give them a share of its fruits, and I command the sun to warm them and give them its light and heat, and I order the sky to move [above them]. In all created things made for them I employ my mercy and love, nor do I withdraw these because of their sins. I give to sinners as I give to the just—and often more to sinners than to the just, because the just are ready to suffer, and I will deprive them of earthly goods in order to give them more abundantly of the goods of heaven.

So my mercy and love shine on my servants sometimes in the persecutions the world's servants inflict on them, proving in them the virtues of patience and charity. By offering constant humble prayer my suffering servants turn it into glory and praise for my name.[116] So whether the wicked will it or not, they offer me glory in this, even though their intent is to insult me.

81

The wicked in this life serve the promotion of virtue in my servants, just as the devils in hell serve as my executioners and promoters. They do justice to the damned and promote the cause of my creatures who are pilgrim travelers in this life, created to reach me, their goal. They are their promoters because they exercise them in virtue by vexing and tempting them in different ways, trying to make them harm each other and steal from one another—and this not just for the sake of the stolen goods or the harm, but to deprive them of charity. But though they think they are so depriving my servants they are in fact strengthening them by proving their patience and courage and perseverance.

In this way the devils give glory and praise to my name, and so my

---

116. Cf. Is. 53:12.

truth is fulfilled in them. For I created them to glorify and praise me, the eternal Father, and to share my beauty. But they rebelled against me in their pride, so they fell and were deprived of seeing me. They do not glorify me in the delight of love, but I, eternal Truth, have sent them to be instrumental in exercising my servants in virtue and to be the executioners of those who because of their sins are damned forever, as well as of those who enter the sufferings of purgatory. So you see, my truth is fulfilled in them, for they glorify me, but not as citizens of eternal life, since they are deprived of that because of their sins. Rather they glorify me as my executioners, for through them is manifested my justice to the damned and to those in purgatory.

82

Who sees and experiences this revelation of my name's being glorified and praised in every created thing and in the devils and in people? The soul who has shed her body and come to me her final goal sees it clearly, and in her vision she knows the truth. Seeing me, the eternal Father, she loves; loving, she is satisfied; being satisfied, she knows the truth; knowing the truth, her will is grounded firmly in mine—so firmly and solidly that nothing can cause her to suffer, for she is in possession of what she had longed for, to see me and to see my name praised and glorified.

She sees this fully and truly in my holy ones, in the blessed spirits, in all other creatures, and in the devils, as I have told you. And even when she sees me offended, a thing that used to grieve her, now she can know no sorrow, but only compassion without pain. She loves those who sin and with loving affection begs me to be merciful to the world.

Suffering has ended for the blessed, but not love. Yes. The Word, my Son, in his painful death on the cross ended the pain of that tormenting desire he had borne from the beginning when I sent him into the world right to the moment of his death for your salvation.[117] Not that he ended his desire for your salvation—no, only the pain. For if my loving charity, which I had revealed to you in his person, had at

---

117. Cf. Let. 242 (to Angelo da Ricasoli): "The cross of desire was greater than was his physical cross. This was his desire: His hunger for our redemption, for the fulfillment of his eternal Father's will, was painful to him until he saw it finished. This was the crucifying desire he bore from the beginning right up to the end." Cf. also Lk. 12:50: "There is a baptism I must still receive, and how great is my distress until it is over!"

that point been ended and finished for you, you would not even exist, because you are created through love. And if I had taken back my love and ceased to love your being, you would not exist. But my love did create you and my love preserves you. And because I am one with my Truth, the incarnate Word, and he is one with me, he put an end to desire's pain, but not its love.

You see, then, how the saints and all souls who have eternal life are desirous of the salvation of souls, but without pain. Their death put an end to their pain, but not to their loving charity. Indeed, they will pass through the narrow gate drunk, as it were, with the blood of the spotless Lamb, dressed in charity for their neighbors and bathed in the blood of Christ crucified, and they will find themselves in me, the sea of peace, lifted above imperfection and emptiness into perfection and filled with every good.

83

Paul, then, had seen and tasted this when I drew him up to the third heaven,[118] to the height of the Trinity. He tasted and knew my Truth, for there he received the Holy Spirit in his fullness and learned the teaching of my Truth, the incarnate Word. Paul's soul was clothed in me, the eternal Father, through feeling and union, just as the blessed are in everlasting life. His soul, though, had not left his body, but the feeling and union were there. But it pleased my goodness to make of him a chosen vessel in the very depths of me, the eternal Trinity. Therefore I stripped him of myself, since no suffering can befall me, and I wanted him to suffer for my name. Then I put before his mind's eye Christ crucified. I clothed him in the garment of his teaching and bound and chained him with the mercy of the Holy Spirit, the fire of charity. He was like a ready vessel, remade by my goodness, for he put up no resistance when he was struck. No, he said, "My Lord, what do you want me to do? Tell me what you want me to do and I will do it."[119] I taught him when I set Christ crucified before his eye and clothed him in my Truth's teaching. Once most perfectly enlightened by the light of true contrition grounded in my charity, through which he repented of his sin, he clothed himself in the teaching of Christ crucified. And he so held on to it (as he revealed to you) that he was never stripped of it. Not for the devil's tempting, not for the thorn in the

---

118. 2 Co. 12:2–4.
119. Cf. Ac. 9:6.

flesh that often fought against him (which my goodness had permitted him to make him grow in grace and merit through humiliation, because he had experienced the height of the Trinity),[120] not for difficulties, not for anything that happened to him did he loosen his hold on the garment of Christ crucified, that is, perseverance in his teaching.[121] No, he took it even more closely into his very flesh. He held it so tightly to himself that he gave his life for it, and he returned to me, God eternal, wearing that garment.

Paul, then, had experienced what it is to enjoy me without the weight of the body, because I made him experience it through the sense of union without actually being separated from his body.

Then, after he had returned to himself, clothed in Christ crucified, his own love seemed to him imperfect compared with the perfection of the love that he had tasted and seen in me and that the holy ones enjoy who are separated from their bodies. Therefore it seemed to him that his body's weight rebelled against him, blocked him off from great perfection, from the fulfilling of desire that the soul receives after death. His memory seemed to him imperfect and weak, and it was, with the imperfection that kept him from being able to remember or hold or receive or enjoy me in truth with the perfection with which the saints receive me. This is why it seemed to him that everything, as long as he was in his body, was for him a perverse law that fought and rebelled against his spirit. It was not a question of struggling with sin. I have already told you that I gave him a guarantee when I said, "Paul, my grace is enough for you."[122] It was a question of struggling with what blocked him from spiritual perfection, from seeing me as I really am. That vision was blocked by his body's law and heaviness, and that is why he cried, "Unfortunate man that I am, who will free me from my body? For I have a perverse law bound up in my members, and it fights against my spirit."[123] And this is the truth: Memory is beleaguered by the body's imperfection; understanding is blocked and fettered by this heaviness of the body and kept from seeing me as I really am; and the will is chained, for weighted down by the body it cannot come to enjoy me, God eternal, without pain. So Paul spoke the truth when he said that he had a law bound up in his body that fought against his spirit.

---

120. Cf. 2 Co. 12:7.
121. Cf. Rm. 8:35.
122. 2 Co. 12:9.
123. Rm. 7:24, 23.

So also my other servants who have arrived at the third and fourth stage of perfect union with me: They cry out with Paul, wishing to be separated and set free from their bodies.

84 .

Death gives these souls no difficulty: They long for it. With perfect contempt they have done battle with their bodies. Therefore, they have lost that natural tenderness which binds soul and body, having dealt the decisive blow to natural love with contempt for bodily life and love for me. They long for death, and so they say, "Who will free me from my body? I long to be set free from my body and to be with Christ."[124] And such as these say along with Paul, "Death for me is in longing, and life in patience." For the soul who has risen to this perfect union longs to see me, and to see me praised and glorified. Afterwards she returns to the cloud that is her body—I mean her feeling, which had been drawn into me by the impulse of love, returns to her body. I told you that all the body's feelings are drawn along by the force of the soul's affection when she is united with me more perfectly than soul is united with body, thus drawing that union into myself. For the body is not capable of bearing such a union constantly. That is why, though I remain in grace and in feeling, I withdraw so far as union is concerned. But I always return with a greater increase of grace and with more perfect union. So it is always with a heightening of my truth that I return, revealing myself to the soul with greater knowledge. And when I withdraw in the way I told you so that the body might return for a while to its senses (which had left because of the union I had effected with the soul and the soul with me), when the body does return to itself, to its senses, the soul is impatient of life. For she sees herself taken away from her union with me, taken away from the company of the immortals who glorify me, and finds herself instead in the company of mortals, whom she sees offending me so miserably.

This is the crucifying desire these souls endure when they see me offended by my creatures. Because of this, and because of their desire to see me, life is insupportable for them. Still, because their will is not their own and has in fact become one with me in love, they can neither will nor desire anything but what I will. Though they long to come to me, they are content to remain with their suffering if I want them to

---

124. Ph. 1:23.

remain, for the greater glory and praise of my name and for the salvation of souls.

So in nothing are they out of harmony with my will, but they run with anguished longing, clothed in Christ crucified, keeping to the bridge of his teaching and glorying in their shame and suffering.[125] The more they have to endure, the more delighted they are. Indeed, suffering many difficulties is for them a kind of refreshment in their longing for death that often, because of their desire and willingness to suffer, softens the pain of their longing to be freed from the body.

These souls not only suffer with patience as do those in the third stage; they in fact glory in enduring many troubles for my name's sake. When they are suffering they are happy; when they are not suffering they are in pain, fearing that I may wish to reward their good works in this life, or that the sacrifice of their desires may not be pleasing to me. But when they are suffering, when I allow them many troubles, they rejoice to see themselves clothed in the sufferings and shame of Christ crucified. Therefore, if it were possible for them to have virtue without weariness, they would not want it, for they would rather delight in the cross with Christ and acquire virtue with suffering than to gain eternal life in any other way.

Why? Because they are enflamed and submerged in the blood, where they find my burning charity. This charity is a fire that comes forth from me and carries off their heart and spirit, accepting the sacrifice of their desires. Then their mind's eye rises up and gazes into my Godhead, and love follows understanding to be nourished there and brought into the union. This is a vision through infused grace that I give to the soul who loves and serves me in truth.

85

By this light set in the mind's eye Thomas [Aquinas] saw me and there gained the light of great learning. Augustine, Jerome, and my other holy doctors, enlightened by my Truth, understood and knew my Truth in the midst of darkness. I am referring to Holy Scripture, which seemed darksome because it was not understood. This was no fault of Scripture, but of the listener who failed to understand. So I sent these lamps to enlighten blind and dense understandings. They raised their mind's eye to know the truth in the midst of darkness, and

---

125. Cf. Ga. 6:14.

I the fire, the one who accepted their sacrifice, carried them off and gave them light, not naturally but beyond all nature, and in the midst of darkness they received the light and so came to know the truth.

So what had seemed darksome before now appears most perfectly lightsome to every sort of person—to the dense as to the discerning. All receive according to their capacity and according to their readiness to know me, for I do not spurn their dispositions. So you see, the eye of understanding has received a light beyond any natural light, infused by grace, and in this light the doctors and the other saints came to know the truth in the midst of darkness, and from the darkness light was made. For understanding existed before Scripture was formed; so learning came from understanding, for in seeing is discernment.

In this way the holy fathers and prophets saw and discerned, and so foretold the coming and death of my Son. This is how the apostles were after the coming of the Holy Spirit who gave them this light above every natural light. This is what the evangelists, doctors, confessors, virgins, and martyrs had: They were all enlightened by this perfect light. They had it in different ways, depending on what was needed for their own salvation and that of others and for proclaiming Holy Scripture. The holy doctors of science did it by proclaiming the teaching of my Truth as it is found in the preaching of the apostles and by interpreting the evangelists' gospels. The martyrs proclaimed with their blood the light of holy faith and the fruitful treasure of the blood of the Lamb. The virgins proclaimed the Word's obedience in charity and purity and obedience. In other words, they demonstrated the perfection of obedience that shines forth in my Truth, who, because of the obedience I laid upon him, ran to the shameful death of the cross.

All this light that is seen in the Old and New Testaments (by the Old I mean the prophecies of the holy prophets) was seen and known by the eye of understanding through the light beyond natural light that I infused by grace.

In the New Testament, how was the evangelical life proclaimed to faithful Christians? By this same light. And because it came forth from the very same light, the New Law did not destroy the Old. No, it bound the two together. The New took away the imperfection of the Old, for the Old had been built solely on fear.

When the Word my only-begotten Son came, he brought the Law to fulfillment by endowing it with love. He lifted the fear of punishment but let holy fear remain. This is how my Truth spoke to the disciples to show them he was not a breaker of the Law: "I have not come to destroy the Law but to fulfill it."[126] It was as if my Truth had told them: The Law is now imperfect, but with my blood I shall perfect it, completing it with what it now lacks. I will take away the fear of punishment and build it on love and holy fear.

What made it clear that this was the truth? The light given by grace, given to whoever wants to receive this light beyond natural light. Every light that comes from Holy Scripture has come and still comes from that light. This is why foolish, proud, and learned people go blind even though it is light, because their pride and the cloud of selfish love have covered and blotted out this light. So they read Scripture literally rather than with understanding. They taste only its letter in their chasing after a multiplicity of books, never tasting the marrow of Scripture because they have let go of the light by which Scripture was formed and proclaimed. Such as these, then, wonder and fall to whining when they see so many uncultured and unschooled in biblical knowledge yet as enlightened in knowledge of the truth as if they had studied for a long time. But this is no wonder at all, for they possess the chief source of that light from which learning comes. But because these proud folk have lost that light they neither see nor know my goodness or the light of grace that is poured out in my servants.[127]

I tell you, therefore, it is far better to walk by the spiritual counsel of a humble and unschooled person with a holy and upright conscience than by that of a well-read but proud scholar with great knowledge. For one cannot share what one does not have in oneself, and because these persons' life is darksome, they often share the light of Holy Scripture in darkness. You will find the opposite in my servants, for they share the light within them in hunger and longing for others' salvation.

I have told you this, my dearest daughter, to let you know the perfection of this unitive state in which souls are carried off by the fire of my charity. In that charity they receive supernatural light, and in that light they love me. For love follows upon understanding. The more they know, the more they love, and the more they love, the more they know. Thus each nourishes the other. By this light they reach that eternal vision of me in which they see and taste me in truth when soul

---

126. Mt. 5:17.
127. Catherine herself, though "uncultured and unschooled," often confounded scholars who engaged her in arguments over biblical interpretation in an attempt to discredit her.

is separated from body. (I told you all this when I described for you the happiness souls receive in me.)

This is that superb state in which the soul even while still mortal shares the enjoyment of the immortals. In fact, she often attains such union that she hardly knows whether she is in the body or out.[128] She tastes the pledge of eternal life through her union with me as well as because her own will is dead. It is by that death that she realizes her union with me, and in no other way could she perfectly accomplish that.

These souls have, then, a taste of eternal life. They have let go of the hell of self-will. But those who live by self-willed sensuality have in that a pledge of hell, as I have told you.

86

Now I, eternal Truth, have let you see with your mind's eye and hear with your feeling's ear how you must behave if you would serve yourself and your neighbors in the teaching and knowledge of my truth. For I told you in the beginning that one comes to knowledge of the truth through self-knowledge. But self-knowledge alone is not enough: It must be seasoned by and joined with knowledge of me within you. This is how you found humility and contempt for yourself along with the fire of my charity, and so came to love and affection for your neighbors and gave them the service of your teaching and your holy and honorable living.

I showed you the bridge as well. And I showed you the three ordinary stairs that are set up in the soul's three powers, and how no one can have the life of grace without climbing all three stairs, without gathering all three powers in my name. Then I revealed to you how these stairs were in a special way a figure of the three spiritual stages, symbolized in the body of my only-begotten Son. I told you that he had made a stairway of his body, and showed it to you in his nailed feet, in his open side, and in his mouth where the soul tastes peace and calm.

I showed you the imperfection of slavish fear and the imperfection of love that loves me for the delight it feels. And I showed you the perfection of the third stage, of those who have attained peace at his mouth. These have run with eager longing across the bridge of Christ crucified. They have climbed the three ordinary stairs, have gathered their souls' three powers and all their works in my name (as I ex-

128. Cf. 2 Co. 12:3.

plained for you more in detail before), and they have climbed the three special stairs and passed from imperfection to perfection. So you have seen how they run on in truth. I also gave you a taste of the soul's perfection as she is adorned with the virtues, as well as the delusions she is subject to before she reaches perfection if she does not use her time well in coming to know herself and me.

I told you about the wretchedness of those who let themselves be drowned in the river because they will not keep to the bridge of my Truth's teaching, the bridge I built for you so you would not drown. Like fools they have chosen to drown in the world's wretched filth.

I have told you all this to make you shake up the fire of your holy longing and your compassion and grief over the damnation of souls. I want your sorrow and love to drive you to pressure me with sweat and tears—tears of constant humble prayer offered to me in the flames of burning desire. And not just for yourself, but for so many others of my creatures and servants who will hear you and be compelled by my love (together with you and my other servants) to beg and pressure me to be merciful to the world and to the mystic body of holy Church, the Church for which you so earnestly plead with me.

You will recall that I already told you I would fulfill your desires by giving you refreshment in your labors, that I would satisfy your anguished longings by reforming holy Church through good and holy shepherds. I will do this, as I told you, not through war, not with the sword and violence, but through peace and calm, through my servants' tears and sweat.[129] I have set you as workers in your own and your neighbors' souls and in the mystic body of holy Church. In yourselves you must work at virtue; in your neighbors and in the Church you must work by example and teaching. And you must offer me constant prayer for the Church and for every creature, giving birth to virtue through your neighbors. For I have already told you that every virtue and every sin is realized and intensified through your neighbors. Therefore, I want you to serve your neighbors and in this way share the fruits of your own vineyard.

Never cease offering me the incense of fragrant prayers for the salvation of souls, for I want to be merciful to the world. With your

---

129. Clearly the Great Schism had not yet erupted at the time this was written. The tone would fit the summer of 1378, when Catherine was so intensely preoccupied with the struggle for peace between Florence and the Holy See, as well as with persuading the recently elected Urban VI of the urgency of clerical reform.

prayers and sweat and tears I will wash the face of my bride, holy Church. I showed her to you earlier as a maiden whose face was all dirtied, as if she were a leper. The clergy and the whole of Christianity are to blame for this because of their sins, though they receive their nourishment at the breast of this bride! But I will tell you about those sins in another place.

87

Then that soul, restless in her great longing, rose up like one drunk from the union she had experienced with God and from what she had heard and tasted of the gentle first Truth. She was anxiously grieving over the foolishness of creatures who do not recognize their benefactor or God's loving charity. Still, she was glad in the hope of the promise God's Truth had given her when he had taught her how she and God's other servants must behave if they wished him to be merciful to the world. So she raised her mind's eye to the gentle Truth with whom she was united, because she wanted to know something about the spiritual stages God had described to her. She saw that the soul passes through these stages with tears, so she wanted Truth to show her the difference among the kinds of tears, what was their source, how they came to be,[130] what fruit was to be had from such weeping, and what different reasons there were for it. And since the truth could be known only from Truth himself, she addressed the question to him. Now nothing can be known in Truth unless the mind's eye can see it. So one who wishes to know must rise up with a desire to know by the light of faith and in Truth, and must open the mind's eye by opening its pupil, which is faith, onto the object of truth.

She knew this, for she had not forgotten what God who is Truth had taught her, that in no other way than this could she learn what she wanted to know of the stages of tears and their fruits. So she rose up above her very self with a longing beyond all telling. And by the light of a lively faith she opened her mind's eye onto eternal Truth, and there she saw and knew the truth of what she had asked. For God revealed himself, that is, his kindness, to her and stooped down to her burning desire and granted her petition.

---

130. The manuscripts vary from here to the end of this sentence. C omits the phrase about the fruit to be had from tears; S, E, F include a repetition of the question of source. In my translation I have opted for the best of both and left out the repetition.

TEARS

88

T hen *God, gentle first Truth, spoke:*
O dearest daughter whom I so love, you have asked me for the
will to know the reasons for tears and their fruits, and I have not
scorned your desire. Open your mind's eye wide, and I will show you,
through the spiritual stages I have described for you, those imperfect
tears whose source is fear.

First of all, there are the tears of damnation, the tears of this
world's evil ones.

Second are the tears of fear, of those who weep for fear because
they have risen up from the sin out of fear of punishment.

Third are those who have risen up from sin and are beginning to
taste me. These weep tenderly and begin to serve me. But because their
love is imperfect, so is their weeping.

The fourth stage is that of souls who have attained perfection in
loving their neighbors[1] and love me without any self-interest. These
weep and their weeping is perfect.

The fifth stage (which is joined to the fourth) is that of sweet tears
shed with great tenderness.

I will tell you, too, about tears of fire, shed without physical weeping, which often satisfy those who want to weep but cannot. And I
want you to know that a soul can experience all of these different
stages as she rises from fear and imperfect love to attain perfect love
and the state of union.

89

I want you to know that all tears come from the heart. Nor is there
any other bodily member that can satisfy the heart as the eyes can. If

---

1. *Nella carità del prossimo.*

the heart is sad the eyes show it. If the sadness is sensual, there will be hearty tears that give birth to death—hearty because they do come from the heart, but deadly because the heart's love is disordered, cut off from me. And because it is disordered it is offensive to me and earns sadness and tears that are deadly. It is true, however, that the seriousness of both sin and weeping depends on how disordered that love is. These, then, are those first, the tears of death, of which I have told you and will tell you more later.[2]

Let us look now at the first of the life-giving tears, the tears of those who recognize their sinfulness and begin to weep for fear of punishment. Their tears are heartfelt but sensual; that is, although they have not yet come to perfect hatred for sin as an offense against me, they do get up with heartfelt sorrow because of the punishment that must follow upon the sin they have committed. So their eyes weep to satisfy the sorrow in their heart.

When the soul begins to practice virtue, she begins to lose this fear. For she knows that fear alone is not enough to win her eternal life (as I told you when I spoke of the soul's second stage[3]). So she rises up in love to know herself and my goodness to her, and she begins to hope in my mercy. In this her heart feels glad, because her sorrow for sin is mixed with hope in my divine mercy.

Now her eyes begin to weep, and her tears well up from the fountain of her heart. But these tears are often sensual because she is not yet very perfect. If you ask me why, I answer: because of the root of selfish love. Not sensual love; she has already risen above that. No, it is a spiritual love in which the soul hungers for spiritual consolations (whose imperfection I have made clear to you) or for the consolations that come through some person she loves with a spiritual love. But let her be deprived of the interior or external consolations she loves (the interior being the consolations she drew from me, and the external those she had got through creatures). Or let temptations come upon her or let other people persecute her. Then her heart is sad, and at once her eyes, sensing the heart's pain and sadness, begin to weep in tender self-pity, a pity springing from spiritual selfishness, because she has not yet

---

2. In the general scheme of this section, there are two principal distinctions: the tears of death (or damnation) and those of life. At this point Catherine takes up in detail the latter, now numbering the tears of fear (which were second in her initial listing) as first. After all of the tears of life have been treated she returns to those of death in greater detail in ch. 93.

3. Cf. ch. 58.

completely put underfoot and drowned her self-will. So she sheds sensual tears, tears of spiritual emotion.

But as she grows and exercises herself in the light of self-knowledge, she conceives a kind of contempt for herself. From this she draws a bit of knowledge of my goodness, aflame with love, and she begins to join and conform her will with mine. She begins to feel joy and compassion: joy for herself because of this impulse of love, and compassion for her neighbors (as I described it for you in the third stage[4]). Then her eyes, which want to satisfy her heart, weep in charity for me and her neighbors with heartfelt love, grieving only for the offense done to me and the harm to her neighbors. For she thinks not of herself but only of being able to praise and glorify my name. And with anguished longing she finds her pleasure in feeding at the table of the most holy cross, that is, in patterning herself after the humble, patient, spotless Lamb, my only-begotten Son, of whom I have made a bridge, as I told you.

So she travels calmly over the bridge, following the teaching of my gentle Truth. She passes through this Word, enduring with true gentle patience every pain and trouble that I permit for her own good. She accepts it courageously, choosing my way over her own. And she suffers not only patiently, but gladly. She considers it a glory to be persecuted for my name's sake so that she might have something to suffer [for me]. This brings the soul to such joy and spiritual peace that no tongue could describe it.

Once she has gone along this way of my only-begotten Son's teaching and set her sights firmly on me, gentle first Truth, she comes to know what she has seen, and knowing it, she loves it. Her will, drawn along on the heels of understanding, tastes my eternal Godhead and knows and sees therein the divine nature joined with your humanity. She takes her rest then in me, the peaceful sea. Her heart is united with me in affectionate love, as I told you at the fourth and unitive stage.[5] When she feels the presence of my eternal Godhead she begins to shed sweet tears that are truly a milk that nourishes the soul in true patience. These tears are a fragrant ointment that sends forth a most delicate perfume.

O most loved daughter, how glorious is the soul who has so truly learned to cross the stormy flood to come to me, the peaceful sea! The

---

4. Cf. ch. 76, 77.
5. Cf. ch. 78.

vessel of her heart is filled with the sea that is my very self, the most high eternal Godhead! And so her eyes, like a channel trying to satisfy her heart's lead, shed tears.

This is that final state in which the soul is both happy and sorrowful. She is happy because of the union with me that she has felt in experiencing divine love. She is sorrowful because she sees my goodness and greatness offended. For she has seen and tasted that goodness and greatness in her knowledge of herself, and it was this self-knowledge that brought her to this final stage. But her sorrow does not mar the unitive state. No, it brings on tears of great sweetness because of the self-knowledge she finds in charity for her neighbors. For in that charity she discovers the lover's lament of my divine mercy and sorrow for her neighbors' sins, and so she weeps with those who weep and rejoices with these who rejoice.[6] These last are those who live in charity, and for these the soul rejoices, for she sees these my servants praising and glorifying my name.

So the second kind of weeping (the third [spiritual stage]) does not stand in the way of the last (the fourth, the second of the unitive stages).[7] Rather, they flavor each other. For if the last kind of weeping, in which the soul found such union, had not been drawn from the second (that is, from the third stage of love for her neighbors), it would not be perfect. So it is necessary for the two to flavor each other. Otherwise the soul would become presumptuous: A subtle breeze of self-conceit would insinuate itself and she would fall from the heights down to the very depths where she first vomited out [her sin].[8]

It is therefore essential that the soul be constant in her charity for her neighbors and in true knowledge of herself. In this way she will feed the flame of my charity within her, because charity for others is drawn from my charity, that is, from the knowledge the soul gained by coming to know herself and my goodness to her, which made her see that I love her unspeakably much. So she loves every person with the

---

6. Rm. 12:15.

7. Catherine's numbers are obviously overlapping here. The third and fourth (last) stages of the spiritual life are, respectively, the first and second unitive stages (cf. ch. 78), and these two are inseparable, the second being simply the perpetuation of the first. Catherine herself defines, in the lines that follow, her reference to "the second kind of weeping" as the tears shed for the sins of others. The "first" kind are those of joy in the soul's union with God. This paragraph and the following are a beautiful, if frustrating, example of Catherine's sometimes convoluted logic!

8. Cf. 2 P. 2:22.

same love she sees herself loved with, and this is why the soul, as soon as she comes to know me, reaches out to love her neighbors. Because she sees that I love them even more than she does, she also loves them unspeakably much.

Since she has learned that she can be of no profit to me, nor return to me the same pure love with which she feels herself loved by me, she sets herself to repaying my love through the means I established—her neighbors. They are the ones to whom you must be of service, just as I told you that every virtue is realized through your neighbors. I have given you these to serve, every one, both in general and individually, according to the different graces you receive from me. You must love with the same pure love with which I love you. But you cannot do this for me because I love you without being loved and without any self-interest. And because I loved you without being loved by you, even before you existed (in fact it was love that moved me to create you in my own image and likeness) you cannot repay me. But you must give this love to other people, loving them without being loved by them. You must love them without any concern for your own spiritual or material profit, but only for the glory and praise of my name, because I love them. In this way you will fulfill the whole commandment of the Law, which is to love me above all things and your neighbor as your very self.[9]

It is true, then, that no one can attain this height without this second state.[10] In other words, the third and second states become one, and the perfection the soul has reached cannot be maintained if she lets go of the love that produced the second kind of tears. Just so, it is impossible to fulfill the law concerning [love for] me, God eternal, apart from [the law concerning love for] your neighbors. These are the two feet of affection on which you must follow the commandments and counsels given you by Christ crucified.

In this way these two states joined into one nourish the soul in virtue and union with me. Not that the one state changes for being joined with the other. On the contrary, it increases the richness of grace by new and different gifts and a wonderful spiritual exaltation, with a knowledge of the truth that although you are mortal you seem in a

---

9. Cf. Mt. 22:37–40.
10. The "second and third" states referred to here are the two kinds of "perfect tears," those of joy in the soul's union with God and those of sorrow for the sins of others.

sense immortal, because your selfishly sensual emotions are dead and your will is dead because of your union with me.

Oh, how sweet is this union to the soul who experiences it! For in the experience she sees my secrets, and from this she may often receive the spirit of prophecy, knowing the future. It is my goodness that does this. Nonetheless, the humble soul should always spurn such gifts—not the gift of my loving charity,[11] but her hankering after her own consolation. She should count herself unworthy of spiritual peace and quiet, and rather nourish virtue within herself. Nor should she rest in her union with me,[12] but rather return to the valley of self-knowledge.

I grant the soul this grace and give her this light to make her continue to grow. For the soul is never so perfect in this life that she cannot become yet more perfect in love. My beloved Son, your head, was the only one who could not grow in any sort of perfection, because he was one with me and I with him. His soul was beatified in his union with my divine nature.[13] But you, his pilgrim members, can always grow to greater perfection. Not that you would advance to another stage once you had reached that final [state of union with me]. But you can make that very union grow in whatever kind of perfection you choose with the help of my grace.

90

Now you have seen the different kinds of tears and the differences among them, as it has pleased my truth to satisfy your desire.

The first kind of tears, the tears of those who are dead in sin, come from a heart that is corrupt. Now the heart is the source of all emotion, which in turn is the source of tears. So because these persons' heart is corrupt, the weeping that comes from it is corrupt and wretched, and so are all their actions.

The second kind of weeping is that of souls who are beginning to know their own sinfulness through the punishment that must be their lot after sinning. This is a common sort of beginning that I in my kindness grant to weak souls who like fools are drowning down there in the

---

11. C has here: "not the effect of my gift of charity," but *effetto* is erased in the manuscript. I have followed the more logical *affetto* of S.

12. Literally, *nel secondo stato*, i.e., the second of the two most perfect stages, that of union.

13. In the theology of Catherine's day, the human soul of Jesus enjoyed the beatific vision from his conception.

river because they shun my Truth's teaching. There are so very many who come as far as this sort of self-knowledge. Without slavish fear of their own punishment they would perish. Some, in a sudden great contempt for themselves, come to consider themselves deserving of punishment. There are others who give themselves in wholesome simplicity to serving me their Creator because they are sorry they have offended me. Those who go the way of great self-contempt are, it is true, more apt to reach perfection than the others. Both will reach it if they exert themselves, but the former will get there sooner. The first sort must take care not to rest in their slavish fear. The others must watch out for tepidity, for if they do not exercise their simplicity it will grow lukewarm within them. This is an ordinary sort of calling.

The third and fourth kinds of weeping belong to those who have risen above fear and attained to love and hope. They taste my divine mercy and receive from me many gifts and consolations, and because of these things their eyes, responding to the heart's emotion, weep. This weeping is still imperfect, because it is mixed with weeping that is spiritually sensual. But if these souls exercise themselves in virtue they reach the fourth stage, where, because their desire has grown, they so unite themselves with my will that they can no longer desire anything but what I will. They are clothed with a charity for their neighbors that gives birth in them to a lover's lament that I am offended and their neighbors hurt.

Such weeping is one with the fifth sort, that of ultimate perfection. Here the soul is united with Truth and the flame of holy desire burns more fiercely within her. The devil flees from this desire and can no longer persecute the soul—not by assaulting her, because love for her neighbors has made her patient, nor by using spiritual or temporal consolations, because she would spurn such things in contempt and true humility.

It is indeed true that the devil never sleeps but teaches you, if you are careless, to sleep when it is profitable to him. But his watching cannot hurt these perfect souls, for he cannot stand the heat of their charity, nor the fragrance of their soul's union with me, the sea of peace. No, the soul cannot be tricked so long as she remains united with me. So the devil flees like a fly from a boiling caldron, because he is afraid of the fire. If the soul were lukewarm he would enter fearlessly—though often enough he perishes there when he finds it hotter than he had imagined! So it happens with the soul when she first reaches perfection. The devil comes in, because she seems to him to be lukewarm, with different sorts of temptations. But if the soul has the least bit of knowledge and heat and hatred of sin, she resists him, binding her will steadfast with the chains of hatred for sin and love for virtue.

Let every soul rejoice who suffers many troubles, because such is the road that leads to this delightfully glorious state. I have told you before that you reach perfection through knowledge and contempt of yourself and knowledge of my goodness. And at no time does the soul know herself so well, if I am within her, as when she is most beleaguered. Why? I will tell you. She knows herself well when she finds herself besieged and can neither free herself nor resist being captured. Yes, she can resist with her will to the point of not giving her consent, but that is all. *Then* she can come to know that [of herself] she is nothing.[14] For if she were anything at all of herself, she would be able to get rid of what she did not want. So in this way she is humbled in true self-knowledge, and in the light of holy faith she runs to me, God eternal. For by my kindness she was able to maintain her good and holy will steadfast when she was sorely besieged, so that she did not imitate the wretched things that were vexing her.

You have good reason, then, to take comfort in the teaching of the gentle loving Word, my only-begotten Son, in times of great trouble, suffering, and adversity, and when you are tempted by people or the devil. For these things strengthen your virtue and bring you to great perfection.

91

I have told you about perfect and imperfect tears, and how they all come from the heart. Whatever their reason, they all come from this same vessel, and so all of them can be called "heartfelt tears." The only difference lies in whether the love is ordered well or ill, is perfect or imperfect.

I still have to tell you, if I would fully answer your desire, about some souls who want the perfection of tears though it seems they cannot have it. Is there another way than physical tears? Yes. There is a weeping of fire, of true holy longing, and it consumes in love. Such a soul would like to dissolve her very life in weeping in self-contempt and for the salvation of souls, but she seems unable to do it.

---

14. *Può cognoscere sè non essere*—a reflection of that central motif: "I am who I am; you are the one who is not."

I tell you, these souls have tears of fire. In this fire the Holy Spirit weeps in my presence for them and for their neighbors. I mean that my divine charity sets ablaze with its flame the soul who offers me her restless longing without any physical tears. These, I tell you, are tears of fire, and this is how the Holy Spirit weeps. Since the soul cannot do it with tears, she offers her desire to weep for love of me. And if you open your mind's eye you will see that the Holy Spirit weeps in the person of every one of my servants who offers me the fragrance of holy desire and constant humble prayer. This, it seems, is what the glorious apostle Paul meant when he said that the Holy Spirit weeps before me the Father "with unspeakable groaning" for you.[15]

So you see, the fruit of these tears of fire is no less than that of physical tears of water. In fact, it is often more, depending on the measure of the soul's love. Such a soul should not be confounded, then, nor think she has lost me because she longs for tears and cannot have them in the way she wishes. She should rather want them in harmony with my will, bowing humbly to yes or no, whichever pleases my divine goodness. Sometimes I prefer not to grant her physical tears in order to make her stand constant in my presence, humbled and tasting me in continual prayer and longing. For if she had what she was asking for, it would not be as profitable to her as she thinks. She would be content to have what she had wanted, and the affection and longing with which she had asked me would slacken off. So it is not to cut her down but to make her grow that I refrain from giving her actual physical tears. Instead I give her spiritual tears, tears of the heart, full of the fire of my divine charity. These are pleasing to me in any situation and any time, so long as the mind's eye, enlightened by faith, never closes out the loving sight of my Truth. For I am the doctor and you the patients, and I prescribe for each of you what is necessary for your health and growth toward spiritual perfection.[16]

This is the truth about the five stages of tears, which I, eternal Truth, have explained to you, my sweetest daughter. Drown yourself, then, in the blood of Christ crucified, the humble, tormented, spotless Lamb, my only-begotten Son. Keep growing in virtue, so that the fire of my divine charity may be fed within you.

---

15. Rm. 8:26.
16. This concept of God's providence is further developed in ch. 142–145.

92

The five stages I have spoken of are like five great channels. Four of them flow freely with an infinite variety of tears that are life-giving if they are used virtuously. How are they infinite? I am not saying that in this life you should weep infinitely much. I call them infinite because of the soul's infinite desire.[17]

I have told you how tears well up from the heart: The heart gathers them up from its burning desire and holds them out to the eyes. Just as green wood, when it is put into the fire, weeps tears of water in the heat because it is still green (for if it were dry it would not weep), so does the heart weep when it is made green again by the renewal of grace, after the desiccating dryness of selfishness has been drawn out of the soul. Thus are fire and tears made one in burning desire. And because desire has no end it cannot be satisfied in this life. Rather, the more it loves, the less it seems to itself to love. So love exerts a holy longing, and with that longing the eyes weep.

But once the soul is separated from the body and has reached me, her final goal, she does not on that account give up her desire so as to no longer desire me and the charity of her neighbors. For charity has entered into her like a great lady, bearing with her the fruit of all the other virtues. What has ended is suffering, because if she longs for me she now possesses me in truth without any fear of being able to lose what she has so long desired. This is how she feeds the flame, for the more she hungers the more she is filled, and the more she is sated, the more she hungers. But her satiety is far from boredom, and her hunger far from pain, for here she lacks no perfection.

So your desire is an infinite thing. Were it not, could I be served by any finite thing, no virtue would have value or life. For I who am infinite God want you to serve me with what is infinite, and you have nothing infinite except your soul's love and desire. This is how I meant there are infinite varieties of tears, and this is the truth, because of the infinite desire that is fused with the tears.[18]

Once the soul has left the body, tears are left behind. But loving charity has drawn to itself and consumed the tears' fruit like water in a furnace. The water has not been left outside the furnace, but the fire's heat has consumed it and taken it into itself. So it is with the soul when

---

17. Cf. I. Colosio, "La infinità del desiderio umano secondo S. Caterina da Siena," *Rassegna di ascetica e mistica* 21 (1970): 355–368.
18. Cf. ch. 4.

she has come to taste the fire of my divine charity, having passed through this life with loving charity for me and for her neighbors, with that unitive love which caused her to shed tears. She never ceases her constant offering of her desires, blessed now and painlessly tearful. Hers are not physical tears now—for she has been dried out in the furnace—but the Holy Spirit's tears of fire.

Now you have seen how these tears are so infinite that even in this life no tongue could tell how many different laments are made in such a state. But I have already told you the differences among the four stages of [life-giving] tears.

93

It remains for me now to tell you of the fruit to be had from tears fused with desire, and what it does for the soul.

I will begin with the fifth [sort of tears],[19] the kind I mentioned to you in the very beginning, the tears of those who live wickedly in the world. They make a god for themselves out of other people and created things, and out of their selfish sensuality, which is the source of every harm that can come to soul or body.

I told you that all tears come from the heart, and this is the truth, for the more the heart loves, the more sorrow it has. Worldly people weep when their hearts are sad, when they have lost something they loved. But their laments are as different as they are many. Do you know how many? As many as their different loves. And because the root, their selfish sensual love, is corrupt, so is everything that comes from it.

Such people are trees that put forth nothing but deadly fruits, putrid flowers, filthy leaves, and branches bent down to the earth, broken by this wind and that. Such are the trees of their souls.

All of you are trees of love: You cannot live without love because I made you for love. The soul who lives virtuously sets her tree's root in the valley of true humility. But those who live wickedly have set their root in the mountain of pride, and because it is badly planted it produces fruit not of life but of death. Their fruits are their actions, and they are all poisoned by a multitude of different sins. If they do produce one or another fruit of good action, it is spoiled because the root from which it comes is rotten. In other words, if a soul is living in

---

19. Catherine is once again reversing her numbers. In her original listing the tears of the damned were first.

deadly sin, no good that she does has any value for eternal life because it is not done in grace.

Still, no one must take this as a reason to leave off doing anything good, for every good is rewarded and every sin punished. The good that is done outside of grace is worth nothing for eternal life, but my divine goodness and justice will give it a less than perfect reward, just as the deed that was offered me was less than perfect.[20] Sometimes it is rewarded with material goods. Sometimes I lend such persons more time (as I told you when I was speaking of these matters in another place), giving them an opportunity to correct themselves. Sometimes when I do this I even give them the life of grace through the ministry of my servants who are acceptable and pleasing to me, as I did for the glorious apostle Paul when, because of Saint Stephen's prayer, he rose up from his infidelity and his persecution of the Christians. So you see, no matter what state people may be in, they should never desist from doing good.

I told you that these souls' flowers are putrid, and this is the truth. Their flowers are the stinking thoughts of their hearts. They are displeasing to me, and are [nothing but] hatred and contempt to their neighbors. Like thieves they steal honor from me their Creator and give it to themselves.

This flower of theirs gives off a stench of false and wicked judgment, and this in two ways. The first concerns me. They make wicked judgments on my hidden judgments and every mysterious way of mine. They judge with hatred what I have done in love. They judge with lies what I have done in truth, and with death what I have done for the sake of life. They condemn and judge everything by their own sick vision, since they have blinded their mind's eye with their selfish sensuality and covered over the pupil of holy faith so that they might neither see nor know the truth.

Their other rash judgment is against their neighbors, and great harm often comes from it. For these wretched people do not know themselves; yet they would set themselves up as knowing the hearts and intentions of others, and on the basis of some action they see or some word they hear they would judge the intentions of the heart. My servants pass judgment only for good, because they are grounded in me, the highest Good. But these others pass judgment only for evil, because they are grounded in wretched evil. And their judgments often

---

20. C omits "just as . . . perfect."

lead to hatred, murder, and contempt for their neighbors, and pull them far away from the love of virtue that marks my servants.

Their leaves follow the same pattern, one by one: the words that spill out from their mouths, vilifying me and my only-begotten Son's blood, and hurting their neighbors. They care for nothing but to curse and condemn my works, to blaspheme and speak evil of every rational creature, as their words follow their judgments. They forget, to their own misfortune, that the tongue was made only to honor me, to confess their own sins, and to work for the love of virtue and their neighbors' well-being. Such are wretched sin's filthy leaves, because the heart that produces them is not sincere but heavily stained with duplicity and wickedness.

What a danger do such wicked words pose! They not only rob souls of grace, but bring temporal harm as well. You have seen and heard how words have caused revolutions, the ruin of cities, murders, and many other evils, when words entered the heart of the one to whom they were said more deeply than a sword could have entered.[21]

This tree, I tell you, has seven branches that bow down to the very earth. It is from these branches that the flowers and leaves come in the way I described for you. The branches are the seven deadly sins, and each is loaded with a multitude of different sins whose common bond is the root and trunk of selfish love and pride. It is this root that produces the branches and the flowers (thoughts), the leaves (words), and the fruit (evil deeds). The branches (the deadly sins) are bowed down to the very earth, that is, they turn nowhere but to the dirt of the weak disordered world. Souls in deadly sin look to nothing but how they might find nourishment in the earth. Their appetite is insatiable, but they are never satisfied. They are insatiable and insupportable to their very selves. But it is quite fitting that they should be forever restless, because they have set their desire and will on what will give them nothing but emptiness.

This is why they can never be satisfied: They are always hankering after what is finite. But they are infinite in the sense that they will never cease to be, even though because of their deadly sin they have

---

21. The tone very likely reflects Catherine's experience in Florence in the late spring and early summer of 1378. There was constant fighting in those months, a great deal of political intrigue. Catherine herself was the victim of the duplicity of those she trusted, and in June barely missed the assassin's knife. She regretted missing her chance for martyrdom but suffered deeply from the slander and deceit that repaid her peace-making efforts.

ceased to be in grace. People have been set above all other created things, not created things above people, nor can people be satisfied or content except in what is greater than they. But there is nothing greater than they except I myself, God eternal, and therefore only I can satisfy them. When people lose me because of their sins they are in constant pain and torment, and so they weep. Then come the winds, and they strike the tree of selfish sensuality, the very heart of their beings.[22]

94

There are four winds: prosperity and adversity, fear and conscience.

The wind of prosperity feeds pride with presumptuousness, with self-exaltation and vilification of others. Those in authority rule with great injustice and vanity, with physical indecency and filthy mind, with self-importance, and with all the other faults that flow from these, more than your tongue could recount. This wind of prosperity—is it corrupt in itself? No, nor are any of the others. What is corrupt is the tree's chief root, and this makes everything else rotten. I who bestow everything that exists am supremely good, so what comes with this prosperous wind is good. But it causes the wicked to weep because it does not satisfy their heart. For they want what they cannot have; because they cannot have it they suffer; and in their suffering they weep, because the eyes like to respond to the heart.

Then comes the wind of slavish fear, which makes them afraid of their own shadow, afraid to lose what they love. Or they fear the loss of their own lives or their children's or someone else's. Or they are afraid they will lose their position, or others will lose theirs—and all this because of their selfish love for themselves or for honor or wealth. Such fear lets them enjoy nothing in peace. They do not hold what they have with respect for my priorities, and so they are dogged by slavish, cringing fear, made the wretched slaves of sin. Now one can consider oneself as good as what one serves. And sin is a nothing, so these souls have become nothings.[23]

---

22. *Dove egli è fatto ogni suo principio.*

23. Cf. Rm. 6:15, 19–21. "Does the fact that we are living by grace and not by law mean that we are free to sin? Of course not. You know that if you agree to serve and obey a master you become his slaves. . . . If I may use human terms to help your natural weakness: As once you put your bodies at the service of vice and immorality, so now you must

While the wind of fear is battering them the wind of trouble and adversity (the very thing they feared) joins in and takes away their possessions, sometimes this thing or that, sometimes life itself, when the power of death deprives them of everything. Sometimes, though, it takes only now one thing, now another: health, children, riches, position, honors—whatever I the gentle doctor see to be necessary for their salvation and so allow it to happen. But if their weakness has turned to rottenness and they are wholly lacking in discernment, the fruit of patience spoils. Then impatience sprouts, along with outrage and complaining and hatred and contempt for me and everyone else, and what I have given for life becomes death to the receivers, with grief in proportion to their selfishness.

This leads to the tormented weeping of impatience, which dries up the soul and kills it by taking away the life of grace. It dries up and consumes the body as well so that [these wretched souls] are blinded both spiritually and physically. It deprives them of all pleasure and hope, because they have lost what gave them pleasure, what they had set their love and faith and hope in. So they weep. Their weeping in itself is not so bad; what is bad is their disordered love and grief, the source of their tears. For death and suffering are not caused simply by weeping, but by the root from which the weeping springs, from the heart's disordered selfish love. If their hearts were in order and alive with grace, their weeping too would be in order, and would constrain me, God eternal, to be merciful to them. Why, then, did I tell you that their tears are death-dealing? Because tears are the messenger that lets you know whether life or death is in the heart.

I said that there is also a wind of conscience. My divine kindness creates this wind after I have tried to lure them with love through prosperity, and used fear to steer their hearts through misfortune to love virtuously, and tried giving them troubles so that they would recognize the world's fragility and inconstancy. But none of this pleases some people. So, because I love you all so unspeakably much, I send a prod of conscience to rouse these people to open their mouths and vomit out the filth of their sins in holy confession. They have been unwilling to receive my grace in any other way, so now I reproach them directly. But they, obstinate as they are, flee from the prod of con-

---

put them at the service of righteousness for your sanctification. When you were slaves of sin, you felt no obligation to righteousness, and what did you get from this? Nothing but experiences that now make you blush, since that sort of behavior ends in death."

science and go right on amusing themselves with their wretched pleasures in spite of me or anyone else. All this happens because their root is corrupt and the whole tree with it, and everything is deadly for them.[24] Their suffering, their weeping, their bitterness are constant.

If they do not correct themselves while they have time and can use their free choice, they will pass from this finite weeping into that which is infinite. That which is finite will become infinite for them because their tears are shed with infinite contempt for virtue, that is, with the soul's desire grounded in infinite hate.

It is true that, had they wanted to, they could have escaped this with the help of my divine grace while they were still free, even though I said that this hate is infinite. It *is* infinite insofar as the soul's being and capacity to love are infinite, though her actual hating and loving are not infinite. So as long as you are in this life you can hate and love as you choose.

If you end in love of virtue you will receive an infinite reward. If you end in hate you will remain forever in hate and receive eternal damnation, just as I said when I told you how some souls drown in the river. They cannot even desire anything good, deprived as they are of my mercy and the love of their fellows.[25] But the saints enjoy mutual charity, and they also love you who are pilgrim travelers in this world, put here by me to reach your final goal in me, eternal Life.

Neither prayers nor almsgiving nor any other work is of any value to [those who are damned]. They are members cut off from the body of my divine charity, because while they were alive they wanted nothing to do with obedience to my holy commandments in the mystic body of holy Church and in that sweet obedience through which you drink the blood of the spotless Lamb, my only-begotten Son. Therefore they reap the fruit of eternal damnation with weeping and gnashing of teeth.[26]

These are the devil's martyrs of whom I told you. The devil shares with them the fruit he himself has. You see, then, that this kind of weeping yields the fruit of suffering in this finite life, and in the end gives them the never-ending company of the devils.

---

24. Cf. Mt. 7:16–18; Lk. 6:43–44.
25. *Carità fraterna.*
26. Cf. Mt. 22:1–14.

95

I still must tell you about the fruits those receive who for fear of punishment begin to rise up from sin toward grace. This, as I have told you, is the ordinary call.

What fruit do these receive? They begin to empty their soul's house of filth when free choice sends them the message of fear of punishment. After they have cleansed their soul of sin they receive peace of conscience and they ready their desire and open their mind's eye to look at their dwelling place. Before it was emptied they could not see it for all the filth of so many different sins. Now they begin to receive consolations, because the worm of conscience is quiet, as if waiting to eat the food of virtue.

It is just like a man who, once he has purged his stomach and vomited out the bile, has an appetite for food. So these souls wait for the hand of free choice to offer them lovingly the food of virtue, for as soon as it is offered they are eager to eat it.

This is how it really happens. When the soul has used this first fear to cleanse her will of sin, she receives the second fruit, which is the second stage of tears, that in which she begins in loving affection to furnish her house with virtue. Even though she is still imperfect, if she rises above her fear she receives consolation and joy. Her love has won joy from my Truth, for I am her love. Because of the joy and consolation she finds in me she begins to love very tenderly, for she feels the agreeableness of the consolation that comes to her from me or from creatures because of me.

Once she has entered into her soul's house after it has been cleansed by fear, she exercises love there and so begins to receive the fruit of my divine goodness, the same goodness that gave her that house. After love has entered to take possession, she begins to enjoy many different consoling fruits, and if she perseveres in this, she receives the reward of preparing her table. That is, after the soul has passed from fear to love of virtue, she takes her place at her table.

When she has attained the third stage of tears, she prepares the table of the most holy cross in her heart and spirit. When it is set, she finds there the food of the gentle loving Word—the sign of my honor and your salvation, for which my only-begotten Son's body was opened up to give you himself as food. The soul then begins to feed on my honor and the salvation of souls with hatred and contempt for sin.

What fruit does the soul receive from this third stage of tears? I will tell you. She receives a courage grounded in holy contempt for her selfish sensuality, along with the pleasant fruit of true humility and a patience that relieves her of every outrage and suffering. The knife of contempt has killed her selfish will, which was the source of all suffering—for only the sensual will is scandalized and led to impatience by insults and persecutions and the loss of spiritual or material consolations. But because this soul's will is dead, she begins with tender and tearful longing to taste the fruit of the tears of gentle patience.

O mildest of fruits! How sweet are you to those who taste you, and how pleasing to me! For in the midst of bitterness you are sweet. You give peace when the soul is assaulted. When her little boat is on the stormy sea and perilous winds lash against her with great waves, you remain peaceful and calm and wholly without malice, covering the little boat with God's gentle will. For in that will you have become the mantle of true and burning charity that no water can penetrate.

O dearest daughter, this patience is a queen who stands guard upon the rock of courage. She is an invincible victor. She does not stand alone, but with perseverance as her companion. She is the very heart of charity, and it is she who reveals whether the mantle of this charity is a wedding garment or not. She lets it be known if it is torn by imperfection, for she senses at once its opposite, which is impatience.

All of the virtues can at times simulate perfection when they are really imperfect, but they cannot deceive patience.[27] For if this gentle patience, the very heart of charity, is present in the soul, she shows that all the virtues are alive and perfect. But if she is absent, it is clear that all the virtues are imperfect and have not yet arrived at the table of the most holy cross. For it is here that patience was conceived in knowledge of self and of my goodness, and brought to birth through holy contempt, and anointed with true humility.

I never deny the food of my honor and the salvation of souls to this patience. Indeed, she feeds on this food constantly. Look at her, dearest daughter, in my gentle and glorious martyrs. How constantly they fed on souls! Their death was life-giving. They raised the dead and drove out the darkness of deadly sin. The world with all its gran-

---

27. E has "me"; C, S, F have "you." The logical reference in the context is a direct address to patience. Catherine has shifted back and forth between second and third person references to patience in these paragraphs.

deur, with all its lords and their power, could not defend itself against them and the power of this queen, gentle patience.[28] This virtue stands like a lamp set on a lampstand.[29]

Such is the glorious fruit that comes of tears joined with charity for others. The soul eats with the bleeding spotless Lamb, my only-begotten Son, with tormented restless longing, with unbearable pain that I her Creator should be offended. It is not a distressing pain, because true patience kills every fear and selfishness that cause such pain. No, it is a consoling pain grounded in charity, which grieves only for the offense to me and the harm to her neighbors. Such pain makes the soul grow fat. She rejoices in it because it is a sure sign that I am within her by grace.

96

I have told you about the fruit of the third kind of tears. Next comes the fourth and last, the stage of unitive tears. This is not separate from the third, as I have told you. The two are joined together just as charity for me and for your neighbors: They season each other. But the soul has grown so much by the time she reaches the fourth stage that she not only suffers patiently but gladly longs for suffering, so much so that she spurns every amusement, no matter what the source, simply to be able to pattern herself after my Truth, Christ crucified.[30]

Such a soul receives the fruit of spiritual calm, an emotional union with my gentle divine nature in which she tastes milk, just as an infant when quieted rests on its mother's breast, takes her nipple, and drinks her milk through her flesh. This is how the soul who has reached this final stage rests on the breast of my divine charity and takes into the mouth of her holy desire the flesh of Christ crucified. In other words, she follows his teaching and his footsteps, because she had learned in the third stage that she could not follow after me, the Father. For no pain can befall me, the eternal Father, but it can befall my beloved Son, the gentle loving Word. And you cannot walk without pain, but must achieve proven virtue through suffering. So the soul rests on the breast of Christ crucified who *is* my love,[31] and so drinks in the milk of virtue. In this virtue she gets the life of grace and tastes within herself my

---

28. Cf. Heb. 11:33–38.
29. Cf. Mt. 5:15.
30. Cf. Ph. 3:8.
31. S has "truth."

divine nature, which gives the virtues their sweetness. This is the truth: The virtues were not sweet to her before, but now they are, because they are practiced in union with me, divine Love. In other words, the soul has no concern for her own profit other than for my honor and the salvation of souls.

See then, gentle daughter, how delightfully glorious is this state in which the soul enjoys such union at charity's breast that her mouth is never away from the breast nor the breast without milk. Thus the soul is never without Christ crucified nor without me the eternal Father, whom she finds when she tastes the high eternal Godhead. O who could imagine how that soul's powers are filled! Her memory is filled with constant remembrance of me as she lovingly drinks in my blessings. It is not so much my blessings in themselves, but my loving charity in giving them to her. Especially it is the blessing of creation, for she sees that she is created in my image and likeness. At the first stage she had recognized the punishment that follows ingratitude for this blessing, and so she rose up from her wretchedness through the blessing of the blood of Christ in which I created her anew in grace. I cleansed her soul's face of the leprosy of sin, and so she discovered the second stage. There she tasted the sweetness of loving me, and disgust for the sin in which she saw she had been so displeasing to me that I had taken out her punishment on the body of my only-begotten Son.

After this she discovered the coming of the Holy Spirit, who convinced and will continue to convince the soul of truth.[32] When does the soul receive this light? After she has recognized my benefits to her in the first and second stages, she receives the perfect light. Then she knows the truth about me the eternal Father: that in love I have created her to give her eternal life. This is the truth, and I have revealed it to her in the blood of Christ crucified. Once the soul has come to know this, she loves it, and she shows her love by genuinely loving what I love and hating what I hate. Thus she finds herself in the third stage of charity for her neighbors.[33]

So the memory, all imperfection past, is filled at this breast because it has remembered and held within itself my blessings.

Understanding receives the light. Gazing into the memory it comes to know the truth, and shedding the blindness of selfish love it remains in the sunlight of Christ crucified in whom it knows both God

---

32. Cf. Jn. 16:8.
33. Thus S, E, F. C has "in the *midst* of charity...."

and humanity. Beyond this knowledge, because of the union [with me] that she has realized, the soul rises to a light acquired not by nature nor by her own practice of virtue but by the grace of my gentle Truth who does not scorn any eager longing or labors offered to me.

Then the will, which follows understanding, unites itself [with me] in a most perfect and burning love. And if anyone should ask me what this soul is, I would say: She is another me, made so by the union of love.

What tongue could describe the marvel of this final unitive stage and the many different fruits the soul receives when its powers are so filled? This is that sweet gathering together that I told you about when I spoke of the three ordinary stairs, based on the word of my Truth. The tongue cannot describe it, but the holy doctors have shown it well when, enlightened by this glorious light, they explained Holy Scripture.

Thus you know of the glorious Thomas Aquinas that he gained his knowledge more from the study of prayer and the lifting up of his mind and the light of understanding than from human study. He was a light that I sent into the mystic body of holy Church to disperse the darkness of error. And if you turn to the glorious evangelist John, what light he imbibed at the priceless breast of Christ my Truth! And with that light he preached the Gospel for such a long time!

And so the light runs on, all of you showing it forth, now one way, now another. But the inmost feeling, the ineffable sweetness and perfect union—you cannot describe it with your tongue, which is a finite thing! This, it would seem, is what Paul meant when he said, "Eye cannot see, nor ear hear, nor heart imagine how great is the joy and reward the soul who serves me in truth will receive in the end."[34] Oh, how lovely, how lovely beyond all loveliness, is the dwelling place of the soul's perfect union with me! Not even the soul's own will stands between us, because she has become one thing with me. She gives forth a fragrance to the whole wide world, the fruit of constant humble prayers. The fragrance of her longing cries out for the salvation of souls; with a voice without human voice she cries out in the presence of my divine majesty.

These are the fruits of union that the soul eats in this life in this final stage, which is reached through labor, tears, and sweat. So she passes in true perseverance from the life of grace in this union, which,

---

34. Thus C. S, E, F have "the soul who loves me in truth. . . . " Cf. 1 Co. 2:9.

though perfect in terms of grace, is still imperfect. But so long as she is bound to her body in this life she cannot be filled with what she longs for. She is indeed bound by a perverse law—a law that has been put to sleep by her love for virtue but is not dead, and so can rise up again if she lets go of the instrument of virtue that keeps it asleep. This is why it is called an "imperfect union." But it is this imperfect union that leads the soul to that everlasting perfection that cannot be taken from her by anything at all, as I told you it is with the blessed. Then she finds joy among those who are truly joyful in me, eternal Life, supreme and eternal Goodness without end. These who receive eternal life are the opposite of those who receive eternal death as the fruit of their weeping. The blessed come from their weeping to gladness. They receive everlasting life with the fruit of their tears and flaming charity; they cry out and offer tears of fire for you in my presence.

Now I have finished telling you about the stages of tears and their perfection, and the fruit the soul receives from these tears: that the perfect receive eternal life, and the wicked eternal damnation.

97

T*hen that soul was restless with a tremendous longing because Truth had so tenderly satisfied her by telling her about these stages of tears. And in love as she was, she said:*

Thanks, thanks to you, high eternal Father, fulfiller of holy desires and lover of our salvation! Out of love you gave us love in the person of your only-begotten Son when we were still at war with you. This abyss of your flaming charity lets me ask you for grace and mercy so that I may come to you in sincerity in the light, and not run along darksomely after the teaching of your Truth. You have clearly shown me his truth to make me see two other real or possible delusions I fear. Before I go on, eternal Father, I wish you would explain these to me.

Here is the first: Sometimes people will come to me or to another of your servants asking for counsel in their desire to serve you and wanting me to instruct them. I know, gentle eternal God, that you have already told me, "I am one who takes delight in few words and many deeds." Still, if it would please your kindness to say a few more words on this, you would be doing me a great favor.

Also, sometimes when I am praying for your creatures and especially for your servants, it happens in the course of my prayer that I find this one spiritually well disposed, apparently rejoicing in you, and another seems to me to have a darksome spirit. Eternal Father, should I or can I judge the one to be in light and the other in darkness? Or if I should see one going the way of great penance and another not, should I judge that the one who does greater penance is more perfect than the other? I ask you, lest I be deluded by my own lack of insight, to be more specific about what you have told me in general terms.

Here is the second thing I want to ask you about: Be more clear to me about the sign you told me the soul receives to tell whether a spiritual visitation is from you, God eternal, or not.

If I remember well, you told me, eternal Truth, that [if the visitation is from you] it leaves the spirit glad and encouraged toward virtue. I would like to know whether this gladness can be disguised spiritual selfishness, for if that is the case I would hold only to the sign of virtue.

These are the things I am asking you so that I may be able to serve you and my neighbors in truth, and not fall into any false judgments about your creatures and your servants. For it seems to me that passing [rash] judgment alienates the soul from you, and I do not want to fall into that trap.

TRUTH

98

That soul's hunger and thirst, her sincerity and the longing with which she asked to be able to serve him pleased God eternal. So he looked on her with compassionate mercy and said:

O dearest daughter whom I so love, you who are my bride, rise above yourself and open your mind's eye. Look at me, infinite Goodness, and see my unspeakable love for you and my other servants. And open the sensitive ear of your desire. This is the only way you will see and hear, for the soul who does not have my Truth for the object of her mind's eye can neither hear nor know my truth. Therefore I want you to rise above your senses so that you may more surely know the truth. Then I will satisfy you, for I am pleased with your desire and your questioning. Not that you can increase my pleasure: It is I who make you grow, not you me. But the very pleasure I take in my creation pleases me.

So that soul obeyed. She rose above herself to know the truth about what she had asked. Then God eternal said to her:

So that you may better understand what I am about to tell you, let me begin at the source of the answer: the three lights that come forth from me, the true Light.

The first is an ordinary light in those whose charity is ordinary. (I will repeat what I have already told you about this, that, and many other things even though you have already heard them, so that your meager understanding may better comprehend what I want you to know.) The other two lights belong to those who have risen above the world and are seeking perfection. Beyond this I shall explain what you have asked me to, being more specific about what I have already touched on more broadly.

You know that no one can walk in the way of truth without the light of reason that you draw from me, the true Light, through the eye of your understanding. You must have as well the light of faith, which you possess as my gift from holy baptism unless you have put it out with your sins. In baptism, through the power of my only-begotten Son's blood, you received the form of faith. If you exercise this faith by virtue with the light of reason, reason will in turn be enlightened by faith, and such faith will give you life and lead you in the way of truth. With this light you will reach me, the true Light; without it you would come to darkness.[1]

There are two lights drawn from this [first] light that you must have, and to the two I will add yet a third.

The first is that you must all be enlightened to know the transitory things of this world, that they all pass away like the wind. But you cannot know this well unless you first know your own weakness, how ready that perverse law bound up in your members makes you to rebel against me your Creator. Not that this law can force any one of you to commit the least sin unless you want to, but it certainly does fight against the spirit. Nor did I give this law so that my people should be conquered, but so that they might increase and prove virtue in their souls. For virtue can be proved only by its opposite. Sensuality is the opposite of the spirit, so it is through sensuality that the soul proves the love she has for me her Creator. When does she prove it? When she mounts hatred and contempt against it.

I gave the soul this law also to keep her truly humble. So you see, while I created her in my image and likeness and made her so honorable and beautiful, I gave her as well the vilest thing there is, this perverse law. In other words, I bound her into a body formed from the vilest earth so that when she saw her beauty she would not lift up her head in pride against me. So the weak body is a reason for humility to those who have this light [of mine]. They have no reason at all to be proud, but they do have reason for true and perfect humility. This perverse law, then, no matter how it fights, cannot force the least sin. Rather it is reason for you to learn to know yourself and to know how inconstant is the world.

The eye of understanding ought to see this through the light of holy faith, which is that eye's pupil. This is that essential light which everyone in every situation must have to share in the life of grace, in the fruit of the spotless Lamb's blood. This is the ordinary light, and

---

1. Cf. Jn. 12:35–36.

everyone must have it. Those who do not have it are damned. Because they do not have the light they are not living in grace, for without the light they do not recognize the evil of sin or its cause, so they cannot shun its cause or hate it. Likewise, those who do not recognize good and the cause of good, that is, virtue, can neither love nor desire me, Goodness itself, or the virtue I have given you as a means and instrument for grace from me, the true Good.

So you see how much you need this light, for your sin consists simply in loving what I hate and hating what I love. I love virtue and I hate vice. So whoever loves vice and hates virtue offends me and loses my grace. Such people behave as if they were blind. Not recognizing the cause of vice, sensual selfishness, they have neither contempt for themselves nor knowledge of vice and the evil vice brings upon them. Nor do they know virtue or me, the Source of life-giving virtue, or the dignity they should preserve in themselves by coming to grace through virtue.

So you see, lack of knowledge is the cause of their evil. How necessary it is, then, for you to have this light!

99

But once the soul has gained this ordinary light she ought not rest content. For as long as you are pilgrims in this life you are capable of growing and should grow. Those who are not growing are by that very fact going backward. Either you should be growing in that ordinary light that you have gained with the help of my grace, or you should be making a genuine effort to advance to the second and more perfect light, to rise from the imperfect to the perfect. For the light gives the soul the will to advance to perfection.

In this second light there are two sorts of perfect souls. The perfect are those who have risen above the ordinary worldly way of living, and there are two sorts. The first are those who give themselves perfectly to punishing their bodies by performing severe and enormous penances. To keep their sensuality from rebelling against reason, these have all set their object more in mortifying their bodies than in slaying their selfish wills. They feed at the table of penance, and they are good and perfect if their penance has its root in me and is guided by the light of discernment. In other words, they must truly know themselves and me, be very humble, and be wholly subject to the judgments of my will rather than to those of other people.

But if they are not thus truly and humbly clothed in my will, they may often sin against their very perfection by setting themselves up as judges over those whose way is not the same as theirs. Do you know why this happens? Because they have invested more effort and desire in mortifying their bodies than in slaying their selfish wills. They are always wanting to choose times and places and spiritual consolations in their own way, and even earthly troubles and conflict with the devil (the way I told you about in the second, imperfect, stage). They are their very own deceivers, deceived by that selfish will that I have called "spiritual self-will," and in their self-delusion they say: "I would like to have this consolation rather than this conflict or trouble with the devil. Nor is it for myself that I say this, but to be more pleasing to God and to have more grace in my soul. For it seems to me I could serve and possess him better in this way than in that."

In this way they often fall into suffering and weariness, and so become insupportable to themselves and sin against their very perfection. And they are not even aware that they are lying there in the filth of their pride. But there they lie. For if it were not so, if they were truly humble and not presumptuous, they would see by the light that I, gentle first Truth, name the situation, the time, and the place, consolations or trials, whatever is necessary for salvation and to bring souls to the perfection for which I chose them. And they would see that everything I give is for love, and that therefore they should accept everything with love and reverence. This is what the others do, those who reach the third stage, as I shall tell you. These two sorts of people both live in this most perfect light.

100

Those who reach the third stage (which follows after the other) are perfect in every situation once they have come into this glorious light. No matter what I send them, they hold it in due reverence, as I mentioned when I spoke to you about the third and unitive stages of the soul. They consider themselves deserving of sufferings and outrages from the world, worthy to be deprived of any consolation at all that may be theirs. And just as they consider themselves deserving of suffering, so they also count themselves unworthy of any fruit that may come to them from their suffering. These have known and tasted in the light my eternal will, which wants only your good and permits you these things so that you may be made holy in me.

After the soul has come to know my will she clothes herself in it and attends only to how she may keep and intensify her perfection for the glory and praise of my name. In the light of faith she fixes her mind's eye on Christ crucified, my only-begotten Son, loving and following his teaching, which is rule and way for the perfect and imperfect alike. She sees how the Lamb my Truth is in love with her and instructs her in perfection, and seeing it, she falls in love with him. Perfection is what she came to know when she saw this gentle loving Word, my only-begotten Son, finding his nourishment at the table of holy desire by seeking honor for me his eternal Father and salvation for you. In this desire he ran eagerly to his shameful death on the cross and fulfilled the obedience that I his Father had laid on him. He did not shun toil or shame, did not hold back because of your ingratitude and foolish failure to recognize the great favor he had done you. The hounding of the Jews could not hold him back, nor the jeering insults and grumbling, nor the shouts of the people. He went through it all like a true knight and captain whom I had put on the battlefield to wrest you from the devils' hands. He freed you from the most perverse slavery there could be. This is why he instructed you in his way, his teaching, his rule. And this is why you can approach the gate to me, eternal Life, with the key of his precious blood that was poured out with such burning love, with hatred and contempt for your sins.

It is as if this gentle loving Word, my Son, were saying to you: "Look. I have made the road and opened the gate for you with my blood. Do not fail, then, to follow it. Do not sit down to rest out of selfish concern for yourself, foolishly saying you do not know the way. Do not presume to choose your own way of serving instead of the one I have made for you in my own person, eternal Truth, incarnate Word, the straight way hammered out with my own blood."

Get up, then, and follow him, for no one can come to me the Father except through him. He is the way and the gate through whom you must enter into me, the sea of peace.[2]

When[3] the soul, then, has come to taste this light after so delightfully seeing and knowing it, she runs to the table of holy desire, in love as she is and eager with a lover's restlessness. She has no eyes for herself, for seeking her own spiritual or material comfort. Rather, as one who has completely drowned her own will in this light and knowledge, she shuns no burden, from whatever source it may come. She even endures the pain of shame and vexations from the devil and other

---

2. Jn. 14:6, 10:9.
3. F adds, "I say, then, that this is the soul's perfection:"

people's[4] grumbling, feasting at the table of the most holy cross on honor for me, God eternal, and salvation for others.

She seeks no recompense either from me or from others, because she is stripped of any mercenary love, of any loving me for her own profit. She is clothed in perfect light, and loves me sincerely without any other concern than the glory and praise of my name. She does not serve me for her own pleasure or her neighbors for her own profit, but only for love.

Souls such as these have let go of themselves, have stripped off their old nature, their selfish sensuality, and clothed themselves in a new nature, the gentle Christ Jesus, my Truth, and they follow him courageously.[5] These are they who have sat down at the table of holy desire, and have set their minds more on slaying their selfish will than on mortifying and killing their bodies. They have, it is true, mortified their bodies, but not as their chief concern. Rather, they have used mortification as the instrument it is to help them slay their self-will. (I told you this when I was explaining my statement that I would have few words and many deeds.) And this is what you should do. Your chief desire ought to be to slay your selfish will so that it neither seeks nor wants anything but to follow my gentle Truth, Christ crucified, by seeking the honor and glory of my name and the salvation of souls.

Those who live in this gentle light do just this. Therefore they are always peaceful and calm, and nothing can scandalize them because they have done away with what causes them to take scandal, their self-will. They trample underfoot all the persecutions the world and the devil can hound them with. They can stand in the water of great troubles and temptations, but it cannot hurt them because they are anchored to the vine of burning desire.[6]

They find joy in everything. They do not sit in judgment on my servants or anyone else, but rejoice in every situation and every way of living they see, saying, "Thanks to you, eternal Father, that in your house there are so many dwelling places!" And they are happier to see many different ways than if they were to see everyone walking the same way, because this way they see the greatness of my goodness

---

4. E has "wicked men's."
5. Cf. Ep. 4:22–24. "You must give up your old way of life; you must put aside your old self, which gets corrupted by following illusory desires. Your mind must be renewed by a spiritual revolution so that you can put on the new self that has been created in God's way, in the goodness and holiness of the truth."
6. Cf. Sg. 8:7; Jn. 15:5.

more fully revealed. In everything they find joy and the fragrance of the rose. This is true not only of good things; even when they see something that is clearly sinful they do not pass judgment, but rather feel a holy and genuine compassion, praying for the sinner and saying with perfect humility, "Today it is your turn; tomorrow it will be mine unless divine grace holds me up."

O dearest daughter, let the love of this sweet marvelous state take hold of you. Look at those who run along in this glorious light and their own magnificence. Their spirits are holy and they feast at the table of holy desire. By this light they have come to find their nourishment in the food of souls for the honor of me the eternal Father. They are clothed in the lovely garment, the teaching, of the Lamb, my only-begotten Son, with flaming charity.

They do not waste their time passing false judgment, either against my servants or the world's servants. They are not scandalized by any grumbling on anyone's part: if it is against themselves they are happy to suffer for my name,[7] and when it is against someone else they bear with it in compassion for their neighbor, grumbling neither against the grumbler nor the victim, because their love for me and for their neighbor is well ordered. And because their love is well ordered, dearest daughter, they are never scandalized in those they love, nor in any person, because in this regard they are blind,[8] and therefore they assume no right to be concerned with the intentions of other people but only with discerning my merciful will.

They are faithful to the teaching that you know my Truth gave you early in your life when you asked with great longing to be led to perfect purity.[9] You know that when you were wondering how you might attain this, your desire was answered while you were asleep. The voice sounded not only in your mind but in your ear as well—so much so, if you recall, that you returned to your bodily senses when my Truth spoke thus to you:

"Do you wish to reach perfect purity and be so freed from scandal that your spirit will not take scandal in anything at all? Then see that

---

7. Cf. Ac. 5:41.

8. *Il loro parere è morto e non vivo.*

9. The teaching that follows corresponds in part to the "Spiritual Document" or "Narration of a Teaching," which William of Flete reports having received from Catherine in 1376. It is to be found in the *Biblioteca Communale da Siena* (T.II.F.—cc. 29–30) and in Milan: *Brera* (AD. IX. 11—c. 56). An English translation can be found in A. T. Drane, *St. Catherine of Siena and her Companions,* vol. 2, pp. 359–362.

you remain unitied with me in loving affection, for I am supreme and eternal purity. I am the fire that purifies the soul. So the nearer the soul comes to me the more pure she will become, and the more she departs from me the more unclean she is. This is why worldly folk fall into such wickedness, because they have left me. But the soul who unites herself directly with me shares in my own purity.

"There is another thing you must do to attain this union and purity: You must never pass judgment in human terms on anything you see or hear from anyone at all, whether it concerns you or someone else. You must consider only my will for them and for you.

"And if you should see something that is clearly a sin or fault, snatch the rose from that thorn. In other words, offer these things to me in holy compassion. As for any assault against yourself, consider that my will permits it to prove virtue in you and in my other servants. And assume that the offender does such a thing as an instrument commissioned by me. For often such a person's intention is good; there is no one who can judge the hidden heart.

"When you cannot see clearly and openly whether the sin is deadly, you must not pass judgment in your mind, but be concerned only about my will for that person. And if you do see it, you must respond not with judgment but with holy compassion. In this way you will attain perfect purity, for if you act this way your spirit will not be scandalized either in me or in your neighbors. For you cast contempt on your neighbors when you pay attention to their ill will toward you rather than my will for them. Such contempt and scandal alienates the soul from me, blocks her perfection, and to some extent deprives her of grace—in proportion to the seriousness of the contempt and hatred she has conceived for her neighbor because of her judgmental thoughts.

"Things go just the opposite for the soul who is concerned for my will. For I will only your well-being, and whatever I give, I give it so that you may reach the goal for which I created you. The soul who considers things in this light remains always in love for her neighbors, and so she remains in my love. And because she remains in my love she remains united with me.

"So if you would attain the purity you ask of me, there are three principal things you must do. You must be united with me in loving affection, bearing in your memory the blessings you have received from me. With the eye of your understanding you must see my affectionate charity, how unspeakably much I love you. And where the human will is concerned you must consider my will rather than people's evil intentions, for I am their judge—not you, but I. If you do this, all perfection will be yours."

This, if you remember well, was the teaching my Truth gave you.

Now I tell you, dearest daughter, those who have learned this teaching taste the pledge of eternal life even in this life. If you keep this teaching in mind you will fall neither into the devil's trap (for you will recognize it) nor into the traps you asked me about. Still, to satisfy your desire I will tell you more clearly how you may never think judgmentally but only in holy compassion.

101

I told you that these souls receive the pledge of eternal life. They receive the pledge, I tell you, but not the full payment. This they are waiting to receive in me, Life everlasting, where they will have life without death, satiety without boredom, and hunger without pain. For their hunger will be anything but painful, because they will possess what they long for. And their satiety will be anything but boring, because I will be their flawless life-giving food.

This is how they receive and enjoy the pledge in this life: The soul begins to hunger for the honoring of me, God eternal, and for that food which is the salvation of souls. And because she is hungry she feasts on that charity for her neighbors which she so hungers and longs for, for her neighbors are indeed a food that, when she feeds on it, never satisfies her. She remains insatiably and continually hungry. Thus, like a pledge, this hunger is a beginning of the certainty I give the soul, and because of it she expects to receive the full payment. The pledge is not in itself perfect, but because of faith it carries the certainty of reaching its fulfillment and its full payment. Just so, this soul who is in love with my Truth and clothed in his teaching, and has already in this life received the pledge of charity for me and her neighbors, is herself not yet perfect, but she waits for the perfection of immortal life.

When I say that this pledge is not perfect, I mean that the soul who enjoys it has not yet reached the sort of perfection that will know no suffering in herself or in others. [She still suffers] for the wrong she herself does me when the perverse law bound up in her members chooses to fight against the spirit. And she suffers because of the sins of others. So far as grace is concerned she is indeed perfect, but she has not yet attained the perfection of my saints who have reached me, everlasting Life, for their desires know no pain, while yours still do. My servants [in this life] find their nourishment at the table of holy desire, and they are at once both happy and sorrowful, just as my only-begotten Son was on the wood of the most holy cross. His flesh was sad and tormented, but his soul was happy because of his union with the divine nature. Just so, these servants of mine are happy because their longing is one with me, clothed in my gentle will. But they are sorrowful because of their compassion for their neighbors and because they are without sensual consolations and pleasures, which is distressing to their selfish sensuality.

102

Now listen well, dearest daughter, so that you will understand more clearly what you asked me about.

I told you about the ordinary light that all of you need, no matter what your situation, and this concerned those whose charity is ordinary. Then I told you about those who walk in perfect light, and here I pointed out two distinct ways. There were those who have risen above this world and are concerned with mortifying their bodies. And there were those who in all things slay their self-will, the perfect souls who find their nourishment at the table of holy desire.

Now I want to speak more particularly to you (and in speaking to you I will address others as well), and respond to your desire.

There are three specific things I want you to do so that ignorance will not stand in the way of the perfection I am calling you to, and so that the devil will not feed the root of presumption within your soul under the guise of charity for your neighbors. For this would lead you into false judgments, which I have forbidden you. You would think you were judging rightly when in fact you were judging wrongly by following what you saw, for often the devil would make you see too much of the truth in order to lead you into falsehood. He would do this to make you set yourself up as judge of other people's spirits and intentions, something of which, as I told you, I alone am judge.

Here is one of the three[10] things I want you to hold fast to: that your judgment should always be qualified, and this is how: Even if your neighbors' sins are clearly shown to your spirit not just once or twice but many times, you should still not confront them with specific sins. Rather, when they come to visit you, you should correct their bad habits in a general way and lovingly and kindly plant the virtues [in

---

10. C, E have "two things"; S, F have "three things"; the latter reading fits the context.

their place], adding severity to your kindness when you must. And if it seems to you that I am often showing you some person's sins, unless you see that it is clearly a revelation do not confront that person specifically, but rather keep to the more certain way and so avoid the devil's deceit and malice. For the devil would like to catch you with this inviting hook, often making you pass judgment on something that is not there in your neighbors, and so you would scandalize them.

So let silence or a holy argument for virtue be in your mouth to discourage vice. And when you think you discern vice in others, put it on your own back as well as theirs, acting always with true humility. Then if the vice is truly there, such people will change their ways all the sooner, seeing themselves so gently understood. That agreeable reproof will constrain them to change their ways, and they will tell you what you wanted to say to them. As for yourself, you will be reassured, and you will have cut the devil off in his path so that he can neither deceive you nor hinder your soul's perfection.

I want you to know also that you should not trust everything you see. Rather put it behind your back and choose not to see it, holding fast only the sight and knowledge of yourself and my generosity and goodness to you. This is how those souls behave who have reached the final stage of which I have told you. Because they return continually to the valley of self-knowledge, their exaltation and union with me is never blocked. This, then, is the first of the three things I told you I want you to do so as to serve me in truth.[11]

103

Now I will tell you about the [second], which is this: If it sometimes happens (as you asked me to explain) that you have prayed specifically for certain individuals and in your prayer have seen some light of grace in the one for whom you were praying while you see in the other (and both are my servants) a confused and darksome spirit, you neither should nor can assume that the second person is guilty of serious sin, for often as not your judgment would be false. And I want you to know that when you are praying for someone it may happen that at one time you will find that person enlightened and filled with holy desire in my presence, so much so that it seems that soul is grow-

---

11. This approach to the shortcomings of others is reflected very strongly in Catherine's own letters and in the stories her early biographers relate of her confrontations with individuals she knew to be in the wrong.

ing fat on such goodness, as if charity's affection would have you share each other's good. But at another time you will find that same person's spirit apparently far away from me and all full of darkness and troubles, so that it seems burdensome for you to keep praying and holding that soul in my presence.

Sometimes this happens because of some fault on the part of the person for whom you are praying. More often, however, it is not because of any fault but because I, God eternal, have withdrawn [the sense of my presence] from that soul, as I often do to lead souls to perfection (as I told you when I was speaking of the spiritual stages[12]). Though I have not taken away my grace, I have withdrawn the feeling of delight and consolation. This is why the spirit remains sterile and dry and in pain. And I make the person who is praying for this soul feel the pain as well. I do this because of the gracious love I have for the soul who is being prayed for, so that the one who is praying may help disperse the cloud that hangs over that spirit.

So you see, dearest and sweetest daughter, how foolish and reprehensible would be any judgment you or anyone else might make by assuming on appearances alone, just because I had revealed to you the darkness that soul was in, that it was because of sin. For now you have seen that that soul had not lost grace, but only the feeling of delight and the sense of my presence that I had given before.

I will, then, and so should you—you and my other servants—that you concentrate on coming to know yourselves perfectly, so that you may more perfectly know my goodness to you. Leave this and every other kind of judgment to me, because it is my prerogative, not yours.[13] Give up judgment, which belongs to me, and take up compassion with hunger for my honor and the salvation of souls. And with restless longing preach virtue and reprove vice in yourself and in others in the manner I have just described for you.

In this way you will come to me in truth, and you will show that you have remembered and observed the teaching given you by my Truth, that is, to discern my will rather than to judge other people's intentions. This is how you must act if you would be genuinely virtuous and live in the ultimate most perfect and glorious light, feasting on the food of souls at the table of holy desire for the glory and praise of my name.

---

12. Cf. ch. 60.
13. Cf. Mt. 7:1; Rm. 12:19.

104

I have told you, dearest daughter, about two; now I will tell you about the third thing I want you to be careful of. Reprove yourself if ever the devil or your own short-sightedness should do you the disservice of making you want to force all my servants to walk by the same path you yourself follow, for this would be contrary to the teaching given you by my Truth. It often happens, when many are going the way of great penance, that some people would like to make everyone go that very same way. And if everyone does not do so, they are displeased and scandalized because they think these others are not doing the right thing. But you see how deluded they are, because it often happens that those who seem to be doing wrong because they do less penance are actually better and more virtuous, even though they do not perform such great penances, than those who are doing the grumbling.

This is why I told you earlier that if those who eat at the table of penance are not truly humble, and if their penance becomes their chief concern rather than an instrument of virtue, they will often, by this sort of grumbling, sin against their very perfection. So they should not be foolish, but should see that perfection consists not only in beating down and killing the body but in slaying the perverse selfish will. It is by this way of the will immersed in and subjected to my gentle will that you should—and I want you to—want everyone to walk.

This is the lightsome teaching of this glorious Light, by which the soul runs along in love with my Truth and clothed in him. I do not for all that despise penance, for penance is good for beating the body down when it wants to fight against the spirit. Yet I do not want you, dearest daughter, to impose this rule on everyone. For all bodies are not the same, nor do all have the same strong constitution; one is stronger than another. Also, it often happens that any number of circumstances may make it right to abandon the penance one has begun. But if you took penance as your foundation, or made it so for others, that foundation would be weak and imperfect, and the soul would be bereft of consolation and virtue.

Then, when you were deprived of the penance you had loved and taken as your foundation, you would think you had lost me. And thinking you had lost my kindness, you would become weary and very sad, bitter and confused. So you would abandon the exercises and the fervent prayer you had been accustomed to when you were doing your penance. With that penance left behind because of circumstances, prayer simply would not have the same flavor it had for you before.

All this would happen if your foundation were in your love for penance rather than in eager desire for true and solid virtue.

So you see what great evil would follow on taking penance alone for your foundation. You would foolishly fall to grumbling about my servants. And all this would bring you weariness and great bitterness. You would be putting all your effort into mere finite works for me; but I am infinite Good and I therefore require of you infinite desire.

It is right, then, that you should build your foundation by slaying and annihilating your self-will. Then, with your will subjected to mine, you would give me tender, flaming, infinite desire, seeking my honor and the salvation of souls. In this way you would feast at the table of holy desire—a desire that is never scandalized either in yourself or in your neighbors, but finds joy in everything and reaps all the different kinds of fruit that I bestow on the soul.

Not so do the wretched souls who do not follow this teaching, the gentle straight way given by my Truth. In fact, they do the opposite. They judge according to their own blindness and lame vision. They carry on like frantic fools and deprive themselves of the goods of earth as well as those of heaven. And even in this life they have a foretaste of hell.

105

Now, dearest daughter, I have satisfied your desire by clarifying what you asked me to. I have told you how you should reprove your neighbors if you would not be deluded by the devil or your own meager insight, that is, that you should reprove in general terms, not specifically, unless you have had a clear revelation from me, and humbly reprove yourself along with them.

I also told you, and I will tell you again, that nothing in the world can make it right for you to sit in judgment on the intentions of my servants, either generally or in particular, whether you find them well or ill disposed.

And I told you the reason you cannot judge, and that if you do you will be deluded in your judgment. But compassion is what you must have, you and the others, and leave the judging to me.

I told you also the teaching and principal foundation you should give to those who come to you for counsel because they want to leave behind the darkness of deadly sin and follow the path of virtue. I told you to give them as principle and foundation an affectionate love for virtue through knowledge of themselves and of my goodness for them. And they should slay and annihilate their selfish will so that in nothing will they rebel against me. And give them penance as an instrument but not as their chief concern—not equally to everyone but according to their capacity for it and what their situation will allow, this one more and this one less, depending on their ability to manage these external instruments.

I told you that it is not right for you to reprove others except in general terms in the way I explained, and this is true. But I would not because of that have you believe that when you see something that is clearly sinful you may not correct it between that person and yourself, for you may. In fact, if that person is obstinate and refuses to change, you may reveal the matter to two or three others, and if this does not help, reveal it to the mystic body of holy Church.[14] But I told you that it is not right for you to hand anyone over merely on the basis of what you see or feel within you or even what you see externally. Unless you have clearly seen the truth or have understood it through an explicit revelation from me, you are not to reprove anyone except in the manner I have already explained. Such is the more secure way for you because the devil will not be able to deceive you by using the cloak of neighborly charity.

Now, dearest daughter, I have finished telling you what is necessary if you would preserve and augment your soul's perfection.

106

Now I will say something about what you asked me concerning the sign I said I give the soul for discerning the visitations she may receive through visions or other consolations. I told you how she could discern whether or not these were from me. The sign is the gladness and hunger for virtue that remain in the soul after the visitation, especially if she is anointed with the virtue of true humility and set ablaze with divine charity.

---

14. Cf. Mt. 18:15–17.

But you asked me whether there could be any delusion in such gladness. You wanted to know this so that you might hold to what is more certain, that is, the sign of virtue that cannot be a delusion. I will tell you therefore what sort of delusion there can be and by what token you can discern whether the gladness is or is not in truth.

This is how one can be deluded. I want you to know that people are glad when they have what they love and desire. And the more a soul loves what she has, the less she sees or is careful to discern with prudence where that thing came from. She finds so much pleasure in the consolation that her gladness over receiving what she loves does not let her see or care about such discernment. Thus people who are very fond of spiritual consolation and find great pleasure in it hanker after visions and set their hearts more on the enjoyment of consolation than (as they should) on me. This is exactly what I told you about those who are still imperfect. They look more to the gift of consolations they receive from me the giver than they do to the loving charity with which I give.

This is how such souls can be deluded in their gladness beyond the other delusions I have clearly told you of elsewhere. How are they deluded? Let me tell you. First they conceive this great love for consolation. Then, whenever they receive a consolation or vision in any way whatever, they are glad because they see what they love and want to have. But often it can be from the devil, and all they feel is this gladness. And I have told you that when the gladness is from the devil the spiritual visitation comes with gladness but lingers with pain and the pricking of conscience, without any desire for virtue.

Now I tell you, sometimes a soul may have this gladness and rise from prayer still glad. But if such gladness is found to be devoid of any burning desire for virtue and is not anointed with humility and set ablaze in the furnace of my divine charity, then that visitation and whatever consolation or vision the soul has received are from the devil and not from me, in spite of the sign of gladness the soul feels. Because her gladness is not joined with love for virtue you can clearly see that her gladness comes from her love for her own spiritual consolation. The reason she is joyful and glad is that she has what she wanted. For it is characteristic of any love whatever to feel gladness when one receives what one loves.

So you cannot trust gladness in itself, even if your gladness should last as long as you have the consolation and even longer. Undiscerning love will not recognize in this gladness the devil's deception because it has not prudence as its counterpart. But if it is accompanied by prudence it will see whether or not this gladness is accompanied by love for virtue, and in this way it will know whether the spiritual visitation is from me or from the devil.

This is the sign by which you can discern that gladness is indeed signaling a visitation from me: if it is joined with virtue. This is truly a clear sign to show you what is delusion and what is not, which spiritual gladness comes from me in truth and which comes from spiritual selfishness, that is, from love and affection for one's own consolation. The visitation that comes from me is accompanied by gladness with love for virtue; that which comes from the devil brings merely the gladness, and when one takes a closer look, there is no more virtue than there was before. Such gladness comes only from love for one's own consolation.

I want you to know that not everyone is deluded by this gladness. It is only these imperfect souls who hanker after pleasure and consolation and are more concerned about my gift than about me the Giver. But there are others who are sincere and without any self-interest. These, afire as they are with love, look only to me the Giver, and not to the gift. They love the gift because of me the Giver, and not because of their own consolation. These cannot be deluded by such gladness.

This is at once a sign to them when the devil in his deceitfulness would come under the guise of light and reveal himself to their spirits with a sudden great gladness. These souls are not obsessed with love of consolation, so their spirits, with truthful prudence, recognize his deceit. The gladness soon passes, leaving them in darkness. But this only makes them humble themselves in true self-knowledge, and scorning all consolation they embrace and hold fast the teaching of my Truth. And the devil, confounded, crawls away and never again returns in this guise.

Those, on the other hand, who are in love with their own consolation often receive such, but they can recognize their delusion by the fact that they find in it gladness without virtue. One does not see them coming out of this experience with humility and true charity, with hunger for honoring me, God eternal, and for the salvation of souls.

All this my goodness has done to provide for you, the perfect and imperfect alike, whatever your situation may be, so that you may never be deluded so long as you guard the light of understanding with its pupil of holy faith that I have given you, never letting the devil cast his shadow over it or covering it over with your own selfishness. For unless you yourselves give it up, there is no one who can take this light from you.

107

Now I have told you everything, dearest daughter, and have enlightened your mind's eye concerning the ways the devil could deceive you. I have satisfied your desire by responding to what you asked me, because I do not spurn my servants' desires. I give to those who ask, and even invite you to ask. And I am very displeased with those who do not knock in truth at the door of Wisdom, my only-begotten Son, by following his teaching. Following his teaching is a kind of knocking that calls out to me the eternal Father with the voice of holy desire in constant humble prayer. And I am that Father who gives the bread of grace through this door, my gentle Truth.[15] Sometimes, to test your desires and your perseverance, I pretend not to hear you. But I do hear you, and I give you whatever you need, for it is I who gave you the very hunger and voice with which you call to me, and when I see your constancy I fulfill your desires insofar as they are ordered in accord with my will.

My Truth invited you to call out thus when he said, "Call and you will be answered; knock and it shall be opened to you; ask and it shall be given to you." So I am telling you what I want you to do. Never relax your desire to ask for my help. Never lower your voice in crying out to me to be merciful to the world. Never stop knocking at the door of my Truth by following in his footsteps. Find your delight with him on the cross by feeding on souls for the glory and praise of my name. And with a restless heart bewail the death of this child, humanity,[16] whom you see reduced to such misery that your tongue could not tell it.

Through this lamentation and crying out it is my will to be merciful to the world. This is what I require of my servants and this will be a sign to me that you love°me in truth. Nor will I spurn your desires, as I have told you.

---

15. Cf. Mt. 7:7–11.
16. S, F have "the death of the human race." C, E have *il morto del figliuolo de l'umana generazione.*

108

T hen that soul, truly like one drunk, seemed to be beside herself and separated from her bodily senses because of her loving union with her Creator. She lifted up her spirit and gazed into eternal Truth with her mind's eye. And as she had come to know the truth
she was in love with truth, and she said:

O high eternal goodness of God! Who am I, wretched as I am, that
you, high eternal Father, have revealed to me your truth and the hidden snares of the devil and the delusion of selfishness I and others can
be subject to in this pilgrim life, so that we might not be deceived either by the devil or by ourselves? What moved you to this? Love. For
you loved me without being loved by me. O fire of love! Thanks,
thanks to you, eternal Father!

I am imperfect and full of darkness. Yet you, perfect and lightsome, have shown me perfection and the lightsome path of your only-
begotten Son's teaching. I was dead and you revived me. I was sick and
you gave me medicine—and not only the medicine of the blood that
you gave to the sick human race in the person of your Son. You gave
me as well a medicine against a hidden sickness I had not recognized,
by teaching me that I can never sit in judgment on any person, especially on your servants. For I, blind and weak as I was from this sickness, have often judged others under the pretext of working for your
honor and their salvation.

So I thank you, high eternal Goodness, for revealing your truth
and the deceitfulness of the devil and of selfish passion, and so making
me aware of my weakness. I ask you therefore for grace and mercy,
that today I may make an end once for all of straying from the teaching
you have given in your kindness to me and to whoever is willing to follow it. For without you nothing can be done.[17]

To you then I run and in you I take shelter, eternal Father, and
what I ask I ask not for myself only, Father, but for the whole world,
and in particular for the mystic body of holy Church. Let this truth
and this teaching that you, eternal Truth, have given to me, wretched
as I am, shine forth in your ministers.

And I ask you especially for all those you have given me, whom I
love with a special love and whom you have made to be one thing with
me. They will be my refreshment, for the glory and praise of your

---

17. Cf. Jn. 15:5.

name, when I see them running along this straight and lovely path, sincere and dead to every selfish will and opinion, never judging or taking scandal or grumbling against their neighbors. And I beg you, most gentle Love, let none of them be taken from my hands by the infernal devil, so that in the end they may reach you, eternal Father, their final goal.[18]

And I would make yet another request, for those two pillars, the fathers[19] you have appointed for me on earth to guide and teach me, who am so wretchedly weak, from the beginning of my conversion until now. Unite them and make of their two bodies a single soul. Let neither of them be concerned for anything but to fulfill in themselves, and in the ministries you have put in their care, the glory and praise of your name through the salvation of souls. And let me, unworthy wretched slave more than daughter, treat them with due reverence and holy fear for love of you, for your honor, for their peace and calm, and for the edification of our neighbors.

I am certain, eternal Truth, that you will not spurn my desire and the petitions I have addressed to you. For I know from having seen what you have been pleased to reveal to me, and even more from experience, that you are receptive to holy desires. I, your unworthy servant, will try as you give me grace to be faithful to your command and your teaching.

O eternal Father, I remember your telling me once, when you were speaking of the ministers of holy Church, that at another time you would talk more at length about the sins these ministers are committing this very day. Therefore, if it would please your goodness, say something about this, so that I may have reason to intensify my sorrow and compassion and restless longing for their salvation. For I recall that you have already said that through the suffering and tears and sorrow, the sweat and constant prayers of your servants, you

---

18. Cf. Jn. 17:9–15.
19. One of these fathers is certainly Raymond of Capua, the other probably Tommaso della Fonte, her earlier confessor and her constant companion throughout her life. Some have thought the second to have been the Augustinian hermit William of Flete, in whom Catherine also confided a great deal, but this is the less likely guess, especially in view of Catherine's petition regarding the relationship between the two in question. Raymond was far closer to Tommaso della Fonte than to William.

would refresh us by reforming the Church with good and holy ministers. Therefore, I make my petition so that this may grow in me.

109

Then God eternal looked on her with mercy. He did not spurn her desire but accepted her petition. Wishing to fulfill this last request[20] that she had made because of his promise, he said:

O dearest daughter whom I so love! I will fulfill your desire in what you have asked of me only if you for your part will not be foolish or indifferent. For that would be much more serious for you and worthy of greater reproach now than before, because you have come to know more of my truth. Make it your concern, then, to offer prayers for all people and for the mystic body of holy Church and for those I have given you to love with a special love. Do not be guilty of indifference about offering prayers and the example of your living and the word of teaching. Reprove vice and commend virtue. Do all this to the greatest extent of your power.

Concerning the two pillars I have given you and of whom you have spoken to me (and you spoke truly), make yourself a channel for giving each of them what he needs, according to their disposition and what I, your Creator,[21] give to you, for without me none of you can do anything.[22] I for my part will fulfill your desires. But never fail—neither you nor they—to trust me, for my providence will not fail you. Let each of them receive humbly what he is ready to receive, and let each of them administer what I give him to administer, each in his own way, as they have received and will continue to receive from my goodness.

---

20. Not the last of the petitions Catherine enumerates in the Prologue (ch. 9), but the last in the present exchange. The "promise" referred to is the promise of mercy that is reiterated at the end of each response from God and that Catherine takes as the basis for each new petition (Cavallini).

21. E has "Redeemer."

22. Jn. 15:5.

THE MYSTIC BODY
OF HOLY CHURCH

110

Now I will answer what you asked me concerning the ministers of holy Church. First, so that you may better come to know the truth, open your mind's eye and consider their excellence and the great dignity in which I have placed them. But because things can be better known by looking at their opposites, I want to show you the dignity of those who use virtuously the treasure I have put into their hands, so that you may better see the wretchedness of those who today are feeding at the breast of this bride.

Then that soul obediently gazed into Truth, where she saw resplendent the virtues of the truly joyful. Then God eternal said:

Dearest daughter, first I want to tell you of the dignity in which my goodness has established them. This is beyond the love that I have shown in general to all my creatures by creating you in my image and likeness and re-creating all of you in grace through my only-begotten Son's blood. You attained such excellence because of the union I effected between my Godhead and human nature that your excellence and dignity is greater than that of the angels. For it was your nature I assumed, not that of the angels. So, as I told you, I, God, became a man and humanity became God through the union of my divine nature with your human nature.[1]

This greatness is given to every person in general, but from among the rest I have chosen my ministers for your salvation, so that through them the blood of the humble spotless Lamb, my only-begot-

---

1. Cf. Thomas Aquinas, *Sermon* (Opusc. 57): "The only-begotten Son of God, wishing to make us sharers in his divinity, assumed our nature so that, once made man, he made men gods."

ten Son, might be administered to you. It is the sun I have given them to administer, for I have given them the light of learning, the heat of divine charity, and the color that is fused with the heat and the light, the blood and body of my Son. His body is indeed a sun, for it is one thing with me, the true Sun. Such is the unity that the one can neither be separated nor cut off from the other, any more than the sun can be divided—neither its heat from its light nor its light from its color, so perfect is its unity.

This Sun never leaves its orbit,[2] never divides. It gives light to all the world, to everyone who wants to be warmed by it. This Sun is not defiled by any uncleanness; its light is one. So is this Word, my Son. His most gracious blood is a sun, wholly God and wholly human, for he is one thing with me and I with him. My power is not separate from his wisdom; nor is the heat, the fire of the Holy Spirit, separate from me the Father or from him the Son, for the Holy Spirit proceeds from me the Father and from him the Son, and we are one and the same Sun.

I am that Sun, God eternal, whence proceed the Son and the Holy Spirit. To the Holy Spirit is appropriated fire, and to the Son, wisdom. And in that wisdom my ministers receive a gracious light for administering this light with lightsome gratitude for the blessing they received from me the eternal Father when they followed the teaching of this Wisdom, my only-begotten Son.

This light has in it the color of your humanity, the one united with the other. So the light of my Godhead became that light made one with the color of your humanity. And that color became lightsome when it became impassible by virtue of the Godhead, the divine nature.[3] The person of the incarnate Word was penetrated and kneaded into one dough with the light of my Godhead, the divine nature, and with the heat and fire of the Holy Spirit, and by this means you have come to receive the light. And to whom have I entrusted it? To my ministers in the mystic body of holy Church, so that you might have life when they give you his body as food and his blood as drink.

I have said that this body of his is a sun. Therefore you could not be given the body without being given the blood as well; nor either the body or the blood without the soul of this Word; nor the soul or

---

2. Catherine, it is to be remembered, lived a full century before Copernicus.
3. One of Catherine's few references to the resurrection of Christ, but one deep in its theological implications.

body without the divinity of me, God eternal. For the one cannot be separated from the other—just as the divine nature can nevermore be separated from the human nature, not by death or by any other thing past or present or future. So it is the whole divine being that you receive in that most gracious sacrament under that whiteness of bread.

And just as the sun cannot be divided, so neither can my wholeness as God and as human in this white host.[4] Even if the host is divided, even if you could break it into thousands and thousands of tiny bits, in each one I would be there, wholly God and wholly human. It is just as when a mirror is broken, and yet the image one sees reflected in it remains unbroken. So when this host is divided, I am not divided but remain completely in each piece, wholly God, wholly human.

Nor is the sacrament itself diminished by being divided, any more than is fire, to take an example. If you had a burning lamp and all the world came to you for light, the light of your lamp would not be diminished by the sharing, yet each person who shared it would have the whole light. True, each one's light would be more or less intense depending on what sort of material each brought to receive the fire. I give you this example so that you may better understand me. Imagine that many people brought candles, and one person's candle weighed one ounce, another's two or six, someone else's a pound, and yet another's more than that, and they all came to your lamp to light their candles. Each candle, the smallest as well as the largest, would have the whole light with all its heat and color and brightness. Still, you would think that the person who carried the one-ounce candle would have less than the one whose candle weighed a pound. Well, this is how it goes with those who receive this sacrament. Each one of you brings your own candle, that is, the holy desire with which you receive and eat this sacrament. Your candle by itself is unlit, and it is lighted when you receive this sacrament. I say it is unlit because by yourselves you are nothing at all. It is I who have given you the candle with which you can receive this light and nourish it within you. And your candle is

---

4. Here and in the pages that follow, the distinction between God and Christ is often hazy. As much logic as there is in Catherine's references here must lie in her insistence that in the Incarnation the Son did not come "alone," and that the Incarnation unites humanity to the indivisible divine nature. In the manuscript I am mainly following (C), an early "reviser" has crossed out every occurrence of the first person pronoun whenever it is conjoined with the expression "God and human," and in later manuscripts the same pronouns are entirely omitted—apparently in an attempt to bring Catherine's theology back into line. But the haziness is too pervasive to be so simply eliminated.

love, because it is for love that I created you, so without love you cannot have life.

Your being was given to you for love, and in holy baptism, which you received by the power of the blood of this Word, you were made ready to share this light. There is no other way you could come to share it. Indeed, you would be like a candle that has no wick and therefore can neither burn nor even receive the light. So if you would bear this light, you must receive the wick that is faith. And to this grace that you receive in baptism you must join your own soul's love. For I created your soul with a capacity for loving—so much so that you cannot live without love. Indeed, love is your food.

Once the soul is so prepared, where is she to be lighted? At the flame of my divine charity, by loving and fearing me and following the teaching of my Truth. And she will take fire more or less intensely depending on the material she brings to this flame. For although you all have one and the same material (that is, you were all created in my image and likeness, and all of you who are Christians have the light of holy baptism), nevertheless each of you can grow in love and virtue as you choose and as I give you grace. Not that you change the form I gave you. But you do grow and build up the virtues in love by exercising your free choice virtuously and lovingly while you have time (for once time has passed for you, you can no longer grow). So you can grow in love.

It is with this love that you come to receive my gracious glorious light, the light I have given you as food, to be administered to you by my ministers. But even though all of you receive the light, each of you receives it in proportion to the love and burning desire you bring with you. It is just like the example I gave you of the people whose candles received the flame according to their weight. Each of you carries the light whole and undivided, for it cannot be divided by any imperfection in you who receive it or in those who administer it. You share as much of the light (that is, the grace you receive in this sacrament) as your holy desire disposes you to receive.

But anyone who would approach this gracious sacrament while guilty of deadly sin would receive no grace from it, even though such a person would really be receiving me as I am, wholly God, wholly human. But do you know the situation of the soul who receives the sacrament unworthily? She is like a candle that has been doused with water and only hisses when it is brought near the fire. The flame no more than touches it but it goes out and nothing remains but smoke. Just so, this soul brings the candle she received in holy baptism and throws the water of sin over it, a water that drenches the wick of baptismal grace that is meant to bear the light. And unless she dries the wick out with the fire of true contrition by confessing her sin, she will physically receive the light when she approaches the table of the altar, but she will not receive it into her spirit.[5]

If the soul is not disposed as she should be for so great a mystery, this true light will not graciously remain in her but will depart, leaving her more confounded, more darksome, and more deeply in sin. She will have gained nothing from this sacrament but the hissing of remorse, not because of any defect in the light (for nothing can impair it) but because of the water it encountered in the soul, the water that so drenched her love that she could not receive this light.

So you see, in no way can the heat and color and brightness that are fused in this light be divided—not by the scant desire the soul brings to this sacrament, nor by any fault in the soul who receives it or in the one who administers it. It is like the sun, which is not contaminated by the filth it shines on. Nothing can contaminate or divide the gentle light in this sacrament. Its brightness is never diminished and it never strays from its orbit, though the whole world shares in the light and heat of this Sun. So this Word, this Sun, my only-begotten Son, never strays from me, the eternal Sun and Father. In the mystic body of holy Church he is administered to everyone who will receive him. He remains wholly with me and wholly you have him, God and human, just as I told you in the example of the lamp. Though all the world should ask for his light, all would have it whole, and whole it would remain.[6]

111

O dearest daughter, open wide your mind's eye and look into the abyss of my charity. There is not a person whose heart would not melt in love to see, among all the other blessings I have given you, the blessing you receive in this sacrament.

And how, dearest daughter, should you and others look upon this mystery and touch it? Not only with your bodily eyes and feeling, for here they would fail you. You know that all your eyes see is this white

---

5. S omits "but she will not receive it into her spirit" (*ma non mentalmente*).
6. Cf. the hymn *Lauda Sion: "Sumit unus, sumunt mille . . . nec sumptus consumitur"* ("Let one or a thousand eat . . . though eaten it would not be consumed").

bit of bread; this is all your hand can touch and all your tongue can taste, so that your dull bodily senses are deceived.[7] But the soul's sensitivity cannot be deceived, unless she so chooses by extinguishing the light of holy faith by infidelity.

What tastes and sees and touches this sacrament? The soul's sensitivity. How does she see it? With her mind's eye, so long as it has the pupil of holy faith. This eye sees in that whiteness the divine nature joined with the human; wholly God, wholly human; the body, soul, and blood of Christ, his soul united with his body and his body and soul united with my divine nature, never straying from me. This, if you remember, is what I revealed to you early in your life and that not only to your mind's eye but to your bodily eyes as well, although because of the great light you soon lost your bodily sight and were left with only your spiritual vision.

I revealed this to you when you had set yourself to resist the battle the devil was giving you in this sacrament, to make you grow in love and in the light of most holy faith. You know that you had gone to the church at dawn to hear Mass, and that before that the devil had been tormenting you. You went to stand at the altar of the crucifix, though the priest had come out to Mary's altar. You stood there considering your sinfulness, fearing that you might have offended me while the devil had been troubling you. And you were considering also how great was my charity that I should have made you worthy to hear Mass at all, since you considered yourself unworthy even to enter my temple. When the celebrant reached the consecration you looked up toward him. And at the words of consecration I revealed myself to you. You saw a ray of light coming from my breast, like the ray that comes forth from the sun's circle yet never leaves it. Within this light came a dove, and dove and light were as one and hovered over the host by the power of the words of consecration the celebrant was saying. Your bodily eyes could not endure the light, and only your spiritual vision remained, but there you saw and tasted the depths of the Trinity, wholly God, wholly human, hidden and veiled under that whiteness. Neither the light nor the presence of the Word, whom in spirit you saw in this whiteness, took away the whiteness of the bread. Nor did the one stand in the way of the other. I did not block your sight either of me, God

---

7. Cf. the hymn *Adoro Te:* "*Visus, gustus, tactus in te fallitur, sed auditu solo tuto creditur.*" (In this section of the *Dialogue* Catherine borrows frequently from the Eucharistic poetry of Thomas Aquinas.)

and human, in that bread, or of the bread itself. Neither the whiteness nor the feel nor the taste was taken away from the bread.

I in my kindness showed this to you. It was your mind's eye, with the pupil of holy faith, that had vision in the end. So the spiritual must be the principal vision, because it cannot be deceived. It is with this eye, then, that you must contemplate this sacrament.

How is this sacrament touched? With the hand of love. This hand it is that touches what the eye has seen and known in this sacrament. The hand of love touches through faith, confirming as it were what the soul sees and knows spiritually through faith.

How is this sacrament tasted? With holy desire. The body tastes only the flavor of bread, but the soul tastes me, God and human. So you see, the body's senses can be deceived, but not the soul's. In fact, they confirm and clarify the matter for her, for what her mind's eye has seen and known through the pupil of holy faith, she touches with the hand of love. What she has seen she touches in love and faith. And she tastes it with her spiritual sense of holy desire, that is, she tastes the burning, unspeakable charity with which I have made her worthy to receive the tremendous mystery of this sacrament and its grace.

So you see, you must receive this sacrament not only with your bodily senses but with your spiritual sensitivity, by disposing your soul to see and receive and taste this sacrament with affectionate love.

112

Dearest daughter, contemplate the marvelous state of the soul who receives this bread of life, this food of angels, as she ought. When she receives this sacrament she lives in me and I in her. Just as the fish is in the sea and the sea in the fish, so am I in the soul and the soul in me, the sea of peace.[8] Grace lives in such a soul because, having received this bread of life in grace, she lives in grace. When this appearance of bread has been consumed, I leave behind the imprint of my grace, just as a seal that is pressed into warm wax leaves its imprint when it is lifted off. Thus does the power of this sacrament remain there in the soul; that is, the warmth of my divine charity, the mercy of the Holy Spirit, remains there. The light of my only-begotten Son's wisdom remains there, enlightening the mind's eye.[9] [The soul] is left strong, sharing in

---

8. Cf. ch. 12. Also Augustine, *Confessions*, Bk. 7, ch. 5.
9. S, E, F add: "to know and see the teaching of my Truth and this wisdom."

my strength and power, which make her strong and powerful against her selfish sensuality and against the devil and the world.

So you see, the imprint remains once the seal is lifted off. In other words, once the material appearances of the bread have been consumed, this true Sun returns to his orbit. Not that he had ever left it, for he is united with me. But my deep charity gave him to you as food for your salvation and for your nourishment in this life where you are pilgrim travelers, so that you would have refreshment and would not forget the blessing of the blood.[10] I in my divine providence gave you this food, my gentle Truth, to help you in your need.

See, then, how bound and obligated you are to love me in return, since I have loved you so much, and because I am supreme eternal Goodness, deserving to be loved by you.

113

O dearest daughter, I have told you all this so that you may better know how I have dignified my ministers, and thus grieve the more over their wickedness. If they themselves had considered their dignity, they would not have fallen into the darkness of deadly sin nor muddied the face of their souls. Not only have they sinned against me and against their own dignity, but even had they given their bodies to be burned they would not have been able to repay me for the tremendous grace and blessing they have received, for it is impossible to have a greater dignity than theirs in this life.

They are my anointed ones and I call them my "christs," because I have appointed them to be my ministers to you and have sent them like fragrant flowers into the mystic body of holy Church. No angel has this dignity, but I have given it to those men whom I have chosen to be my ministers. I have sent them like angels, and they ought to be earthly angels in this life.

I demand purity and charity of every soul, a charity that loves me and others, and helps others in whatever way it can, serving them in prayer and loving them tenderly. But much more do I demand purity in my ministers, and that they love me and their neighbors, administering the body and blood of my only-begotten Son with burning love and hunger for the salvation of souls, for the glory and praise of my name.

---

10. Cf. 1 Co. 11:25–26.

Just as these ministers want the chalice in which they offer this sacrifice to be clean, so I demand that they themselves be clean in heart and soul and mind. And I want them to keep their bodies, as instruments of the soul, in perfect purity. I do not want them feeding and wallowing in the mire of impurity, nor bloated with pride in their hankering after high office, nor cruel to themselves and their neighbors—for they cannot abuse themselves without abusing their neighbors. If they abuse themselves by sinning, they are abusing the souls of their neighbors. For they are not giving them an example of good living, nor are they concerned about rescuing souls from the devil's hands, nor about administering to them the body and blood of my only-begotten Son, and myself the true Light in the other sacraments of holy Church. So, by abusing themselves they are abusing others.

114

I want them to be generous, not avariciously selling the grace of my Holy Spirit to feed their own greed.[11] They ought not do so; I will not have them do so. Rather, as they have received charity freely and generously from my goodness, so ought they to give to everyone who humbly asks, lovingly, freely, and with a generous heart, moved by love for my honor and the salvation of souls.[12] Nor ought they to take anything in payment for what they themselves have not bought but have received gratuitously so that they might administer it to you. But alms they may and should accept. So also should those act who are the receivers, for their part giving alms when they are able. For my ministers ought to be provided by you with material help in their needs, and you ought to be provided for and nourished by them with grace and spiritual gifts, that is, with the holy sacraments I have established in holy Church for them to administer to you for your salvation.[13]

And I want you to know that they give you incomparably more than you give them, for there is no comparison between the finite and passing things with which you help them, and myself, God, who am infinite and have appointed them in my providence and divine charity to minister to you. With all of your material possessions you could never repay the incomparable spiritual gifts you receive—not only this mystery, but everything whatever that is administered to you by any-

---

11. Cf. Ac. 8:18–20.
12. Cf. Mt. 10:8.
13. Cf. 1 Co. 9:11.

one as a spiritual favor, whether through prayer or any other means.

Now I tell you that whatever my ministers receive from you they are obliged to distribute in three ways by dividing it into three parts: one for their own livelihood, one for the poor, and the rest for what is needed for the Church. If they use it in any other way they would offend me.

115

This is how my gentle glorious ministers conduct themselves. I told you that I wanted you to see the excellence that is theirs beyond the dignity I have given them by making them my christs. When they exercise this dignity virtuously they are clothed in this gentle glorious Sun that I have entrusted to their ministry.

Consider those who have gone before them: the gentle Gregory, Sylvester,[14] and the other successors of the chief pontiff Peter, to whom my Truth gave the keys of the heavenly kingdom when he said, "Peter, I am giving you the keys of the heavenly kingdom; whatever you loose on earth shall be loosed in heaven, and whatever you bind on earth shall be bound in heaven."[15]

Listen well, dearest daughter. By showing you the magnificence of their virtues I shall show you more fully the dignity to which I have appointed these ministers of mine. This is the key[16] to the blood of my only-begotten Son, that key which unlocked eternal life, closed for so long a time because of Adam's sin. But after I gave you my Truth, the Word, my only-begotten Son, he suffered and died, and by his death he destroyed your death[17] by letting his blood be a cleansing bath for you. Thus his blood and his death, by the power of my divine nature joined with his human nature, unlocked eternal life.

And to whom did he leave the keys to this blood? To the glorious apostle Peter and to all the others who have come or will come from now until the final judgment day with the very same authority that Pe-

---

14. St. Gregory the Great, who was pope from 590 to 604, and St. Sylvester I, 314 to 335.

15. Mt. 16:19.

16. There is a double image here. Christ's blood is the key to eternal life. This key, his blood, is in turn locked within the "wine cellar" of the Church's "mystic body" (the sacramental heart of the Church), to which the pope holds the key. He unlocks the wine cellar and appoints ministers to carry the blood (the sacraments) to the people.

17. Cf. Preface for Easter: " . . . by dying he destroyed our death" (now one of the Acclamations after the Consecration of the Mass: "Dying you destroyed our death; rising you restored our life; Lord Jesus, come in glory!").

ter had. Nor is this authority lessened by any sinfulness on their part; nor can that sinfulness deprive the blood or any other sacrament of its perfection. I have already told you that no uncleanness can defile this Sun, nor is its light lost because of any darkness of deadly sin that may be in the minister or in those who receive it. Their sin cannot injure the sacraments of holy Church or lessen their power. But grace is lessened and sin increased in those who administer or receive them unworthily.

Christ on earth,[18] then, has the keys to the blood. If you remember, I showed you this in an image when I wanted to teach you the respect laypeople ought to have for these ministers of mine, regardless of how good or evil they may be, and how displeased I am with disrespect. You know that I set before you the mystic body of holy Church under the image of a wine cellar. In this wine cellar was the blood of my only-begotten Son, and from this blood all the sacraments derive their life-giving power.

Christ on earth stood at the door of this wine cellar. He had been commissioned to administer the blood, and it was his duty to delegate ministers to help him in the service of the entire universal body of Christianity. Only those accepted and anointed by him were to thus minister. He was the head of the whole clerical order, and he appointed each one to his proper office to administer this glorious blood.

Because he has sent them out as his helpers, it is his task to correct them for their faults, and it is my will that he do so. For by the dignity and authority I have bestowed on them I have freed them from slavery, that is, from submission to the authority of temporal rulers. Civil law has no power whatever to punish them; this right belongs solely to the one who has been appointed to rule and to serve according to divine law. There are my anointed ones, and therefore it has been said through Scripture: "Dare not to touch my christs."[19] Therefore, a person can do no worse violence than to assume the right to punish my ministers.[20]

---

18. "Christ on earth" is Catherine's favorite name for the pope as Christ's vicar.

19. Ps. 105:15.

20. This passage reflects the prevailing Church-state relationship of the Middle Ages, a relationship that was being severely challenged at the time the *Dialogue* was being written. This challenge was, in fact, at the root of the struggles between the papacy and the Italian city-states that Catherine tried so desperately to mediate, and many references in these chapters suggest that they may very likely have been written during Catherin's third and last stay (spring-summer of 1378) with the Florentines, who had been under papal interdict since the spring of 1376.

116

And if you should ask me why I said that this sin of those who persecute holy Church is graver than any other sin, and why it is my will that the sins of the clergy should not lessen your reverence for them, this is how I would answer you: Because the reverence you pay to them is not actually paid to them but to me, in virtue of the blood I have entrusted to their ministry. If this were not so, you should pay them as much reverence as to anyone else, and no more. It is this ministry of theirs that dictates that you should reverence them and come to them, not for what they are in themselves but for the power I have entrusted to them, if you would receive the holy sacraments of the Church. For if you refuse these when it is in your power to have them, you would live and die condemned.

So the reverence belongs not to the ministers, but to me and to this glorious blood made one thing with me because of the union of divinity with humanity. And just as the reverence is done to me, so also is the irreverence, for I have already told you that you must not reverence them for themselves, but for the authority I have entrusted to them. Therefore you must not sin against them, because if you do, you are really sinning not against them but against me. This I have forbidden, and I have said that it is my will that no one should touch them.

For this reason no one has excuse to say, "I am doing no harm, nor am I rebelling against holy Church. I am simply acting against the sins of evil pastors." Such persons are deluded, blinded as they are by their own selfishness. They see well enough, but they pretend not to see so as to blunt the pricking of conscience. If they would look, they could see that they are persecuting not these ministers, but the blood. It is me they assault, just as it was me they reverenced. To me redounds every assault they make on my ministers: derision, slander, disgrace, abuse. Whatever is done to them I count as done to me. For I have said and I say it again: No one is to touch my christs. It is my right to punish them, and no one else's.

But the wicked show how little they reverence the blood, how little they value the treasure I have given them for their souls' life and salvation. You could receive no greater gift than that I should give you myself, wholly God and wholly human, as your food.

But by not paying me reverence in the persons of my ministers, they have lost respect for the latter and persecuted them because of the many sins and faults they saw in them. If in truth the reverence they had for them had been for my sake, they would not have cut it off on account of any sin in them. For no sin can lessen the power of this sacrament, and therefore their reverence should not lessen either. When it does, it is against me they sin.

There are many reasons that make this sin more serious than any other, but I will tell you of three principal ones.

The first is that what they do to my ministers they do to me.[21]

The second is that they are violating my command, for I forbade them to touch [my christs]. They scorn the power of the blood they received in holy baptism, for they disobediently do what I have forbidden. They are rebels against the blood because they have become irreverent persecutors, like rotten members cut off from the mystic body of holy Church. And if they persist in this irreverent rebellion and die in it, they will end in eternal damnation. Still, if even at the end they humble themselves and admit their sin and want to be reconciled with their head—even though they cannot do it actually—they will receive mercy. But let no one count on having the time for this, since no one can be certain of it.

The third reason this sin is more serious than any other is that it is committed deliberately and with selfish malice. They know they cannot do it in good conscience, but they do it nonetheless and sin. And it is a sin committed in perverse pride without any bodily pleasure: Indeed, both body and soul are eaten up by it. Their souls are eaten up because they are deprived of grace and chewed up by the worm of conscience. Their material possessions are consumed in the service of the devil. And their bodies die of it like animals.

So this sin is committed directly against me. It is unmitigated by any profit to the sinner or any pleasure except the sooty spite of pride—a pride born of selfish sensuality and of that perverse slavish fear that led Pilate to kill Christ, my only-begotten Son, rather than risk losing his power. So do these behave.[22]

All other sins are committed either through stupidity or ignorance or through the sort of malice that, though conscious of the evil being done, sins for the sake of disordered pleasure or profit. Such sinners

---

21. Cf. Lk. 10:16. Cf. also Let. 377 to the rulers of Florence.
22. Cf. Jn. 19:12. Cf. also Let. 123: "This is the perverse fear and love that killed Christ, for Pilate, fearing to lose his power, closed his eyes to the knowledge of the truth. . . . And it seems to me the whole world is full of such Pilates who through blind fear think nothing of persecuting God's servants, hurling their rocks of insults, slander, and hounding."

bring harm to their own soul and offend me and their neighbors—me because they are not praising and glorifying my name, their neighbors because they are not giving them the joy of their charity. But they are not actually persecuting me, because while they are sinning against me, it is themselves they are harming, and their sin displeases me because of the harm it does to them.

But this other is a sin committed directly against me. Other sins have some pretext; they are committed with some excuse, with some middle ground—for I told you that every sin as well as every virtue is realized through your neighbors. Sin is committed through lack of charity for God and your neighbors, and virtue is practiced out of the warmth of charity. If you sin against your neighbors you sin against me through them.

But among all my creatures I have chosen these ministers of mine. They are my anointed ones, stewards of the body and blood of my only-begotten Son—your human flesh joined with my divinity. When they consecrate they stand in the place of Christ my Son. So you see, this sin is directed against this Word, and because it is done to him it is done to me, because we are one and the same. These wretches persecute the blood and so deprive themselves of the treasure and fruit of the blood. Thus I consider this sin, committed not against my ministers but against me, the more serious because the persecution as well as the honor is not (nor do I so consider it) owed to them but to me, that is, to this glorious blood of my Son, for we are one and the same. Therefore I tell you, if all the other sins these people have committed were put on one side and this one sin on the other, the one would weigh more in my sight than all the others. I have shown you this so that you would have more reason to grieve that I am offended and these wretched souls damned, so that the bitter sorrow of you and my other servants by my kind mercy might dissolve the great darkness that has come over these rotten members who are cut off from the mystic body of holy Church.

But I find hardly anyone who will grieve over the persecution that is waged against this glorious precious blood, while there are many who persecute me constantly with the arrows of disordered love and slavish fear and self-conceit. Blind as they are, they count as honor what is shameful, and as shame what is honorable, that is, to humble themselves before their head.

Through these sins they have risen up and continue to rise up to persecute the blood. *(117)* I spoke the truth when I told you that they are persecuting me. So far as their intention is concerned, they persecute me in whatever way they can. Not that I in myself can be harmed or persecuted by them, for I am like the rock that is not hurt by what is thrown at it, but glances it back at the one who threw it.[23] Just so, the impact of the filthy sins they hurl can do me no harm, but their arrows glance back at them poisoned with guilt. This guilt deprives them of grace in this life because they lose the fruit of the blood, and in the end, unless they change their ways through heartfelt contrition and holy confession, they will come to eternal damnation, cut off from me and bound over to the devil. They have, in fact, made a compact, they and the devil, for as soon as they have lost grace they are bound in sin with the chain of hatred for virtue and love of vice. And this chain they have put into the devil's hands with their free choice. This is what he binds them with, for in no other way could they be bound.

This chain binds the persecutors of the blood one with the other, and as members bound up with the devil they have taken on the function of the devils. The devils make every effort to lead my creatures astray, to lure them away from grace and drag them down into the guilt of deadly sin, so that others may share the evil that is in themselves. This is what such people do, neither more nor less. As the devil's members they go about undermining the children of the bride of Christ, my only-begotten Son, undoing them from the bond of charity and binding them up in the wretched chain where they will be deprived of the fruit of the blood along with themselves. The links of this chain are pride and self-importance, along with the slavish fear that makes them lose grace rather than risk losing their temporal powers. So they fall into greater confusion than ever, since they have forfeited the honor of the blood. Their chain is welded with the seal of darkness, so that they do not recognize into what great trouble and wretchedness they have fallen and are making others fall. This is why they do not change their ways. They do not know themselves, but blind as they are they take pride in their own spiritual and bodily ruin.

O dearest daughter, grieve without measure at the sight of such wretched blindness in those who, like you, have been washed in the blood, have nursed and been nourished with this blood at the breast of holy Church! Now like rebels they have pulled away from that breast

---

23. Cf. Pr. 26:27. "A stone will come back on the person who starts it rolling."

out of fear and under the pretext of correcting the faults of my ministers—something I have forbidden them to do, for I do not want [my
anointed ones] touched by them. What terror should come over you
and my other servants when you hear any mention of that wretched
chain of theirs! Your tongue could never describe how hateful it is to
me! And worse still, they want to take cover under the cloak of my
ministers' sins so as to cover up their own sins. They forget that no
cloak can hide anything from my sight. They might well be able to
hide from creatures, but not from me, for nothing present nor anything at all can be hidden from me. I loved you and knew you before
you came into being.

And this is one reason the wicked of this world do not change
their ways: they do not believe in truth, by the light of living faith, that
I see them. For if they believed in truth that I see them and their sins,
and that every sin is punished and every good rewarded, they would
not commit such evil but would turn away from what they have done
and humbly ask for my mercy. And I, through my Son's blood, would
be merciful to them. But they are obstinate, and so they are rejected by
my goodness and because of their sins fall into the ultimate disaster of
losing the light and, blind as they are, becoming persecutors of the
blood. But no fault on the part of the ministers of the blood can justify
such persecution.

118

I have told you, dearest daughter, something of the reverence that
ought to be given my anointed ones no matter how sinful they may be.
For reverence neither is nor should be given them for what they are in
themselves, but only for the authority I have entrusted to them. The
sacramental mystery cannot be lessened or divided by their sinfulness.
Therefore your reverence for them should never fail—not for their
own sake, but because of the treasure of the blood.

Looking to the contrary, I have shown you ever so little how grave
and displeasing to me and how harmful to themselves is the irreverence of those who persecute the blood. And I have shown you the compact they have made against me by binding themselves together in the
service of the devil, so that you may grieve the more.

I have told you specifically about this sin because of the persecution of holy Church. And I tell you the same of Christianity in general:
anyone who lives in deadly sin is scorning the blood and letting go of

the life of grace. But much more displeasing to me[24] and serious for themselves is the sin of those of whom I have spoken specifically.

119

Now I would refresh your soul by softening your grief over the darksomeness of those wretched ones with the holy lives of my ministers. I have told you that they have taken on the qualities of the Sun, so that the fragrance of their virtues mitigates the stench, and their lightsomeness the dark. By this very light I would have you know more deeply the sinful darksomeness of those other ministers of mine. So open your mind's eye and contemplate me, the Sun of justice, and you shall see these glorious ministers who by their stewardship of the Sun have taken on the qualities of the Sun.

I have told you about Peter, the prince of the apostles, who received the keys of the heavenly kingdom. Just so, I am telling you about others who, in this garden of holy Church, have been stewards of the light, that is, the body and blood of my only-begotten Son. He is the one undivided Sun, and all the Church's sacraments derive their value and life-giving power from his blood. All these of whom I am now telling you were appointed by rank according to their state to be stewards of the Holy Spirit's grace. How have they administered it? By the gracious brightness they have drawn from this true light.

Does this brightness exist by itself? No, for neither can the brightness of grace exist by itself nor can its light be divided: One must either have it whole and entire or not have it at all. Anyone living in deadly sin is by that very fact deprived of the light of grace. And anyone who has grace is spiritually enlightened by knowing me, for I am the giver of grace and of the virtue by which grace is preserved. It is in this light that the soul recognizes the wretchedness of sin and its source, sensual selfishness, and therefore hates it. By hating sin and its source she receives the warmth of divine charity into her will, for the will follows understanding. And she receives the color of this glorious light by following the teaching of my gentle Truth, whence her memory is filled in pondering the blessing of his blood.

So you see, it is impossible to receive this light without also receiv-

---

24. I have followed the more consistent reading of E here. C, S, F have: "This is displeasing to me, and their fault is serious. . . . "

ing its warmth and color, for all three are fused into one and the same thing. Thus it is that the soul cannot have one of her powers disposed to receive me, the true Sun, unless all three of her powers are disposed together in my name. For as soon as the eye of understanding rises above physical sight by the light of faith and contemplates me, the will follows by loving what the eye of understanding has come to see and know, and the memory is filled with what the will loves. And as soon as these three powers are ready, the soul shares in me, the Sun, by being enlightened by my power and the wisdom of my only-begotten Son and the mercy of the Holy Spirit's fire.

So you see, the soul's powers have taken on the qualities of the sun. In other words, once these powers have been filled and clothed with me, the true Sun, they behave as the sun does. The sun warms and enlightens, and with its heat makes the earth bring forth fruit. So also these gentle ministers of mine, whom I chose and anointed and sent into the mystic body of holy Church to be stewards of me the Sun, that is, of the body and blood of my only-begotten Son along with the other sacraments that draw life from this blood. They administer it both actually and spiritually by giving off within the mystic body of holy Church the brightness of supernatural learning, the color of a holy and honorable life in following the teaching of my Truth, and the warmth of blazing charity. Thus with their warmth they cause barren souls to bring forth fruit, and enlighten them with the brightness of learning. By their holy and well-ordered lives they drive out the darksomeness of deadly sin and unfaithfulness, and set in order the lives of those who had been living disordered lives in the darkness of sin and the cold that came of their lack of charity. So you see how these ministers of mine are suns because they have taken on the qualities of me the true Sun. By love they have been made to be one thing with me and I with them.

They have all, according to the positions I have chosen them for, given light to holy Church: Peter with his preaching and teaching and in the end with his blood; Gregory with his learning and [his knowledge of] Sacred Scripture and the mirror of his living; Sylvester by his struggles against unbelievers and above all in the disputations and argumentations for the holy faith that he made in deeds as well as in words with the power he received from me. And if you turn to Augustine, to the glorious Thomas, to Jerome and the others, you will see what great light they have shed on this bride, as lamps set on a lampstand, dispelling errors with their true and perfect humility.

THE DIALOGUE

Hungry as they were for my honor and the salvation of souls, they fed on these at the table of the most holy cross. The martyrs did it with their blood. Their blood was fragrant to me, and with the fragrance of their blood and their virtues and with the light of learning they bore fruit in this bride. They spread the faith: Those who had been in darkness came to their light and they enkindled the light of faith in them. The prelates, who were entrusted with the authority of Christ on earth, offered me the just sacrifice of their holy and honorable lives. The pearl of justice shone in them and in their subjects, but first of all in them, with true humility and blazing charity, with enlightened discernment. Justly they offered me my due of glory and praise and offered themselves their contempt for their selfish sensuality by shunning vice and embracing virtue which charity for me and for their neighbors. With humility they trampled pride underfoot and like angels approached the table of the altar. They celebrated [the Mass] with bodily purity and spiritual sincerity, set ablaze as they were in charity's furnace. Because they had first done justice to themselves, they were just to their subjects as well. They wanted them to live virtuously, and so corrected them without any slavish fear, for their concern was not for themselves but only for my honor and the salvation of souls. They conducted themselves as good shepherds and followers of the good shepherd, my Truth, whom I sent to govern you, my little sheep, and to lay down his life for you.[25]

These ministers of mine followed in his footsteps. Therefore they did not let my members grow rotten for want of correction. But they corrected lovingly, with the ointment of kindness along with the harshness of the fire that cauterizes the wound of sin through reproof and penance, now more, now less, according to the gravity of the sin. Nor did it concern them that such correcting and speaking the truth might bring them death.

They were true gardeners, and with care and holy fear they rooted out the brambles of deadly sin and put in their place the fragrant plants of virtue. Thus their subjects lived in truly holy fear and they grew up as fragrant flowers in the mystic body of holy Church because my ministers fearlessly gave them the correction they needed. Because there was in them no thorn of sin, they kept to the way of holy justice and administered reproof without any slavish fear. This was and is the shining pearl that sheds peace and light on people's spirits and estab-

25. Cf. Jn. 10:11.

lishes them in holy fear with hearts united. I want you, therefore, to know that nothing causes as much darkness and division in the world among both laypeople and religious, clergy and shepherds of holy Church, as does the lack of the light of justice and the invasion of the darkness of injustice.

No rank, whether of civil or divine law, can be held in grace without holy justice.[26] For those who are not corrected and those who do not correct are like members beginning to rot, and if the doctor were only to apply ointment without cauterizing the wound, the whole body would become fetid and corrupt.

So it is with prelates or with anyone else in authority. If they see the members who are their subjects rotting because of the filth of deadly sin and apply only the ointment of soft words without reproof, they will never get well. Rather, they will infect the other members with whom they form one body under their one shepherd. But if those in authority are truly good doctors to those souls, as were those glorious shepherds, they will not use ointment without the fire of reproof. And if the members are still obstinate in their evildoing, they will cut them off from the congregation so that they will not infect the whole body with the filth[27] of deadly sin.

But [those who are in authority] today do not do this. In fact, they pretend not to see. And do you know why? Because the root of selfish love is alive in them, and this is the source of their perverse slavish fear. They do not correct people for fear of losing their rank and position and their material possessions. They act as if they were blind, so they do not know how to maintain their positions. For if they saw how it is by holy justice that their positions are to be maintained, they would maintain them. But because they are bereft of light they do not know this. They believe they can succeed through injustice, by not reproving the sins of their subjects. But they are deceived by their own sensual passion, by their hankering for civil or ecclesiastical rank.

Another reason they will not correct others is that they themselves are living in the same or greater sins. They sense that the same guilt envelops them, so they cast aside fervor and confidence and, chained by slavish fear, pretend they do not see. Even what they do see they do

---

26. Cf. Pr. 16:12. Also, Let. 123: "And I tell you there is no other way the people of the world can preserve themselves spiritually or temporally than by living virtuously, for there is nothing that can cause us to fail other than our own sins and faults."

27. S, E, F have "filth" *(puzza)*; C has "guilt" *(colpa)*.

not correct, but let themselves be won over by flattery and bribes, using these very things as excuses for not punishing the offenders. In them is fulfilled what my Truth said in the holy Gospel: "They are blind and leaders of the blind. And if one blind person leads another, they both fall into the ditch."[28]

Those who have been or would be my gentle ministers did not and would not act this way. I told you that these have taken on the qualities of the sun. Indeed, they are suns, for there is in them no darkness of sin or ignorance, because they follow the teaching of my Truth. Nor are they lukewarm, because they are set ablaze in the furnace of my charity. They have no use for the world's honors and ranks and pleasures. Therefore, they are not afraid to correct. Those who do not hanker after power or ecclesiastical rank have no fear of losing it. They reprove [sin] courageously, for those whose conscience does not accuse them of sin have nothing to fear.

So this pearl [of justice] was not clouded over in these anointed ones, these christs of mine, of whom I have told you. No, it was luminous. They embraced voluntary poverty and sought after lowliness with deep humility. This is why they were not annoyed by people's derision or abuse or slander, or by insult or shame or pain or torture. They were cursed, and they blessed.[29] They endured with true patience, like earthly angels and more than angels—not by nature, but because of the sacramental grace given them from above to be the stewards of the body and blood of my only-begotten Son.

Truly they were angels, for just as the angel I have given you as guardian serves you with good and holy inspirations, so also were these ministers angels—and such they should be—given you by my kindness as your guardians. Therefore, their eyes were constantly fixed on their subjects, true guardians that they were, breathing good and holy inspirations into their hearts (that is, offering tenderly loving desires for them in my presence by constant prayer), and instructing them by word and by the example of their lives. So you see, they were angels, appointed by my burning charity to be lamps in the mystic body of holy Church. They are to be your guardians so that you who are blind may have guides to direct you along the way of truth by giving you good inspirations, along with their prayers and the example of their lives and teaching.

---

28. Mt. 15:14; Lk. 6:39.
29. Cf. 1 Co. 4:9–13.

How humbly they governed and communicated with their subjects! With what hope and lively faith! They had no fear or worry that either they or their subjects would be lacking in temporal goods, so they generously gave out the Church's possessions to the poor. Thus they fulfilled to the utmost their obligation to divide their temporal goods to meet their own needs and those of the poor and the Church. They set nothing aside, and after their death there was no great estate to settle; in fact, some of them left the Church in debt for the sake of the poor—all because of their generous charity and their trust in my providence. They were strangers to slavish fear, so they were confident they would lack nothing, either spiritually or temporally.

This is the sign that people's trust is in me rather than in themselves: that they have no slavish fear. Those who trust in themselves are afraid of their own shadow; they expect both heaven and earth to let them down. This fear and perverted trust in their scant wisdom makes them so wretchedly concerned about acquiring and holding on to temporal things, that they seem to toss the spiritual behind their backs. Not one of them has any concern for the spiritual.

They forget, these faithless proud wretches, that I am the one who provides for everything whatever that may be needed for soul or body. In the measure that you put your trust in me, in that measure will my providence be meted out to you.[30] But these presumptuous wretches do not reflect that I am who I am and they are the ones who are not. From my goodness they have received their very being and every gift beyond that. So consider it useless to wear yourself out guarding your city unless it is guarded by me.[31] Every effort is useless for those who think they can guard their city by their own toil or concern, for I alone am the guardian.

I have given you your being and other gifts beyond that, and it is true that I want you to use these by virtuously exercising my gift of free choice by the light of reason. For I created you without your help, but I will not save you without your help. I loved you before you came into being.

These my loved ones saw and recognized this, and therefore they loved me unspeakably much. Because of their love, their trust in me was generous and they feared nothing. Sylvester was not afraid when

---

30. Mt. 7:2; Mk. 4:24; Lk. 6:38.
31. Cf. Ps. 127:1.

he stood before the emperor Constantine, debating with those twelve judges in front of the whole crowd.[32] He believed with a lively faith that since I was on his side, no one could be against him.[33] So also were all the others fearless, because they were not alone, for those who abide in loving charity abide in me.[34] From me they received the luminous wisdom of my only-begotten Son; from me they received power to be strong and forceful against the tyrannical rulers of the world; and from me they had the fire of the Holy Spirit and shared in the mercy and burning love of this same Holy Spirit. And for anyone who would share in it, this love was and is accompanied by faith and hope, by courage, true patience, and perseverance even to the moment of death. So you see, these ministers of mine were not alone; they were in good company, and therefore they were fearless.

The only ones who are afraid are those who think they are alone, who trust in themselves and have no loving charity. They are afraid of every little thing because they are alone, deprived of me. For it is I who give complete security to the soul who possesses me in love. These my glorious loved ones experienced well that nothing could harm their souls. Indeed, they were the bane of humans and devils alike, who often were left chained by the strength and power I had given my servants over them. This was because I responded to the love and faith and trust they had put in me.

Your tongue could never adequately describe their virtue, nor your mind's eye see the reward they receive in everlasting life—the reward everyone will receive who follows in their footsteps. They stand like precious stones in my sight, for I have accepted their labors and the light they shed with such fragrant virtue in the mystic body of holy Church. Therefore I have set them with the greatest honor in everlasting life. The sight of me makes them gloriously happy, because they gave an example of holy and honorable living, and were lightsome stewards of the light of my only-begotten Son's body and blood as well as all the other sacraments. So I love them very especially, both for the dignity to which I appointed them, that they should be my anointed

---

32. The story is one of those related by Jacopo da Varagine in his *Golden Legend* (ch. XII), a work that was certainly familiar to Catherine. Raymond of Capua tells us that when Catherine stopped at the plague-stricken Varagine on her way back from Avignon in 1376, she advised the townfolk to erect a shrine in honor of their holy fellow-citizen. They did so, and the plague ceased (*B. Raymundi Capuani, Opuscula et Litterae*, [Rome, 1895], pp. 25–30).

33. Cf. Rm. 8:31.

34. Cf. 1 Jn. 4:16.

ministers, and because they were not so foolish or indifferent as to bury the treasure I entrusted to them.[35] They acknowledged that it was from me and used it with care and deep humility, with true and solid virtue.

Because I had appointed them to such dignity for the salvation of souls, they never rested, good shepherds that they were, from gathering the little sheep into the sheepfold of holy Church. In their love and hunger for souls they even laid down their lives to rescue them from the devils' hands.[36] They made themselves weak along with those who were weak. That is, to keep the weak from being confounded with despair and to give them more room to expose their weakness, they would show their own weakness, saying, "I am weak along with you."[37] They wept with those who wept and rejoiced with those who rejoiced.[38] Thus they knew how to give everyone the right food ever so tenderly. They encouraged the good by rejoicing in their goodness, for they were not gnawed up with envy but broad in the generosity of their charity for their neighbors and subjects. Those who were sinful they drew out of their sin by showing that they themselves were also sinful and weak. Their compassion was true and holy, and while correcting others and imposing penances for the sins they had committed, they themselves in their charity did penance along with them. Because of their love, they who were imposing the penance suffered more than those who received it. And sometimes some of them actually did the same penance themselves, especially when they saw that it seemed very difficult for the penitent. And by that act the difficulty became sweet for them.

O my loved ones! They who were superiors became as subjects. They who were in authority became as servants. Though they were healthy, without the sickness and leprosy of deadly sin, they became as if afflicted. Though they were strong, they became as if weak. With the dull and simple they showed themselves as simple, and with the lowly, as lowly. And so with every sort of person they knew how to deal humbly and with charity, giving to everyone the right food.

What made this possible? The hungry longing they had conceived in me for my honor and the salvation of souls. They ran to feast on

---

35. Cf. Mt. 25:14–30; Lk. 19:12–27.
36. Cf. Jn. 10.
37. Cf. 1 Co. 9:22.
38. Rm. 12:15. (C omits "rejoiced with those who rejoiced.")

these at the table of the most holy cross, refusing no labor and evading no toil. Zealous as they were for souls and for the welfare of holy Church and the spread of the faith, they walked through the brambles of trial and exposed themselves to every sort of danger with true patience. They offered me the fragrant incense of eager longing and constant humble prayer. With their tears and sweat they anointed the wounds the guilt of deadly sin had made, and those who humbly received this anointing regained perfect health.

120

Dearest daughter, I have given you but a glimpse of the high dignity to which I have appointed those I have chosen to be my ministers—a mere glimpse, I tell you, in relation to how great a dignity this is.

Because of the dignity and authority I have given them, it never has nor ever will be my will that the hand of civil law should touch them for any sin of theirs. To do so would be a wretched offense against me. No, it is my will that they be held in due reverence, not for what they are in themselves, but for my sake, because of the authority I have given them. Therefore, the virtuous must not lessen their reverence, even should these ministers fall short in virtue. And so far as the virtues of my ministers are concerned, I have described them for you by setting them before you as stewards of the Sun, that is, of my Son's body and blood and of the other sacraments. This dignity belongs to all who are appointed as such stewards, to the bad as well as to the good.

I told you that those who were perfect took on the qualities of the sun. They gave the light and warmth of loving charity to their neighbors, and because of this warmth they bore fruit and caused virtue to spring up in the souls of their subjects. I suggested to you that they are angels, and such is the truth. I have given them to you to be your guardians, to protect you and breathe good inspirations into your hearts by means of their holy prayers, their teaching, and the mirror of their lives. They are to serve you by administering to you the holy sacraments. They are to be like the angel who serves and protects you and inspires you with good and holy thoughts.[39]

So you see how worthy of love they are if, beyond the dignity to which I have appointed them, they are for you a shining example of

---

39. Cf. Heb. 1:14.

virtue as were those I have told you about, and as all of them are in duty bound to be. And you must hold them in great reverence, because they are my beloved children and suns sent into the mystic body of holy Church because of their virtue. For everyone who is virtuous is worthy of love; how much more so these, because of the ministry I have entrusted to them! So because of their virtue and because of their sacramental dignity you ought to love them. And you ought to hate the sins of those who lead evil lives. But you may not for all that set yourselves up as their judges; this is not my will, because they are my christs and you ought to love and reverence the authority I have given them.[40]

You know well enough that if someone filthy or poorly dressed were to offer you a great treasure that would give you life, you would not disdain the bearer for love of the treasure and the lord who had sent it, even though the bearer was ragged and filthy. He might well displease you, but for love of the lord you would do what you could to persuade him to get rid of his filth and put on better clothes. This is how you ought to act in the realm of charity, and this is how I want you to act toward those of my ministers who are out of line, who are covered with the filth of sin and ragged from their abuse of charity when they bring you the great treasures of the Church's sacraments. You receive grace through these sacraments no matter how sinful the bearers may be when you receive them worthily, for love of me, God eternal, the sender, and for love of the life of grace that you receive from this great treasure; for it brings me to you, wholly God and wholly human, that is, the body and blood of my Son united with my divinity. You ought to despise and hate the ministers' sins, and try to dress them in the new clothes of charity and holy prayer, and wash away their filth with your tears. In other words, you should hold them out to me with tears and great desire, so that I in my goodness may clothe them with the garment of charity.

You know well that I want to be gracious to them if only they are disposed to receive it and you to ask it of me. For it is not my will that they should administer the Sun to you out of their darksomeness, nor that they should be stripped of the garment of virtue and filthy with dishonorable living. Indeed, I have appointed them and given them to you to be angels on earth and suns, as I have told you. When they are less than that, you ought to pray for them. But you are not to judge

---

40. Cf. Mt. 23:2–3.

them. Leave the judging to me, and I, because of your prayers and my own desire, will be merciful to them. If they will not change their ways, the dignity they have will be their destruction. And if the great reproof they receive from me, the supreme Judge, at the moment of death does not make them change or reach out for my generous mercy, they will be condemned to eternal fire.

121

Now listen well, dearest daughter, for I want to show you the wretchedness of their lives, so that you and my other servants will have the more reason to offer me humble and constant prayer for them. No matter where you turn, to secular or religious, clerics or prelates, lowly or great, young or old, you see nothing but sin. All of them pelt me with the filth of deadly sin. But their filth harms only themselves, not me.[41]

Up to now I have told you about the excellence of my ministers and the virtues of the good, both to refresh your soul and to make you better appreciate the wretchedness of these wicked ones and see how deserving they are of greater rebuke and more intolerable punishment. By the same token, my chosen and loved ministers, because they have virtuously used the treasure entrusted to them, deserve a greater reward, deserve to stand as pearls in my sight. It is just the contrary for these wretched ones, for they will reap a cruel punishment.

Do you know, dearest daughter—listen with grieving bitterness of heart—do you know where these have set their principle and foundation? In their own selfish self-centeredness. There is born the tree of pride with its offshoot of indiscretion. So, lacking in discernment as they are, they assume honor and glory for themselves by seeking higher office and adornments and delicacies for their bodies, repaying me with abuse and sin. They take to themselves what is not theirs and give me what is not mine. To me should be given glory and my name should be praised; to themselves is due contempt for their selfish sensuality. They ought to know themselves enough to consider themselves

---

41. After having clearly affirmed the incomparable dignity of the priesthood as such, Catherine goes on to fearlessly expose the wretched state of many unworthy ministers. This exposé, even in the crudity of some of its parts, is no mere scandal-mongering. Its only intent is to rouse sorrow and stronger love to wrest from God, by prayer and penance, the grace of reform for the Church and its members. It is essential to read these pages in the spirit in which they were written, or pass over them altogether (Cavallini).

unworthy of the tremendous mystery they have received from me. But they do just the opposite, for, bloated with pride as they are, they never have their fill of gobbling up earthly riches and the pleasures of the world, while they are stingy, greedy, and avaricious toward the poor.

Because of this wretched pride and avarice born of their sensual selfishness, they have abandoned the care of souls and give themselves over completely to guarding and caring for their temporal possessions. They leave behind my little sheep, whom I had entrusted to them, like sheep without a shepherd.[42] They neither pasture nor feed them either spiritually or materially. Spiritually they do administer the sacraments of holy Church (the power of which sacraments can neither be taken away nor lessened by any sin of theirs) but they do not feed them with sincere prayers, with hungry longing for their salvation, with holy and honorable living, nor do they feed their poor subjects with temporal assistance.

I told you they were to distribute their material goods in three portions: one for their own needs, one for the poor, and one for the use of the Church.[43] But these do the opposite. Not only do they not give what they are in duty bound to give to the poor, but they rob them through simony and their hankering after money, selling the grace of the Holy Spirit.[44] Some are so mean that they are unwilling to give to the needy the very things I have given them freely so that they might give them to you—unless their hands are filled [with money] or they are plentifully supplied with gifts [in return]. They love their subjects for what they can get from them, and no more. They spend all the goods of the Church on nothing but clothes for their bodies. They go about fancily dressed, not like clerics and religious, but like lords or court lackeys. They are concerned about having grand horses, many gold and silver vessels, and well-adorned homes. They have and keep what they ought not, all with huge vanity. Their heart babbles out its disordered vanity,[45] and their whole desire is feasting, making a god of their bellies,[46] eating and drinking inordinately. So they soon fall into impure and lustful living.

Woe, woe, to their wretched lives! For what the gentle Word, my only-begotten Son, won with such suffering on the wood of the most

---

42. Cf. Zc. 10–11; Mt. 9:36; Mk. 6:34.
43. Cf. ch. 114.
44. Cf. Ac. 8:20.
45. Cf. Si. 21:29.
46. Ph. 3:19.

holy cross they spend on prostitutes. They devour the souls who were bought with Christ's blood, eating them up in so many wretched ways, and feeding their own children with what belongs to the poor. O you temples of the devil! I appointed you to be earthly angels in this life, but you are devils who have taken up the devils' work! The devils dispense darkness from what is theirs, and administer excruciating torments. With their vexatious temptations they lure souls away from grace to drag them down to the guilt of deadly sin. They exert every effort they can in this. Although no sin can touch the soul who does not want it, they nevertheless do all they can.[47] Thus these wretches, unworthy of being called ministers, are devils incarnate, for by their sins they have patterned themselves after the devils. They perform their task of administering me, the true Light, out of the darkness of deadly sin, and they administer to their subjects and to others the darksomeness of their perverted and evil lives. They are the cause of confusion and suffering to the spirits of those who see their disorderly living. Indeed, they are the cause of confusion and suffering to the consciences of those they succeed in dragging down from the state of grace and the way of truth, for by leading them into sin they make them walk in the way of falsehood.

But those who follow them do not in fact have an excuse for their sin, for no one can be forced into deadly sin either by these visible devils or the invisible ones. No one ought to give attention to their lives or copy what they do. Still, as my Truth admonished you in the holy Gospel, you should do as they tell you.[48] This is the teaching given you in the mystic body of holy Church, borne in Holy Scripture, and brought to you by my trumpeters, the preachers whose duty it is to proclaim my word. But the woe that is their just desert, and their evil lives, you are not to imitate. Nor are you to punish them, for in that you would offend me. Leave them their evil lives and take for yourselves their teaching. And leave their punishment to me, for I am the gentle eternal God, and I reward everything good and punish every sin.

Their dignity in being my ministers will not save them from my punishment. Indeed, unless they change their ways, they will be punished more severely than all the others, because they have received more from my kindness. Having sinned so miserably, they are deserving of greater punishment. So you see how they are devils, just as I told

---

47. This sentence is not in C, but occurs in S, E, F.
48. Mt. 23:3.

you that my chosen ones are angels on earth and do the work of the angels.

122

I told you that the pearl of justice was luminous in those chosen ones. Now I tell you that the jewel these puny wretches wear over their heart is injustice.[49] This injustice proceeds from and is mounted in their self-centeredness, for because of their selfishness they perpetrate injustice against their own souls and against me, along with their dark lack of discernment. They do not pay me my due of glory, nor do they do themselves the justice of holy and honorable living or desire for the salvation of souls or hunger for virtue. Thus they commit injustice against their subjects and neighbors, and do not correct them for their sins. Indeed, as if they were blind and did not know, because of their perverse fear of incurring others' displeasure, they let them lie asleep in their sickness. They do not consider that by wishing to please creatures they are displeasing both them and me your Creator.

Sometimes they administer correction as if to cloak themselves in this little bit of justice. But they will never correct persons of any importance, even though they may be guilty of greater sin than more lowly people, for fear that these might retaliate by standing in their way or deprive them of their rank and their way of living. They will, however, correct the little people, because they are sure these cannot harm them or deprive them of their rank. Such injustice comes from their wretched selfish love for themselves.

This selfishness has poisoned the whole world as well as the mystic body of holy Church and made the garden of this bride a field overgrown with putrid weeds. That garden was well cultivated when it had true workers, that is, my holy ministers, and it was adorned with an abundance of fragrant flowers, because good shepherds whose own lives were honorable and holy kept their subjects from living evil lives. But that is not the case today. In fact, it is just the opposite, because evil shepherds are causing their subjects to be evil. So this bride is full of thorns, full of a multitude of different sins.

Not that she can herself be infected with the filth of sin or that the power of her holy sacraments can suffer any damage. But those who

---

49. Cf. Ws. 5:18. "He will put on justice as a breastplate." Also Ep. 6:14. "So stand your ground, with truth buckled round your waist, and integrity for a breastplate."

feed at the breast of this bride imbide filth into their souls when they surrender the dignity to which I appointed them. Their dignity is not lessened in itself, but only in relation to themselves. Thus because of their sins the blood is disgraced, for laypeople lose the reverence they ought to have for them because of the blood, even though this should not be so. And if they are so irreverent, their guilt is not lessened because of their shepherds' sins. It is only that these wretches have become mirrors of wickedness, whereas I had appointed them to be mirrors of virtue.

123

What is the source of such filth in their souls? Their own selfish sensuality. Their selfishness has made a lady of their sensuality, and their wretched little souls have become her slaves, whereas I made them to be free by the blood of my Son, when the whole human race was freed from slavery to the devil and his rule. Every person receives this grace, but these whom I have anointed I have freed from the world's service and appointed them to serve me alone, God eternal, by being stewards of the sacraments of holy Church.

I have made them so free, in fact, that it has never been my will, nor is it now, that any civil authority should presume to sit in judgment over them. And do you know, dearest daughter, what thanks they give me for such a great gift? This is their thanks: They hound me constantly with so many villainous sins that your tongue could never describe them, and you would faint if you heard them. But I want to tell you at least something about them beyond what I have already said, to give you more reason for tears and compassion.

My ministers should be standing at the table of the cross in holy desire, nourishing themselves there on the food of souls for my honor. And though every person ought to do this, much more should those whom I have chosen to administer for you the body and blood of my only-begotten Son, Christ crucified, and to give you an example of good and holy living by following my Truth in their suffering and in great holy longing as they make your souls their food.

But instead these have made the taverns their table, and there in public they swear and perjure themselves in sin upon miserable sin, as if they were blind and bereft of the light of reason. They have become beasts in their sinning, lustful in word and deed. They do not so much as know what the Divine Office is, and even if they say it from time to time they are saying it with their tongue while their heart is far from me.[50] They are like criminal gamblers and swindlers: After they have gambled away their own souls into the devils' hands, they gamble away the goods of the Church as well, and they gamble and barter away whatever material goods they have been given in virtue of [my Son's] blood. So the poor go without what is due them, and the Church's needs are not provided for.

Because they have made themselves the devil's temple, they are no longer concerned about my temple. Rather, the things that should go for the adornment of the Church and her temples out of respect for the blood go instead to adorn the houses they live in. And worse: They act like husbands adorning their brides; these incarnate devils use the Church's property to adorn the she-devils with whom they live in sin and indecency. Shamelessly they let them come and stay and go. And while they, miserable devils, stand at the altar to celebrate, it does not even bother them to see their wretched she-devils coming up with their children by the hand, to make their offering with the other people!

O devils and worse than devils! At least let your iniquity be hid from the eyes of your subjects! Then at least, though you would still be offending me and harming yourselves, you would not be hurting your neighbors by actually setting your evil lives before their eyes. For by your example you give them reason not to leave their own sinful ways, but to fall into the same sins as yours and worse. Is this the kind of purity I demand of my ministers when they go to celebrate at the altar? This is the sort of purity they bring: They get up in the morning with their minds contaminated and their bodies corrupt. After spending the night bedded down with deadly sin they go to celebrate [Mass]! O tabernacles of the devil! Where are your nightly vigils and the solemn and devout praying of the Office? Where is your constant devoted prayer? In that nighttime you ought to be readying yourselves for the mystery you are to celebrate in the morning. You ought to be taking a deeper look at yourselves, recognizing and acknowledging that you are unworthy of so great a mystery. And you should be taking a deeper look at me, for I in my goodness, not for any merit of yours, made you wor-

---

50. Cf. Is. 29:13; Mt. 15:8; Mk. 7:6.

thy of it, and made you my ministers so that you might serve my other creatures.

124

I am letting you know, dearest daughter, that in this sacrament I demand of you and of them the greatest purity that is possible to humanity in this life—so much so that you for your part as well as they ought to constantly strive to attain it. You should reflect that, were it possible for the angels to be purified, they would have to be purified for this mystery. But this is not possible; they do not need to be purified, for the poison of sin cannot infect them. I am telling you this to make you see what great purity I demand of you and them, and especially of them, in this sacrament. But they do just the opposite to me, for they come to this mystery[51] wholly impure—and not simply with the sort of impurity and weakness to which you are all naturally inclined because of your weak nature (although reason can calm its rebellion if free choice so wills). No, these wretches not only do not restrain their weakness; they make it worse by committing that cursed unnatural sin. As if they were blind and stupid, with the light of their understanding extinguished, they do not recognize what miserable filth they are wallowing in. The stench reaches even up to me, supreme Purity, and is so hateful to me that for this sin alone five cities[52] were struck down by my divine judgment. For my divine justice could no longer tolerate it, so despicable to me is this abominable sin. But the stench displeases not only me, as I have said, but the devils as well, those very devils these wretches have made their masters. It is not its sinfulness that displeases them, for they like nothing that is good. But because their nature was angelic, that nature still loathes the sight of that horrendous sin actually being committed. It is true that it was they who in the beginning shot the poisoned arrows of concupiscence, but when it comes to the sinful act itself they run away.

---

51. S alone has "they come to this mystery."

52. In Gn. 19:24–25 only Sodom and Gomorrah are mentioned, as also in practically every other biblical allusion (cf. Is. 13:19, 1:9; Rm. 9:29; Jd. 7, etc.). But in Ws. 10:6 we find: " . . . the fire raining down on the Five Cities, in witness against whose evil ways a desolate land still smokes . . . ," the five being Sodom, Gomorrah, Admah, Zeboiim, and Zoar.

You know, if you remember well, how before the great Death[53] I
showed you how despicable this sin is to me, and how the world is corrupted by it. At that time, when I lifted your spirit up above yourself
in holy desire, I showed you the whole world, and in people of almost
every walk of life you saw this miserable sin. You saw in that revelation how the devils fled. And you know that your spirit suffered so
from the stench that you thought you would surely die. You could see
nowhere that you and my other servants could go to escape being
touched by this leprosy. It seemed you could not live among the lowly
or the great, the old or the young, religious or clerics, superiors or subjects, masters or servants; for they were all contaminated in mind and
body by this curse. I did not show you then, nor am I telling you now,
which individuals are the exceptions, for I do leave some just ones
among the wicked to hold back my justice[54] so that I may not command the very stones to rise up against them, nor the earth to swallow
them up, nor the beasts to devour them, nor the demons to carry them
off soul and body. Indeed, I am continually finding ways to be merciful
to them, to make them change their ways. And I put my servants who
are healthy and not leprous in their midst to pray for them.

Sometimes I reveal these miserable sins of theirs to my servants
(just as I did to you) so that they may be even more concerned for their
salvation and hold them out to me with greater compassion, praying
for them with sorrow for their sins and the insult they are to me. If
you recall, when I let you smell even a bit of this stench, you were in
such a state that you could stand no more, so that you said to me, "O
eternal Father, be merciful to me and to these creatures of yours! Otherwise take the soul from my body, for I do not think I can stand it
anymore. Or give me some respite by showing me where I and your
other servants can find refuge so that this leprosy will not be able to
harm us or deprive us of our bodily and spiritual purity."

In response I turned and looked on you with pity. I said, and I say
it again now: "My daughter, let your respite be in glorifying and praising my name, in offering me the incense of constant prayer for these
poor wretches who have sunk so low and made themselves deserving of

---

53. The plague of 1374, during which Catherine was prodigal in her care of the
stricken and worked more than one miraculous cure, though she saw seven of her own
nieces and nephews die. Cf. *Leg. Maj.* II, viii.
54. An allusion to Abraham's bargaining with the Lord over Sodom and Gom-
morah. Cf. Gn. 18:23–32.

divine judgment for their sins. And let your place of refuge be my only-begotten Son, Christ crucified. Make your home and hiding place in the cavern of his open side. There, in his humanity, you will enjoy my divinity with loving affection. In that open heart you will find charity for me and for your neighbors, for to honor me his eternal Father and to fulfill the obedience I had placed on him for your salvation, he ran to his shameful death on the most holy cross. Once you see and taste this love you will follow his teaching and find your nourishment at the table of the cross. In other words, charity will make you put up with your neighbors with true patience by enduring pain, torment, and weariness no matter what their source. In this way you will flee and escape the leprosy."

Such is the way I gave and still give to you and the others. For all this, your soul was not relieved of the stench nor your mind's eye of the darksomeness. But my providence was with you. I let you commune in the body and blood of my Son, wholly God and wholly human, by receiving the sacrament of the altar. And there, as a sign that I had spoken truly, the fragrance of this sacrament dispelled the stench, and its light dispersed the darksomeness. And as you know, it pleased my goodness to let that fragrance of the blood remain wonderfully present to your mouth and your bodily taste for several days.

So you see, dearest daughter, how abominable this sin is to me in any person. Now imagine how much more hateful it is in those I have called to live celibately. Among these celibates who have been lifted up above the world, some are religious and some are trees planted as my ministers in the mystic body of holy Church. You cannot imagine how much more I despise this sin in these celibates—even more than in ordinary people of the world. They are lamps set on a lampstand, to be stewards of me the true Sun, giving off the light of virtue and of holy and honorable living. But instead they minister in darksomeness.

Let me show you how darksome they are. Holy Scripture is lightsome in itself, and my chosen ones drew from it with a supernatural light from me the true light, as I have told you elsewhere.[55] But these wretches, because of their bloated[56] pride, indecency, and lust, neither see nor understand anything but the outer crust, the letter, of Scripture. They receive it without any relish, because their spiritual taste is disordered, corrupted even, by selfish love and pride. Their bellies are

---

55. Cf. ch. 85.
56. E has "infinite."

full of uncleanness, hungry only for the fulfilment of their perverted pleasures, glutted with concupiscence and avarice. Nor are they ashamed to commit their sins in public. And many of the wretches practice usury as well, which I have forbidden.

125

How can those who are so sinful bring their subjects to justice and reproach them for their sins? They cannot, for their own sins have left them bereft of any enthusiasm or zeal for holy justice. If they do sometimes attempt it, they make their subjects (who have become sinful along with themselves) say, "Doctor, treat yourself first; then treat me, and I will take the medicine you give me.[57] Your sin is greater than mine, yet you condemn me!"

Those whose reprimands are only words unsupported by a good and well-ordered[58] life are doing wrong. Not that they ought therefore to leave their subjects' sins unreprimanded, good or evil though they themselves may be. But they still are doing wrong in that their reprimand is not accompanied by holy and honorable living. And those do even worse who do not humbly accept the reprimand and change their evil ways, no matter how the reprimand is given, no matter how good or evil the pastor may be. Such people are hurting only themselves and no one else, and they are the ones who will suffer the penalties of their own sins.

All these evils, dearest daughter, come of not administering corrections out of one's own good and holy living. Why do they not correct? Because they are blinded by their selfish self-centeredness. This selfishness is the source of all their evil doings. Subjects and pastors, clerics and religious alike, are looking out for nothing except how they can have all their perverse pleasures and pastimes.

Where, where, my gentle daughter, is the obedience religious ought to have? I established them like angels in holy religion, and they are worse than demons. I appointed them to proclaim my word by their life and teaching, but the words they shout are only empty sounds, producing no fruit in the hearts of their listeners. Their preaching is aimed more at pleasing others or at tickling their own ears than at honoring me. They spend their efforts not on virtuous living but on polished rhetoric.

---

57. Cf. Lk. 4:23.
58. E has "honorable."

Such as these are not sowing my seed in truth. They pay no attention to rooting out vice and planting virtue. So, because they have not rid their own orchard of brambles, they are not concerned about getting them out of their neighbors' orchards. All their pleasure is in adorning their bodies and their cells, and in roaming and gossiping about the city. And just as fish taken out of the water die, so do these religious who live vainly and dishonorably outside their monastic cells.[59] They leave their cells, which ought to be a heaven for them, and wander about the wards of the city seeking out the homes of their relatives and other secular folk, just as it pleases them, wretched subjects that they are, and the wicked superiors who have given them such a long leash. These, wretched shepherds that they are, are not bothered to see their brothers [and sisters] submitting to the devils' power; in fact, they themselves often put them there. And sometimes when they recognize that these religious are incarnate devils, they send them from one monastery to the next to those who are incarnate devils like themselves. Thus each corrupts the other with all sorts of subtle tricks and deceits. The devil may start them out under the pretext of devotion, but because their lives are lustful and wretched their devotional disguise is all too thin. Soon enough the fruits of their "devotions" appear. First are seen the stinking blossoms of dishonorable thoughts and the rotten leaves of their words. And in what wretched ways do they satisfy their desires! The fruits that come of them—you know well, for you have seen them—are their children. Often they carry on so that one after another they leave religious life. He becomes a wanton, and she a public whore.

Superiors are the cause of these and many other evils because they do not keep their eyes on their subjects. They give them plenty of rope and even send them out, and then pretend not to see their wretched behavior. The subjects for their part find no pleasure in their cells. And so, through the fault of both the one and the other, they die in the end. Your tongue could never describe how greatly and in what miserable ways they sin against me. They become the devil's arms, and they throw their venomous filth both within and without: without among seculars and within in the religious community. They are bereft of fra-

---

59. Cf. Cavalca, *Lives of the Fathers:* "Just as a fish taken out of the water cannot long survive on the sand, so it is with the monk who takes up his residence with seculars. Therefore, it is just as essential for the monk to return to his solitude as it is for the fish to return to the water" ("Life of St. Anthony, Abbot," ch. 17).

ternal love.[60] Everyone wants to be the greatest, and everyone wants possessions. So they transgress both the commandment and the vow they have made.[61]

They made a promise to keep the rule and they violate it. Not only do they not observe it; they act like ravenous wolves toward the lambs they see observing the rule, taunting and jeering at them. And they believe, these wretches, that by hounding and taunting and jeering at those good religious who keep the rule they will cover over their own sins; but they expose themselves all the more.

The gardens of religious life are holy: There are saints in them because they were created and founded in the Holy Spirit. So the order as such cannot be spoiled or corrupted because of its members' sins. Therefore those who are making a decision to enter the order should not look at those who are evil, but should sail on the power of the order's arms, which neither are nor can be weak, and keep its rule until death.

I tell you, these great evils have come because of superiors who will not correct and subjects who are wicked. They regard as transgressors those who are sincerely observing the rule, because they do not hold to the customs and ceremonies these others have ordained and observe in the sight of seculars so as to impress them and thus cloak their sins. But you see, they do not fulfill the very first vow, that of obedience, for they do not keep the rule. I will tell you about that obedience in another place.

They further vow to observe voluntary poverty and to be celibate. How do these wretches observe those vows? Take a look at their possessions and all the money they keep for themselves. They stand off from the common charity of sharing their material and spiritual goods with their brothers as the rule of love and their own rule requires. They want to make no one fat but themselves and their beasts. So the one beast feeds the other, while their poor brother dies of hunger and cold.[62] And once they themselves are well dressed and well fed, they have no thought of the others, nor would they be found with them at

---

60. The reference here and in many of the passages that follow concentrates specifically on *male* religious!

61. I.e., the commandment of love and the vow of poverty (Cavallini).

62. Cf. Dante, *Paradiso* 21, 133–134: "Their mantles drape their palfreys, so that then/two beasts pace onwards 'neath a single hide."

THE DIALOGUE

the poor table in the refectory. Their pleasure is rather to be where they can have their fill of meat and satisfy their gluttony.

For such as these it is impossible to keep the third vow, that of celibacy, for a full belly does not make for a chaste spirit. Indeed, they become inordinately excited and lustful, and so go from evil to evil. And much evil comes on them because of their possessions, because if they had nothing to spend they would not live so sumptuously and would not have these capricious affairs. For romance does not last long when one has nothing to give, nor do those friendships that are built not on perfect love but on love of presents or on any delight or pleasure one might find in the other.

O wretches! Stuck in such baseness because of their sins when I had established them in such dignity! They flee from the choir[63] as if it were poison, or if they are there, they cry out with their voices, but their hearts are far from me. It has become habitual for them to approach the table of the altar without any preparation, as if they were going to any ordinary table.

All these evils, and so many others I do not want to tell you lest your ears be infected with the stench, follow upon the sin of evil shepherds who will not correct or punish the sins of their subjects. They have neither concern nor zeal for the observance of the rule because they themselves do not observe it. They are quick to lay heavy commands on the heads of those who want to keep the rule,[64] and punish them for faults they have not committed. All this they do because it is not the pearl of justice that shines in them but [the stone] of injustice. So their giving is unjust. To those who deserve grace and kindness they give penances and contempt. To those who, like themselves, are members of the devil, they give love, pleasures, and rank, entrusting them with the high offices of the order. They live as if they were blind, and they give out offices and govern their subjects as if they were blind. If they do not change their ways, they will carry that blindness right up to the darkness of eternal damnation. There they will have to give an account to me, the supreme judge, for the souls of their subjects. The only account they will be able to give me will be wicked and

---

63. I.e., the Divine Office chanted in community.
64. Cf. Mt. 23:4.

evil. Therefore they will receive from me, and justly, what they deserve.

126

D earest daughter, I have given you but a tiny glimpse of how these religious live, how miserably they wear sheep's clothing within their orders while they are, in fact, wolves.[65] Let me return now to the Church's clergy and ministers and with you grieve over their sins. Beyond what I have already told you, I want to grieve with you over the three pillars of vice I showed you at another time: impurity, bloated pride, and greed—for it is their greed that leads them to sell the grace of the Holy Spirit.

Each of these three vices is dependent on the others, and the foundation of these three pillars is their selfish self-centeredness. As long as these three pillars are standing upright and are not overthrown by the force of love of virtue, they are strong enough to keep the soul obstinately set in every other vice. For all of the vices are born of selfishness because it is from selfishness that the principal vice, pride, is born. Those who are proud are bereft of any loving charity, and their pride is the source of impurity and avarice. Thus are these souls their own jailers, locking themselves up with the devil's chains.

Now, dearest daughter, look with what miserable impurity they defile both their bodies and their spirits. I have already told you something about this. But I want to tell you something more so that you may better appreciate the fountain of my mercy and be more compassionate to the wretched souls it touches. Some of them are such devils that not only do they not reverence the sacrament or value the dignity to which I in my goodness have appointed them, but, as if their love for certain creatures has blotted all this from their memories, when they cannot have what they want from them they resort to diabolical incantations. And the sacrament I have given you as life-giving food they use as witchery to realize their dishonorable intentions and bring their will to prevail. As for the little sheep they ought to be caring for and feeding in body and spirit, they torment them in these and many other ways I will not mention lest I give you even greater pain. As you have seen, they let them wander about in a disoriented state because these incarnate demons have cast spells on them that cause them to do what

---

65. Cf. Mt. 7:15.

they do not want to do. And because of the resistance they put up, they suffer intense physical pain. What is the cause of this? And what is the cause of the many other miserable evils you know so well that I have no need to tell you about them? Their wretched dishonorable lives!

O dearest daughter! How they have debased the flesh that was exalted above all the choirs of angels through the union of my divinity with your humanity! O despicable wretched man, not man but beast! That you should give your flesh, anointed and consecrated to me, to prostitutes and worse! By the wounded body of my only-begotten Son on the wood of the most holy cross, your flesh and that of the whole human race was healed of the wound Adam dealt it by his sin. O wretch! He honored you, and you disgrace him! He healed your wounds with his blood, and more, he made you his minister, and you persecute him with your lustful dishonorable sins! The good shepherd washed the little sheep clean in his blood.[66] But you defile those who are pure: You use your power to hurl them into the dung heap. You who ought to be a mirror of honor are a mirror of dishonor.

You have yielded all your members to the works of wickedness, doing the opposite of what my Truth did for you. I allowed them to blindfold his eyes to enlighten you, and you with your lustful eyes shoot poisoned arrows into your own soul and the hearts of those you look on so miserably! I let them give him vinegar and gall to drink, and you like a perverse beast find your pleasure in delicate foods, making a god of your belly![67] On your tongue are dishonorable empty words. It is your duty with that tongue to admonish your neighbors, to proclaim my word, and to say the Office with your heart as well as your tongue. But I smell nothing but filth coming from your tongue as you swear and perjure yourself as if you were a swindling hoodlum, blaspheming me right and left. I let them bind my Son's hands to free you and the whole of humankind from the bondage of sin, and anointed and consecrated your hands for the ministry of the most holy sacrament, and you use your hands for wretched obscene touching. All the actions you express through your hands are corrupt and directed to the devil's service. O wretch! And I appointed you to such dignity so that you might serve me alone—you and every other rational creature!

I willed that my Son's feet should be nailed, and made his body a stairway for you. I let them open his side so that you might see his in-

66. Cf. Rv. 1:5.
67. Ph. 3:19.

245

most heart. I set him like an open hostelry where you could see and taste my unspeakable love for you when you found and saw my divinity united with your humanity. There you see that I have made the blood—of which you are a steward for me—to be a bath to wash away your sins. And you have made of your heart a temple for the devil! And your will, of which your feet are a symbol, you use to offer me nothing but filth and abuse. The feet of your will carry you nowhere except to the devil's haunts. So with your whole body you persecute my Son's body by doing the opposite of what he did and what you and everyone else are bound and obligated to do.

These bodily instruments of yours have taken up the sound for evil, for your soul's three powers are united in the name of the devil, whereas they ought to be united in my name.

Your memory ought to be filled with the blessings you have received from me, but it is filled with dishonor and many other evils. Your mind's eye, illumined by faith, ought to be fixed on my only-begotten Son, Christ crucified, whose minister you have been made, but you in your miserable vanity have fixed your attention on pleasures and honors and wordly riches. Your will ought to love me alone, unconditionally, but you have wretchedly given it to loving creatures and your own body. In fact, you love your animals more than you love me! What proves this? Your impatience with me whenever I take away something you love, and your displeasure with your neighbors whenever you think they have done you any material harm, so that by your hatred and blasphemy you cut yourself off from my charity as well as theirs. How unfortunate you are! You were made a steward of the fire of my divine charity, but you, for your perverse selfish pleasures and for the bit of harm you suffer from your neighbors, let go of it!

This, dearest daughter, is one of the three wretched pillars I told you of.

127

N ow I want to tell you about the second, avarice.
What my Son gave so generously, you are so miserly with.[68]
You see him with his body torn wide open on the wood of the cross, bleeding from every part; he did not redeem you with gold or silver

---

68. The addressee is once again the sinful minister.

but with his blood in the greatness of his love.[69] He did not redeem just half of the world but the whole human race, past, present, and future. He gave you not only his blood but fire as well, for it was through the fire of love that he gave you his blood. Nor can the fire or the blood be separated from my divine nature, for divinity was perfectly united with human nature. And of this blood made one with my divinity I have made you, wretch, a steward. But you are so avaricious and greedy in your use of what my Son bought on the cross, the souls he redeemed with such great love, and in your use of what he gave you by making you a minister of his blood! Wretch that you are, you are so miserly that you greedily put up for sale the grace of the Holy Spirit,[70] requiring your subjects to buy from you when they ask for what you have received as a gift.[71]

Your gullet is so ready to devour money that you have no appetite to eat souls for my honor. You are so tight in your charity with what you have received so generously that I cannot get through to you with grace nor can your neighbors with love. The temporal goods you received in virtue of this blood you received generously, but you, greedy wretch, are good to no one but yourself. Like a thieving bandit you deserve eternal death for stealing what belonged to the poor and to holy Church and spending it on luxuries with dishonorable women and men as well as with your relatives, on pleasures and on caring for your children.

O miserable wretch! Where are the offspring of the true gentle virtues you ought to have? Where is the burning charity with which you ought to minister? Where is your restless longing for my honor and the salvation of souls? Where is the piercing sorrow you ought to suffer as you see the infernal wolf making away with your little sheep? There is none, because there is no room in your tight heart for love of me or them. You love only yourself with sensual selfishness—a love that poisons you and others as well. You are that infernal devil who swallows up the sheep in your perverse selfishness. Your gullet hankers after nothing else; therefore it concerns you not at all when the invisible devil carries them off. You, the visible devil, have made yourself the instrument that sends them off to hell.

---

69. Cf. 1 P. 1:18–19. S, E, F have: "What my Son gave so generously (you see him with his body torn wide open on the wood of the cross, bleeding from every part) he did not buy with gold or silver, but with his blood in the greatness of his love."

70. Cf. Ac. 8:18–20.

71. Cf. Mt. 10:8.

Who are those who are clothed and fattened on what belongs to the Church? You and the other devils with you, and your beasts, the great horses you keep not because you need them but for your perverse pleasure—whereas you should have them only as you need them and not for pleasure. Such pleasures are for worldly people. Your pleasures ought to be with the poor and in visiting the sick, assisting them in their spiritual and material needs. For no other reason have I made you my minister and given you such dignity. It is because you have made a filthy beast of yourself that you find such pleasure in these beasts of yours. You do not see, for if you did see the punishments that will be yours unless you change your ways, you would not behave as you do. No, you would repent of what you have done in the past and correct the present.

Do you see, dearest daughter, how much reason I have to grieve over such wretchedness? And how generous I have been with them and how miserly they have been with me? For just as I told you, some of them even lend for usury. Not that they set up shop as public usurers do, but they have all sorts of subtle ways of selling time to their neighbors to satisfy their own greed. Now there is nothing in the world that can justify this. Even if it were the smallest of gifts, if their intention is to receive it as the price for the service they have done by lending their goods, this is usury as much as anything else that might be paid for the time [of the loan]. I appointed these wretches to forbid seculars [to practice usury], and here they are doing the same and more. For when someone comes to ask their advice about this matter, because they are guilty of the same sin and have lost the light of reason, the advice they give is darksome, tainted by the passion within their own souls.

This sin and many others are born of the tight, greedy, avaricious heart. One could use the words my Truth said when he entered the temple and found there the sellers and buyers. He chased them out with a whip of cords, saying, "Of my Father's house, which is a house of prayer, you have made a robbers' den."[72]

You see well, sweetest daughter, how true it is that they have made a robbers' den of my Church, which is a place of prayer. They sell and buy and have made the grace of the Holy Spirit a piece of merchandise. So you see, those who want the high offices and revenues of the Church buy them by bribing those in charge with money and pro-

---

72. Mt. 21:13; Mk. 11:17; Lk. 19:46.

visions. And those wretches are not concerned about whether [the candidates] are good or bad, but only about pleasing them for love of the gifts they have received. So they make every effort to set these putrid plants in the garden of holy Church, and for this the wretches will give a good report of them to Christ on earth.[73] Thus both use falsehood and deceit against Christ on earth, whereas they ought to behave sincerely and in all truth. But if my Son's vicar becomes aware of their sin he ought to punish them. He should relieve those of office who will not repent and change their evil way of living. As for those who do the bribing, they would do well to receive imprisonment for their bargaining, both to change their sinful ways and that others may see the example and be afraid to do the same thing any more. If Christ on earth does this, he is doing his duty. If he does not, his sin will not go unpunished when it is his turn to give me an account of his little sheep.

Believe me, my daughter. Today this is not done, and this is why such sins and abominations plague my Church. Those who make appointments to high offices do not investigate the lives of those they appoint, to see whether they are good or bad. Or if they do look into anything, they are questioning and asking information of those who are as evil as they are themselves, and these would not give anything but good testimony because they are guilty of the same sin. They are concerned about nothing but the grandeur of rank and nobility and wealth, about knowing polished rhetoric; and worse, they will recommend their candidate by saying he is good looking! Despicable, devilish things! Those who ought to be looking for the beautiful adornment of virtue are concerned about physical beauty! They ought to be searching out the humble poor folk who in their humility avoid high office, but instead they pick those who in their bloated pride go seeking promotions.[74]

They look for learning. Now learning in itself is good and perfect when the scholar is at the same time good and honorable and humble. But if learning is combined with pride, indecency, and sinful living, it is venomous and understands nothing but the letter of Scripture. It understands in darkness, for it has lost the light of reason and its eye for understanding is clouded over. It was in this light, enlightened by faith, that Holy Scripture was proclaimed and understood by those of

---

73. I.e., the pope.
74. For Catherine's concept of the prerequisites for high ecclestastical office, cf. Let. 209.

whom I have told you more at length elsewhere.[75] So you see, knowledge is good in itself, but not in those who do not use it as it should be used, and it will be a punishing fire to those who do not amend their lives. Therefore, they should look more for good and holy living than for those who are learned but do not know how to direct their own lives. But these wretches do just the opposite: The good and virtuous who are unlearned they consider fools, and they despise them; and the poor they shun because they have nothing to give.

So you see how lies abound in my house. Yet my house ought to be a house of prayer.[76] There the pearl of justice ought to shine, and the light of learning joined with holy and honorable living. There one should find the fragrance of truth. My ministers' possession ought to be voluntary poverty. With true concern they should care for and protect souls, and rescue them from the devils' hands. But their hunger is for riches, and they are so taken up with concern for temporal things that they have abandoned all concern for the spiritual. They attend to nothing but amusements and laughter and increasing and multiplying their material possessions. Miserable wretches! They are not aware that this is the best way to lose them, for if they were filled with virtue and careful for spiritual things as they ought to be, they would have plenty of the temporal as well. So many rebellions has my bride suffered that she should not have had![77] They ought to let the dead be buried by the dead.[78] As for themselves, they should follow the teaching of my Truth and fulfill my will for them by doing what I appointed them to do. But they do exactly the opposite, for they set themselves to burying dead and passing things in their disordered care and affection, stealing their business from the hands of worldly folk. This displeases me and is harmful to holy Church. They ought to leave these things to the worldly, and let the one dead thing bury the other; that is, let those take care of worldly, temporal things who are appointed to do so.

I said, "Let the one dead thing bury the other," and I mean "dead" to be understood in two ways. The first is administering and governing bodily things in deadly sin because of one's disordered care and af-

75. Cf. ch. 85.
76. Cf. Is. 56:7; Jr. 7:11; Mt. 21:13; Mk. 11:17; Lk. 19:46.
77. In most of her letters addressed to Gregory XI Catherine speaks of those who misuse their powers and responsibility in the midst of the strife that engulfed central Italy. Repeatedly she insists on desposing such prelates and replacing them with good ones (Cavallini).
78. Mt. 8:22.

fection. The other stems from the fact that because these things are tangible it is the body's function [to care for them]; and the body is a dead thing because it has no life in itself except as it derives it from the soul, and it shares in life only so long as the soul remains in it.

Therefore, these anointed ones of mine, who ought to be living as angels, should leave dead things to the dead and concern themselves with governing souls. For souls are living things and do not ever die so far as their existence is concerned. So they should govern them and administer to them the sacraments and gifts and graces of the Holy Spirit, and pasture them on spiritual food through their own good and holy lives. In this way will my house be a house of prayer, abounding in grace and filled with their virtues. But because they do just the opposite of this, I can say that it has become a robbers' den. They have become merchandisers in greed, selling and buying, and in their indecency they have made [my house] a receiving place for filthy beasts—made it, in fact, a pigsty where they wallow in the mire of indecency. Thus do they keep their she-devils in the Church as a husband keeps his bride in his house.

So you see how much evil is born of these two fetid and stinking pillars, impurity and greedy avarice. And there is incomparably more than what I have described for you.

128

Now I want to tell you about the third pillar, pride. I have left it till last because it is both end and beginning. For all the vices are seasoned with pride just as the virtues are seasoned and enlivened by charity.

And pride is born from and nurtured by that sensual selfish love which is the foundation of these three pillars and of every sort of evil creatures commit. For those who love themselves inordinately are bereft of my love because they do not love me. By not loving me they offend me because they are not keeping the Law's commandment to love me above all things and their neighbors as themselves. By loving themselves sensually they neither love nor serve me, but rather love and serve the world, because neither sensual love nor the world is patterned after me. So it follows that those who sensually love and serve the world despise me, and those who despise the world love me. This is why my Truth said that no one can serve two opposing masters. Whoever would serve the one would be despised by the other.[79] So you see, selfish love deprives the soul of my charity and clothes her in the vice of pride whence is born every sin because of its foundation in that selfish love.

I sorrow and grieve for every person who lives in this sin, but especially for my anointed ones who ought to be humble both because it is everyone's duty to have this virtue of humility, which nurtures charity, and because they have been made the ministers of the humble spotless Lamb, my only-begotten Son. Are they, together with the whole human race, not ashamed to be proud even as they see me, God, stooped down to humanity by giving you the Word, my Son, in your flesh? And they see this Word, because of the obedience I imposed on him, running to the humiliation of his shameful death on the cross.[80]

He bows his head to greet you, wears the crown [of thorns] to adorn you, stretches out his arms to embrace you, lets his feet be nailed that he may stand with you. And you, miserable wretch, you who were made the steward of such generosity and humility, ought to embrace the cross. But you flee from it and embrace evil impure creatures. You ought to stand firm and unwavering in your following of my Truth's teaching, nailing your heart and mind to him. But you flit about like a leaf in the wind; every little thing sets you flying. If it is prosperity you are moved to inordinate gladness; if it is adversity you are moved to impatience, thus sucking out the marrow of pride, which is impatience. For just as the marrow of charity is patience, so impatience is the marrow of pride. Thus every little thing upsets and scandalizes those who are proud and wrathful.

Pride is so despicable to me that it plummeted down from heaven when the angels revolted in pride. Pride does not ascend to heaven. No, it goes down to the depths of hell. Therefore my Truth said, "Those who exalt themselves (by pride) will be humbled, and those who humble themselves will be exalted."[81]

In any class of people pride displeases me, but much more in these ministers because I have appointed them to a humble state to be stewards of the humble Lamb, and they behave completely contrariwise.

---

79. Cf. Mt. 6:24; Lk. 16:13. In the Gospel text, however, the object of love and hate is not the servant but the master. Catherine reads into the text the reciprocity that is characteristic of her whole understanding of the relationship between the soul and God.

80. Cf. Ph. 2:8.

81. Mt. 23:12; Lk. 14:11, 18:14.

THE DIALOGUE

How can a wicked priest not be ashamed of his pride when he sees me stoop down to you by giving you the Word, my only-begotten Son? I have made priests his ministers; and he the Word, in obedience to me humbled himself to the shameful death of the cross! His head was crowned with thorns, and this wretch holds his head high against me and against his neighbors. He ought to be a humble lamb, but he has made himself a ram with pride for horns, goring everyone who comes near him.[82]

O unhappy man! You forget that you cannot escape from me. Is this the task I gave you, that you should gore me with the horns of your pride and assault both me and your neighbors? And that foolishness and abuse should be your converse with them? Is this the meekness in which you ought to go to celebrate the body and blood of Christ my Son? You have become like a ferocious beast without any fear of me. You devour your neighbors and thrive on dissension. You have taken to playing favorites, receiving those kindly who wait on you and serve your interests, who please you because they are living just as you are, whereas you ought to correct such people and discourage their sinfulness. But you do the opposite by giving them an example for doing worse. If you were good you would correct them, but because you are evil you do not know how to reprimand, nor do the sins of others even displease you.

You scorn the humble and virtuous poor and avoid them. And you have good reason to avoid them, even though you ought not. You avoid them because your stinking vice cannot stand virtue's fragrance. You consider it beneath you to be seen on the doorsteps of my poor. You avoid going to visit them in their need; you even see them dying of hunger and refuse to help them. This is all the work of the horns of pride that will not bow down in the least gesture of humility. Why not? Because they have not given up one ounce of the selfishness that nurtures pride, and therefore they are unwilling to condescend to help the poor with either temporal or material goods unless they are paid for it.

O accursed pride, outgrowth of selfish love! How you have blinded their mind's eye! They seem to themselves to be tender and loving, but you have made them cruel. They think they are gaining what they are actually losing. They think they have pleasures and riches and

---

82. Cf. Cavalca, "Life of St. Anthony, Abbot," ch. 3: " . . . the bellowing bull that threatens to gore one with its horns of pride."

253

great dignity, but their poverty and wretchedness is great because they have not the riches of virtue and have fallen from the heights of grace to the baseness of deadly sin. They think they see, but they are blind because they know neither themselves nor me. They do not know their condition nor the dignity I appointed them to; nor do they know the fragility and scant stability of the world, for if they did they would not make it their god. What has taken away their discernment? Pride. This is how they have become demons, whereas I had chosen them to be earthly angels in this life. And they have fallen from the light of heaven to the darkness of the abyss.[83]

So great has their darkness and wickedness become, and some of them are such incarnate devils, that they often pretend to consecrate [the Eucharist] while not consecrating at all for fear of my judgment and to relieve themselves of any restraint or fear in their wrongdoing. In the morning they get up from their indecency and in the evening from their inordinate eating and drinking. They have to satisfy the people, but when they consider their sinfulness they see that they neither should nor can celebrate with a good conscience. So the smallest glimmer of fear comes upon them—not from hatred for sin, but from their selfish love for their own selves.

Do you see, dearest daughter, how blind they are? They do not turn to heartfelt contrition and contempt for their sin and resolution to amend their ways. No, they choose this solution of not consecrating. Blind as they are, this last error and sin is greater than the first because they are making idolaters of the people by letting them adore this host that is not consecrated as the body and blood of Christ my only-begotten Son, wholly God and wholly human. For this is what it is when it is consecrated. But now it is nothing but bread.

Now you see how great an abomination this is and how great is my patience that I should put up with them.[84] But unless they change their ways every grace will turn into judgment for them.

But what should the people do so as to avoid such a predicament? They should add a qualification to their prayer: "If this celebrant has

---

83. The rendering I have given this sentence is a composite of the variant readings of S, E, F, C, none of which singly presents both poles of a characteristically Catherinian contrast: light:darkness::heaven:abyss. Each of these elements, however, is to be found in one or more of the manuscripts (C: *da l'altezza del cielo al basso della tenebre;* E: *de la luce del cielo nell' abisso*).

84. Cf. Dante, *Paradiso* 21:135. "O patience, what a load dost thou sustain!"

said what he ought to say, I truly believe that you are Christ, the Son of the true and living God,[85] given to me as food by the fire of your immeasurable charity and in memory of your most tender passion and the great blessing of your blood poured out with such burning love to wash away our sinfulness."[86] If they do this, the celebrant's blindness will not lead them into the darkness of adoring what is really something else, and although the wretched celebrant is guilty of sin, the guilt will be his alone.[87]

O sweetest daughter! What keeps the ground from swallowing up such ministers? What keeps my power from turning them into solid immobile statues before all the people to confound them?[88] My mercy. I restrain myself, that is, I restrain my divine justice with mercy in an effort to conquer them by the strength of mercy. But they, obstinate demons that they are, neither see nor recognize my mercy. It is as if they believed that what they have from me is their due, because pride has blinded them and they do not see that what they have is theirs only by grace and not because it is their due.

129

I have told you all this to give you more reason for bitter weeping over their blindness, over seeing them damned, and to give you a deeper knowledge of my mercy. In this mercy you can find trust and great security, offering to me these ministers of holy Church and the whole world, and begging me to be merciful to them. The more you offer me sorrowful and loving desires for them, the more you will prove your love for me. For the service neither you nor my other servants can do for me you ought to do for them instead. Then I will let myself be constrained by the longing and tears and prayers of my servants, and will

---

85. Cf. Mt. 16:16.

86. Cf. Mt. 26:27–28; Lk. 22:19–20.

87. The generality of the advice given here suggests that the practice referred to was not a rare occurrence. (In the liturgical custom of the day the celebrant bowed low over the bread and wine at the time of consecration, his back to the people, and whispered the words in Latin. Thus such a pretense was easy to hide.) Catherine herself experienced it personally when she was ill during her stay at Lucca in 1375. A priest, wishing to expose her, brought an unconsecrated host to her bedside in solemn procession. Catherine showed no sign of reverence, and when the priest rebuked her she in turn reprimanded him for making a jest of the sacrament and exposing herself and others to the possibility of idolatry.

88. Cf. Gn. 19:26.

be merciful to my bride by reforming her with good and holy shepherds.[89]

Once she is reformed with good shepherds, her subjects will certainly change their ways. For in a way, the guilt for the subjects' sins lies with their evil shepherds, because if the latter had reprimanded and if the pearl of justice had been luminous in their holy and honorable living, their subjects would not have behaved this way. But do you know what has come of their perversity? The one has followed in the footsteps of the other. The subjects are not obedient because their superiors were not obedient to their superiors. So they receive from their subjects just what they gave [their own superiors], and shepherd and subject alike are evil.

The cause of all this and of every other sin is pride founded in selfish love. Those who were foolish and proud as subjects are even more foolish and proud as superiors. So great is their foolishness that like blind men they give the office of priesthood to idiots who scarcely know how to read and could never pray the Divine Office. Such men, who because of their ignorance do not know the sacramental words well, will often not consecrate. So in their ignorance they commit the same sin as those who maliciously do not consecrate but only pretend to consecrate. Therefore, superiors ought to choose [for the priesthood] men who are learned and virtuous, and who know and understand what they are saying. But these wretches do the opposite. They are not concerned that a man be knowledgeable. They are not concerned about his age. In fact, it seems to give them pleasure to choose little boys instead of mature men. They are not concerned either that they be holy and honorable in their living, or that they know to what dignity they are coming or the great mystery[90] that is theirs to celebrate. They seem interested only in multiplying people, not virtue.[91] They are blind recruiters of the blind.[92] They do not see that in this as well as in other things I will demand an accounting from them at the moment of death. So after they have made priests so darksomely, they put them in charge of souls even though they see that they do not know how to take charge of themselves.

---

89. A reaffirmation of the principle introduced in ch. 3: Expiation is not a matter of deeds but of desire, that is, of love made more intense by the knowledge of evil (Cavallini).

90. E: "ministry."

91. Cf. Is. 9:3.

92. Cf. Mt. 15:14.

Now how can those who do not know their own sinfulness recognize and correct it in others? They are neither able nor willing to go against themselves. And the little sheep who have no shepherd who cares about them or knows how to guide them easily go astray and are often snatched and devoured by wolves.[93] Because the shepherds are evil they are not careful to have a dog that will bark when it sees the wolf coming. No, their dog is no better than themselves.[94] So these careless ministers and shepherds have neither the dog of conscience nor the rod of justice nor a staff for correcting. Their conscience does not bark to reproach them for their own sins, so they do not reprove the sheep either when they see them going astray and not keeping to the way of truth, not observing my commandments. But if this dog would bark and make them aware of their sins they would take up the rod of holy justice, rescue their sheep from the infernal wolf that wants to devour them, and they would return to the sheepfold.

But if the shepherd has no rod and no dog of conscience his sheep will perish. And he will not even be concerned, because the dog of his own conscience is so weakened for want of feeding that it cannot bark. And the food that must be given to this dog is the blood of the Lamb, my Son. For if the memory, as the vessel of the soul, is filled with the blood, conscience will be nourished by it. In other words, the remembrance of the blood sets the soul afire with hatred for sin and love for virtue, and this hatred and love cleanse the soul of the stain of deadly sin. This so invigorates conscience that it stands guard, and as soon as any enemy of the soul, that is, sin, wants to gain entrance (and not only the will but even the thought of it), conscience barks like a dog, excitedly, until it rouses reason. Thus the soul commits no injustice, because whoever has a conscience has justice.

But these evil men are unworthy to be called rational, much less ministers. Through their sins they have become filthy beasts. They have no dog, for one could say it has become so weakened they may as well have none. And therefore they have no rod of holy justice either. And their sins have made them so timid that they are afraid of their own shadows—not with a holy fear but slavishly. They ought to be readying themselves for death by rescuing souls from the devils' hands, but instead they put them there by not instructing them in good and

---

93. Cf. Jr. 23:1; Ezk. 34:5.
94. Cf. Is. 56:10.

holy living. Nor are they willing to endure a single abusive word for their salvation.

It may happen that one of their subjects is engulfed in very serious sins and deep in debt to others, but because of his inordinate desire not to impoverish his family he will not pay the debts. His ways are common knowledge to many folk and to the wretched priest as well. Nonetheless, they inform him so that, like the doctor he ought to be, he may take care of that soul. Then the wretch may set out to do his duty, but one abusive word or one hostile glance is enough to make him have nothing more to do with the affair. Or sometimes he may be bribed, so that between the bribe and his slavish fear he will surrender that soul to the devils' hands and continue to give him the sacrament of the body of Christ, my only-begotten Son. He sees and knows that that person has not thrown off the darkness of deadly sin. But in spite of that, to please wordly folk, and because of his perverse fear and their bribes, he gives such a one the sacraments and buries him with great honor in holy Church, whereas he ought to throw him out like a beast or a member cut off from the body.

What is the cause of this? Selfish love and its horns of pride. For if that priest had loved me more than anything else and loved the soul of that poor wretch, and had been fearlessly humble, he would have sought that soul's salvation.

You see, then, what great evil comes of these three vices I have set before you as three pillars whence proceed all other sins: pride, avarice, and impurity of mind and body. Your ears could never bear to hear how many evils come from these, as if they were members of the devil. And by their pride and indecency and greed they sometimes cause fearful scruples in those simple folk of good faith who hear of such sins. You have seen those who have been so affected. Fearing that they may be possessed by the devil they go to this wretched priest, believing that he can free them. It is a case of one devil casting out another.[95] But avaricious as he is he accepts their gifts, and like a wretched, dishonorable, lustful beast he tells these poor souls: "This is the only way you can be relieved of your sinfulness." Thus he makes them break their necks as he breaks his own.

O devil and worse than devil! In every way you have become worse than the devil! There are many devils who consider this sin

---

95. Cf. Mt. 12:24–27.

loathsome, but you who are worse than they wallow in it like a pig in the mire. O filthy beast! I ask you to expel demons from souls and bodies by the power of the blood whose minister I have made you, but you send them in instead! Do you not see that the axe of divine judgment is already set to the root of your tree?[96] I tell you, your sins are all gathering interest on your account till the appointed time and place, and unless you atone for them through heartfelt contrition and penance, your priesthood will not profit you at all; rather you will be miserably punished. You will bear the penalties for those others as well as for yourself, and you will be more cruelly tormented than they. Beware, then, of using the demon of greed to cast out demons! And beware of the other evil: that when persons bound in deadly sin come to you to be freed, you should bind them still more tightly by falling into sin with them in yet new ways.

If you recall, [daughter], you saw with your own eyes a person to whom this happened. Indeed, such a shepherd without a dog of conscience smothers the consciences of others as well as his own.

I have appointed [my priests] to sing psalms and hymns through the night by praying the Divine Office. But instead they have learned to cast spells and summon devils. Through the devil's trickery they make the creatures they love so sinfully come to them at midnight (though sometimes what seems to come really is not there). Now is this how I appointed you to spend the night watch? Certainly not. I willed that you should spend it in vigilant prayer, so that in the morning you would be prepared to celebrate [Mass] and give the people the fragrance of virtue, not the stench of vice. You were appointed to an angelic state so that you might keep company with the angels in holy meditation in this life, and in the end forever enjoy the sight of me together with them. But you find your pleasure in being a devil and keeping company with the devils even before the moment of death arrives.

But the horns of your pride have pierced through the pupil of most holy faith in your mind's eye, and so you have lost the light and cannot see how wretched you are. You do not really believe that every sin is punished and every good rewarded, for if you did you would not behave as you do. You would neither seek nor want the devil's company; in fact, you would be terrified even at the mention of his name. But

---

96. Cf. Mt. 3:10; Lk. 3:9.

because you follow his will you take delight in him and in his works. O blinder than blind! I wish you would ask the devil what pay he can offer you for the service you give him! He would answer that he will give you the same reward he himself has, for there is nothing else he can give but those excruciating torments and the fire in which he burns forever, into which he fell because of his pride from the heights of heaven. And you, earthly angel, are falling from the heights because of your pride—from priestly dignity and the treasure of virtue into the poverty of wretchedness and, unless you change your ways, into the depths of hell.

You have made the world and yourself your god and lord. Now talk to the world with all the pleasures you have taken from it in this life. And talk to that selfish sensuality of yours through which you have used this world's goods—in spite of the fact that I appointed you to the priesthood so that your sensuality should despise yourself and the world. So tell the world and your selfishness to give an accounting of you before me, the supreme Judge. They will answer that they cannot help you. They will make fun of you and say, "You will have to do that accounting for yourself." And there you will stand, before me and the world, confounded and disgraced.

You do not see how damned you are, because the horns of your pride have blinded you. But you will see it at the moment of death, and then you will not be able to take refuge in any virtue of yours, because you have none. Your only refuge will be my mercy, if you put your trust in that sweet blood whose minister you had been made. This [last refuge] will never be taken away from you or anyone else so long as you have the will to put your trust in the blood and in my mercy. But let no one be so foolhardy, nor you so blind, as to wait for that last moment.

Consider that at that last moment, if you have lived sinfully, the devils and the world and your own weakness will accuse you. They will not tempt you. They will not show you pleasure where there is bitterness, nor perfection in what is imperfect, nor light for darkness as they were in the habit of doing during your lifetime. In fact, they will show you the truth of reality. The dog of conscience that had been so weakened will begin to bark so incessantly that it will all but drive your soul to despair. But no one ought to despair. No, reach out trustingly for the blood, no matter what sins you have committed, for my mercy, which you receive in the blood, is incomparably greater than all the sins that have ever been committed in the world. But, as I have said, let no one dillydally, for it is a dreadful thing to be caught unarmed on the battlefield among so many enemies.

130

O dearest daughter, these wretches I have told you about pay no attention to these things. If they did, neither they nor the others would fall into such sins. Rather they would behave as those do who live virtuously, who choose death before they would willfully offend me and befoul the face of their souls and degrade the dignity to which I appointed them. Rather their souls' dignity and beauty would increase. Not that the dignity of the priesthood as such can be increased by virtue or lessened by sin. But the virtues give the soul an adornment and dignity beyond the simple beauty that is hers from the beginning when I created her in my image and likeness.

These [good priests] know the truth of my goodness and their own beauty and dignity because pride and selfish love have not clouded over or taken away the light of reason in them. They have given up [their pride] for love of me and the salvation of souls. But these other poor wretches, because they are entirely bereft of light, are not at all concerned that they are going from vice to vice till in the end they wind up in the ditch. And they make a barnyard of the temple of their souls and of the garden of holy Church.

O dearest daughter, how I detest this! Their houses ought to be gathering places for my servants and the poor. The bride they hold ought to be the breviary, and the books of Holy Scripture their children. There they should take their pleasure in sharing instruction with their neighbors and finding a holy life for themselves. But their houses are gathering places for evil and indecent people. Their bride is not the breviary (indeed, they have treated this bride, the breviary, like an adulteress) but a wretched she-devil who indecently lives with them. Their books are their brigade of children, and shamelessly they romp about with these children whom they have begotten in such brutish baseness.

On Sundays and solemn feasts, when they ought to be glorifying and praising my name in the Divine Office and offering me the incense of humble devoted prayers, they are playing and amusing themselves with their she-devils, and going about with seculars, trapping and fowling as if they were seculars or even courtly lords.

O wretched man! What has become of you? You ought to be hunting souls for the glory and praise of my name in the garden of holy

Church, and you are going about in the woods! But because you have become a beast, you harbor within your soul the animals of so many deadly sins. This is why you have become a trapper and fowler of beasts: because the orchard of your soul has become a wild tangle of brambles. That is why you have found your pleasure in wandering through deserted places looking for wild beasts.[97]

Blush for shame and look at your sins, for wherever you turn you have reason to be ashamed. But you are not ashamed, because you have lost all true and holy fear of me. Like a shameless whore you boast about your exalted position in the world and your fine family and your brigade of children. And if you have no children you are trying to have some so as to have heirs to leave behind. But you are a thieving bandit, because you know very well that your heirs are supposed to be none other than the poor and holy Church. O devil incarnate! Without any light you seek what you ought not to be seeking; you boast and brag about what ought to deeply confound you and make you ashamed in my presence (for I see your inmost heart) and in the presence of all creation. You are confused, but the horns of your pride keep you from seeing your confusion.

O dearest daughter, I set them on the bridge on my Truth's teaching to serve you pilgrims with the sacraments of holy Church, and they are instead in the wretched river beneath the bridge, and there in the river of worldly pleasures and baseness they exercise their ministry. They are not even aware that the wave of death is upon them and that they are being carried along together with their lords the devils whose servants they have been and whom they have allowed to guide them along the path of the river without any anchor-hold. Unless they change their ways they will be swept on to eternal damnation with such reproach that your tongue could never describe it. And it will be much worse for them as priests than for seculars. The very same sin is punished more severely in them than in others whose calling was in the world. And their enemies will rise up to accuse them more reproachfully at the moment of death.

131

I have told you how the world and the devils and their own selfish sensuality accuse them, and this is the truth. Now I want to tell you more at length about the fate of these wretches, so that you may have

97. Cf. Mt. 12:43-45.

greater compassion for them, for the struggles allotted to the souls of the just are far different from those of sinners, and so is their death. The death of the just is so much more peaceful in proportion to their perfection.

I want you to know, then, that the will is the seat of all the pain people suffer, for if the will is fully in accord with my will there is no pain in suffering. Not that the soul is relieved of all burdens, but to the will that carries them willingly for love of me they are not painful because there is gladness in carrying what is seen to be my will. Because of the holy contempt such souls have for themselves, they have declared war on the world, the devil, and their selfish sensuality. So when they come to the moment of death they die in peace because they have conquered their lifelong enemies. The world cannot accuse them because they recognized its deceitfulness and therefore renounced the world and all its pleasures. Their frail sensuality and body do not accuse them because they treated it as a servant under the restraint of reason, making their flesh pliable with penance and vigils and constant humble prayer. Their selfish will they slew with hatred and contempt for sin and love for virtue. They totally destroyed the tender loving bond between body and soul that naturally makes death seem hard and fearsome.

The virtue of the just goes beyond nature, for this natural fear is extinguished in them. Their holy contempt and their desire to return to their goal is so strong that this natural tenderness cannot do battle against them, and their conscience is quiet because during their lifetime it was a good watchdog, barking whenever enemies came by with a will to capture the city of the soul. Just as a dog stationed at the gate barks when it sees enemies, and by its barking wakes up the guards, so this dog of conscience would wake up the guard of reason, and reason together with free choice would discern by the light of understanding who was a friend and who an enemy. To friends, that is, the virtues and holy thoughts of the heart, they would give warm affectionate love by exercising them with great care. To enemies, that is, vice and perverse thoughts, they would deal out hatred and contempt, striking them down with the sword of hatred and love by reason's light and free choice's hand. So at the moment of death their conscience does not gnaw but rests peacefully because it has been a good watchdog.

It is true that the soul, in humility and because at the time of death she better appreciates the value of time and the precious gems of virtue, reproaches herself because it seems to her that she has made poor use of her time. But this is not a distressing pain but one that fattens the soul,[98] for it makes her gather everything together within her, putting herself in the presence of the blood of the humble spotless Lamb, my Son. She does not turn back to look at her past virtues because she does not want to place her trust in them but only in the blood wherein my mercy is to be found. And just as she lived mindful of the blood, so in death she is immersed and inebriated in the blood. The devils cannot reproach her for sin because in her lifetime she conquered their malice with wisdom, but now they come around to see whether they can still make some small gain. So they come in horrible forms to frighten her with their hideously foul appearance and with all sorts of fantasies. But because there is none of sin's venom in the soul, their appearance does not frighten her as it would someone else who had lived sinfully in the world.

When the devils see that the soul has entered into the blood ablaze with charity, they cannot bear it, but from far off they keep shooting their arrows. But their fighting and screaming does no harm to that soul, for she has already begun to taste eternal life. Her mind's eye with its pupil of most holy faith sees me, her infinite eternal reward whom she is waiting to possess—not because she deserves it but as a gift of my grace in the blood of Christ my Son. So she stretches out her arms of hope and reaches out for it with the hands of love, entering into possession even before she is actually there. And as soon as she has passed through the narrow gate of the Word, immersed in his blood, she comes to me, the sea of peace. For we are joined as one: I the sea with him the gate, because I and my Truth, my only-begotten Son, are one and the same thing.

What happiness it is to the soul to see herself so gently brought to this passing! For she tastes the joy of the angels, and because she has lived in charity for her neighbors, she shares the joy of all those who are truly joyful in loving one another. Such is the reward of those who so gently pass over. But it is even greater for my ministers who have lived like angels. For they lived in this life with deeper knowledge and more intense hunger for my honor and the salvation of souls. I am not speaking simply of the light of virtue, which everyone in general can have. These, once they had attained the light of virtuous living, which

---

98. Cf. Dante, *Paradiso* 10, 94–96: "I was a lamb of the holy flock, obeying/that Dominic, who hath a pathway shown,/where good is fattening, if there be no straying." (Dante, however, uses *s'impingua*, whereas Catherine uses *ingrassa*.)

is a light beyond nature, went on to attain the light of learning by which they came to know more of my Truth. Now those who know more love more, and those who love more receive more. What you deserve is meted out to you according to the measure of your love.[99]

And if you should ask me whether others who are not learned can attain this degree of love, [I would answer that] although it is possible, exceptional cases do not dictate the general rule, and I am speaking to you in generalities. In fact, their dignity is greater in virtue of their priesthood because I have directly entrusted to them the task of eating souls for my honor. Although all of you have the duty of warmly loving your neighbors, to my priests is entrusted the ministry of the blood and the care of souls, and if they do this conscientiously with love for virtue they receive more than others do.

Oh, how blissful are their souls when they reach the moment of death! Because they proclaimed and defended the faith for their neighbors, it has become incarnate for them in the marrow of their souls. It is with this faith that they see their place in me. They lived in hope, trusting in my providence and not at all in themselves or in their own knowledge. And because they ceased trusting in themselves they were not inordinately attached to any created person or thing and so lived in voluntary poverty. Therefore [at the moment of death], this hope of theirs reaches out toward me with great joy.

Their hearts were vessels of affection that carried my name.[100] They proclaimed it with burning love, both by the example of their good and holy living and by their teaching of the word to their neighbors. So now this heart of theirs rises up with unspeakable love and with this thrust of love seizes me, its goal. It brings to me the pearl of justice, which it had always kept in sight by being just to everyone and doing its duty with discernment. Therefore it offers me the justice of true humility and glory and praise for my name in thanks to me for the grace to have run its course with a pure and holy conscience. But to itself it offers indignation, considering itself unworthy to have received and still be receiving such grace.

Their conscience bears them good witness to me,[101] and in justice

---

99. Cf. Mt. 7:2.
100. Cf. Ac. 9:15. It is interesting to note here how Catherine's allusion probably reflects her hearing rather than reading of this particular passage. The Latin *vas electionis* (Italian *vassello d'elezione*) is heard as *vas delectionis* (Italian *vassello di dilezione*).
101. Cf. Rm. 9:1.

I reward it with the crown of justice[102] adorned with pearls of virtue, that is, the fruit their charity has drawn from the virtues.

O earthly angel! Blessed are you that you have not been ungrateful for the benefits you have received from me, and that you have not been guilty of negligence or foolishness. Conscientiously and with true light you kept your eyes on your subjects, and as a faithful, courageous shepherd you followed the teaching of the true good shepherd, the gentle Christ Jesus my only-begotten Son. This is why you are now passing through him [the gate] so regally, immersed and bathed in his blood, with your herd of little sheep. For by your holy teaching and life you have led many of them to everlasting life, preserved many of them in grace.

O dearest daughter, the sight of the devils cannot harm these souls. Because of the sight of me, which they see in faith and possess in love, and because there is none of the venom of sin in them, this darksome terror can neither harm nor frighten them. They have no slavish fear but only holy fear. So they are not afraid of the devils' delusions; because of the supernatural light of grace and the light of Holy Scripture, they recognize them for what they are and they suffer neither darkness nor spiritual distress from them. Thus gloriously they pass, bathed in the blood, hungry for the salvation of souls, all ablaze with charity for their neighbors, coming through the gate of the Word and entering into me. And my goodness assigns them their places, measuring out to all according to the measure of loving charity they have brought to me.

132

O dearest daughter, it does not go nearly so well with those other miserable wretches of whom I have told you. How darksome and terrifying is their death! At the moment of death the demons accuse them with such terrifying and darksome faces—and you know how horrible they are—that a person would choose any suffering that can be endured in this life rather then endure this sight. Even the sting of their conscience is reawakened and gnaws away at them pitilessly. They had made their selfish sensuality and perverse pleasures lord over their reason, and now these miserably accuse them. For now they know the truth about what they did not discern before, and they are deeply confounded over their error. They lived their lives like infidels,

---

102. Cf. 2 Tm. 4:8.

unfaithful to me, because their selfish love had covered over that pupil which is the light of most holy faith. And now the devil taunts them with their infidelity in order to lead them to despair.

Oh, how hard this struggle is for them! For it finds them unarmed, without the weapon of loving charity. As members of the devils, they have completely lost it. So they have neither the supernatural light of grace nor that of learning. They never understood learning because the horns of pride kept them from tasting its sweet marrow. And now in these great struggles they do not know what to do. They were never nourished in hope because they put their trust not in me or in the blood whose steward I had made them, but only in themselves and in worldly honors and pleasures. They did not see, these wretched devils incarnate, that everything was theirs only on loan, and that as debtors they have to give an accounting to me. Now they find themselves naked and virtueless, and wherever they turn they hear nothing but great confounding reproach.

The injustice they practiced during their lifetime so accuses their conscience that they dare not ask for anything but justice. I tell you, their shame and confusion is so great that their only hope is to put their trust in my mercy if only this one time in their whole life. Granted, because of their sins it is really presumptuous, for those who have used the arm of mercy to offend can hardly call this putting their trust in mercy. It is more presumption that trust, but at least they have accepted mercy's action. Thus, if when they come to the point of death they acknowledge their sin and unload their conscience in holy confession, the offensiveness of their presumptuousness is removed and what remains is mercy. With this mercy they gain access to hope if only they are willing. If this were not the case there is no one who would not despair, and despair would bring eternal damnation with the devils.

Thus does my mercy work to bring them to hope during their lifetime. I do not do this to give them leave to abuse my mercy but so that charity and the consideration of my goodness may make them open up. But these wretches abuse my mercy to the full, for they use the hope my mercy has given them to sin against me. Still I keep them in hope of my mercy so that at the point of death they will have something to take hold of and will not be completely crushed by their reproach and so end in despair. For this sin of ultimate despair is much more displeasing to me and harmful to them than all the other evils they have committed. And this is why: Other sins are committed with some selfish sensual pleasure, and sometimes they are regretted, and they can be regretted in such a way that the regret will win my mercy. But the motive for despair is not weakness, because there is to be found in it no pleasure but only intolerable pain. Despair spurns my mercy by considering one's sinfulness greater than my goodness and mercy. So once one has fallen into this sin there is no repentance, no true sorrow for having offended me (as one should be sorry). True, there is sorrow for one's own damnation but none for the offense done to me. Thus, the end is eternal damnation.

So you see, this single sin is what leads them to hell, and in hell they are tormented for this and for all the other sins they have committed. If they had repented in sorrow for having offended me and had put their trust in my mercy, they would have found mercy. For, as I have told you, my mercy is incomparably greater than all the sins anyone could commit. Thus it displeases me greatly when they consider their sins to be greater, and this is that sin which is not forgiven either here or hereafter.[103] Because despair displeases me so much it is my will that they should put their trust in my mercy even at the point of death, after they have spent their life in wickedness. So while they are still alive I use this gentle trick to make them put immense trust in my mercy. For if they are nurtured within this hope, when they come to die and hear those harsh reproaches, they will not be as inclined to let go of it as they would be if they had not been nurtured in it.

All this is given them by the fiery abyss of my unspeakable charity. But because they have abused it with their darksome selfish love, the source of all sin, they have not known it in truth. This is why, so far as their will is concerned, the gentleness of my mercy is for them considered a great presumption. And this is another reproach their conscience gives them through the appearance of the demons: that the time and generosity of my mercy in which they had put their trust should have made them open up in charity and love for virtue, and thus virtuously spend the time that I in my love had given them; but they used that time and that expansive trust in my mercy to sin miserably against me.

O blind and worse than blind! You buried the pearl, the talent I had entrusted to you so that you might realize a profit from it. You, presumptuous as you were, chose not to do my will. You buried your

---

103. Cf. Mt. 12:32.

268

talent in the earth of your perverse self-centered selfishness, and now it is giving you its return in the fruit of death.[104]

O you wretch! How great is the punishment you are receiving now in the end! And your wretchedness is not hidden from you, for the worm of your conscience is no longer asleep, but is gnawing away.[105] The devils are screaming at you and giving you the wages they are in the habit of giving to their servants: confusion and reproach. And to prevent your escaping from their hands at the point of death, they want to bring you to despair. This is why they confound you, so that later they can share with you what is theirs by right.

O wretch! The dignity I appointed you to shows itself luminous as it is for your shame, knowing that you have kept and used it in such sinful darkness. The Church's goods remind you that you are a debtor and a thief, and ought to have given what you owed to the poor and to holy Church. Next your conscience reminds you that it was on public prostitutes that you spent those goods, and on supporting your children and enriching your relatives, and you swallowed them up in feasting, on adornments for your house, on all sorts of silver vessels. And you should have been living in voluntary poverty.

Your conscience displays before you the Divine Office, which you set aside, not caring that you were falling into deadly sin. Even if you said it with your mouth, your heart was far from me.[106] You ought to have had charity for your subjects and hunger for nurturing them in virtue, giving them the example of your own life, disciplining them with the hand of mercy and the rod of justice. But because you did just the opposite, your conscience reproaches you in the horrible appearance of the demons.

And you who have been in authority: If you have been unjust in bestowing high office on your subjects or in putting them in charge of others, if you have been careless in your appointments, all this now comes before your conscience. For flattering words and human respect should not have ruled you in this, but only regard for virtue and my honor and the salvation of souls. And because you did wrong in this, you are being reproached for it. It will be to your greater suffering and

---

104. Cf. Mt. 25:14–30.
105. Cf. Is. 66:24; Mk. 9:43–48.
106. Mt. 15:8; Is. 29:13.

confusion to have what you have wrongly done and wrongly left un-
done set before your conscience in the light of understanding.

I want you to know, dearest daughter, that white is more clearly
seen next to black, and black next to white. This is how it happens to
these wretches—all of them in general, but especially to these [evil
ministers]. Just as the just begin to see their happiness more clearly at
death, so these wretched souls are presented with the sight of their evil
lives. There is no need for anyone else to show them, for their own
conscience sets before them the sins they have committed and the virtues they ought to have practiced. Why the virtues? So as to shame
them the more. For when vice and virtue are set side by side, vice is
better known [for what it is] in contrast to virtue, and the more they
know this the more ashamed they are. And in contrast to their sinfulness they are more aware of how perfect virtue is. Thus their grief is
the greater because they see that their lives are lacking in any virtue.

And I want you to know that because of this knowledge they have
of virtue and vice they see all too well the reward that follows the virtuous and the punishment that follows those who have wallowed in the
darkness of deadly sin.

I grant this knowledge not to lead them to despair but to lead them
to perfect self-knowledge and hope-filled shame over their sinfulness
so that they may atone for their sins with discerning shame and placate
my wrath by humbly asking for mercy.

As for the virtuous, it intensifies their joy and their knowledge of
my charity, for they attribute to me, not to themselves, the grace of
having followed virtue and walked in the way of my Truth. Therefore
they exult in me. With this true knowledge they receive and enjoy
their gracious end, in the way I have told you of elsewhere.[107] So these
just who have lived in burning charity exult in joy, while the darksome
wicked are confounded in pain. The darksome sight of the demons
does not bother or frighten the just; only sin can cause them fear and
harm. But those whose lives have been guided by lust and wickedness
find fear and hurt in the sight of the demons. Not the hurt of despair,
unless they so choose, but the pain of reproach and the reawakening of
conscience, and fear and fright at the demons' horrible appearance.

See, then, dearest daughter, how different are the pain and struggle the just and the wicked experience in death, and how different are
their ends. I have described for you and shown to your mind's eye only

---

107. Cf. ch. 41.

the smallest bit—so little as to be almost nothing in comparison with the reality of the punishment of the one and the reward of the other.

Now you see how blind people are, especially these wretches, for because they have received more from me and been more enlightened by Holy Scripture, they are so much the more obligated. So they reap more unbearable confusion. Because they knew more of Holy Scripture in their lifetime, in death they know more clearly how greatly they have sinned and are allotted greater torment than others, just as the lot of good [ministers] is more magnificent.

It happens to them as it does to unfaithful Christians who are allotted greater torment in hell than are pagans, because they had the light of faith and renounced it, whereas the pagans never had it. Just so, these evil ministers will be more severely punished than other Christians who were guilty of the very same sin, because of the ministry I entrusted to them when I made them stewards of the sun of the holy sacrament, and because they had the light of learning by which to discern the truth for themselves as well as for others if they had so chosen. It is therefore just that they should be more severely punished.

But these wretches do not know this. For if they had the least regard for their position they would never have come to such an evil pass. They would have been what they should have been. But they are not. Indeed, the whole world is corrupt, and they behave much more badly than their worldly peers. With their filthiness they defile the face of their own souls and corrupt their subjects and suck the blood of my bride, holy Church. By their sins they have left her pallid. The loving charity they ought to have had for this bride they lavished on themselves, thinking of nothing but snitching her grapes one by one,[108] taking her high offices and lucrative positions when they should have been seeking after souls. Thus their evil lives lead the laity (though these are not thereby excused) to irreverence and disobedience toward holy Church.

133

I could tell you of a great many sins, but I do not want to pour any more filth into your ears. I have told you this much to respond to your

---

108. The verb *piluccare* has the literal sense of picking grapes off the vine one by one and nibbling them as one goes. The imagery thus ties in with that of the Church as vineyard and wine cellar of the blood of Christ, of which the clergy are meant to be tenders and stewards.

desire, and to make you more concerned to offer me tenderly grieving and loving desires on their behalf. I have told you as well about the dignity in which I have established them, and about the treasure, the holy sacrament (wholly God and wholly human) that is administered to you by their hands. I gave you the figure of the sun so that you might see that no sin of theirs can lessen the power of this sacrament, and that therefore it is not my will that they should be treated with less reverence. I showed you also the superb state of my virtuous ministers in whom the pearl of virtue and holy justice shines resplendent. I showed you how displeased I am with the sin of those who persecute holy Church, what disrespect they show for the blood. When they persecute [my ministers] I regard it as done not against them but against the blood, for I have forbidden anyone to touch my christs.[109]

Now I have told you about their pernicious lives and how wretchedly they live, what pain and confusion they suffer in death and how much more cruelly than any others they are tormented after death. So I have kept my promise. I have granted you what you asked when you wanted me to keep the promise I had made to you.

Now I repeat that, in spite of all their sins and even if they were worse yet, I do not want any secular powers meddling in the business of punishing them. If they do, their sin will not go unpunished unless they themselves atone for it with heartfelt contrition and conversion. Both the one and the other are devils incarnate: In divine justice the one devil punishes the other, but both are guilty of sin. The secular has no excuse in the sin of the cleric, nor the cleric in the sin of the secular.

Now, dearest daughter, I invite you and all my other servants to weep over these dead. Be as little sheep in the garden of holy Church, grazing there in holy longing and constant prayer. Offer these to me on their behalf so that I may be merciful to the world. Do not let either assault or prosperity cause you to abandon this grazing. I mean, I do not want you to raise your heads either in impatience or in inordinate gladness. Rather, be humbly attentive to my honor, the salvation of souls, and the reform of holy Church. This will be a sign to me that you and the others love me in truth. You know well, for I have shown you, that I want you and the others to be little sheep who graze contin-

---

109. Cf. Ps. 105:15.

ually in the garden of holy Church, putting up with weariness right up to the moment of death. If you do this, I will fulfill your longings.

134

T hen that soul was like one drunk with restlessness and on fire with love, her heart cut through with bitter sorrow. So she turned to the supreme eternal Goodness and said:

O eternal God, light surpassing all other light because all light comes forth from you! O fire surpassing every fire because you alone are the fire that burns without consuming! You consume whatever sin and selfishness you find in the soul. Yet your consuming does not distress the soul but fattens her with insatiable love, for though you satisfy her she is never sated but longs for you constantly. The more she possesses you the more she seeks you, and the more she seeks and desires you the more she finds and enjoys you, high eternal fire, abyss of charity!

O supreme eternal Good! What moved you, infinite God, to enlighten me, your finite creature, with the light of your truth? You yourself, the very fire of love, you yourself are the reason. For it always has been and always is love that constrains you to create us in your own image and likeness, and to show us mercy by giving your creatures infinite and immeasurable graces.

O Goodness surpassing all goodness! You alone are supremely good, yet you gave us the Word, your only-begotten Son, to keep company with us, though we are filth and darksomeness. What was the reason for this? Love. For you loved us before we existed. O good, o eternal greatness, you made yourself lowly and small to make us great! No matter where I turn, I find nothing but your deep burning charity.

Can I, wretch that I am, repay the graces and burning charity you have shown and continue to show, such blazing special love beyond the general love and charity you show to all your creatures? No, only you, most gentle loving Father, only you can be my acknowledgment and my thanks. The affection of your very own charity will offer you thanks, for I am she who is not. And if I should claim to be anything of myself, I should be lying through my teeth! I should be a liar and a daughter of the devil, who is the father of lies.[110] For you alone are who you are, and whatever being I have and every other gift of mine I

---

110. Cf. Jm. 8:44, 58.

have from you, and you have given it all to me for love, not because it was my due.

O most gentle Father, when the human race lay sick with Adam's sin you sent as doctor the gentle loving Word, your Son.[111] Now, when I lie sick in the weakness of my foolish indifference, you, God eternal, most mild and gentle doctor, have given me a medicine at once mildly sweet and bitter so that I may be healed and rise up from my weakness. It is mild to me because you have shown yourself to me with your mild charity. It is sweeter than sweet to me because you have enlightened my mind's eye with the light of most holy faith. In this light, as you have been pleased to reveal it, I have come to know what dignity and grace you have bestowed on the human race by administering [to us your Son], wholly God and wholly human, in the mystic body of holy Church, and I have come to know the dignity of the ministers you have appointed to administer you to us.

I was hoping you would keep the promise you had made me, and you gave me so much more, giving me what I did not even know how to ask for. So I really know in truth that the human heart does not so much as know how to desire or ask for all that you give. Thus I see that you are who you are, infinite eternal Good, and we are the ones who are not. And since you are infinite and we finite, you give what is too great for your creatures either to know how or be able to desire. [We cannot imagine] how you know how and are able and want to satisfy our souls and fill them with things we have not asked for, nor how gently and pleasantly you give them. This is how I have come to receive light in your generous charity as you have revealed your love for the whole human race and especially for your anointed ones who ought to be earthly angels in this life. You have revealed the virtue and blessedness of those anointed ones of yours who have lived in holy Church as lamps alight with the pearl of justice. Because of this I have better understood the sinfulness of those who live in wickedness, and so I have conceived a tremendous grief for the offense done to you and the harm done to all the world, for they do harm the world by being mirrors of evil whereas they ought to be mirrors of virtue. Because you have revealed this to me, the wretched cause and instrument of so many sins, and lamented over their iniquity, I have found unbearable sorrow.

Immeasurable Love! By revealing this you have given me a bitter-

---

111. Cf. Mt. 9:12; Lk. 5:31.

sweet medicine so that I might rise up once and for all from the sickness of foolish indifference and run to you with concern and eager longing. You would have me know myself and your goodness, and the sins committed against you by every class of people and especially by your ministers, so that I might draw tears from the knowledge of your infinite goodness and let them flow as a river over my wretched self and over these wretched living dead. Therefore it is my will, ineffable Fire, joyous Love, eternal Father, that my desire should never weary of longing for your honor and the salvation of souls. And I beg you, let my eyes never rest, but in your grace make of them two rivers for the water that flows from you, the sea of peace. Thank you, thank you, Father! In granting me both what I asked of you and what I did not ask because I did not know how, you have given me both the invitation and the reason to weep and to offer tender, loving, tormented longings in your presence with constant humble prayer.

Now, I beg you, be merciful to the world and to holy Church. I am asking you to grant what you are making me ask. Alas for my wretched sorrowful soul, the cause of all evil! Do not delay any longer in granting your mercy to the world; bow down and fulfill the longing of your servants. Alas! It is you who make them cry out: so listen to their voices. Your Truth said that we should call and we would be answered, that we should knock and the door would be opened for us, that we should ask and it would be given to us.[112] O eternal Father, your servants are calling to you for mercy. Answer them then. I know well that mercy is proper to you, so you cannot resist giving it to whoever asks you for it. Your servants are knocking at the door of your Truth. They are knocking because in your Truth, your only-begotten Son, they have come to know your unspeakable love for humankind. Therefore your burning charity neither can nor should hold back from opening to those who knock with perseverance.

Open, then, unlock and shatter the hardened hearts of your creatures. If you will not do it for their failure to knock, do it because of your infinite goodness and for love of your servants who are knocking at your door for them. Grant it, eternal Father, because you see how they stand at the door of your Truth and ask.[113] And for what are they asking? For the blood of this door, your Truth. In this blood you have

---

112. Mt. 7:7; Lk. 11:19.
113. Cf. Rv. 3:20.

washed away iniquity and drained the pus of Adam's sin.[114] His blood is ours because you have made of it a bath for us, and you neither can nor will refuse it to those who ask it of you in truth. Give then the fruit of the blood to these creatures of yours. Put into the scales the price of your Son's blood so that the infernal demons may not carry off your little sheep. Oh, you are a good shepherd to have given us your only-begotten Son to be our true shepherd who in obedience to you laid down his life for your little sheep[115] and made of his blood a bath for us. It is this blood that your servants, hungry as they are, are asking for at this door. They are asking you through this blood to be merciful to the world and make holy Church blossom again with the fragrant flowers of good holy shepherds whose perfume will dispel the stench of the putrid evil flowers.

You said, eternal Father, that because of your love for your creatures, and through the prayers and innocent sufferings of your servants, you would be merciful to the world and reform holy Church, and thus give us refreshment.[116] Do not wait any longer, then, to turn the eye of your mercy. Because it is your will to answer us before we call, answer now with the voice of your mercy.

Open the door of your immeasurable charity, which you have given us in the door of the Word.[117] Yes, I know that you open before we knock, because your servants knock and call out to you with the very love and affection you gave them, seeking your honor and the salvation of souls. Give them then the bread of life, the fruit of the blood of your only-begotten Son, which they are begging of you for the glory and praise of your name and for the salvation of souls. For it would seem you would receive more glory and praise by saving so many people than by letting them stubbornly persist in their hardness. To you, eternal Father, everything is possible. Though you created us without our help, it is not your will to save us without our help. So I beg you to force their wills and dispose them to want what they do not want. I ask this of your infinite mercy. You created us out of nothing. So, now that we exist, be merciful and remake the vessels you created and formed in your image and likeness; re-form them to grace in the mercy and blood of your Son.[118]

---

114. Cf. Rv. 1:5.
115. Jn. 10:11.
116. Cf. ch. 15.
117. Cf. Jn. 10:7.
118. Cf. Rm. 9:20–23.

DIVINE PROVIDENCE

135

T hen the high eternal Father turned the eye of his mercy toward her with ineffable kindness, as if to show her that in all things his providence for humankind never fails anyone who is willing to receive it. And he uttered a tender complaint about humankind, saying:

O my dearest daughter, as I have told you so often, I want to be merciful to the world and provide for my reasoning creatures' every need. But the foolish take for death what I give for life, and are thus cruel to themselves. I always provide, and I want you to know that what I have given humankind is supreme providence. It was with providence that I created you, and when I contemplated my creature in myself I fell in love with the beauty of my creation. It pleased me to create you in my image and likeness with great providence. I provided you with the gift of memory so that you might hold fast my benefits and be made a sharer in my own, the eternal Father's power. I gave you understanding so that in the wisdom of my only-begotten Son you might comprehend and know what I the eternal Father want, I who gave you graces with such burning love. I gave you a will to love, making you a sharer in the Holy Spirit's mercy, so that you might love what your understanding sees and knows.[1]

All this my gentle providence did, only that you might be capable of understanding and enjoying me and rejoicing in my goodness by seeing me eternally. And as I have told you many times,[2] I wanted to make it possible for you to reach this goal. Heaven had been closed because of Adam's sin. He did not know his own dignity, considering

---

1. Cf. ch. 51.
2. Cf. ch. 21ff.; 26ff.

with what ineffable love and providence I had created him. So he fell into disobedience, and from disobedience into impurity, because of pride and his desire to please a woman. For he was so concerned about pleasing and bowing to his companion, even though he did not believe what she said, that he consented to disobey my command rather than offend her. And this disobedience has been and is the source of all the evils that have come after it. All of you have been infected with this venom. (Later I shall tell you how dangerous this disobedience is so as to recommend obedience to you.) So, to take away this death, dearest daughter, I gave humankind the Word, my only-begotten Son, thus providing for your need with great prudence and providence.

I say "with prudence" because with the bait of your humanity and the hook of my divinity I caught the devil, who could not recognize my Truth. This Truth, the incarnate Word, came to destroy and put an end to his lie, which he had used to deceive humankind.

Just think, dearest daughter! I could have used no greater prudence and providence than to give you the Word, my only-begotten Son. On him I imposed a great obedience in order to draw out the venom that through disobedience had befallen the human race. Thus he, in love as he was and truly obedient, ran to his shameful death on the most holy cross, and by his death gave you life, not by the power of humanity but by the power of my Godhead. For I in my providence had joined my Godhead, the divine nature, with your human nature to make satisfaction for the sin that had been committed against me, infinite Goodness. That sin demanded infinite satisfaction. In order to make satisfaction to me (because I am infinite), and for past, present, and future humanity, human nature, which had sinned and was finite, had to be united with something infinite. Now no matter how greatly people sin they can find perfect satisfaction if they are willing to return to me during their lifetime, because you have received perfect satisfaction through that union of my Godhead with your humanity. This was the work of my providence, that through a finite deed (for the Word's suffering on the cross was finite) you have received infinite fruit by the power of the Godhead.

I, God your Father, the eternal Trinity, in my infinite eternal providence, saw to it that humankind was reclothed when you had lost the garment of innocence and were stripped of all virtue and perishing from hunger and dying from the cold in this life of pilgrimage. You were subjected to every sort of misery. The gate of heaven had been locked and you had lost all hope of attaining it. If you could only have taken hold of this hope it would have been a comfort for you in this life. But you did not have it, and great was your distress. But, I, supreme providence, saw to this need of yours. Constrained not by any justice or virtue of yours but by my own goodness, I clothed you anew in the person of this gentle loving Word, my only-begotten Son. He, by stripping himself of life, clothed you anew in innocence and grace.[3] You receive this innocence and grace in holy baptism by the power of the blood that washes away the stain of original sin in which you were conceived, which you contracted from your father and your mother.

My providence provides for this not with bodily pain as was the custom in Old Testament circumcision, but with the gentleness of holy baptism. Thus have you been clothed anew. I made you warm again when my only-begotten Son revealed to you through his pierced body the fire of my charity hidden under the ashes of your humanity. And would this not warm the frozen human heart? Yes, unless it is so obstinate and blinded by selfishness that it does not see how unspeakably much I love you.

My providence has given you food to strengthen you while you are pilgrim travelers in this life. And I have so weakened your enemies that no one but you yourself can harm you. The road is cemented with the blood of my Truth so that you may reach the end for which I created you.

And what food is this? It is the body and blood of Christ crucified, wholly God, wholly human, the food of angels and the food of life. It is a food that satisfies the hungry soul who finds joy in this bread, but not those who are not hungry, for it is a food that must be taken with the mouth of holy desire and tasted in love. So you see how I have provided for your strengthening.

136

I have also given you the solace of hope, if only you will contemplate in the light of most holy faith the price of the blood that has been paid for you and that gives you firm hope and assurance of salvation. Through the disgrace of Christ crucified I have given you honor. For while you have offended me with all the members of your body, the blessed Christ my most gentle Son has borne the worst of torments in his whole body, and by his obedience has dispelled your disobedience.

---

3. Cf. Ga. 3:27.

From his obedience you have all contracted grace, just as you had all contracted blame from disobedience.[4]

This is the gift of my providence, which has seen to your need for salvation in so many different ways from the beginning of the world until today, and will continue to do so right up to the end. I, the true and just doctor, give you whatever I see your weakness needs to make you perfectly healthy and to keep you healthy. My providence will never fail those who want to receive it. Whoever wants to experience my goodness in my providence has only to look at those who hope in me, who knock and call out not just with words but with love enlightened by most holy faith. I do not mean those who knock and shout only with empty words, calling out to me, "Lord! Lord!" I tell you, unless they make their requests of me with some other virtue, I will acknowledge them not with mercy but with justice.[5] So I tell you, my providence will not fail those who truly hope in me, but it will fail those who hope not in me but in themselves.

You know that it is impossible to put your trust in two contradictory things. This is what my Truth meant in the holy Gospel when he said, "No one can serve two masters. For if you serve the one, the other will despise you."[6] There is no service without hope, for servants serve in the hope of pleasing their master or at least in the hope of receiving some payment and profit. They would never serve their master's enemy. Such service would be hopeless, leaving the servants deprived of what they had expected to receive from their master. Consider, then, dearest daughter, how it goes with the soul. Either she must serve and hope in me, or she will serve and hope in the world and herself. Insofar as she serves the world with a sensual service apart from me she is serving and loving her own selfish sensuality, hoping to find sensual pleasure and profit in this love and service. But because her hope is set on empty finite passing things, her hope will fail her and she will never, in effect, attain what she desires. So long as she hopes in herself and in the world she will not put her trust in me. For worldly desires are despicable to me, so hateful to me that I gave up my only-begotten Son to the shameful death of the cross. The world has nothing in common

---

4. Cf. Rm. 5:19.

5. Cf. Mt. 7:21–23; Lk. 6:46; Mt. 25:11–12.

6. Cf. Mt. 6:24; Lk. 16:13. This is the second time Catherine cites this passage, both times making the servant the object of the second master's contempt, whereas in the Gospel text the master is the object.

with me, nor I with it. But the soul who perfectly hopes in me and serves me with her whole heart and will must necessarily put no hope in herself or in the world or in her own weakness.[7]

This true and perfect hope is more or less perfect in proportion to the soul's love for me, and thus she experiences my providence more or less perfectly. Those who serve me in the simple hope of pleasing me receive and enjoy it more perfectly than those who serve in hope of the reward or pleasure they might find in me.

The former are those in the final spiritual stage, whose perfection I have described for you. The others are those of the second and third stages, whose hope is set on pleasure and reward, the imperfect ones of whom I told you when I was speaking of the stages of the soul.[8]

But in no way will my providence ever fail either the perfect or the imperfect, so long as they do not become presumptuous or put their trust in themselves. Presumption and trust in oneself, because they come from selfish love, darken the mind's eye by depriving it of the light of most holy faith. Then the soul walks without the light of reason and therefore does not discern my providence. Not that she does not experience it. There is no one, just or sinner, for whom I do not provide. I created and made everything in my goodness, because I am who I am and without me nothing has been made—except sin, which is nothingness. So these souls certainly receive of my providence, but they do not understand it because they do not know it, and not knowing it they do not love it, and therefore they receive no fruit of grace from it. Though everything is upright, they see it all distorted. Blind as they are they see light as darkness and darkness as light. So, because their service and trust are set on darkness, they fall to complaining and impatience.

How can they be so foolish? Ah, dearest daughter, how can they believe that I, supreme eternal Goodness, could want anything but their good in the small things I permit day by day for their salvation, after they have experienced in great things how I want nothing other than their sanctification? For all their blindness they can hardly, with the least bit of natural light, fail to see my goodness and the blessings of my providence. They find it undeniably in the first creation as well as in the new creation that has been theirs in the blood when I re-created them in grace. This is something so clear and obvious that they

---

7. Cf. Mt. 6:25–34.
8. Cf. ch. 58–80.

cannot deny it. But then they falter in their own shadow because they have not used this natural light virtuously. Foolish as they are they do not see how constantly I have provided for the world in general and for all of them individually according to their particular situations. And because none of you are stable in this life but are continually changing until you reach your final stable state, I am constantly providing for what you need at any given time.

137

In general I provided for you in the Law of Moses in the Old Testament, and in many other holy prophets.[9] In fact, I want you to know that before the coming of the Word my only-begotten Son, the Jewish people were never without a prophet to strengthen them and give them hope in their prophecies that my Truth, Prophet of prophets, would release them from slavery and make them free, would unlock heaven for them with his blood after it had been locked for so long. But once the gentle loving Word had come, no other prophet rose up among them. Thus they were assured that the one they had been waiting for had come, and there was no further need for prophets to announce him. But they did not recognize him and still do not recognize him because of their blindness.[10]

After the prophets I provided for you in the coming of the Word, who was your mediator with me, God eternal. And after him I sent the apostles, the martyrs, the doctors and confessors. All these things my providence has done, and so, I tell you, will I continue to provide for you right up to the end. This is the general providence granted to everyone who is willing to receive its fruit.

And in my providence I give to each of you in particular the manner of life and death I choose. Hunger, thirst, loss of worldly position, nakedness, cold, heat, insults, abuse, slander—all these things I allow people to say and do to you. Not that I am the source of the malice and ill will of those who do these evil and harmful things; I only grant them their existence and time. I did not give them existence to sin against me and their neighbors, but so that they might serve me and others with loving charity. But I permit these actions either to test the virtue of patience in the soul who is their object, or to make the sinners aware of what they are doing.

---

9. Cf. Lk. 16:29–31.
10. Cf. Jn. 1:10–11.

Sometimes I let the whole world be against the just, and in the end they die a death that leaves worldly people stunned in wonder. It seems to them unjust to see the just perishing now at sea, now in fire, now mangled by beasts, now physically killed when their houses collapse on top of them. How unreasonable these things seem to the eye unenlightened by most holy faith! But not so to the faithful, for through love they have found and experienced my providence in all those great things. Thus they see and grasp that I do what I do providentially, only to bring about your salvation. Therefore they hold everything in reverence. They are not scandalized in themselves nor in my works nor in their neighbors, but pass through everything with true patience. My providence is never denied to anyone; it seasons everything.

Sometimes people think that the hail and storms and lightning I rain upon their bodies are cruel. In their judgment I have no care for their well-being. I have done these things to rescue them from eternal death, but they believe the opposite.

Thus do worldly people try to distort my every work and interpret it after their own base understanding. *(138)* But I want you, most beloved daughter, to see how patiently I have to bear with my creatures whom I have made in my image and likeness with such tender love.[11]

Open your mind's eye and gaze into me. I set before you something particular that had happened. If you recall, you asked me to provide for this, and as you know, I have seen to it that this person regained his position without danger of death.[12] And just as I provided for this particular case, so it is with everything in general.

T hen that soul opened her mind's eye enlightened by most holy faith. She looked upon his divine majesty with eager longing because his words had given her a deeper knowledge of his Truth in

---

11. Cf. Rm. 9:22–23.

12. Hurtaud speculates that the reference here is to Niccolò di Tuldo. Taurisano rejects this opinion and holds that the allusion is to Nanni di Ser Vanni, whom Catherine had converted and who was later freed from a critical situation through her prayers (*Leg. Maj.* II, vii). The question is complicated by another reference to "the particular case" in ch. 139, which explicitly alludes to a death sentence, something that would pertain to Niccolò but not to Nanni. With regard to Niccolò, however, Catherine's long letter (273) to Raymond about his conversion and death gives no indication of the devotion to Mary mentioned in ch. 139. In any case, Cavallini considers the two cases distinct.

his gentle providence. In obedience to his command she gazed into the abyss of his charity and saw how he is supreme eternal Goodness, and how through love alone he created us and redeemed us with the blood of his Son. It is with this very love that he gives what he gives and permits. Trials and consolations and all other things are given for love and to provide for our salvation, and for no other purpose. And the blood she saw poured out with such burning love made it clear to her that this is the truth.

Then the high eternal Father spoke:

They are blinded, as it were, by their selfish self-centeredness, taking scandal with great impatience. (I am speaking now both in general and in particular, reviewing what I have told you.) These people judge as bad and hateful and for their harm and destruction what I do in love for their own good, to deliver them from eternal suffering and to win for them and give them eternal life. Why then do they complain about me? Because they put their hope not in me but in themselves. I have already told you that this is why they end in such darksomeness that they have no knowledge. So they hate what they ought to hold in reverence. And proud as they are they want to pass judgment on my hidden judgments, all of which are righteous. But they act like the blind who, by the touch of the hand or the taste of the tongue or the sound of the voice, would judge whether something is good or bad, according to their scant, base, sick knowledge. They do not want to keep to my ways, though I am the true Light and the one who nourishes them spiritually and physically, and without me they can have nothing.

And if anyone serves me, it is I who have given that person the will and the inclination, the power and the knowledge to be able to do it. Yet like fools they want to walk by feeling about with their hands, though their touch is deceptive because it has no light to discern color. So also is their taste deceptive because it cannot see the unclean animals that sometimes find their way into their food. Their ear is deceived by the pleasantness of sound because it cannot see who is singing, and that singer, if one is not on one's guard, can use pleasure to kill.

This is how they act. As if they were blind, because they have lost the light of reason, they touch the world's pleasures with the hand of sensual feeling and think they are good. But because they do not see, they are not wary of this blanket that is intertwined with thorns, with wretchedness and great anxiety, such that the heart that possesses it apart from me becomes insupportable to itself.

So also these pleasures seem sweet and mild to the mouth of desire that loves them inordinately, but what it really has is the unclean beast of a crowd of deadly sins that make the soul unclean, making her less and less like me and depriving her of the life of grace. And unless she goes in the light of most holy faith to be cleansed in the blood, eternal death is hers.

What she hears is her own selfishness, which seems to her to sound sweet. Why so? Because she is chasing after the love of her selfish sensuality and does not see that she is being deceived by its sound, and so she runs on after it with inordinate pleasure and finds herself led into the ditch, bound with the chains of guilt, betrayed into the hands of her enemies—all because she was blinded by selfish love and the trust she had put in herself and her own knowledge, not keeping close to me, her way and her guide.

This way was made by the Word, my Son. He said that he is Way, Truth, and Life. And he is Light, so that those who walk with him cannot be deceived or walk in darkness.[13] And no one can come to me except through him, for he is one thing with me.[14] I have already told you that I have made him a bridge for you so that all of you would be able to reach your goal. But in spite of all this, these people do not trust me, though I want nothing other than their sanctification. It is to this end, with great love, that I give and permit everything. But they are always scandalized in me, and I support and bear with them in great patience because I loved them without their ever loving me.[15] And they are forever hounding me with great impatience and hatred, with complaining and infidelity. They with their blinded vision want to set themselves up as investigators of my hidden judgments, which are made justly and out of love. And they do not yet even know themselves, so they see falsely. For those who do not know themselves do not know me or my justice in truth.

139

Do you want me, daughter, to show you how greatly the world is deluded about my mysteries? Then open your mind's eye and gaze into me, and you will see into the particular case I promised to tell you about. And as with this case, so could I tell you in general about others.

---

13. Cf. Jn. 14:6, 8:12.
14. Cf. Jn. 10:30.
15. Cf. 1 Jn. 4:10.

Then that soul, in obedience to the high eternal Father, gazed into him with eager longing, and God eternal showed her the condemnation of the person in question.[16] *He said:*

I want you to know that I permitted this to happen to rescue him from the sentence of eternal damnation under which he stood, so that he might have life through his own blood in the blood of my Truth, my only-begotten Son. For I had not forgotten the reverence and love he had for Mary, my only-begotten Son's most gentle mother. For my goodness, in deference to the Word, has decreed that anyone at all, just or sinner, who holds her in due reverence will never be snatched or devoured by the infernal demon. She is like a bait set out by my goodness to catch my creatures. So it was in mercy that I did this. That is, though I did not make the evil intent of the wicked, I permitted what people consider cruel because their selfish self-centeredness has deprived them of light and thus keeps them from knowing my truth. But if they would be willing to lift the cloud they would know my truth and love it, and thus they would hold all things in reverence and at harvest time they would reap the fruit of their labors.

Have no doubt, my daughter, that I will fulfill your desires and those of my servants regarding what you asked of me. I am your God. I repay every labor and fulfill holy desires whenever I find people knocking in truth and with light at the door of my mercy, so that they may not stray or falter in their hope in my providence.

140

Now that I have told you about this particular case, I return to what is more general.

You cannot imagine how great is people's foolishness. They have no sense or discernment, having lost it by hoping in themselves and putting their trust in their own knowledge.[17] O stupid people, do you not see that you are not the source of your own knowledge? It is my goodness, providing for your needs, that has given it to you.

What shows you this? That which you experience in yourselves: Say you want to do something you neither can do nor know how to do. Sometimes you have the knowledge but not the ability, and at other times you have the ability but not the knowledge.[18] Sometimes you do

---

16. Cf. note 12 above.
17. Cf. Pr. 26:12, 28:26.
18. S omits this sentence.

not have time, or if you have the time you lack the desire. I grant all this to provide for your salvation, so that you may know that you are nothing of yourselves and may have reason to humble yourselves and not become proud. So you find change and privation in everything, for things are not at your command. Only my grace is firm and stable and cannot be taken away from you or changed unless you change it by departing from this grace and turning to sin.

How, then, can you lift up your head against my goodness? You cannot, if you would follow reason, nor can you put your hope in yourselves or trust in your own knowledge. But because you have become senseless beasts[19] you do not see that all things except my grace are changing. And why do you not put your trust in me your Creator? Because your trust is in yourselves. Am I not faithful and loyal to you? Of course I am. And this is not hidden from you because you experience it continually.

O dearest sweetest daughter, humankind was neither loyal nor faithful to me. They violated the obedience I had imposed on them and so fell into death. But I was faithful to them, keeping for them that for which I had created them because I wanted to give them the supreme eternal Good.[20] And to fulfill this my truth, I joined my Godhead, the highest of heights, with the lowliness of their humanity, so that they were redeemed and restored to grace through the blood of my only-begotten Son. He proved it. But it seems they do not believe that I am powerful enough to help them, or strong enough to aid and defend them against their enemies, or wise enough to enlighten their understanding, or merciful enough to want to give them what is necessary for their salvation, or rich enough to enrich them, or beautiful enough to give them beauty, or that I have food to feed them or garments to reclothe them. Their actions show me that they do not believe it, for if they believed it in truth, it would show in the work of good holy actions.

Yet they experience continually that I am strong, because I keep them in existence and defend them against their enemies. They see that no one can resist my power and strength. Still, they do not see it because they do not want to see it.

With my wisdom I have organized and I govern all the world with such order that nothing is lacking and nothing could be added to it. Ev-

---

19. Cf. Ps. 49:12; 1 Co. 2:14.
20. Cf. Ps. 145:13–14.

erything is provided for in soul and body. Nor was it your will that constrained me to do this, because you did not even exist. No, it was only my mercy. Constrained by my very self, I made the heavens and the earth, the sea and the vault of the sky to move above you, the air so that you might breathe, fire and water each to temper the other, and the sun so that you would not be left in darkness. All these I made and put in order to serve the needs of humankind. The sky adorned with birds, the earth bringing forth its fruits, the many animals all for the life of humankind, the sea adorned with fish—everything I made with the greatest order and providence.

After I had made everything good and perfect,[21] I created the rational creatures in my own image and likeness, and I put them in this garden. But because of Adam's sin the garden where first there were fragrant flowers, innocently pure and so very sweet, brought forth thorns. Everything had been obedient to Adam, but because of his sin of disobedience, he found rebellion in himself and in all creatures. The world and humankind became wild—another world. But by sending into the world my Truth, the incarnate Word, I saw to it that he should take away the wildness and uproot the thorns of original sin. And I made it a garden watered by the blood of Christ crucified, and planted there the seven gifts of the Holy Spirit after rooting out deadly sin. All this happened only after my only-begotten Son's death.

It was prefigured in the Old Testament when Elisha was asked to raise up the young man who was dead. At first he did not go. Instead he sent Gehazi with his staff, telling him to put it on the boy's back. Gehazi went and did as Elisha had told him but the boy did not rise. When Elisha realized that he had not risen, he went himself and member for member laid himself out on the boy. He breathed sharply seven times into the boy's mouth and the boy took seven breaths as a sign that he had come back to life.[22]

Gehazi was prefigured in Moses, whom I sent to lay the staff of the Law on the dead human race. But this law did not give you life.[23] So I sent the Word my only-begotten Son, who was prefigured in Elisha. He laid himself out on this dead child by joining the divine nature

---

21. There is an echo here of the divine complacency over the work of creation, "and God saw that it was good," repeatedly expressed in Gn. 1 and reechoed in Ps. 104. But Catherine underscores the beauty of creation in the birds and the fish, ornaments of the sky and sea, and in the harmony of opposites (Cavallini).
22. 2 K. 4:27–35.
23. Cf. Jn. 1:17; Rm. 3:20.

with your human nature. Member for member he joined this divine nature with yours: my power, the wisdom of my Son, the mercy of the Holy Spirit—all of me, God, the abyss of the Trinity, laid upon and united with your human nature.

After this union the gentle loving Word accomplished the other by running like one in love to the shameful death of the cross, where he laid himself out. And after this union he gave the seven gifts of the Holy Spirit to this dead child, blowing into the soul's mouth of desire and driving out death in holy baptism. The soul breathes as a sign that she has life, casting out of herself the seven deadly sins. Thus has she become a garden adorned with sweet, mild fruits.

It is true that the keeper of this garden, free choice, can cultivate it or let it grow wild, just as he pleases. If he sows there the venom of selfish self-centeredness from which grow the seven capital sins and all the others that sprout from these, he is in fact keeping out the seven gifts of the Holy Spirit and depriving the soul of all virtue. There is no courage because she is so weakened. There is no moderation or prudence because she has lost the light by which she had used reason. There is no hope or justice because she has become unjust: She puts her hope in herself and believes with a dead faith in herself; her trust is in creatures rather than in me her Creator. There is no love or piety because she has driven it out by her love of her own weakness. She has become cruel to herself, so she cannot be devoted to her neighbors. Bereft of every good, she has fallen into the worst of evils.

What can bring her to life again? This same Elisha, the incarnate Word, my only-begotten Son. How? This gardener must use hate to uproot the thorns of sin (for unless he hates them he will never pull them out), and run with love to conform the soul to the teaching of my Truth by watering her with his blood. That blood is poured over her head by my minister when she goes to confession with heartfelt contrition and contempt for sin, making satisfaction and resolving not to sin again.

This is how the garden of the soul can be cultivated during her lifetime. For once this life is past there is nothing she can do.

141

You see, then, how I in my providence have reconciled the second world, humankind. The first world was left bringing forth troublesome thorns so that in all things humankind still finds rebellion. I did not do this for want of providence or concern for your well-being but with great providence and concern for your well-being, to take away your trust in the world and make you run straight to me, your goal. Thus the vexation of troubles, if nothing else, will make you raise your heart and will above the world. But people are so foolishly ignorant of the truth and so weak when it comes to worldly pleasures that even with all these wearisome thorns they find in them they seem unwilling to rise above them, unconcerned about returning to their homeland. Imagine, daughter, what they would do if they found perfect pleasure and painless rest in the world!

This is why in my providence I allow the world to bring forth so many troubles for them, both to prove their virtue and that I may have reason to reward them for their suffering and the violence they do themselves. So my providence has ordained and provided in all things with great wisdom. I have given because I am rich and I was and am able to give, and my wealth is infinite. Everything was made by me, and without me nothing can exist. Therefore, if it is beauty you want, I am beauty. If you want goodness, I am goodness, for I am supremely good. I am wisdom. I am kind; I am compassionate; I am the just and merciful God. I am generous, not miserly. I give to those who ask of me, open to those who knock in truth, and answer those who call out to me. I am not ungrateful but grateful and mindful to reward those who will toil for me, for the glory and praise of my name. I am joyful, and I keep the soul who clothes herself in my will in supreme joy. I am that supreme providence who never betrays my servants' hope in me in soul or body.[24]

How can people see me feeding and nurturing the worm within the dry wood, pasturing the brute beasts, nourishing the fish in the sea, all the animals on the earth and the birds in the air, commanding the sun to shine on the plants and the dew to fertilize the soil, and not believe that I nourish them as well, my creatures made in my image and likeness? As a matter of fact, all this is done by my goodness to serve them. No matter where they turn, spiritually and materially they will find nothing but my deep burning charity and the greatest, gentle, true, perfect providence. But they do not see it, because they have let go of the light and do not let themselves see. This is why they are scandalized and hold back in their charity for their neighbors. Their thoughts are greedily on tomorrow, though my Truth forbade this when he said, "Do not be concerned about tomorrow; each day has

---

24. Cf. Rm. 10:12.

enough worries of its own."[25] He was reproaching you for your infidelity and showing you my providence and the shortness of time when he said, "Do not be concerned about tomorrow." It is as if my Truth were saying, "Do not be concerned about what you cannot be sure of having; today is enough." And he taught you to ask first for the kingdom of heaven, that is, a good holy life, for I your heavenly Father know well enough that you need these lesser things. That is why I made the earth and commanded it to give you its fruits.[26]

These wretches who in their lack of trust hold back their hearts and hands from charity for their neighbors have never read the teaching given by the Word my Truth, because they are not following in his footsteps. They become insupportable even to themselves. And from this trusting in themselves rather than in me comes every evil. They set themselves up as judges of other people's intentions; they do not see that it is my right to judge—mine, not theirs. My will they neither understand nor judge rightly, except when it seems to hold some worldly advantage or pleasure for them. But if this fails them, because it was there they had set their whole will and hope, they think they have neither felt nor received either my providence or any kindness. They think they have been deprived of everything good. And because they are blinded by their selfish passion, they do not recognize the wealth within, nor the fruit of true patience. Rather they draw death from it, and even in this life have a foretaste of hell.

But for all this I in my goodness do not cease to provide for them. Thus I command the earth to give its fruits to the sinner as well as to the just. I send the sunshine and the rain upon their fields—often, in fact, the sinner will have more than the just.[27]

This my goodness does to endow the souls of the just more fully with spiritual riches when for my love they are stripped of material goods because they have renounced the world and all its pleasures and even their own will. These are the ones who fatten their souls, enlarging them in the abyss of my charity. They abandon all concern not only for worldly riches but for themselves as well. Then I become their spiritual provider, and materially I employ a special providence beyond the general: my mercy, the Holy Spirit, becomes their servant. If you remember well, you know from having read it in the lives of the

---

25. Mt. 6:34.
26. Cf. Mt. 6:31–33; Lk. 12:29–31.
27. Cf. Mt. 5:45.

holy fathers[28] that when that holy hermit was ill who had wholly surrendered himself to the glory and praise of my name, my mercy provided and I sent an angel to care for his needs. His body had the help it needed and his soul experienced wonderful joy and delight in the angel's company.

Such a soul has the Holy Spirit as a mother who nurses her at the breast of divine charity. The Holy Spirit has set her free, releasing her, as her lord, from the slavery of selfish love. For where the fire of my charity is, the water of selfishness cannot enter to put out this sweet fire in the soul. This servant, the Holy Spirit, whom I in my providence have given her, clothes her, nurtures her, inebriates her with tenderness and the greatest wealth. Because she has left all she finds all. Because she has stripped herself of herself she is clothed in me. She has made herself the servant of all in humility, so now she is made mistress over the world and her own sensuality. Because she became blind in her own sight she is now in perfect light. Because she put no trust in herself she is crowned with living faith and fulfilled hope. She has a taste of eternal life, free of every distressing pain and bitterness. She judges all things rightly because in all things she discerns my will. She has seen by the light of faith that I will nothing other than her holiness, and this has made her patient.

Oh, how blessed is this soul who while still in her mortal body enjoys the reward of immortality! She holds all things in reverence, the left hand as well as the right, trouble as well as consolation, hunger and thirst as well as eating and drinking, cold and heat and nakedness as well as clothing, life as well as death, honor as well as disgrace, distress as well as comfort. In all things she remains solid, firm, and stable, because her foundation is the living rock. She has seen and known, by the light of faith and with firm hope, that I give everything I give with the same love and the same concern for your salvation, and that I provide for everything. Thus in great labor I give great strength; I do not impose a heavier burden than the soul can bear, if only she is ready and willing to bear it for love of me. In the blood I have made it clear that I do not want sinners to die, but rather to be converted and live,[29] and throughout their life I give them whatever I give them.

---

28. Domenico Cavalca had written a popular version of *The Lives of the Fathers* in Tuscan, and Catherine was familiar with this work. This and the *Golden Legend* of Jacopo da Varagine were the sources of most of her allusions to anecdotes from the lives of the saints.
29. Ezk. 33:11.

The soul who has stripped herself of herself has seen this, so she rejoices in what she sees and experiences in herself and in others. She is not afraid that she will lack the lesser things because by the light of faith she is guaranteed the greater things. Oh, how glorious is this light of most holy faith by which she sees and has come to know and knows my Truth! She has this light from the Holy Spirit, whom I have given her as a servant. It is a supernatural light the soul receives from my goodness when she makes good use of the natural light I have given her.

142

Do you know, dearest daughter, how I provide for these servants of mine who put their trust in me? In two ways, for all my providence for my rational creatures is for both soul and body. And whatever I do to provide for the body is done for the good of the soul, to make her grow in the light of faith, to make her trust in me and give up trusting in herself, and to make her see and know that I am who I am and that I can and will and know how to assist her in her need and save her.

I have given the soul the sacraments of holy Church for her life, to be her food. Heavy physical bread is given as food for the body. But because the soul in incorporeal, she lives by my word. Thus my Truth in the holy Gospel said that people do not live by bread alone, but by every word that comes from me,[30] that is, by following with spiritual understanding the teaching of my incarnate Word. This Word and the holy sacraments give you life in virtue of the blood.

So you see, spiritual sacraments are given to the soul. Although they are performed and given by means of the body, that act of itself would not give the soul the life of grace unless the soul received it with the disposition of true holy spiritual desire. And this desire is in the soul, not in the body. This is why I told you that the sacraments are spiritual and are given to the soul because the soul is incorporeal. And though they are carried by means of the body it is the soul that receives them.

Sometimes, to intensify her hunger and holy desire, I will let her desire them when she cannot have them. Because she cannot have them her hunger grows, and with her hunger her self-knowledge grows because in her humility she considers herself unworthy. Then I make her worthy, and often I provide this sacrament in different ways.

---

30. Mt. 4:4; Lk. 4:4.

You know that this is true, for you will recall having heard and experienced it yourself. Because my mercy, the Holy Spirit whom I in my goodness have given, stands ready to serve the soul, he will inspire some minister to give her this food. And the minister, constrained by my burning charity in this Holy Spirit who pricks his conscience, is thus moved to feed that soul's hunger and fulfill her longing. Sometimes I will make her wait until the last moment, and then when she has given up all hope, she will get what she longs for.

Could I not provide at the beginning as well as later? Of course. But I do this to intensify the light of faith in her so that she will never fail to hope in my goodness. I want to make her cautious and prudent, so that she will not foolishly turn back and relax her hunger. This is why I make her wait.

Just so, you remember the soul who once came to the church with great hunger for communion.[31] When the celebrant came to the altar she asked for the body of Christ, wholly God, wholly human, but he refused. The tears and longing grew in her; and in him, when he came to the offering of the chalice, the pricking of conscience grew, urged on by that servant, the Holy Spirit, who was providing for that soul. And as he provided and worked on that heart within, it began to show outwardly, and the priest said to the server, "Ask her if she wants to receive communion, for I will willingly give it to her." And if she had the tiniest bit of faith and love before, it now grew to overflowing fullness with such great longing that it seemed as if the life wanted to leave her body. And this is why I had permitted it, to make her grow and to dry up in her any selfish unfaithfulness or any trust she had in herself.

At that time I provided through another person. At other times the Holy Spirit himself as servant provides without using such an intermediary, as has happened more than once to many persons and happens every day to my servants. But I will tell you about two wonderful examples which you know, to make you grow in faith, and for the praise of my providence.

You remember having heard about that soul who was standing in my temple, the holy church, on the feast of the conversion of the glori-

---

31. Catherine is speaking of herself. Cf. *Leg. Maj.* II, xii, where Raymond tells of the opposition she encountered in those who were scandalized at her frequent ("not every day, but frequently," says Raymond) communions.

ous apostle Paul, my gentle trumpeter.[32] She was so longing to approach this sacrament, the bread of life, the food of angels given to humanity, that she tried almost every priest who came out to celebrate. In my providence she was denied by all of them, because I wanted her to learn that although everyone else might fail her, I her Creator would never fail her. Therefore, at the last Mass I employed the means I am about to tell you: I used a tender trick to make her drunk with my providence.

This was the trick: She had said that she wanted to receive communion, but the server did not want to tell the celebrant. When she saw that the priest was not answering negatively, she waited with great longing to be able to receive communion. The Mass came to an end, and finding herself let down, her hunger and longing intensified tremendously because in true humility she considered herself unworthy. She reproached herself for her presumption, because it seemed to her that she had been presumptuous to approach so great a mystery. Then I who exalt the humble drew to myself this soul's love and longing and gave her knowledge in the abyss of the Trinity, myself, God eternal. I enlightened her understanding in my own the Father's power, in the wisdom of my only-begotten Son, and in the mercy of the Holy Spirit—for we are one and the same thing. That soul was so perfectly united with me that her body was lifted up from the earth, because in this unitive state I am telling you about, the union of the soul with me through the impulse of love is more perfect than her union with her body. And in this great abyss, to satisfy her longing, she received holy communion from me. And as a sign that I had in truth satisfied her, for several days she sensed in a wonderful way, in her bodily taste, the savor and fragrance of the blood and body of Christ crucified, my Truth. Thus was she renewed in the light of my providence, having tasted it so sweetly. All of this was visible to her, but invisible to the eyes of others.

But the second instance was visible to the minister who was involved.[33] That soul had a great longing to hear Mass and receive communion, but physical pain prevented her going to the church at her usual time. She came in late, however, at the consecration. He was at

---

32. The story, again about Catherine herself, is related in *Supplementum* Pt. II, Tr. 6, 14.

33. Raymond of Capua, who himself tells the story in great detail, *Leg. Maj.* II, xii.

one end of the church and she took her place at the other, since obedience had forbidden her to stand closer.[34] She stood there weeping copiously and saying, "O my wretched soul, do you not see what great grace you have received simply to be in the holy temple of God and to have seen his minister—you who deserve to live in hell for your sins?" But her desire was not for all that stilled. The more she plunged into the valley of humility, the more she was raised up. It was granted her to know my goodness in faith and hope, and to trust that the Holy Spirit, her servant, would nourish her hunger. And then I gave her what she did not even know how to desire in such a fashion.

This is how it was: When the priest came to break the host for his own communion, as he broke it a tiny piece fell off. By my permission and power this tiny bit of the host left the altar and went to the other end of the church where she was standing. She felt that she had received communion, but in her great burning desire she thought that, as had often happened before, I had satisfied her invisibly. But it did not seem so to the celebrant, who, when he could not find that piece of host, experienced unbearable sorrow. If my mercy as servant had not revealed to his spirit who had had it, he would have remained in doubt until she finally told him about it.

Could I not have relieved her of her physical weakness and let her come on time so that she could have received the sacrament from the celebrant? Yes, but I wanted her to experience that with or without the help of another person, in any situation or at any time whatever, in any fashion she knew how to desire and even more in any fashion she could not know how to desire, I know how to and can and will satisfy her in wonderful ways.

I have told you enough, dearest daughter, about the providence I employ toward souls who hunger for this sweet sacrament. So also in all the others, as there is need, do I employ this gentle providence.

Now I will tell you a little bit how I employ my providence within the soul without the mediation of the body as external instrument. Though I spoke about it when I was telling you about the stages of the soul, I still want to tell you more about it.[35]

---

34. It was Tommaso della Fonte who had forbidden Catherine to stand near the altar, an attempt to keep her and her very expressive devotion at some distance from the rest of the congregation.
35. Cf. ch. 60, 63, 64, 68, 70, 78.

143

The soul is either living in deadly sin, or imperfectly in grace, or she is perfect. Toward all I am generous in my providence, but in different ways, very wisely, as I see people have need.

Worldly people who are dead in mortal sin I wake up with the pricking or weariness they feel within their hearts in new and different ways—so many ways your tongue could never describe them. Sometimes, because of the insistence of the pains and pricking of conscience within their souls, they abandon the guilt of deadly sin. And sometimes their heart conceives love for deadly sin or for creatures apart from my will. But I always pluck the rose from your thorns. So I deprive them of places and times for fulfilling their own wishes until they are so tired of the interior suffering their sinfulness has brought them when they cannot fulfill their perverse wishes that they return to their senses. And the pricking of their conscience and heartfelt compunction lead them to throw away their madness. It can truly be called madness because, while they thought they had set their affection on something, when they begin to see they find nothing there. True, the creature they loved with such a wretched love was and is something, but what they got from it was nothing because sin is a nothing. But from this nothingness of sin, a thorn that pierces the soul, I pluck this rose to provide for their salvation.

What constrains me to do this? Not they, for they neither seek me nor ask for my help and providence except in sin and worldly pleasures and riches and honors. It is love that constrains me, because I loved you before you came to be. Without having been loved by you, I loved you unspeakably much. This is what constrains me to do it, along with the prayers of my servants. For the Holy Spirit, my mercy, waits on these and gives them love for me and warm affection for their neighbors, so that with immeasurable charity they seek their salvation. They spare no effort to placate my wrath and tie the hands of my divine justice, which the wicked deserve to have me employ against them. These servants of mine constrain me with their humble tears and constant prayer. And what makes them cry out? My providence seeing to the needs of those dead ones. Thus it has been said that I do not want sinners to die but to be converted and live.[36]

---

36. Ezk. 33:11.

Fall in love, daughter, with my providence! Open your spiritual and bodily eyes, and you will see how the evil who live in such wretchedness, stinking of death, beclouded and darksome for want of light, go about singing and laughing, spending their time on vanities, pleasures, and indecency. They are all lustful, drunkards, and gluttons, so much so that they make a god of their bellies.[37] They are hateful, spiteful, and proud, full of every wretchedness (you know these wretched things more vividly than I described them to you!) and they do not know their own condition. They are traveling the road that leads to eternal death unless they change their ways while they are still alive, and they go along singing! Would not people think a person truly stupid and mad who was condemned to death and went to execution singing and dancing, showing signs of mirth?[38] Of course! So stupid, and incomparably more, are these wretches, for the spiritual condemnation and death penalty they are receiving is much greater than that of the body. They are losing the life of grace and are to be infinitely punished if they die condemned, whereas these others are losing only bodily life, suffering only a finite punishment. Yet they go along singing! Blinder than blind! Stupid and mad beyond all stupidity!

My servants live in weeping, in bodily distress and contrition of heart, in watching and constant prayer, sighing and lamenting, torturing their flesh to win the salvation of these others. And they make fun of them! But their ridicule will fall on their own heads, and the penalty of sin will come to those who deserve it, while the reward for labors borne for love of me will be given to those my goodness has made deserving of it. For I am your just God, and I give to all as they deserve.[39] But ridicule and persecution and ingratitude do not make my servants slacken their pace; in fact, their concern and desire grow. What makes them knock with such hunger at the door of my mercy? My providence, for at one and the same time I procure the salvation of these wretches and increase my servants' virtue and the reward for [40] their loving charity.

---

37. Ph. 3:19.

38. The fate of prisoners condemned to death, the sight of the death cart with its tortures, and even execution itself were familiar to Catherine. See especially her letter (260) to the prisoners of Siena, her letter (273) to Raymond telling of the execution of Niccolò di Tuldo, and Raymond's account (Leg. Maj. II, vii) of her converting two prisoners on their way to execution in Siena.

39. Cf. Ps. 62:12.

40. S has "the fire of" instead of "the reward for."

Endless are the ways of my providence toward sinners to draw them out of the guilt of deadly sin.

Now I will tell you about what my providence does for those who have risen up from sin but are still imperfect. I will not go over the spiritual stages, because I have already adequately described these for you, but I will say something briefly.

144

D o you know, dearest daughter, how I raise the soul out of her imperfection? Sometimes I vex her with evil thoughts and a sterile mind. It will seem to her that I have left her completely, without any feeling whatever. She does not seem to be in the world, because she is in fact not there; nor does she seem to be in me,[41] because she has no feeling at all other than that her will does not want to sin.

I do not allow enemies to open this gate of the will, which is free. I do let the devils and other enemies of humankind beat against other gates, but not against this, which is the main gate guarding the city of the soul. The guard that stands at this gate, free choice, I have made free to say yes or no as he pleases.

The gates of this city are many. There are three main gates—memory, understanding, and will—and the last, if it so chooses, always holds firm and guards the others. But if the will gives its consent, the enemy of selfish love and all the other enemies that follow after it come in. Then understanding surrenders to the darkness that is the enemy of light, and the recollection of injury makes memory surrender to the hatred that is the enemy of loving charity for one's neighbors. The soul harbors memories of worldly pleasures and delights in as many different ways as there are different sins against the virtues.

As soon as these gates are opened, the wickets of the body's senses all open up, as instruments that respond to the soul. So you see how a person's disordered will that has opened all its gates responds by means of these organs so that all its sounds, that is, its works, are wasted and contaminated.[42]

---

41. E omits "because . . . in me."

42. Elements of two metaphorical levels begin to move in and out here in an intriguingly inextricable fashion. One level is that of the city and its gates, within which gates are wickets, smaller doors that open and shut far more easily than the huge gates. The second level, introduced in this paragraph, is that of the organ. To follow the imagery it is helpful to recall that in the usage of Catherine's day *organo* had several interrelated lay-

The eyes offer nothing but death, because they have been given to seeing what is dead by looking wantonly where they ought not. Their vanity, lightness, and indecency are the cause of death to themselves and to others. What a wretch you are! I gave you eyes to look at the sky and everything else and the beauty of creation through me, and to look at my mysteries, and you use them to look at the mire and wretchedness and so earn death with them.

Your ears also take pleasure in dishonorable things, in listening judgmentally to what your neighbors have done. But I gave you your ears to listen to my word and to pay heed to your neighbors' needs.

I gave you your tongue to proclaim my word, to confess your own sins, and to work for the salvation of souls. But you use it to blaspheme me your Creator, to destroy your neighbors by feeding on their flesh, complaining and judging good deeds as bad and evil as good. You curse and lie. With your lustful words you endanger yourself and others. You spit out words that cut through your neighbors' hearts like a knife, words that provoke them to anger. Oh, how many evils and murders, what dishonor, what anger and hatred and loss of time come from this member![43]

When it comes to smell, you sin as much as you take perverse pleasure in what you smell. And as for taste, you think of nothing but filling your belly with insatiable gluttony, with disordered appetite that hankers after an endless variety of foods. Wretched soul, you did not consider when you opened the gate that this inordinate eating would lead to firing up the weak flesh and corrupt you with perverse desire.

Your hands, which were made to serve your neighbors when you see them sick and to help them with alms in their need, you use to take what belongs to your neighbors, and for filthy miserable touching. Your feet were given you to serve by carrying your body to places that are holy and useful to you and your neighbors for the glory and praise of my name, but you use them to carry your body to vile places in all

---

ers of meaning. The primary sense was that of instrumentality, as in the bodily organs or the senses as organs (instruments) of the soul. In the musical realm, everything that carried music in an instrumental way was *organo:* the human voice, especially in polyphony; any instrument or orchestration of instruments; finally, the instrument we know as the organ. The overlap of the two metaphors, city and organ, comes through the "gates and wickets" that are common to both.

43. Cf. Jm. 3:6.

sorts of ways, gossiping and being disagreeable, corrupting others with your own wretchedness, however your perverse wretched will pleases!

I have told you all this, dearest daughter, to give you reason to weep at the sight of the noble city of the soul come to such misery, and to let you see what great evil comes forth from its main gate, the will, which I never give the soul's enemies leave to enter. But, as I have told you, I do let these enemies beat at the other gates. Thus I let understanding be battered by spiritual darkness, and memory seem to be bereft of any thought of me. And sometimes it will seem that all the body's other senses are being beseiged in different ways. Though they are seeing and touching and hearing and smelling and walking in holy things, everything will seem to be a source of inconstancy, dishonor, and corruption.

But all this is not meant to be deadly. I do not will the soul's death so long as she is not so stupid as to open the gate of her will. I let her enemies stand outside, but I do not allow them to enter. They cannot enter unless her own will chooses to let them in.

And why do I keep this soul, surrounded by so many enemies, in such pain and distress? Not for her to be captured and lose the wealth of grace, but to show her my providence, so that she will trust not in herself but in me. Then she will rise up from her carelessness and her concern will make her run for protection to me her defender, her kind Father, the provider of her salvation. I want her to be humble, to see that of herself she is nothing and to recognize that her existence and every gift beyond that comes from me, that I am her life. She will recognize this life and my providence when she is liberated through these struggles, for I do not let these things last forever. They come and go as I see necessary for her. Sometimes she will think she is in hell, and then, through no effort of her own, she will be relieved and will have a taste of eternal life. The soul is left serene. What she sees seems to cry out that God is all aflame with loving fire, as she now contemplates my providence. For she sees that she has come [safely] out of this great flood not by any effort of her own. The light came unforeseen. It was not her effort but my immeasurable charity, which wanted to provide for her in time of need when she could scarcely take any more.

Why, when she was faithful to prayer and other necessary things, did I not relieve her with light and take away the darkness? Since she was still imperfect, I did not want her taking credit for what was not hers.

So you see how the imperfect soul comes to perfection by fighting these battles, because there she experiences my divine providence,[44] whereas before this she only believed in it. I have now guaranteed it to her through experience, and she has conceived perfect love because she has come to know my goodness in my divine providence[45] and has thus risen above her imperfect love.

I even make use of a holy trick, just to raise her up from imperfection: I make her conceive a special love for certain people, beyond a general spiritual love. In this way she practices virtue, lets go of her imperfection, strips her heart of every other sensual love for creatures—even any selfish passion for her father and mother, sisters and brothers—and she loves them for my sake. And with this well-ordered love I have given her she chases out the disordered love with which she had loved creatures in the beginning. So you see how she dispels this imperfection.

But listen to another thing this sort of love does. It provides a test of whether or not the soul perfectly loves me and those I have given her. This is why I gave them to her: to test this so that she might have something on which to base her discernment. For without this discernment she would neither find displeasure in herself, nor pleasure in what is mine within her. This is how she comes to this discernment, for I told you before that she is still imperfect. And there is no doubting that so long as her love for me is imperfect, her love for other people will also be imperfect, for perfect charity for others depends on perfect charity for me. So she will love others with the same measure of perfection or imperfection with which she loves me. And how does this [special love] let her know this? In many ways. In fact, she has barely to open her mind's eye, and not a moment will pass without her seeing and experiencing it. But because I have made this clear to you elsewhere, I will say but little about it here.

Whenever the soul loves someone with a special love, she feels pain when the pleasure or comfort or companionship she has become accustomed to, and which gave her great consolation, is lessened. Or she suffers if she sees that person keeping more company with someone else than with her. This pain makes her enter into knowledge of herself. And if she is willing to walk wisely in the light as she ought, she will come to love that special person more perfectly, for with self-

---

44. E: "So you see how the imperfect soul experienced my divine providence, . . ."
45. S omits "whereas . . . providence."

knowledge and the contempt she has conceived for her selfish feelings, she will cast off imperfection and come to perfection. Once she is more perfect, a greater and more perfect love for others in general will follow, as well as for the special person my goodness has given her. This goodness of mine provides for that collision between self-contempt and love for virtue during this life of pilgrimage. But let her not be so foolish as to fall into confusion and spiritual weariness in time of suffering, or into sadness of heart and lack of effort. This would be dangerous: What I had given her for life would become death and destruction for her. Let her not act like this, but rather with healthy concern and humility let her consider herself unworthy of what she desires when she does not have the consolation she would like. In the light let her see that virtue, which should be the chief reason for her love, is not lessened in her if she is willing to endure with hunger and patience every suffering, whatever its source, for the glory and praise of my name. In this way she will fulfill my will for her and reap the fruit of perfection. For I have permitted the struggles and the special love and everything else to bring her to the light of perfection.

This is how I employ my providence with the imperfect, and in so many other ways that your tongue could never tell them.

145

N ow I will tell you about the perfect, how I provide for them to preserve them, to prove their perfection, and to make them keep growing. For there is no one in this life, no matter how perfect, who cannot grow to greater perfection. So among other things I use the way my Truth described when he said, "I am the true vine, my Father is the vinedresser, and you are the branches."[46] He is the true vine because he proceeds from me, the Father, and whoever remains in him by following his teaching will bear fruit. And so that your fruit may grow and be perfect, I prune you by means of trials: disgrace, insults, mockery, abuse, and reproach, with hunger and thirst, by words and actions, as it pleases my goodness to grant to each of you as you are able to endure. For trial is a sign that shows whether the soul's charity is perfect or imperfect.

Patience is proved in the assaults and weariness I allow my ser-

---

46. Jn. 15:1–5.

vants, and the fire of charity grows in the soul who has compassion for the soul of her abuser. For she grieves more over the offense done to me and the harm done to the other than over her own hurt. This is how those behave who are very perfect, and so they grow. And this is why I permit all these things. I grant them a stinging hunger for the salvation of souls so that they knock day and night at the door of my mercy, so much so that they forget themselves (as I described for you in the state of the perfect[47]). And the more they abandon themselves, the more they find me.

And where do they seek me? In my Truth, by walking perfectly along the way of his gentle teaching. They have read this gentle glorious book, and as they have read they have learned how, because he wanted to obey me completely and show how much he loved me and the human race, he ran through pain and shame to the table of the most holy cross. There in his suffering he ate as his food the human race. Thus, by suffering and in a human fashion he showed me how much he loved my honor.

I tell you, these beloved children of mine who have attained the highest perfection through perseverance and watching and constant humble prayer show me that they love me in truth and that they have learned well by following this holy teaching of my Truth in their suffering and in the burdens they bear for their neighbors' salvation. They have found no other way than this to show their love for me. Indeed, any other way there may be to show their love is based on this principal way, for every good work is done through your neighbors. For no good can be done except in charity for me and your neighbors; if it is not done in this charity it cannot be good even though the action in itself may be virtuous.[48] In the same way evil is done for want of charity. So you see how through this means that I have established for you these souls show their perfection and the genuineness of their love for me by constantly winning their salvation by the sufferings they endure. Then I purify them so their trials will make them produce better and sweeter fruit, and their patience sends up a great fragrance to me.

Oh, how mild and sweet is this fruit, and how profitable to the soul who suffers innocently! If they only saw it, there would be no one who would not seek suffering with great solicitude and joy. In order to give them this great treasure I provide a weight of great labor for them,

---

47. Cf. ch. 78.
48. Cf. 1 Co. 13:1–3.

lest the virtue of patience grow rusty within them. Then, when the time comes for it to be tested, they will not, for not having used it, find it rusty with that impatience which corrodes the soul.

Sometimes I resort to a pleasant trick with them to keep them humble. I make their feelings fall asleep so that it seems to them they feel nothing either in their will or their emotions, as if they were asleep though not, I say, dead. For the sensual emotions slumber in the perfect soul but they do not die. This is why, if they relax their efforts or let the flame of holy desire grow dim, these emotions will awaken stronger than ever. Therefore let no one, however perfect, trust them. It is essential to remain in holy fear of me, for many who would otherwise not have fallen have fallen miserably in this way. Thus I say the emotions seem to be asleep; it seems they do not feel the weight of great suffering and heavy burdens. But bit by bit, in some tiny thing that really is nothing, that they themselves will later laugh at, their feelings are so aroused that they are stupified. My providence does this to make them grow and go down into the valley of humility. For then they will wisely rise up above themselves and not be lost, but will chastise their emotions with contempt and reproach, and this chastising will put them more perfectly to sleep.

Sometimes my providence leaves my great servants a pricking, as I did to my gentle apostle Paul, my chosen vessel. After he had received my Truth's teaching in the depths of me the eternal Father, I still left him the pricking and resistance of his flesh.[49]

Could I and can I not make it otherwise for Paul and the others in whom I leave this or that sort of pricking? Yes. Then why does my providence do this? To give them opportunity for merit, to keep them in the self-knowledge whence they draw true humility, to make them compassionate instead of cruel toward their neighbors so that they will sympathize with them in their labors.[50] For those who suffer themselves are far more compassionate to the suffering than are those who have not suffered. They grow to greater love and run to me all anointed with humility and ablaze in the furnace of my charity. And through these means and endless others they attain perfect union—such union and knowledge of my goodness that while they are still in their mortal bodies they taste the reward of the immortals. Though they are still imprisoned in their bodies it seems to them they are outside. And be-

---

49. Cf. 2 Co. 12:7.
50. Cf. Heb. 4:15, 5:2–3.

cause they have come to know so much of me, they love me much. And whoever loves much will have great sorrow; therefore those whose love grows will know more sorrow.[51]

In what sorrow and pain are they left? Not from any assault to themselves, nor from bodily suffering, nor from the vexations of the devil, nor from any other painful thing that could happen directly to themselves. They grieve only for offenses committed against me, for they see how deserving I am of love and service. And they grieve for the harm that comes to souls when they see them walking so blindly through the world's darkness. For in their loving union with me they have contemplated and known how ineffably I love my creatures, seeing how they reflect my likeness, and they have fallen in love with my creatures' beauty for love of me. Therefore they feel unbearable sorrow when they see them straying from my goodness. These sufferings are so great that they make every other suffering diminish in them until they regard nothing as being done to themselves.

I provide for them. How? By revealing myself to them, letting them see in me, with great bitterness, the wickedness and wretchedness of the world and the damnation of souls individually and collectively, as it pleases my goodness to make them grow in love and sorrow. Then, prodded by burning desire they cry out to me in firm hope and with the light of most holy faith, asking my help in such great need. Thus my divine providence sees at one and the same time to the help of the world by letting myself be constrained by my servants' sorrowful tender restless longing, and to their own nurturing and growth in this way to greater and more perfect knowledge and union with me.

You see then in how many different ways I provide for these perfect ones, for as long as you are alive you can still grow in perfection and merit. This is why I purge them of every selfish and disordered love, whether temporal or spiritual, and prune them by means of many trials so that they may produce more and better fruit. And because of the great suffering they endure when they see me offended and souls deprived of grace, every lesser emotion of theirs is quelled, until they consider any burden they could bear in this life to be less than nothing. This is why they care equally about trial and consolation, because they are not seeking their own consolation. They do not love me with a mercenary love for their own selfish pleasure; rather, it is the honor and glory and praise of my name they seek.

51. Cf. ch. 5.

You see then, dearest daughter, how I extend my providence to every person in an endless variety of wonderful ways unknown by darksome folk—for darkness cannot comprehend the light.[52] My ways are known only to those who have the light, perfectly or imperfectly, according to the perfection of their lightsomeness. This light is won in the soul's knowledge of herself, which makes her rise above the darkness in perfect contempt.

146

I have told you and you have seen less than a whiff of a droplet, a nothing in comparison to the sea of my providence for my creatures, now that I have spoken to you in general and in particular. Now I will go through the same stages, telling you about how I provide through the sacrament for the soul's growth in hunger, and how I provide within the soul's emotions by administering grace through the service of the Holy Spirit. The wicked receive it to the lessening of grace within them. The imperfect are brought to perfection. And the perfection of the perfect is augmented and made to grow, because they are prepared to grow, and I want to make of them good and perfect mediators for those who are at war with me. For I have already told you, if you recall, that it is by means of my servants and their great sufferings that I would be merciful to the world and reform my bride.

Truly these last can be called another Christ crucified, my only-begotten Son, because they have taken his task upon themselves. He came as a mediator to put an end to the war and reconcile humanity to me in peace by suffering even to the shameful death of crucifixion. In the same way must these be crucified and become mediators in prayer, in word, in good holy living, setting themselves up as an example to others. The precious stones of virtue shine in their patience as they bear others' sins. These are the hooks with which they catch souls. They throw out their nets to the right, not to the left, as my Truth told Peter and the other disciples to do after the resurrection,[53] for the left hand of selfishness is dead in them, and the right is alive with a true, sincere, gentle, and divine love, with which they cast the nets of holy desire into me, the peaceful sea. And to join the story of what took place before the resurrection with the story of what took

52. Cf. Jn. 1:5.
53. Jn. 21:6.

place after,[54] know that when they draw the net back in and count the catch in self-knowledge, they take in such an abundance of soul-fishes that they have to call on a partner to help take them out of the net because they cannot do it alone. Both in the casting and in the tightening of the net they need the partner of true humility; they have to call out lovingly to their neighbors and ask them to help take in these soul-fishes.

You can see and experience in my servants how true this is. The weight of these souls they have caught in the net of holy desire seems so great to them that they call for company and would have everyone help them because in humility they consider themselves inadequate. This is why I told you that they call on humility and charity for their neighbors to help them take in these fishes. When they pull in the net they take them in in great numbers, even though many escape from the net because of their sins and are not caught. The net of desire had certainly been held out to all, because the soul who is hungry for my honor is never content with a fraction but wants them all. She asks the good to help her get the fishes into her net so that they may be preserved and become more perfect. She would have the imperfect become perfect. She would have the bad become good. The darksome unbelievers she would have turn to the light of holy baptism. She wants them all, whatever their condition, because she sees them all in me, created by my goodness in such burning love and redeemed by the blood of my only-begotten Son, Christ crucified.

So she has taken them all into the net of her holy desire, but many escape because they depart from grace by their sins, both the unbelievers and those who are living in deadly sin. Not that they should therefore not be included in that desire by constant prayer. For though souls by their sins may depart from me and from the loving company they ought to keep with my servants and from the reverence they ought to have, my servants do not and should not lessen the warmth of their charity for them. Thus they cast out this gentle net on the right side.

O gentlest daughter, consider for one moment what the glorious apostle Peter did (as it is told in the Holy Gospel that my Truth had him do) when my Truth commanded him to cast the net into the sea. Peter answered that he had worked hard all night and had not been able to catch anything. "But at your word and command I will cast it,"

54. Cf. Lk. 5:4–8; Jn. 21:1–8.

he said. And when he did so he caught such an abundance that he could not bring it in alone. So he called the disciples to help him. This truly happened so, but I am using it as a figure for what I have told you, and you will find it appropriate. And I would have you know that all the mysterious ways my Truth used in the world, both with and without the disciples, serve as figures within the souls of my servants and in all manner of folk, so that in everything you can have a rule and teaching by contemplating it with the light of reason. And everyone, dense or quick, of low or great understanding, can play a part, if only they are willing.

I told you that Peter, at the Word's command, cast out the net. Thus he was obedient, believing with a lively faith that he could take a catch. So he caught plenty, but not during the night. Do you know what nighttime is? It is the darksome night of deadly sin, when the soul is bereft of the light of grace. During this night the soul catches nothing at all, because she casts her desire not in the living sea but in the dead, where she finds only sin, which is nothingness. In vain does she wear herself out in great unbearable pain without any profit. She makes a martyr of herself for the devil, not for Christ crucified. But when the day breaks and she leaves sin behind to return to grace, the commandments of the Law appear before her mind, telling her to cast this net of hers into the word of my Word by loving me above all things and her neighbor as herself. Then in obedience and by the light of faith with firm hope she casts her net into his word by following the teaching and the footsteps of this gentle loving Word and the disciples. And I have already told you how she takes a catch and whom she calls, so I will not repeat any more.

147

I have told you this much so that with the light of understanding you might know how great was my Truth's providence in working his mysteries and all his deeds while he was in your company. And I wanted you to know what you must do and how those act who have reached the highest perfection. Consider also that one does it more perfectly than another, depending on how promptly they go to obey this word and with what perfect light, having given up all trust in themselves and taking refuge only in me their Creator. Those souls who obey by keeping the commandments and counsels both in act and in spirit cast their nets more perfectly than do those who keep the commandments in act but the counsels only in spirit. Anyone who does not keep the counsels in spirit cannot be keeping the commandments in act, for the two are bound together. So one's catch will be as perfect as one's cast. But those who are perfect catch plenty and with great perfection.

Oh, how they have harmonized their organs through that good gentle guard, free choice, who stands at the gate of the will! All their senses make one sweet sound, which comes forth from the center of the city of the soul because all her gates are both opened and closed. Her will is closed to selfishness and open to desire and love of my honor and affection for her neighbors. Her understanding is closed to the sight of the world's pleasures and vanity and wretchedness, all of which are a night that darkens the understanding of those who look on them perversely. But her understanding is open and fixed with light-someness on the light of my Truth. Her memory is locked to sensual thoughts of the world and herself, but open to receive and remember my blessings. The soul's movements, then, make a jubilant sound, its chords tempered and harmonized with prudence and light, all of them melting into one sound, the glorification and praise of my name.

Into this same sound where the great chords of the soul's powers are harmonized, the small chords of the body's senses and organs are blended. Just as I told you, when I was speaking to you about the wicked, that they all give a dead sound when they let in their enemies, so those who welcome as friends true and solid virtues give a sound of life, every instrument playing in good holy actions. Every member does the work given it to do, each one perfect in its own way: the eye in seeing, the ear in hearing, the nose in smelling, the taste in tasting, the tongue in speaking,[55] the hands in touching and working, the feet in walking. All are harmonized in one sound to serve their neighbors for the glory and praise of my name, to serve the soul with good, holy, virtuous actions, obediently responding to the soul as its organs. They are pleasing to me, pleasing to the angels, pleasing to those who are truly joyful who wait with great joy and gladness for the day they will share each others' happiness, and pleasing to the world. Whether the world is willing or not, the wicked cannot but feel the pleasantness of this sound. And many, many continue to be caught on this instrumental hook: They leave death behind and come to life.

All the saints have gone fishing with this organ. The first to sound forth the sound of life was the gentle loving Word when he took on your humanity. On the cross he made a sweet sound with this human-

---

55. S omits "the tongue in speaking."

ity united with the Godhead, and he caught the children of the human race. He also caught the devil, for he took away from him the lordship he had had for so long because of his sin.

All the rest of you sound forth when you learn from this maestro. The apostles learned from him and sowed his word throughout the world. The martyrs and confessors, the doctors and virgins, all caught souls with their sound. Consider the glorious virgin Ursula: She played her instrument so sweetly that she caught eleven thousand from the virgins alone, and from all sorts of folk she caught more with this same sound. And so with all the others, one in this way, another in that. What is the reason? My infinite providence, which gave them these instruments and taught them how and what to play. And everything I give and permit them in this life is a way for them to improve their instruments if they choose to discern it and do not choose to cast off the light and see by the cloud of their own self-centeredness, self-complacency, and self-opinionatedness.

148

Enlarge your heart, daughter, and open your mind's eye to the light of faith. See with what great love and providence I have created and ordained humankind to rejoice in my supreme eternal reward. I have provided for everything in soul and body, for the imperfect and the perfect, for the good and the bad, spiritually and temporally, in heaven and on earth, in this mortal life and in the immortal.

In this mortal life, so long as you are pilgrims, I have bound you with the chain of charity. Whether you want it or not, you are so bound. If you should break loose by not wanting to live in charity for your neighbors, you will still be bound by it by force. Thus, that you may practice charity in action and in will, I in my providence did not give to any one person or to each individually the knowledge for doing everything necessary for human life. No, I gave something to one, something else to another, so that each one's need would be a reason to have recourse to the other. So though you may lose your will for charity because of your wickedness, you will at least be forced by your own need to practice it in action. Thus you see the artisan turn to the worker and the worker to the artisan: Each has need of the other because neither knows how to do what the other does. So also the cleric and religious have need of the layperson, and the layperson of the religious; neither can get along without the other. And so with everything else.

Could I not have given everyone everything? Of course. But in my providence I wanted to make each of you dependent on the others, so that you would be forced to exercise charity in action and will at once.

I have shown you my generosity, goodness, and providence toward people. But they let themselves be guided by their own darksome weakness. Your bodily members put you to shame, because they all together practice charity, while you do not. Thus, when the head is aching, the hand helps it. And if the finger, that tiniest of members, hurts, the head does not snub it because it is greater and more noble than all the other parts of the body. No, it comes to its aid with hearing and sight and speech and everything it has. And so with all the other members.[56] But those who are proud do not behave that way. They see a poor person, one of their members, sick and in need, and do not help. They refuse to give not only of their possessions but even a single word. Indeed, they reproachfully and scornfully turn away. They have plenty of wealth, but they leave the poor to starve. They do not see that their wretched cruelty throws filth into my face, and that their filth reaches down even to the depths of hell.

I provide for the poor, and for their poverty they will be given the greatest of riches. But the others unless they change their ways will be severely reproached by my Truth as is said in the holy Gospel: "I was hungry and you gave me nothing to eat; I was thirsty and you gave me nothing to drink; I was naked and you did not clothe me, in prison and you did not visit me." And at the last moment it will do them no good to excuse themselves by saying, "I never saw you, for if I had I would have done it." The wretches know well enough—and my Truth said that whatever is done to his poor is done to him. Thus they will justly be eternally punished with the devils.[57]

So you see, I have provided on earth that they should never end in eternal grief.

Look up into me, everlasting Life; look up to the angels and the citizens of this everlasting life who have won eternal life by the power of the Lamb's blood. I have so ordered their charity that no one simply enjoys his or her own reward in this blessed life that is my gift without its being shared by the others. This is not how I have willed it to be. Rather, their charity is so well ordered and perfect that the great find joy in the reward of the small, and the small find joy in the reward of the great. I mean small in the sense of capacity, not that the small are

56. Cf. 1 Co. 12:14–26.
57. Mt. 25:42–46.

any less full than the great. As I have told you elsewhere, each has his or her own measure.[58]

Oh, how intimate is this charity! How united they are with me and with each other! For I am the source of what they have and they acknowledge this with holy fear and due reverence. When they see this they immerse themselves in me, and in me they see and know the dignity I have given them. The angelic communicates with the human, that is, with the souls of the blessed, and the blessed with the angels. Thus all of them in this joyous charity rejoice in each others' reward and exult in me with jubilation and mirth without any sadness, sweet without any bitterness, because while they lived and died they enjoyed me in loving charity through charity for their neighbors. What so ordained it? My wisdom, with gentle, wonderful providence.

And if you turn to purgatory, there you will find my gentle immeasurable providence toward those poor souls who foolishly wasted their time. Now, because they are separated from their bodies, they no longer have time in which to merit. Therefore I have provided that you who are still in mortal life should have time for them. I mean that by giving alms and having my ministers say the Divine Office, by fasting and praying while you are in the state of grace, you can by my mercy shorten their time of punishment. O tender providence![59]

I have told you all this about the soul's interior life and your salvation to make you fall in love with my providence and clothe yourself in the light of faith and firm hope. Thus you will free yourself of selfishness and, in all that is yours to do, trust in me without any slavish fear.

149

Now I want to tell you just a little bit about the ways I have to help my servants who trust in me in their bodily needs. I provide for all of them, but they receive my help perfectly or imperfectly according to how perfect or imperfect, how detached from the world and themselves, they are. Take for example my poor—those who are poor in spirit and in will, that is, in spiritual intent. I do not simply say "poor," because there are many who are poor but would rather not be. These are rich so far as their will is concerned, and beggars insofar

---

58. Cf. ch. 41.
59. This entire paragraph is in S but not in C. (There are a few linguistic elements that suggest the paragraph is *possibly* not Catherine's.)

as they neither trust in me nor willingly bear the poverty I have given them as medicine for their souls because wealth would have been bad for them and would have been their damnation.

My servants, on the other hand, are poor but not beggars. Beggars often do not have what they need and suffer great want. But the poor, though they do not enjoy plenty, have their every need fulfilled; I never fail them so long as they put their trust in me. True, I sometimes bring them to the brink so that they will better see and know that I can and will provide for them, so that they will fall in love with my providence and embrace true poverty as their bride.[60] Then their servant, the Holy Spirit, my mercy, when he sees that they lack anything that is necessary for their bodies, will light a nudging spark of desire in the hearts of those who are able to help, and these will come to help them in their need. The whole life of my gentle poor is thus cared for by the concern I give the world's servants for them. While it is true that in order to prove their patience and faith and perseverance I allow them to suffer reproach and insult and abuse, at the same time my mercy constrains the very persons who treat them ill to give them alms and help them in their need. Such is my general providence for my poor.

But sometimes, for my great servants, I act directly, by myself alone, without any human intermediary, as you know from your own experience. And you have heard how your glorious father Dominic, in the early days of the Order, was once so in need that when it came time to eat, the brothers had nothing. My beloved servant Dominic, trusting by the light of faith that I would provide, said, "Sons, take your places at table." The brothers obeyed him, and at his word sat down. Then I who provide for those who trust in me sent two angels with the whitest of bread, so much that they had great plenty for several meals.[61] This was an instance of providence worked by the Holy Spirit's mercy without any human intermediary.

Sometimes I provide by multiplying a little bit of something that

---

60. A trace of Franciscan influence. Catherine's father was a Franciscan tertiary.

61. The incident occurred at old St. Sixtus in Rome and was recorded by Sister Cecilia, Dominic's first biographer. Two brothers had gone begging but had received nothing but a single loaf of bread, and this they had given to a poor man. So they returned to the convent empty-handed. Nonetheless, Dominic had the dinner bell rung. After the prayers two young men entered the refectory with baskets of the whitest of bread and distributed it to the brothers, beginning with the youngest. When they came to St. Dominic, they bowed and vanished. This is the source of the Dominican custom of serving the youngest at table first.

would never have been enough, as you know I did for that gentle virgin Saint Agnes.[62] From her childhood right up to the end she served me with true humility and such firm trust that she never had any hesitations concerning herself or her family. So with her lively faith, at the command of Mary this poor young thing without any temporal goods began to establish a monastery. You know that the place had been a brothel. She didn't think, "How will I be able to do this?" But with my providence she quickly made it a holy place, a monastery for religious. There in the beginning she gathered eighteen young virgins, though she had nothing unless I would provide. Among other things, I once let them go three days without bread, with nothing but greens to eat. You might ask me, "Why did you do this in spite of the fact that you told me that you never fail your servants who trust in you and that they always have what they need? It seems to me that these women did not have what they needed, because the human body cannot live on nothing but greens. (I am speaking about people in general, not about the perfect. But even if Agnes was perfect the others were not so perfect.)" I would answer you that I did it and permitted it to make Agnes drunk with my providence. As for those who were still imperfect, in the miracle that followed afterward they would have material to build their principle and foundation in the light of most holy faith. As for any human body to which a similar thing would happen, I would make it so amenable to those greens or anything else that it would fare better on that little bit of greens, or sometimes even without any food, than it had done before on bread and all the other things that are given for human life. And you know that this is so because you have experienced it yourself.[63]

I told you I provide by multiplying things. At the time I was telling you about, Agnes turned her mind's eye to me in the light of faith and said, "My Father and Lord, my eternal bridegroom, did you make me take these daughters away from their fathers' homes to die of hunger? Provide, Lord, for their need." It was I who made her ask. I was pleased to test her faith, and her humble prayer was pleasing to me. I stretched out my providence to a certain person who was standing in

---

62. Agnes Segni of Montepulciano (1268–1317). She was not canonized until 1726, but Catherine like her contemporaries did not hesitate to give her the title of Saint.

63. Catherine spent most of the last ten years of her life unable to take any nourishment except at times "a bit of raw lettuce." When she did try to eat because of criticism or for fear of giving scandal, she would be forced almost immediately to leave the room to regurgitate (Cf. *Leg. Maj.* I, vi).

spirit before me, and I constrained him by my inspiration to bring them five little rolls. I revealed this to Agnes' mind, and she turned to her sisters and said, "Go to the turn, my daughters, and bring that bread." When they had brought it back they took their places at table. I gave her such power as she divided up the bread that all of them ate their fill and so much was left on the table that they had plenty for their bodily need yet another time.[64]

This is the providence I use with my servants who are poor by choice, and not simply by choice but for spiritual reasons. For without that spiritual intention it would be worthless. They would be like the philosophers who for love of science and their will to learn it spurned riches and became poor by choice because they knew naturally that worrying about worldly riches would prevent their reaching the scientific goal they had set before their mind's eye as their sole end. But because their choice of poverty was not spiritual, not made for the glory and praise of my name, it did not bring them grace or perfection but eternal death.

150

But alas, dearest daughter, see how those philosophers put to shame the miserable lovers of wealth who do not follow the knowledge offered them by nature to gain the supreme eternal Good! For the philosophers, knowing wealth was a hindrance for them, threw it off. But these people would make wealth a god. It is clear that this is so from the fact that they grieve more when they lose their wealth and temporal possessions than when they lose me, the supreme eternal wealth.

If you will look well, you will see that every sort of evil comes from this perverse desire and will for wealth.[65] Pride comes from it, because they want to be superior. It brings forth injustice to themselves and to others. It brings forth avarice, because their hunger for money makes them think nothing of robbing their brothers [and sisters] or taking what belongs to the Church, what has been bought with the blood of the Word, my only-begotten Son. It generates trafficking in the flesh of their neighbors and selling time as usurers who like thieves sell what is not theirs to sell. It generates gluttony for too much

---

64. Catherine was twice a guest at the monastery founded by St. Agnes and could have heard the story, if not from nuns who had witnessed the incident, certainly at least as an oral tradition still closely linked with its source (Cavallini).
65. Cf. 1 Tm. 6:10.

and too many foods. And indecency, for if they had nothing to spend they would not be keeping company with such wretchedness.

How many murders! How much hatred and spite toward their neighbors! What cruelty and unfaithfulness to me, because they presume on themselves as if they had acquired their wealth by their own power! They do not see that they neither gain nor keep it by their own power but only by mine.[66] They lose their trust in me and trust only in their riches. But their trust is empty, for it will fail as soon as they have no more riches. Either they will lose them in this life by my dispensation and for their own good, or they will lose them in death. Then they will know how fickle and empty their trust was. It impoverishes and kills the soul. It makes people cruel to themselves. It takes away the worth of the infinite and makes it finite; that is, their desire, which ought to be united with me, infinite Good, is united with and set on the love of something finite. They lose their taste for virtue and for the fragrance of poverty, they lose their lordship by becoming the servants of riches.[67] They are never satisfied, because they love something that is less than themselves. All created things were made to serve people,[68] not for people to become their servants, and people ought to be serving me, for I am their end.

To what dangers and sufferings people will submit themselves on land and sea to acquire greath wealth, to return later to their own city with pleasures and honors! Yet they neither try nor care to acquire the virtues or to suffer the least bit of pain to have them, though these are the riches of the soul. They are totally immersed [in their wealth], and their heart and affection, which ought to be serving me, they have set on wealth, loading their conscience with all sorts of unlawful gains. See to what wretchedness they come, what it is they serve: not firm and stable things but changeable things, so that today they are rich, tomorrow poor. Now they are high up, now low. Now they are feared and respected by the world because of their wealth, and now they are ridiculed for having lost it. They are treated with reproach and shame and no compassion, because they were loved and made themselves loved for their riches and not for their virtue.[69] If they had made them-

---

66. E: "my permission."
67. Cf. Ga. 4:9.
68. Cf. Ps. 8:6, cited in Heb. 2:7–8.
69. Taurisano (*Dialogo*, 1947, p. 431) notes in this passage a reflection of the state of affairs in Siena during Catherine's time, when the failure of the famous bankers, the

selves loved and been loved for their virtue, they would have lost neither respect nor love, because they would have lost only their temporal possessions but not the riches of virtue.

Oh, what a heavy weight these are to their conscience! They are so heavy that they can neither run along this road of pilgrimage nor pass through the narrow gate.[70] Thus my Truth said in the holy Gospel that it is more impossible for a rich person to enter eternal life than for a camel to pass through the eye of a needle.[71] Such are those who possess or desire wealth with miserably disordered affection. For there are many who are poor, as I have told you, who by their disordered affection possess the whole world with their will if only they could have it. They cannot pass through the gate because it is narrow and low. Only if they throw their load to the ground and restrain their affection for the world and bow their head in humility will they be able to pass through. And there is no other gate but this that leads to eternal life.

The gate is broad that leads to eternal damnation, and blind as they are it seems they do not see their own destruction, for even in this life they have a foretaste of hell. They are always suffering because they are wanting more than they can have. They suffer over what they do not have, and what they lose they lose with grief. Their grief is as great as was their love in possessing. They lose all affection for their neighbors and have no care for acquiring virtue.

O rottenness of the world! Not the things of the world in themselves, because I created everything good and perfect. But rotten are those who seek and keep these things with disordered love.

Dearest daughter, your tongue could never tell how many are the evils that come from this. They see and experience them every day, but they do not want to see or recognize their harmfulness.

151

I have touched on these few things because I want you to know better the treasure of spiritually motivated voluntary poverty. Who knows it? My beloved poor servants who in order to be able to travel this road and enter through this narrow gate have thrown to the ground the burden of riches.

Buonsignori, involved many Sienese families and set off a serious crisis in the city's business and finances (Cavallini).

70. Cf. Mt. 7:13–14.
71. Cf. Mt. 19:24; Mk. 10:25; Lk. 18:25.

THE DIALOGUE

Some throw it down both in fact and in spirit: These are those who observe both the commandments and the counsels in fact as well as in spirit. The others observe the counsels in spirit only, stripping themselves of attachment to wealth, so that they do not possess it with disordered love but with holy fear. In fact, they are not so much possessors of it as distributors for the poor. This is good, but the first way is perfect, more fruitful and less encumbered, and there my providence is more clearly reflected in actuality. (I will finish telling you about this when I am speaking in praise of true poverty.) Both the one and the other bow their heads, making themselves small in true humility. But because I have told you elsewhere about the second—if you remember well, I did tell you something about it[72]—I will now tell you only about the first.

I have shown you how every evil, harm, and suffering, in this life and in the next, comes from selfish love of riches.

Now, on the opposite side, I am telling you that every good, peace, rest, and calm comes from poverty. Only look at the faces of those who are truly poor: how happy and joyful they are! The only thing that saddens them is when I am offended, and this sadness fattens rather than distresses the soul. Through poverty they have gained the highest of riches. By leaving darkness behind they discover the most perfect light for themselves. By leaving behind worldly sadness they have come to possess happiness. In place of mortal goods they find the immortal. The greatest of consolations is theirs. Their labors and suffering are refreshment to them. They are just and love everyone with a familial love. They do not play favorites.

In whom do the virtues of most holy faith and true hope shine forth? Where does the fire of divine charity burn? In those who, by the light of their faith in me, supreme eternal wealth, raise their hope above the world and above all empty riches to embrace true poverty as their bride along with her servants. And do you know what these servants of poverty are? Contempt for oneself and true humility, which serve and nurture the soul's love for poverty. With this faith and hope, ablaze with the fire of charity, my true servants leaped and leap above riches and selfishness. Just so, the glorious apostle Matthew leaped up from his tax booth and, leaving his great wealth behind, followed my Truth,[73] who taught you the way and the rule by teaching you to love

---

72. Cf. ch. 47.
73. Cf. Mt. 9:9; Mk. 2:14; Lk. 5:27.

and follow this poverty. And he taught you not only with words but by his example as well, from his birth right up to the end of his life. For you he took poverty as his bride, though he was wealth itself by his union with the divine nature, for he is one thing with me and I with him, eternal wealth.

And if you would see him humiliated and in great poverty, look at God made man, clothed in the lowliness of your humanity.

You see this gentle loving Word born in a stable while Mary was on a journey, to show you pilgrims how you should be constantly born anew in the stable of self-knowledge, where by grace you will find me born within your soul. You see him lying among the animals, in such poverty that Mary had nothing to cover him up with. It was winter, and she kept him warm with the animals' breath and a blanket of hay. He is the fire of charity but he chose to endure the cold in his humanity.

All the while he lived he chose to suffer, whether his disciples joined him or not, as when once because of their hunger the disciples plucked ears of corn and ate the grain.[74]

At the end of his life, stripped naked, scourged at the pillar, parched with thirst, he was so poor on the wood of the cross that neither the earth nor the wood could give him a place to lay his head. He had nowhere to rest it except on his own shoulder. And drunk as he was with love, he made a bath for you of his blood when this Lamb's body was broken open and bled from every part.[75]

Out of his misery he gave you great wealth. From the narrow wood of the cross he extended his generosity to everyone. By tasting the bitterness of the gall he gave you the most perfect sweetness. From his sadness he gave you consolation. He was nailed to the cross to loose you from the chains of deadly sin. By becoming a servant he rescued you from slavery to the devil and set you free. He was sold to ransom you with his blood. By choosing death for himself he gave you life.

How truly, then, has he given you love as your rule by showing you more love than you could ever show, giving his life for you who were enemies to him and to me the high eternal Father. The foolish ones who so offend me and scorn the great price he paid do not recognize this. He gave you true humility as your rule by humbling himself in his shameful death on the cross. He gave you lowliness as your rule

---

74. Mt. 12:1.
75. Cf. Jn. 19:34.

by suffering such disgrace and great reproach. And he gave you true poverty as your rule, for Scripture laments in his name, "The foxes have dens, the birds have nests, but the Virgin's Son has nowhere to lay his head."[76] Who knows this? Those who are enlightened by most holy faith. In whom do you find this faith? In the spiritually poor who have taken as their bride Queen Poverty, for they have cast away the riches that bring on the darkness of infidelity.

This queen's realm is never at war, but is always peaceful and calm. She overflows with justice, because the thing that perpetrates injustice is cut off from her. Her city walls are strong, because their foundation is not in the earth, nor on the sand that every little wind scares up from the earth,[77] but on the living rock,[78] the gentle Christ Jesus my only-begotten Son. There is no darkness within her, but fire without any cold,[79] because this queen's mother is divine charity. This city's adornment is compassion and mercy, because the cruel tyrant wealth has been put out. There is benevolence, that is, neighborly affection, among all its citizens. There is enduring perseverance and prudence, for poverty does not act or govern her city imprudently but watches over it with great concern and prudence. Thus the soul who takes this gentle queen, poverty, as bride is made master of all these riches, for the two go hand in hand. The only condition is that the plague of hankering after wealth not come upon that soul, for then she would be cut off from that good and find herself outside the city in the greatest misery. But if she is loyal and faithful to this bride, she will bestow her wealth on her forever and ever.

Who sees such excellence? The soul in whom the light of faith is shining. This bride clothes her spouse anew in purity by taking away the wealth that had made her unclean. She deprives her[80] of wicked companions and gives her good ones instead. She drains out from her the pus of carelessness by casting out care for the world and riches. She draws out what is bitter and leaves what is sweet; she pulls out the thorns and leaves the rose. She empties the soul's stomach of the rotten

---

76. Cf. Mt. 8:20; Lk. 9:58.
77. S, F omit "nor . . . earth."
78. Cf. Mt. 7:24–29; Lk. 6:47–49.
79. S, F omit "but . . . cold."
80. The metaphors become crossed here. Poverty is the bride (feminine), but her spouse (masculine in Catherine's Tuscan) is the soul (always feminine in Catherine's references). English has no really adequate way of dealing with the overlap: I have opted for consistency with the soul's femininity, which is the more constant thread even here.

humors of disordered love and makes it light, and as soon as it is emptied she fills it with the food of virtues that bring the greatest sweetness. She gives the soul hatred and love as servants so that she will clean her dwelling place. Thus hatred for vice and selfish sensuality sweep out the soul, and love for virtue adorns her. She relieves her of all doubt by taking away her slavish fear and gives her confidence and holy fear instead.

The soul who takes Queen Poverty as bride finds all the virtues, all the graces and pleasures and delights she could desire and more. She has no fear of vexation, for no one is at war against her. She has no fear of hunger or want, because her faith sees and trusts me, her Creator and the source of all wealth and providence, for I always feed and nurture her. Have you ever found a servant of mine, a spouse of poverty, who died of hunger? No. There have been some who had great and overflowing riches and have perished because they trusted in their riches rather than in me. But I never fail those who never fail in their hope. I provide for them as a kind compassionate father. And with what glad generosity they come to me, because they have come to know by the light of faith that my providence always has and always will provide for every spiritual and temporal need. True, I let them suffer to make them grow in faith and hope and so that I may reward them for their labors, but I never fail to give them anything they need. In everything they sweetly experience the depth of my providence, tasting in it the milk of divine tenderness, and this is why they do not fear the bitterness of death. Rather they run on with eager longing, dead as they are to selfish feelings about themselves and riches, arm in arm with poverty their bride. They are people in love and alive in my will, ready to endure heat, cold, and nakedness, hunger and thirst, anguish and abuse and even death, in their desire to give their life for love of Life (that is, for me, for I am their life), and to shed their blood for love of the blood.

Look at the poor apostles and the other glorious martyrs, Peter, Paul, Stephen. Look at Lawrence, who seemed to be not over the fire but over the most pleasant of flowers, joking, as it were, with the tyrant and saying, "This side is cooked; turn it over and start eating!"[81] The fire of divine charity was so great that in his soul's feeling he regarded the lesser fire as nothing. And to Stephen the stones seemed

---

81. Cf. the Office for the feast of St. Lawrence: *"assatus est iam: versa et manduca."* Also, *The Golden Legend*, ch. CXII, i.

like roses. What was the reason? The love with which he had taken true and perfect poverty as his bride. He had left the world behind for the glory and praise of my name and espoused poverty by the light of most holy faith with firm trust and ready obedience. These souls became obedient both in fact and in spirit to the commandments and to the counsels given them by my Truth.

They are desirous of death and scornful and impatient of life, not because they wish to escape toil and weariness, but because they want to be united with me, their end. And why are they not afraid of death as people naturally are? Because poverty their bride has made them secure by taking away their attachment to themselves and to riches. Thus, with virtue they have trampled their natural love underfoot and have received this divine light and love that are beyond nature. How could those in such a state be sad about death? For their desire is to leave this life behind, and it pains them to see it so prolonged. Could those who have so eagerly spurned worldly pleasures and riches be sorry to leave them behind? It is not surprising, for one who does not love is not sad; indeed, it is a pleasure to leave behind what one hates. So wherever you turn you find in these souls perfect peace and calm and every good thing. And in the wicked who possess things with such disordered love you see the greatest evil and unbearable suffering. Even though on the outside they may seem the opposite, in truth it is always so.

Who would not have judged that poor Lazarus was supremely miserable and the rich man quite happy and content? Yet such was not the case, for that rich man with all his wealth suffered more than poor Lazarus tormented by his leprosy. For the rich man's [selfish] will was alive, and this is the source of all suffering. But in Lazarus this will was dead and his will was so alive in me that he found refreshment and consolation in his pain. He had been thrown out by others, especially by the rich man, and was neither cleansed nor cared for by them, but I provided that the senseless animals should lick his sores. And you see how at the end of their lives Lazarus has eternal life and the rich man is in hell.[82]

So the rich are left sad while my poor are happy. I hold them to my breast and give them the milk of great consolation. Because they leave everything they possess me completely. The Holy Spirit becomes the nurse of their souls and their little bodies in every situation. I make

---

82. Lk. 16:19–22.

the animals provide for them in this way and that, depending on their need. If a hermit is ill I make another hermit leave his cell to help him. You know how often I have pulled you out of your cell to satisfy the needs of the poor. Sometimes I have let you experience this yourself by using this same kind of providence to help you when you were in need, and even when creatures failed you, I your Creator did not.[83] In every way I provide for [my poor]. How does it happen that people who have wealth and take such good care of their bodies and have so many clothes are always sickly—and then when they come to despise themselves and embrace poverty with just enough clothes to cover their bodies they become strong and healthy and it seems nothing can hurt them, that neither cold nor heat nor coarse foods can harm their body? My providence is the reason, for I provide and deprive and care for those who completely surrender themselves.

So you see, most beloved daughter, how great is the contentment and delight of these beloved poor of mine.

152

Now I have told you just a little bit about my providence for all manner of folk. I showed you how I have done and do all I do in providence for your salvation,[84] from the beginning (when I created the first world and then the second, my human creation, giving you existence and creating you in my image and likeness) right up to the end. Everything you have received since you began to be I have given for this purpose. The wicked people of the world who have thrown away the light do not see this. I have told you how they are scandalized at me because they have no knowledge. Yet I bear with them patiently, waiting for them right up to the end, providing for their needs (although they are sinners) in these temporal things and in the spiritual, just as I do for the just. I have also described for you the imperfect nature of riches, a bit about the wretched behavior of those who are inordinately attached to them, and the magnificence of poverty, the wealth she bestows on the soul who chooses to espouse her along with her sister, lowliness. I will describe this lowliness for you when I tell you about obedience.

I have also shown you how pleasing and dear to me such a soul is,

---

83. Cf. *Leg. Maj.* II, iii.
84. Cf. 1 Th. 4:3.

and how I provide for her. I have told you all this to commend this virtue to you along with the most holy faith that brings one to this marvelous state. I wanted to make you grow in faith and in hope, to make you come knocking at the door of my mercy. Believe with lively faith that I will fulfill your longing and that of [all] my servants, along with great suffering even to the point of death. But take courage and rejoice in me, because I am your defender and your consoler.

I have spoken enough now about my providence. You asked me to provide for my creatures' needs, and you have seen that I am no scorner of truly holy desires.

153

Then that soul was as if drunk with love of true holy poverty. She was filled to bursting in the supreme eternal magnificence and so transformed in the abyss of his supreme and immeasurable providence that though she was in the vessel of her body it seemed as if the fire of charity within her had taken over and rapt her outside her body. And with her mind's eye steadily fixed on the divine majesty she spoke to the high eternal Father:

O eternal Father! O fiery abyss of charity! O eternal beauty, O eternal wisdom, O eternal goodness, O eternal mercy! O hope and refuge of sinners! O immeasurable generosity! O eternal, infinite Good! O mad lover! And you have need of your creature? It seems so to me, for you act as if you could not live without her, in spite of the fact that you are Life itself, and everything has life from you and nothing can have life without you.[85] Why then are you so mad? Because you have fallen in love with what you have made! You are pleased and delighted over her within yourself, as if you were drunk [with desire] for her salvation. She runs away from you and you go looking for her. She strays and you draw closer to her:[86] You clothed yourself in our humanity, and nearer than that you could not have come.

And what shall I say? I will stutter, "A–a," because there is nothing else I know how to say.[87] Finite language cannot express the emotion of the soul who longs for you infinitely. I think I could echo Paul's

---

85. Cf. Jn. 1:3–4.
86. The text here has "me"—a delightful slip that puts the whole of this ecstatic outburst out of the detached third person into the very intimate first.
87. Cf. Jr. 1:6.

words: The tongue cannot speak nor the ear hear nor the eye see nor the heart imagine[88] what I have seen! What have you seen? "I have seen the hidden things of God!"[89] And I—what do I say? I have nothing to add from these clumsy emotions [of mine]. I say only, my soul, that you have tasted and seen the abyss of supreme eternal providence.

I thank you now, high eternal Father, for the measureless kindness you have shown me, though I am miserably undeserving of any favor.

But because I see that you are a fulfiller of holy desires, and that your Truth cannot lie, I wish now that you would speak to me a little about the power and excellence of obedience just as you, eternal Father, promised me you would, so that I might fall in love with this virtue and never cut myself off from obedience to you. Please, in your infinite kindness, tell me how perfect it is, where I can find it, what would take it away from me, who gives it to me, and what is the sign that I do or do not have it.

---

88. Cf. 1 Co. 2:9.
89. *"Vidi arcana Dei!"* Catherine's sole use of Latin in the *Dialogue.* Cf. 2 Co. 12:4, though these exact words do not occur there.

OBEDIENCE

154

T*hen the high eternal compassionate Father looked on her with
mercy and said:*

O dearest, gentlest daughter! Your holy longing and just petitions
deserve to be heard. I am supreme Truth, and I will fulfill my truth by
keeping my promise and granting your wish. You ask me where you
may find obedience, what can take it away, and how you may know
whether or not you have it. My answer is that you will find it in its
fullness in the gentle loving Word, my only-begotten Son. His obedience was so ready that to realize it he ran to his shameful death on the
cross.

What takes obedience away? Look at the first man. What took
away the obedience that I the eternal Father had laid on him was the
pride that came from his selfish love and his desire to please his companion. This is what gave him disobedience in place of the perfection
of obedience, death in place of the life of grace, wretched filthiness in
the place of innocence. And it was not only he who fell, but the whole
human race with him, as I have told you.[1]

The sign that you have this virtue is patience, and impatience is
the sign that you do not have it. (As I tell you more, you will find that
this is so.)

Notice that there are two ways of observing obedience. The one is
more perfect than the other, but like the commandments and the counsels the two are not separate but united.[2] The one is good and perfect;
the other is most perfect. But only the obedient can attain eternal life,

---

1. Cf. ch. 135; also 14, 21.
2. Cf. ch. 47.

for eternal life, which had been locked by Adam's disobedience, was unlocked by the key of obedience.

When I saw that humankind, whom I so loved, were not returning to me their end, my infinite goodness constrained me to put the key of obedience into the hand of the gentle loving Word, my Truth, and he like a doorman unlocked heaven's gate. Without this key and this doorman, my Truth, no one can enter. This is why he said in the holy Gospel that no one can come to me, the Father, except through him.[3] When he rose beyond human companionship through his ascension to return triumphantly to me into heaven, he left you this sweet key of obedience. As you know, he left it in the hands of his vicar, Christ on earth, whom you are all obliged to obey even to the point of death. Whoever refuses to obey him is, as I have told you elsewhere,[4] living in damnation.

Now I want you to see and know this most excellent virtue and its source in the humble spotless Lamb. What was the source of this Word's obedience? His love for my honor and your salvation. And what was the source of this love? The light of his soul's clear vision of the divine Essence and eternal Trinity, for he always saw me, God eternal.

This vision effected most perfectly in him that fidelity which the light of most holy faith effects imperfectly in you. Because he was faithful to me his eternal Father, he ran like one gloriously in love along the way of obedience. Love never stands alone, but has as her companions all the true solid virtues, because all the virtues have life from charity's love. (The virtues existed differently in the Word, however, from the way they do in you.) And among love's companions is patience, the very marrow of love and the clear sign of whether the soul is in grace and is loving in truth or not. This is why charity, the mother, has given obedience patience as a sister and has so joined the two together that the one can never be lost without the other. Either you have both or you have neither.

Obedience has a wet nurse, true humility, and the soul is as obedient as she is humble, and as humble as she is obedient. This humility is also charity's governess and wet nurse, and she nurtures the virtue of obedience with the very same milk. The garment this nurse gives the soul is self-abasement, the clothing of disgrace and mockery and

---

3. Jn. 14:6.
4. Cf. ch. 65, 66.

abuse,[5] the choice of my pleasure over her own. In whom will you find all this? In the gentle Christ Jesus, my only-begotten Son. Who has ever been more humble than he?[6] He was saturated with disgrace and abuse. To please me, he despised his own pleasure, that is, his bodily life.[7] And who has ever been more patient than he? He was never heard to cry out in complaint;[8] no, he embraced insults with patience. In love as he was, he fulfilled the obedience that I his eternal Father had laid upon him.

In him, then, you will find this virtue in her fullness. He left her to you as a rule and teaching that he first lived himself. She is a straight path leading to life. And he is himself the Way. This is why he said that he is Way and Truth and Life and that whoever walks by this way walks in the light. Those who walk in the light cannot unwittingly stumble or be tripped up,[9] because they have cast off the darkness of selfish love that had been the cause of their falling into disobedience. For, as I have told you, the source and companion of obedience is humility. But disobedience comes from pride, which in turn comes from selfish love for oneself and deprives one of humility. Selfish love gives disobedience impatience as a sister and pride as wet nurse. And in the darkness of infidelity she runs along the darksome way that leads to eternal death.

All of you ought to read this glorious book [the Word], for here you will find this and all the other virtues written.

155

Now that I have shown you where to find obedience, whence she comes, who is her companion and who her wet nurse, I will speak to you about the obedient and the disobedient side by side, and about general obedience and special, that is, the obedience of the commandments and that of the counsels.

Your entire faith is founded on obedience, for it is by obedience that you show your fidelity. My Truth imposed on all of you in general the commandments of the Law, the chief of which is to love

---

5. S, E, F omit "mockery and abuse."
6. Cf. Ph. 2:7.
7. Cf. Rm. 15:3.
8. Cf. Is. 53:7.
9. Cf. Jn. 14:6, 8:12, 11:9–10.

me above all things and your neighbors as your very self. And the others are so bound up with this one that those who observe this one necessarily observe them all, and those who let go of this one let go of them all.[10] Those who observe this double commandment observe all the others; they are faithful to me and to their neighbors; they love me and are affectionate toward my creatures. Therefore they are obedient and submit themselves to the commandments of the Law and to other people for my sake. And they humbly and patiently endure every sort of labor and slander.

The Word's obedience was so superb that all of you draw grace from it, just as you had drawn death from disobedience.[11] But it would not be enough for it to be in him alone and not be exercised by you here and now. I have already told you that this obedience is a key that unlocked heaven, a key that he put into the hands of his vicar. This vicar puts it into the hands of each of you when you receive holy baptism, promising to obey [me] and to renounce the devil, the world, and all their pleasures and ostentation. So each of you individually has it, the very Word's key. And unless you walk by the light of faith and with the hand of love to open heaven's gate with this key, you will never enter there, even though it has been opened by the Word. For I created you without your help, without your ever asking me, because I loved you before you even existed,[12] but I will not save you without your help.

You must, then, carry the key in your hand; you must walk, not sit—walk along the way of my Truth's teaching and not sit down by setting your heart on finite things as do those fools who follow the old man, their first father. They do what he did, for he threw the key of obedience into the filthy mire and smashed it with the hammer of pride and let it get rusty with selfishness. Not until the Word my only-begotten Son came was this key of obedience picked up again. He purified it in the fire of divine charity after he had picked it out of the mire and washed it with his blood. With the knife of justice he straightened it and on the anvil of his body he hammered out your iniquities.[13] He repaired it so perfectly that no matter how you might damage it with

---

10. Cf. Mt. 22:37–40.
11. Cf. Rm. 5:19.
12. E omits "without your ever asking ... existed."
13. Cf. Ps. 129:3.

your free choice, by your same free choice you can, with the help of my grace and using these same instruments, repair it again.

Oh, blind and worse than blind are you who care nothing about repairing this key of obedience after you have damaged it! Do you think the disobedience that locked heaven will open it for you? Do you think the pride that fell from there can rise back up? Do you think you can go to the wedding with your garment torn and filthy? Do you think you can walk when you are sitting there bound in the chains of deadly sin? Or that you can open the door without a key? Do not imagine that you can, because your imagination would be deceived. You have to be set free. Leave deadly sin behind by a holy confession with heartfelt contrition, satisfaction, and resolution to sin no more. Then you will throw off your ugly filthy garment and with a [proper] wedding garment, in the light and with the key of obedience in your hand, you will run to unlock the door. Tie this key on tightly with the cord of lowliness and contempt for yourself and the world. Attach it to desire to please me your Creator. You ought to make yourself a belt of this desire, so that you will not lose the key.[14]

Know, my daughter, that many people have taken hold of the key of obedience when they have seen by the light of faith that in no other way can they escape eternal damnation. But they hold it in their hand without tying it with this cord or fastening it to this belt. In other words, they do not clothe themselves perfectly in the desire to please me but are only interested in pleasing themselves. They have not tied on the cord of lowliness by desiring to be considered lowly; rather, they have found their pleasure in being praised by others. They are likely to lose the key. Let them only experience a little too much physical or spiritual weariness, and unless they are very careful they will all too often loosen the grip of their desire and lose it. This is a loss that can be recovered, if they are willing, so long as they are alive. But if they are not willing they will never find it. And who will show them that they have lost it? Impatience. For patience was joined with obedience, and the absence of patience shows that obedience is not in the soul.

Oh, how delightful and glorious is this virtue! She embraces all the

---

14. Cf. Is. 11:5. "Integrity is the loincloth round his waist, faithfulness the belt about his hips."

other virtues because she is conceived and born of charity. In her is laid the foundation stone of most holy faith. She is a queen, and whoever espouses her will never know evil but only peace and calm. No matter how the sea's stormy waves may pound her, they cannot hurt the marrow of the soul. She feels no hatred when she is hurt because she wants to be obedient and knows that she has been commanded to forgive. She does not suffer when her own wishes are not fulfilled, because obedience has set her priority in desiring only me, and I know how to and can and will fulfill her desires. Obedience has stripped her of worldly joys. And so in all things—it would take too long to tell you everything—she finds peace and calm once she has espoused this queen, obedience, whom I have given you as a key.

O obedience! You sail on without weariness until you arrive safely at the port of salvation. You pattern yourself after the Word, my only-begotten Son, boarding the ship of the most holy cross to suffer so as not to violate the Word's obedience or depart from his teaching. You make of it your table, where you feast on souls in your affection for your neighbors.

You are anointed with true humility, so you do not hanker after your neighbors' possessions against my will. You are straight, not winding, because you keep your heart direct and true, loving my creatures freely and without guile.

You are a dawn bearing the light of divine grace. You are a warming sun, never without charity's heat. You make earth blossom: The instruments of soul and body all bring forth fruit for the soul's own life and that of others.

You are wholly joyous, for you have not marred your face with impatience but have kept it pleasant with the pleasantness of patience, wholly and strongly serene. You are great in your perseverance—so great that you reach from heaven to earth—for it was with you that heaven was unlocked. You are a pearl hidden and unknown, trampled on by the world, humbling yourself in submission to others.[15]

Your authority is so great that no one can have authority over you, because you have left behind the deadly servitude of selfish sensuality that had deprived you of your dignity. Once this enemy was slain by contempt for doing your own will, you regained your freedom.

---

15. Cf. Mt. 13:44–46, 7:6.

156

I tell you, dearest daughter, all of this was done by my kind providence, which provided that the Word should reclaim this key to obedience. But worldly people, bereft of all virtue, do just the opposite. Like animals running loose (because they are without the restraint of obedience) they run on from bad to worse, from sin to sin, from wickedness to wickedness, from darkness to darkness, from death to death. They finally end up in death's ditch with the worm of conscience constantly gnawing away at them. And even though it is possible for them to take up again the obedience of willingness to obey the Law's commandments if they have time and are sorry for their disobedience, it is very difficult because they are so in the habit of sinning. So let no one be so presumptuous as to wait for the moment of death to pick up the key of obedience. It is true that everyone can and should have hope so long as there is time, but no one should be so confident of this as to put off amending his or her life.

And what causes them to be so unfortunate and blind that they do not know this treasure? The cloud of selfish love and wretched pride that made them depart from obedience and fall into disobedience. Because they are not obedient they are not patient, and in their impatience they suffer intolerably. It has drawn them away from the way of truth and leads them along the way of falsehood so that they become servants and friends of the devils, and unless they change their ways, in their disobedience they will go along with their masters the devils to eternal punishment. But my beloved children who are obedient to the Law rejoice and exult in the eternal sight of me with the humble spotless Lamb, the maker, fulfiller, and giver of the Law. In this life they have tasted peace in its observance, and in the blessed life they receive and are clothed in the most perfect peace. Here there is peace without any war, every good without any evil, security without any fear, wealth without poverty, satiety without boredom, hunger without pain, light without darkness, supreme Good not finite but infinite, shared by all the truly joyful.

What has established them in such a great reward? The blood of the Lamb by whose power the key of obedience shed its rust so that you would be able to use it to unlock the gate. So it is obedience that has opened it for you by the power of the blood.

O stupid fools! Do not wait any longer to come up out of the filthy mire. It seems you roll about in the mire of sensuality as pigs roll about in the mud. Leave behind injustice and murders, hatred and spite, the detraction, complaining, [rash] judgment, and violence you have used against your neighbors, the thievery and betrayal and perverse pleasures and delights of the world. Cut off pride's horns and so dissipate the hatred you have in your hearts for those who do you harm. Compare the harm you do to me and to your neighbors with what is done to you, and you will find that in comparison to what you do to me and them your own hurt is nothing. It is easy to see that by harboring hatred you insult me because you violate my commandment, and you hurt your neighbors by depriving them of loving charity. I commanded you to love me above all things and to love your neighbors as your very selves. This was not qualified in any way that might say: If they hurt you, do not love them. No, [your love must be] free and sincere, because the command was given you by my Truth, who observed it with sincerity. You ought to observe it with the same sincerity, for if you do not, you are hurting yourselves and harming your souls by depriving yourselves of the life of grace.

So take up, take up the key of obedience by the light of faith. Walk no more in such blindness and cold, but rather cling to this obedience with burning love so that with all who observe the Law you may come to taste eternal life.

157

There are some, dearest daughter, in whom the gentle loving fire of love for this obedience grows so strong (and since there is no fire of love without hatred for selfish sensuality, this hatred grows as the fire grows) that for love and hatred they are not content with ordinary obedience to the Law's commandments. These you are all obliged to obey if you wish to have life, and otherwise you would have death. But these souls take on a special obedience that follows on great perfection: They become observers of the counsels in fact as well as in spirit.

They bind themselves more strictly in self-contempt and to slay their will completely. Either they bind themselves to the yoke of obedience in a religious order, or they submit their will outside religious life to some other person so as to advance more speedily to unlock heaven. These have chosen the most perfect obedience.

I have told you about ordinary obedience. Now, because I know you want me to speak about the more special and most perfect kind of obedience, I will tell you about it. This second kind of obedience does not leave the first behind; it is simply more perfect, for (as I have already told you) the two are so bound together that they cannot be separated.

I have told you where ordinary obedience comes from, where it is found, and what takes it away. Now, without drawing you away from this beginning, I will tell you about special obedience.

158

The soul who has lovingly taken on the yoke of obedience to the commandments by following my Truth's teaching and exercising herself in virtue will from there attain the second kind of obedience by the same light by which she came to the first. For by the light of most holy faith she will have come to know my truth in the blood of the Lamb: the truth of my ineffable love for her and her own inability to respond to me as perfectly as she ought. So with this light she begins seeking how and where she might better pay her debt to me, trampling underfoot her own weakness and killing her [selfish] will. Her search leads her by the light of faith to religious life. The Holy Spirit made this [way of life] and set it there like a ship ready to receive souls who want to race on to perfection and to bring them to the port of salvation.

The captain of this ship is the Holy Spirit, who lacks nothing. His religious subjects who violate his orders can hurt only themselves, never this ship. Yet the captain may let it run into the waves through the fault of those who are at the helm, the miserable wicked shepherds he had appointed to be superiors and pilots of the ship. In herself this ship is so delightful that your tongue could never describe her.

This soul, I tell you, in whom the fire of desire and holy self-contempt has grown, when she has found the place by the light of faith, enters it dead if she is truly obedient and has perfectly observed the ordinary commandments. If she enters it imperfect it does not mean she cannot attain perfection. She will attain it if she is willing to exercise herself in obedience. In fact, the majority of those who enter are imperfect. Some enter perfect, some as children, some through fear, some to do penance, some because they are attracted to it. But from that point on the only thing that counts is that they exercise themselves in virtue and persevere until death. For there are many who seemed to be perfect when they entered but later have turned back or have stayed in the order but with great imperfection. So you cannot pass judgment on the fact or manner of their entry. That is ordained by me, and I call people in different ways. You can judge only by the fact of their persevering there in true obedience.

This ship is rich. Her subjects need never worry about what they need spiritually or temporally, for if they are truly obedient and observe the rule they will be provided for by the captain, the Holy Spirit. I told you, when I was talking about my providence, that though my servants might be poor they are not beggars. It is the same with these souls: They will have whatever they need.

Those who have observed and now observe the rule have sure experience of this. Thus you see that when the orders blossomed with the virtues of true patience and familial charity, they were never lacking in temporal sustenance but had more than they needed. But as soon as stinking selfishness and noncommunal living entered in and obedience fell by the wayside, they found themselves wanting in temporal goods.[16] The more they possessed, the more they found themselves reduced to begging. It is only just that they should experience even in the least things the fruit that comes from disobedience. For if they were obedient they would be observing the vow of poverty, not keeping private property and living private lives.

Here is found a wealth of holy ordinances established in great order and light by those who had been made temples of the Holy Spirit.

Consider the great order with which Benedict governed his ship.

Consider Francis. With what fragrantly perfect poverty and what pearls of virtue he governed his order's ship! He steered it along the way of high perfection—and he was the first to practice it—giving it true holy poverty as a bride. He himself had espoused her by embracing lowliness. Uninterested in doing his own pleasure, he had no desire to please anyone else against my will. Indeed, he wanted the world to revile him. He disciplined his body, slew his [selfish] will, and clothed himself in shameful sufferings and disgrace for love of the humble Lamb, with whom he was nailed to the cross in love.[17] In fact,

---

16. The theme of poverty has already been treated at length under the heading of providence (Cf. especially ch. 119–151). Here it returns in the realm of obedience as a reproof to the inherent danger of noncommunal ("private") living arrangements to which different historical circumstances (not the least of which was the plague of 1348) had contributed (Cavallini).

17. Cf. Ga. 2:19.

by a singular grace, the wounds of my Truth appeared in his body to show in the vessel of his body what was in his soul's affection. Thus did he make a path for the others.

But you will say to me, "And are not all the other orders founded on this same thing?" Yes, but it is not the principal aspect of all of them. True, all are founded on this, but it happens as it does with the virtues. All the virtues have their life from charity; nonetheless, this virtue is peculiar to one, that to another, though all are grounded in charity. So it is with these people. True poverty was peculiar to the poor Francis, and in love he made this poverty the rule of his ship, with many strict ordinances, for perfect people, not ordinary, for good ones and few. I say "few" because there are not many who choose this perfection. But because of their sins the members multiplied but their virtue grew less. There was nothing wrong with the ship, but its subjects were disobedient and its pilots wicked.

And look at the ship of your father Dominic, my beloved son. He governed it with a perfect rule, asking [his followers] to be attentive only to my honor and the salvation of souls with the light of learning. He wished to build his foundation on this light, while not for all that giving up true and voluntary poverty. He had that as well, and as a sign that he had it and that its opposite displeased him, he left as a bequest to his sons his curse and mine[18] if they should have or keep any property individually or collectively. It was a token that he had chosen Queen Poverty as his bride.[19]

But for his more proper object he took the light of learning in order to stamp out the errors that were rising up at that time. He took up the task of the Word, my only-begotten Son. Clearly he appeared as an apostle in the world, with such truth and light did he sow my word, dispelling the darkness and giving light. He was a light that I offered the world through Mary and sent into the mystic body of holy Church as an uprooter of heresies. Why did I say "through Mary"? Because Mary gave him the habit—a task my goodness entrusted to her.[20]

---

18. C omits "and mine."

19. Cf. *Legenda Aurea*, ch. XVIII: "And he forbade them, with all the severity he could muster, to ever let any temporal possessions invade his order. In his own name and in the name of God almighty he called down a terrible curse on anyone who would be so bold as to defile the Order of Preachers with the dust of earthly riches."

20. The story is told by Jacopo da Varagine (*Leg. Aurea*, ch. XVIII) and is found as well in various collections. Master Reginald had decided to enter the Order of Preachers when he was struck with a violent fever. Then the Virgin Mary appeared to him, and

Where would he have his children eat by the light of learning? At the table of the cross. On that cross is set the table of holy desire where one eats souls for love of me. He wanted his children to do nothing else but stand at this table by the light of learning to seek only the glory and praise of my name and the salvation of souls. And so that they might attend to nothing else, he relieved them of worry about temporal things and wanted them to be poor. Was he lacking in faith or did he fear they would not be provided for? Certainly not, for he was clothed in faith and trusted firmly in my providence.

He wanted them to be obedient in doing what they are appointed to do. And because indecent living beclouds the mind's eye (and not only the mind's: This miserable vice makes bodily vision fail as well), he established the third vow, continence, and wanted them to observe it completely in true perfect obedience. For he did not want that light by which they would better and more perfectly acquire the light of learning to be impeded. But today this vow is ill kept. And people pervert the light of learning into darkness with the darksomeness of pride. Not that this light in itself becomes darksome, but pride sheds darkness upon their souls. Obedience cannot coexist with pride. I have already told you that people are as humble as they are obedient and as obedient as they are humble. It is rare that a person who sins against the vow of obedience does not also sin against continence and true poverty.[21]

So Dominic set his ship in order by rigging it with three strong ropes: obedience, continence, and true poverty.[22] He made it thoroughly royal by not tying it to the guilt of deadly sin.[23] Enlightened by me, the true light, he was providing for those who were less perfect. For, though all who observe the rule are perfect, still even in [this way

---

after anointing him mysteriously "she showed him the habit of the order and said, 'This is the habit of your order.' " Three days later Reginald got well, and the earlier primitive Dominican habit was modified: The woolen scapular shown by Mary replaced the linen surplice.

21. S, E, F omit "and true poverty."

22. C omits "So . . . poverty."

23. "Before this constitution was written, I recall that I heard from older brethren that this was the intention of the Order, namely, that the Constitutions did not oblige under sin. For this reason Blessed Dominic said at the chapter of Bologna for the encouragement of faint-hearted friars that even Rules do not always bind under sin; for if this were what was believed, he would want to go about forever through the monasteries and destroy all monastic Rules with his knife. I was told this by a friar who heard him say it" (Humbert of Romans *Opera* II, 46).

of] life one is more perfect than another, and both the perfect and the not-so-perfect fare well on this ship. Dominic allied himself with my Truth by showing that he did not want the sinner to die but rather to be converted and live.[24] He made his ship very spacious, gladsome, and fragrant, a most delightful garden.

But those wretches who have violated rather than kept the rule have made it a dense wilderness with little fragrance of virtue or light of learning in those who nurse at the order's breast. I do not say "in the order," because the order in itself, as I have told you, is wholly delightful. Things were not so in the beginning when the order blossomed with men of great perfection. They were like Saint Paul, so enlightened that no darksome error appeared in their sight without being dispersed.

Consider the glorious Thomas.[25] With his mind's eye he contemplated my Truth ever so tenderly and there gained light beyond the natural and knowledge infused by grace. Thus he learned more through prayer than through human study. He was a blazing torch shedding light within his order and in the mystic body of holy Church, dispelling the darkness of heresies.

Consider my Peter, virgin and martyr.[26] With his blood he shed light amid the darkness of many heresies, hating them so much that he was ready to give his life [in the struggle against them]. As long as he lived his sole concern was to pray, preach, debate with the heretics, and to fearlessly proclaim the truth and spread the faith. He bore witness to it not only during his lifetime but right up to the very last moment of his life. Thus at the point of death, having neither voice nor ink, after he had been struck down he dipped his finger into his own blood. This glorious martyr had no paper, so he bore witness to the faith by bending down and writing on the ground, *"Credo in Deum."* His heart was ablaze in the furnace of my charity. Therefore he did not

---

24. Cf. Ezk. 33:11.

25. Thomas Aquinas (1225–1274), one of the three Dominicans canonized by Catherine's time. Taurisano states that "when this *Dialogue* is carefully studied in the light of Thomas, it will be said that Catherine was a most faithful and wise disciple of the holy doctor." More recent research, however, often leans in the opposite direction, holding that Catherine was in fact far more influenced by the earlier Augustinian bent of the order than directly by the works of Thomas. The most tenable position seems to lie in the simple observation that Catherine absorbed and integrated everything that came her way, and her writings reflect many sources.

26. Peter of Verona, third of the saints of the Dominican Order canonized by Catherine's time. He was martyred in 1252.

slacken his pace or turn back even though he knew he would have to die. (I had revealed his death to him beforehand.) Like a true knight without any slavish fear he went forth onto the battlefield.

I could tell you about many others who, though they never suffered actual martyrdom, did so in spirit, as did Dominic. What workers this father sent into his vineyard to uproot the thorns of vice and to plant the virtues!

Truly Dominic and Francis were two pillars of holy Church: Francis with the poverty that was his hallmark and Dominic with learning.

159

I have told you about the places, these ships set in order by the Holy Spirit by means of these pilots. (I told you that the Holy Spirit is captain of these ships established in the light of most holy faith because with this light my mercy, this same Holy Spirit, would be their ruler.) I also showed you the perfection of these places, these orders. Now I will speak to you about the obedience and disobedience of those who live on these ships, speaking about all of them at once rather than individually, that is, not referring to any one order more than another. I will show you side by side the sinfulness of the disobedient and the virtue of the obedient, so that you may better know the one through the other. And I will show you how those who want to enter the ship of the order ought to walk.

How ought those walk who would enter into perfect special obedience? By the light of most holy faith, for by this light they will know that they must slay their selfish will with the knife of contempt for every selfish sensual passion and espouse the bride charity will give them, the bride, I say, of true ready obedience with her sister patience and her wet nurse humility. Without this wet nurse obedience would die of hunger, because obedience will quickly die in a soul who does not have this little virtue of humility.

Nor is humility alone. She has a servant, contempt for the world and for oneself, who keeps the soul lowly, hungry for shame rather than honor. Just so dead ought those who are old enough approach the ship of the order. But no matter how they enter (I told you I call people in different ways[27]), they ought to acquire and preserve in themselves this perfection: to take up generously and readily the order's key of obedience, the key that unlocks the smaller door in heaven's gate. Just as a material door has a smaller opening, so these souls have undertaken to unlock this smaller door. They have gone beyond the big key of ordinary obedience[28] that unlocks heaven's gate, and have taken up a slender key to pass through the lower narrower door. This smaller door is not, for all that, separate from the larger gate, as you can see materially. Once they have taken up this slender key they must hold onto it and never throw it away.

The truly obedient have seen by the light of faith that they cannot pass through this smaller door loaded with riches and their own will without great toil and loss of life. Nor can they go through holding their head high without cracking it and then in their pain bowing it whether they want to or not. Therefore they throw off the burden of riches and of their own will by observing the vow of voluntary poverty. They have no wish for possessions, since they see by the light of faith how these could destroy them: They would be sinning against obedience by not observing their promised vow of voluntary poverty.

[The disobedient] walk proudly, carrying the head of self-will high. And if they are sometimes forced to obey they do not bow down in humility but pass through [the door] proudly. So their head is bent by a force that breaks their self-will, because they obey with contempt for the order and their superior.

Little by little these souls come to ruin in yet another way, by sinning against the vow of continence. For those who have not kept their appetites in order or stripped themselves of temporal possessions take up many associations and find that all too many of their friends love them for their own profit. From association they move on to close friendship and tend their body with pleasures because they do not have humility as their wet nurse nor her sister, lowliness. Therefore they are self-complacent and live comfortably and delicately, not like religious but like nobles, without watching or praying. Because of these and many other things that happen to them because they have money to spend (for these things would not happen to them if they had nothing to spend), they fall into bodily or spiritual impurity. For if some-

27. Cf. ch. 158.
28. Thus S; C has "big ordinary key of obedience."

times they abstain physically, whether for shame or because they have no means, they do not abstain spiritually. It is impossible to keep one's mind pure while indulging in a great social life, bodily delicacy, and inordinate eating without watching and prayer.

This is why those who are perfectly obedient see from a distance, by the light of most holy faith, the evil and harm that would come to them from having temporal possessions and walking under the weight of self-will. They see well that they have no choice but to pass through this small door. But they would pass through it not to their life but to their death, if they have not unlocked it with the key of obedience. I have said they must pass through it, and this is so, for unless they leave the ship of the order they must, whether they want to or not, pass through the narrow door of obedience to their superiors.

Therefore those who are perfectly obedient rise above themselves and take control of their selfish sensuality. But rising above their emotions with a lively faith they have set contempt in their soul's house as a servant to chase away the enemy of self-love. For their mother, charity, has espoused them to obedience with the ring[29] of faith, and they do not want this bride to be offended. This is why they chase away the enemy and put there their bride's companion and her wet nurse. Contempt has chased away the enemy, and love for obedience has put there those who love the bride, obedience, that is, true and solid virtues and the customs and observances of the order. Thus does this gentle bride enter into the soul with her sister patience and her wet nurse humility, along with humility's companions, lowliness and self-contempt. As soon as the bride has entered she possesses peace and calm because she has put out her enemies. She stands in the garden of true continence with understanding's light as her sun. And at the center of her understanding is the pupil of faith with my Truth as its object, for its object is truth. She has the fire to warm her and all her companions and servants, because she keeps the observances of the order with the fire of love.

Who are the enemies who stand outside? Their chief is the selfish love that produces pride, the enemy of charity and humility. Impatience stands against patience, disobedience against true obedience, unfaithfulness against fidelity. Presumption and trust in oneself clash with the true hope the soul ought to have in me. Injustice cannot harmonize with justice, nor can foolishness harmonize with prudence, nor

---

29. S, E, F: "light."

intemperance with temperance, nor disregard for the customs[30] of the order with observance of the rule; nor can evil relations with those who lead wicked lives harmonize with good relationships. They are enemies.

These also are cruel enemies: There is anger against benevolence,[31] cruelty against compassion, wrath against mildness, contempt for virtue against love for virtue, indecency against purity, indifference against concern, foolishness against discernment, excessive[32] sleeping against watching and constant prayer.

Because the soul has come to know by the light of faith that all of these are enemies who would defile her bride, holy obedience, she has commanded contempt to chase them out and love to put her friends inside. Thus contempt with his knife has slain perverse self-will, which, nurtured by selfish love, had given life to all these enemies of true obedience. Once this chief's head is cut off who had maintained all the others, the soul is left in peace with no one at all to war against her. There is no one or nothing that could, because she has cast off what used to keep her sad and bitter.

What does war against the obedient? Insult or injury? No, because they are patient, and patience is the sister of obedience. Are the burdens of the rule heavy for them? No, because obedience makes them observant. Does a solemn command cause them pain? No, because they have trampled self-will underfoot and have no wish to question or judge their superiors' will, but by the light of faith they discern my will in them, believing in truth that my mercy makes them command or not command as is necessary for their salvation. Are they displeased or put out at having to do the more lowly tasks of the order? Or at having to endure the derision and reproach, the abuse and slander that are often their lot, or at being considered of no account? No, because they have conceived a love for lowliness. They have a most perfect contempt for themselves and they rejoice in patience, exulting in joy and gladness with their bride, holy obedience. Nothing makes them sad but to see me their Creator offended.

They associate with those who fear me in truth, and if they must have to do with those who are cut off from my will, they do so not by imitating their sins but by drawing them out of their wretchedness.

---

30. S, F: "commandments."
31. F: "obedience."
32. S, E, F omit "excessive."

For in familial charity they want to offer them the good they themselves have, seeing that it would be to the greater glory and praise of my name to have more than just themselves observing the rule. Therefore they try to call both religious and layfolk with word and prayer, using whatever way they can to draw them out of the darkness of deadly sin. Thus the relationships of the truly obedient, because of their well-ordered affection and generous charity, are good and perfect whether they are with the just or with sinners.

They make a heaven of their cell, and find their pleasure in speaking and keeping company with me, the high eternal Father, in loving affection. They avoid idleness by constant humble prayer. And when, by the devil's illusion, their cell is filled with distractions, they do not sit down on the bed of indifference in the arms of idleness nor try to use reason to investigate their heart's thoughts and fancies. No, they flee idleness by rising above themselves with contempt for sensual emotion and with true humility and patience endure this spiritual weariness. They resist with watching and humble prayer, fixing their mind's eye on me, seeing by the light of faith that I am their helper and that I know how to and can and will help them. I open the arms of my kindness, and I permit them these things so that they may be more conscientious about fleeing from themselves and coming to me. And if mental prayer seems to fail them because of their great spiritual weariness and darkness, they take up vocal prayer or physical exercise and by this means avoid idleness. Enlightened, they see in me that it is for love I send them these things, so they proceed in true humility, considering themselves unworthy of spiritual peace and calm like the other servants of God, and deserving of suffering. Because in their mind they have already humbled themselves with self-contempt and reproach, it seems they cannot have enough of suffering. Their hope never falters as with faith, holding the key of obedience, they cross over this stormy sea in the ship of the order. Thus do they dwell in their cell, and there avoid idleness.

The obedient want to be the first to enter choir and the last to leave. And when they see a fellow religious more conscientiously obedient than themselves they are envious with a holy envy and try to steal this virtue without wishing that it be lessened in the other. (If they should wish that, they would be cut off from charity for their neighbor!)

The obedient never eat elsewhere than in the [common] refectory but are regular in their presence there and take pleasure in being at table with the poor.[33] And as a token that such is their pleasure, so as not to have reason to eat elsewhere they have cast off temporal possessions and keep the vow of poverty perfectly—so perfectly that they consider their physical need a reproach. Their cell is filled with the fragrance of poverty, not of garments, and they have no worry that thieves might come to rob them or that rust or moths will spoil their clothes.[34] If something is given to them they would not think of storing it up but share it freely with their fellow religious, never worrying about tomorrow but taking what they need from the present day, concerned only about the kingdom of heaven[35] and how they might be more truly obedient. And so that they might better keep themselves humble they submit themselves equally to the lowly and the great, the poor and the rich. They make themselves the servants of all, never refusing any labor, but lovingly serving everyone. The obedient have no desire to obey in their own way, to choose the time and the place; they would rather follow the rule and their superiors.

The truly perfect and obedient do all this painlessly and without spiritual weariness. With this key [of obedience] in hand they pass through the narrow door of the rule easily and without violence because they have kept and still keep their vow of voluntary poverty, true continence, and perfect obedience. They have rejected the exaltation of pride and humbly bowed their head to obedience, so they do not break their necks in impatience. They are patient, strong, and persevering, for those virtues are friends of obedience. They bypass the devils' assaults by mortifying and subduing their flesh, stripping it of delights and pleasures and clothing it in the labors of the order, faithfully and without disdain. Like little ones who do not remember their father's beatings or the hurts inflicted on them, these little ones do not remember any hurts or burdens or beatings they might receive from their superiors in the order. No, when their superiors call them they go back to them humbly, not obsessed with hatred or anger or bitterness, but with meekness and good will.

These are the little ones my Truth told the disciples about when they were arguing among themselves about who of them was the greatest. He said: "Let the little ones come to me, for the kingdom of heaven

---

33. The assumption is not that they like to eat, but that in the common refectory the food is meager.
34. Cf. Mt. 6:19–20; Lk. 12:33.
35. Cf. Mt. 6:33–34.

is for such as these. Whoever will not be humble like this child will not enter the kingdom of heaven."[36] For those who humble themselves, dearest daughter, will be exalted, and those who exalt themselves will be humbled.[37] This is exactly what my Truth said.

It is just, then, that I the eternal Father should exalt these humble little ones. They have humbled and subjected themselves in true holy obedience for love's sake, not stubbornly resisting the rule or their superiors. With the true citizens of the blessed life they shall be rewarded for their every labor, and even in this life they shall have a foretaste of eternal life.

160

The word of the gentle loving Word my only-begotten Son is fulfilled in them. Peter said to him, "Master, we have left everything for love of you and have followed you. What will you give us?" My Truth answered him, "I will give you a hundred for your one, and you will possess eternal life."[38] It was as if my Truth wanted to say, "You have done well, Peter. There is no other way you could have followed me. But I will give you a hundred for one even in this life." And what is this hundred, most beloved daughter, that is followed by eternal life? Of what was my Truth speaking? Of temporal possessions? Not really, though sometimes I do multiply the temporal goods of those who give alms. But then what was he referring to? To those who give their own will, which is but a single will, I return a hundred for this one.

Why do I use the number one hundred? Because hundred is a perfect number: You cannot add any more without beginning again at one. In the same way, charity is the most perfect, beyond all the other virtues. One cannot climb to any virtue more perfect. True, you can begin again at self-knowledge and add hundreds of numbers in merit, but you will always come back to the number hundred. This is the hundred that is given to those who give the one that is their will, whether in ordinary obedience or in this special obedience. And along with this hundred you have eternal life, because it is charity alone who comes as a lady bringing with her the fruit of all the virtues, leaving the other virtues themselves outside as she enters into me, eternal Life. It is in me that these souls enjoy eternal life because I am eternal Life.

---

36. Mt. 10:14–15; Lk. 18:16–17; Mt. 19:14, 18:3.
37. Mt. 23:12; Lk. 14:11, 18:14.
38. Mt. 19:27–29; Mk. 10:28–30; Lk. 18:28–30.

Faith does not climb this high, because these souls possess experiential-
ly and in essence what they had believed in faith. Nor does hope, because these souls possess as their own what they had hoped for. And so
it is with all the other virtues. Charity alone enters as queen and possesses me as I possess her.

You see, then, how these little ones receive for their one a hundred, and eternal life as well, for here they receive the fire of my divine
charity, symbolized in the number hundred. And because they have received this hundred from me their joy of heart is wonderful, for no sadness befalls charity, only joy: Charity makes the heart expansive and
generous, not double or narrow. The soul who is pierced by this tender
arrow does not show one thing with her face and tongue when she has
another in her heart. Nor does she serve or behave deceitfully or ambi-
tiously with regard to her neighbors, because charity is open with everyone. Therefore the soul who possesses charity never falls into pain
or distressing sadness, nor does she argue with obedience; no, she is
obedient even to the point of death.

161

The wretched disobedient, who remain on the ship of the order
causing such pain to themselves and to others, behave the opposite and
in this life taste the earnest of hell. They are always sad, spiritually
confused, and uneasy of conscience, disgusted with the rule and their
superiors. They are insupportable even to themselves. What a specta-
cle, my daughter, are those who take up the key of obedience to the
rule only to live in disobedience! They are slaves of disobedience and
have taken her as mistress along with her companion, impatience, nurtured by pride and self-complacency. And the source of this pride is
their selfish love for themselves. Everything here is the exact opposite
of what I have told you about true obedience. How can these wretches,
bereft of charity, be otherwise than in pain? They are forced to bow
the head of their will while pride holds it high. Their every wish is out
of harmony with what the rule would have. The rule demands obedience of them, but they love disobedience; the rule demands voluntary
poverty and these disobedient souls evade it by wanting and possessing
wealth; the rule would have continence and purity, but they want indecency.

My daughter, when religious violate these three vows they fall
into ruin, into such miserable sins that their appearance seems not that
of religious but of devils incarnate, as I have told you more in detail

elsewhere.[39] I will, however, still tell you something about their delusion and the fruit they draw from disobedience, so as to commend and extol obedience.

These wretches are deluded by selfish love, since their mind's eye is fixed in dead faith on selfish sensual pleasure and on worldly things. They have climbed above the world with their body and remained there with their affection. And since obedience seems a burden to them, they choose to flee it by disobeying. But they fall into the greatest weariness of all because they simply must obey, if not for love, then by force. It would be better for them and less burdensome to obey for love.

Oh, how deluded they are! And no one is deceiving them but themselves. By choosing to please themselves they displease themselves, for the very actions they perform because of the obedience imposed on them disgust them. They want to live in pleasure and make their eternal life in this life. But the rule would have them be pilgrims, and constantly shows them this, for when they settle down in one place and want to stay there because of the pleasure and delight they find there, and they are transferred, they suffer from the change because their will is alive to resist it. And if they do not obey they are subjected to the necessity of bearing the burdensome discipline of the rule. Thus they live in continual torment.

You see their delusion, then: Though they want to flee pain they fall into it. The way of true obedience is a way of truth built on the obedient Lamb, my only-begotten Son, who takes the pain out of it. But their blindness does not let them see this. Therefore they travel along the way of falsehood, thinking they will find pleasure there, but they find pain and bitterness. Who guides them there? Their love for their selfish passion to disobey.

Like fools they want to sail this stormy sea on their own power, confiding in their own pitiful knowledge, rather than sail on the strength of the rule and their superiors. While it is true that they stay on the ship of the order physically, they are not there in spirit. In desire they have left, by not observing the rules and customs of the order or the three vows they promised at their profession to observe. There they are in the stormy sea, pounded by dangerous contrary winds, attached to the ship only by their clothes—for they wear the habit on their bodies but not in their hearts.

---

39. Cf. ch. 125.

THE DIALOGUE

They are not religious but people in costume: human in form but in fact and in their living worse than animals. Do they not see that it is more wearisome to sail on their own power than on the order's? And do they not see that they are in danger of eternal death if the cloth that holds them should be torn from the ship? For as soon as they are torn away in death there will be no saving them. No, they do not see it, because the cloud of selfish love, the source of their disobedience, deprives them of the light and prevents them from seeing their evil fate. So they are miserably deluded.

What fruit do these wretched trees produce? The fruit of death, because the root of their affection is planted in the pride they have drawn from self-centeredness and self-complacency. This is why everything that comes from them is rotten. The blossoms, the leaves, the fruit, the branches of their tree are all spoiled. The three branches—obedience, poverty, and continence—which are held in the ill-planted trunk of the will, are rotten. The leaves these trees produce, that is, their words, are so rotten you would not find them in the mouth of a worldly ruffian. If they should have to proclaim my word, they do it with polished rhetoric, but it is not sincere, because their concern is not to pasture souls on the seed of my word, but to speak with great polish.

Look at these trees' blossoms, all the different stinking evil thoughts they welcome willingly and with pleasure and delight, avoiding neither the place nor the paths that bring these to them. In fact, they seek them out in order to accomplish their sin, the fruit that kills them by taking away the life of grace and giving them eternal death. What is the stench given off by this fruit produced by their blossoms? The stench of disobedience: In the thoughts of their hearts they choose to question and pass evil judgments on the will of their superiors. And the stench of indecency, for they delight in all sorts of relationships in a pretense of devotion.

Wretch! You do not see that you will come out of this show of devotion with a whole parade of children! This is what your disobedience gets you! You have not taken the virtues for children as have the truly obedient.

My daughter, when they find themselves denied what their perverse will would have they try to trick their superiors with flattery or sharp words, disrespect and reproach. They are intolerant of their fellow religious, nor can they endure the slightest reproachful word without at once bringing forth the poison fruit of impatience, anger, and

349

hatred against them. What others do for their good they take as evil, and thus scandalized they live in pain, body and soul. Why are they displeased with their fellow religious? Because they were looking to their own sensual pleasure.

They avoid their cell as if it were poison. They fell into disobedience when they left the cell of self-knowledge; therefore they cannot stand their material cell.

As for the refectory, they would no more appear there than with their enemies so long as they have anything to spend, but if they have nothing to spend, necessity brings them there. The obedient, then, do well in choosing to observe the vow of poverty, not having anything to spend, so that money will not take them away from the sweet table of the refectory where the obedient nourish themselves in peace and calm of soul and body. They are not concerned about cooking or providing for themselves as are these wretches who find the refectory bitter to their taste and therefore avoid it.

They want to always be the last to enter choir and the first to leave. They come near me with their lips, but their heart is far away.[40]

They are happy to escape the chapter [of faults][41] whenever they can for fear of the penance, and treat being there like a mortal enemy, with shame and confusion in their spirit—something they did not feel in committing the faults, not blushing even to commit deadly sin. What is the reason? Disobedience.

They are strangers to watching and prayer—not only mental prayer, but often they do not even say the Divine Office to which they are obliged. Nor do they know familial charity, for they do not love others as themselves: They love not with a reasonable love but bestially. So many are the evils that fall on the head of the disobedient and so many are their pitiful fruits that your tongue could never describe them!

O disobedience! You strip the soul of every virtue and clothe her in every vice! O disobedience! You deprive the soul of the light of obedience, take away her peace, and give her war! You take away her life and give her death! You drag her away from the ship of obedience to the rule and drown her in the sea by making her sail[42] under her own

---

40. Cf. Mk. 7:6; Is. 29:13.
41. In the chapter hall the community gathered daily. Each member admitted publicly any transgressions of the rule and accepted a penance from the superior.
42. S: "swim."

power rather than the order's. You clothe her in every misery and make her die of hunger by depriving her of the food of the merit of obedience. You give her continual bitterness. You deprive her of all delight and sweetness and good, and make her live in every sort of evil. Even in this life you make her endure the earnest of excruciating torments, and if she does not correct herself before her clothes are torn from the ship in death, you, disobedience, will lead her to eternal damnation along with the devils who fell from heaven because they rebelled against me and are on their way to the depths. Thus will it be for you who are disobedient, who have rebelled against obedience. You have thrown away the key with which you should have opened the gate of heaven, and with the key of disobedience you have opened hell.

162

O dearest daughter! How many are there who today pasture in this ship? Many, but few are truly obedient. True, between the perfect and these wretches there are a good number who live mediocre lives in the order, neither evil nor yet as perfect as they should be. They simply keep their conscience free of deadly sin: They are lukewarm or even coldhearted, and unless they exercise their life a bit with the observances of the rule, they are in great danger. Therefore they have to be very careful not to fall asleep, and to rise up from their tepidity, for if they stay there they are apt to fall. And even if they do not fall, they will be standing by their own judgment and human pleasure, colored the color of the order, but more concerned about observing the ceremonies of the rule than the rule itself. And often for want of light they are quick to fall into judging those who observe the rule more perfectly than they do, though they may be less perfect in all the ceremonies of which their judges are so observant.

Thus it is in every respect dangerous to be content with mediocre obedience. Such obedience is cold, very burdensome, and very painful. Because it seems to the cold heart wearisome to carry it, these souls bear great burdens with little fruit. They sin against the perfection into which they entered and which they are obliged to observe. And though they do less evil than the others of whom I told you, they still do evil. For they do not leave lay life to live with the ordinary key of obedience but to unlock heaven with the key of obedience to the rule. This little key ought to be tied with the strong cord of lowliness, of self-abasement, attached to the belt of humility and held tightly in the hand of burning love.

Know, dearest daughter, that these mediocre souls are capable enough of reaching great perfection if they want to, for they are closer to it than are these other wretches. But in another way it is more difficult for them to rise above their imperfection than it is for the wicked to rise above their misery. And do you know why? Because the wicked see clearly that they are doing wrong; conscience makes it clear to them. Because of the selfishness that has debilitated them they do not make an effort to get out of this sinfulness, though they see by a natural light that what they are doing is evil. So if anyone should ask them, "And is it not evil for you to do this?" they would say, "Yes, but I am so weak that I do not think I can get out." Although they are not telling the truth (for with my help they can get out if they want to), at least they know they are doing wrong, and with that knowledge it is easy for them to get out if they want to.

But these tepid souls who are doing neither great evil nor great good do not recognize how cold or imperilled they are. Because they do not recognize it they care neither to get up nor to be told. And if they are told, the coldness of their heart makes them stay bound up in their old habits.

What way is there to make them get up? Let them take the wood of self-knowledge along with contempt for their self-complacency and self-conceit, and put these into the fire of my divine charity, espousing once again, as if they were entering the order just then, holy obedience as their bride with the ring of most holy faith. And let them fall asleep no more in this state, for that is very displeasing to me and harmful to them. Rightly could this word be addressed to them: "Accursed tepid souls! I would rather you were simply ice! Unless you change you will be vomited out of my mouth!"[43] In the same way I told you that if they do not get up they are likely to fall, and if they fall they will be reproached by me. I would rather you were ice. In other words, I would rather you had remained as layfolk, with ordinary obedience which, in comparison with the fire of the truly obedient, is as good as ice. This is why I said, "I would rather you were simply ice."

I have explained this word to you so that you would not fall into the error of thinking I would rather have people in the ice of deadly sin than in the lukewarmness of imperfection. No, I could never will the guilt of sin. This poison is not in me. In fact, it so displeased me in humanity that I did not will that it should go unpunished. And because

---

43. Cf. Rv. 3:15–16.

humanity was not enough to bear the punishment consequent on sin I sent the Word, my only-begotten Son, and he in obedience hammered it out on his own body.

Let them, then, rise up through exercise, watching, and constant humble prayer. Let them look into the mirror of their rule and of the pilots of this ship who were as human as they, nourished by the same food, born in the very same way. And I am the same God now as I was then. My power is not weakened, my will wants your salvation no less, nor does my wisdom want less to give you light to know my Truth.

So they can do it if they want to, if only they set it before their mind's eye, shedding the cloud of self-centeredness and running on in the light with the perfectly obedient. In this way they will get there and not otherwise. This is where the remedy is.

163

This is the true remedy the truly obedient possess, and they have it new again every day. They increase the virtue of obedience by the light of faith. They desire slander and abuse and to be laden with heavy burdens by their superiors so that the virtue of obedience and her sister patience will not rust and will not fail them or work only with great difficulty when they need to use them. Therefore they constantly sound the instrument of desire, wasting no time, because they are hungry for these things. Obedience is a solicitous spouse who does not want to stand idle.

O delightful obedience! O pleasant obedience! Gentle obedience! Lightsome obedience, because you have lifted the darkness of selfish love! O life-giving obedience, giving the life of grace to the soul who has chosen you as bride after you have taken away the death[44] of self-will that had brought war and death to the soul!

You are generous, for you make yourself subject to every rational creature! You are kind and compassionate: Kindly and meekly you carry every great burden because you are accompanied by strength and true patience. You are crowned with perseverance; the importunity of superiors or the lack of discretion with which they may impose great burdens on you does not make you falter. By the light of faith you carry everything. You are so joined to humility that no creature can take her from the hand of holy desire in the soul who possesses you.

And what shall we say, dearest most beloved daughter, about this

---

44. E: "love."

marvelous virtue? She is a good without any evil. She stands hidden in the ship so that no contrary wind can harm her. She makes the soul sail on the strength of the rule and her superiors, not on her own; for the truly obedient will not have to render an account of themselves to me, but the superiors to whom they are subject will.

Fall in love, dearest daughter, with this glorious virtue. Do you want to show your gratitude for the blessings you have received from me the eternal Father? Be obedient. For obedience shows whether you are grateful, because it proceeds from charity. It shows if you are not foolish, because it proceeds from the knowledge of my Truth. Thus it is a good that is known in the Word, who taught you the way of obedience as your rule by becoming obedient himself even to the point of his shameful death on the cross. In his obedience, the key that unlocked heaven, is founded the general obedience given to you as well as this special obedience, as I told you at the beginning of this discussion of obedience.[45]

This obedience sheds a light on the soul that shows that she is faithful to me and faithful to the rule and to her superior. In this light of most holy faith she has forgotten herself, not seeking herself for her own sake, because in obedience acquired by the light of faith she has shown that within her will she is dead to every selfish emotion. Such sensual emotion seeks what belongs to others rather than to her, as do the disobedient who question the will of those who command and pass judgment on it according to their own base opinions and darksome vision, but do not question their own perverse[46] will that brings them death.

The truly obedient, by the light of faith, judge rightly about the will of their superiors. Therefore, they do not seek their own will but bow their head and nourish their soul with the fragrance of true holy obedience. And this virtue grows in the soul as much as she grows in the light of most holy faith, because charity, the mother of obedience, proceeds from the light of faith.[47] For the soul loves me and humbles herself by the same light of faith by which she knows herself and me. And the more she loves and is humble, the more obedient she is. And obedience and her sister patience show whether the soul is in truth

---

45. Cf. ch. 154.
46. C, E, F omit "perverse."
47. S, F omit "because . . . faith."

clothed in the wedding garment of charity, the garment with which you gain entrance into eternal life.

Thus obedience unlocks heaven, but she herself remains outside, while charity, who gave [the soul] this key, enters in with the fruit of obedience. Every virtue, as I have told you, remains outside while this one alone enters. But it is appropriate that obedience should be the key that opens [the gate], because heaven was locked by the sin of the first man, and by the obedience of the humble spotless Lamb my only-begotten Son, eternal life, which had been so long locked, was unlocked.

164

He left you obedience to guide and teach you, giving it to you as a key with which you can open [the gate] leading to your goal. He left it to you as a commandment in ordinary obedience. He left it to you as a counsel if you are willing to go on to great perfection and pass through the narrow door of the rule. There are also those who do not have a rule but are nonetheless on the ship of perfection: These are those who observe the perfection of the counsels outside any order, who have renounced worldly riches and vanities, some in the state of virginity, some in the fragrance of continence after they have lost their virginity. These observe obedience by subjecting themselves to some other person whom they try to obey with perfect obedience until they die.

And if you should ask me, "Who has the greater merit: those who belong to an order or these others?" I answer you that the merit of obedience is not measured by the act or the place or the person commanding (that is, good or bad, lay or religious), but by the measure of love in the person obeying. This is the measure with which it is measured.

For the imperfection of a bad superior does not harm the truly obedient. Sometimes, in fact, it benefits them, for with persecution and the indiscreet weight of heavy commands the virtue of obedience is gained along with patience her sister. Nor does a less than perfect place harm them—imperfect, I say, because there is no state more perfect, more firm, more stable than religious life. This is why I set before you as imperfect the place of those who hold the small key of obedience by observing the counsels outside any order. I am not suggesting that their obedience is less perfect or less meritorious, because all obedience, and every other virtue, is measured by the measure of love.

Still it is true that in many other ways, both because of the vow religious make into the hands of their superior and because they endure more, obedience is better proved in the order than outside it.[48] For their every external act is bound into this yoke, and they cannot free themselves of it as they choose without the guilt of deadly sin, because it has been vowed and approved by holy Church.

But it is not so for these others. Because of their love they have bound themselves voluntarily to obedience, but not by a solemn vow. Therefore they could for legitimate reasons, though not through their own fault, abandon obedience to this particular other person without being guilty of deadly sin. But they would not be free of very serious sin if they were to abandon it through their own fault.

Do you know what is the difference between the two [ways]? In the one case, they have lent something and then taken back what they had given in love. They had the intention of not asking to have it back but never made a positive contract about it. The others have given it by contract in profession, when they renounced their very selves into the hands of their superiors and promised to observe obedience, continence, and voluntary poverty. And their superiors promised, if they would observe it until death, to give them eternal life.

So in observance and place and manner, the one is more perfect and the other less. Those in religious life are more secure, and should they fall they are more likely to get up again because they have more help. The others are more uncertain and less secure, and more likely, should they happen to fall, to turn back, because they know they are not bound by a public vow. Religious who are not yet professed may leave before their profession, but not after.

But as for merit, I have told you before and I tell you again that it is given according to the measure of love in the truly obedient, so that all, no matter what their state in life, can have perfect merit, since it is dependent solely on love.

I call some to one state and some to another, according to each one's disposition. But all are filled according to this same measure of love. If a layperson loves more than a religious, that layperson receives more, and vice versa. And so with all the others.

---

48. I have followed the more consistent reading of S, E, F here. C inserts "the obedience of religious life is more meritorious" at the head of the sentence, a clause that contradicts what was just said in the previous paragraph.

165

I have sent all of you into the vineyard of obedience to work in different ways. Each of you will be rewarded according to the measure of your love, not according to your work or the time spent. In other words, those who come early will not get more than those who come late, as it is said in the holy Gospel. My Truth gave you the example of those who were standing idle and were sent by the lord to work in his vineyard. He gave as much to those who went out at dawn as to those who went out at the first hour, as much to those who went out at the third hour and to those who went out at the sixth and the ninth and near evening as to the first. My Truth was showing you that you are rewarded not according to your work or your time but according to the measure of your love.[49] Many are sent in their childhood to work in this vineyard. Some enter later, and some even in their old age. These last sometimes, because they see how short a time they have, come in with such burning love that they catch up with those who enter in their childhood and have walked slowly. It is from the love of obedience, then, that the soul receives her merit; it is there she fills her vessel in me, the sea of peace.

There are many who hold this obedience so ready and have so incarnated it within their souls that they not only want to see the rightness of the intention of those who command them, but they scarcely wait for the words to come out of their mouths. By the light of faith they understand their superiors' intention. Thus the truly obedient obey the intention more than the word, assuming that their superiors' will is within my will, and that they give their commands by my permission and will. They obey the word because they have first obeyed their superiors' will with their own, seeing by the light of faith and discerning their superiors' will in me.

The person you read about in *The Lives of the Fathers* showed well how he first obeyed with his will. He was just beginning to write the letter *O*, no great thing, when his superior gave him a command. He did not so much as give himself time to finish that letter, but ran at once to obey. So to show how pleased I was I gave you a sign: My mercy completed the other half in gold.

This glorious virtue is so pleasing to me that there is no virtue to

---

49. Cf. Mt. 20:1–16.

which I have given such miraculous signs and testimonies as I have to this one, for this one proceeds from the light of faith.

To demonstrate how pleasing it is to me, the earth obeys this virtue, and so do the animals. Water sustains the obedient, and if you turn to the earth, it obeys the obedient. You have seen this: You will recall having read it in *The Lives of the Fathers*.[50] A certain disciple was given a dry stick by his abbot, who commanded him in obedience to plant it in the earth and water it every day. Obedient as he was by the light of faith, he did not presume to say, "How could this be possible?" Without wishing to know whether it was possible he did as he was told, so in virtue of his obedience and faith the dry wood grew green again and produced fruit, as a sign that that soul had risen above the dryness of disobedience and once grown green had borne the fruit of obedience. Therefore the holy fathers called the apple on that wood "the fruit of obedience."

And if you consider the irrational animals, [you will see] the very same thing. That same disciple, commanded by obedience, in his purity and obedience captured a dragon and brought it to his abbot. But the abbot, true doctor that he was, so that he might not be caught by the wind of vainglory and to test his patience, chased him away with the reproach, "You beast! You have brought the beast in chains!"

And if you look at fire, it is the same. Thus you have in Holy Scripture that many were put into the fire rather than violate my command, or to obey me more promptly, and the fire did not hurt them— like those three young men in the furnace[51] and many others one could tell about.

When Maurice was commanded in obedience to rescue the disciple who was drowning in the water, the water held him up. He did not think of himself, but by the light of faith was concerned only about fulfilling his superior's command, and he walked over the water as if he were walking on the ground to rescue that disciple.

In absolutely everything, if only you open your mind's eye, you will find how I have shown you the excellence of this virtue.

Everything else should be left behind for obedience. If you were lifted up in such contemplative spiritual union with me that your body was suspended above the ground, if you were given a command in obedience (I am speaking in general and of no particular instance, since

---

50. S omits "in *The Lives of the Fathers*."
51. Dn. 3:12–24.

one instance cannot make a law), if you could you should make every effort to rouse yourself in order to fulfill that command. Remember, though, that you should never rise from prayer at the appointed time except for the sake of charity or obedience.[52] I am telling this to make you see how prompt I want my servants' obedience to be, and how pleasing obedience is to me.

The obedient merit by whatever they do. If they eat, they are eating obedience. If they sleep it is obedience. Whether they go or stay, fast or keep vigil, obedience is doing it all. If they serve their neighbors it is obedience. If they are in choir or in the refectory or in their cell, who guides them there and makes them stay? Obedience, by the light of most holy faith. It was by this light that they threw themselves into the arms of the order and their superiors, dead to every selfish desire, humbled and contemptuous of themselves.

With this obedience they have been at rest in the ship, content to have it guided by their superiors. Thus they have sailed the stormy sea of this life in great calm, with serene spirit and tranquil heart, because obedience together with faith has taken away all darkness from them. They are courageous and confident because by shedding their own will, the source of all weakness and disordered fear, they have shed weakness and fear.

And what do these spouses of obedience eat and drink? They eat knowledge of themselves and of me, knowing their sinfulness and that of themselves they are nothing, and knowing that I am who I am. In me they taste and eat my truth, having come to know it in the Word incarnate who is my Truth. And what do they drink? The blood by which the Word has shown them my truth and my ineffable love for them. In this blood he shows his obedience, an obedience I his eternal Father imposed on him for your sake, and this makes them drunk. And once they are drunk with the blood and the Word's obedience, they lose themselves and every knowledge and opinion of their own and possess me in grace, tasting me in affectionate love by the light of faith in holy obedience.

Their whole life proclaims peace, and at their death they receive what their superiors promised them at their profession, eternal life, the vision of peace and supreme eternal tranquillity and rest—an immeasurable reward. No one can imagine how great it is, because it is infi-

---

52. E omits "Remember . . . obedience." (Probably, however, a copyist's error, as the omission extends from one occurrence of *obedienzia* to the next.)

nite. This infinite good cannot be fully contained by anything less than itself any more than the vessel dipped into the sea can contain the whole sea but only as much as it can hold. Only the sea itself can fully contain itself. In the same way I, the sea of peace, am the only one who can fully contain and value myself. And this makes me rejoice in myself. And the joy and good that I have in myself I share with you, with each of you according to your own capacity. I fill you and do not leave you empty. In my gift of perfect blessedness, you know and contain as much of my goodness as I have given you to know.

The obedient, then, by the light of faith in truth, are set ablaze in the furnace of charity, anointed with humility, inebriated with the blood. With humility's sister patience and with lowliness, with courage and perseverance, and with all the other virtues (that is, with the fruit of the virtues) they have received their reward from me their Creator.

CONCLUSION

166

Now, dearest daughter whom I so love, I have satisfied your desire from your first request right up to this last about obedience. If you remember well, in the beginning you asked me with restless longing, and it was I who made you ask in order to make the fire of my charity grow within your soul. You asked four petitions.

The first was for yourself. I have satisfied this by enlightening you with my truth and showing you how you might come to know this truth that you longed to know. I explained to you how to attain knowledge of the truth through knowledge of yourself and of me by the light of faith.

The second thing you asked me was that I should be merciful to the world.

Your third petition was for the mystic body of holy Church. You begged me to relieve her of darkness and persecution, and wanted me to punish you for the sins of others. On this matter I explained to you that no suffering that could be given in finite time could of itself atone for sin committed against me, the infinite Good. But such suffering can atone if it is united with the soul's desire and heartfelt contrition. And I told you how. I also answered you that I want to be merciful to the world, and showed you that mercy is proper to me, for in my immeasurable mercy and love for humankind I sent the Word, my only-begotten Son. And to show it to you really clearly, I set him before you in the image of a bridge stretching from heaven to earth through the union of my divine nature with your human nature.

I also showed you, to enlighten you even more with my Truth, how the bridge is mounted by three stairs, the soul's three powers. And concerning this Word, the bridge I showed you, I also used these three stairs as an image of his body. In his feet, his open side, and his mouth, I in turn suggested three spiritual stages: the imperfect, the perfect, and finally the most perfect state in which the soul attains the excellence of unitive love. At each stage I showed you clearly what it is that takes away the soul's imperfection and makes her attain perfection, what is the way by which she travels, and what are the hidden deceits of the devil and her own spiritual selfishness. And in these stages I spoke to you about the three reproaches my mercy gives. The first, I told you, is given during this life. The second is given at death to those who are dying in deadly sin without hope; I told you that these travel beneath the bridge along the way of the devil, and I told you about their miseries. The third reproach is that of the final general judgment. And I told you something of the punishment of the damned and the glory of the blessed, when all will have back the endowment of their body.

I also promised you, and I promise you now, that through the sufferings of my servants I shall reform my bride. So I invited you to suffer as I grieve with you over my ministers' wickedness. I showed you the dignity to which I have appointed them, and the reverence I require laypeople to have for them. I showed you why their sinfulness is no reason for you to lessen your reverence for them, and how such irreverence displeases me. And I told you about the virtue of those who live as angels, at the same time touching upon the excellence of the sacrament [of the Eucharist].

In further reference to the above-mentioned stages, because you wanted to know about the stages of tears and their source, I told you about these, paralleling the spiritual stages and the stages of tears. I told you that all tears come from the heart's fountain, and one by one I told you how. I described for you four stages of tears, as well as a fifth that brings forth death.

I responded to your fourth petition, that I should provide for a special case that had arisen. I did provide, as you know. On the basis of this I explained my providence to you in general and in particular, letting you see from the beginning of the world's creation right up to the end how I have done and continue to do everything with divine providence, giving and permitting all that I do for your good—trials and consolations both spiritual and temporal—so that you may be sanctified in me and my truth may be fulfilled in you.[1] And this is that truth:

---

1. Cf. Jn. 17:17–19.

that I created you so that you might have eternal life; and this truth has been revealed to you in the blood of the Word, my only-begotten Son.

Finally, I satisfied your desire, in fulfillment of my promise to you, by telling you about the perfection of obedience and the imperfection of disobedience. I told you where obedience comes from and what takes it away. I set it before you as an ordinary key, and so it is. And I told you about special obedience, about the perfect and the imperfect, about those within the order and those outside it, and I told you distinctly about each of these. I told you of the peace obedience gives and the war that is the gift of disobedience. I told you how greatly deluded the disobedient are, and showed you how death came into the world through Adam's sin.

Now, in conclusion, I the eternal Father, supreme eternal Truth, am telling you that in the obedience of the Word, my only-begotten Son, you have life. Just as all of you contracted death from the first—the old—man, so all of you who are willing to carry the key of obedience have contracted life from the new man, the gentle Christ Jesus. I made of him a bridge for you because the road to heaven had been destroyed. If you travel along this delightful straight way, which is a lightsome truth, holding the key of obedience, you will pass through the world's darknesses without stumbling. And in the end you will unlock heaven with the Word's key.[2]

Now I invite you to weep, you and my other servants. And through your weeping and constant humble prayer I want to be merciful to the world. Run along this road of truth dead [to yourselves], so that you may never be reproached for walking slowly. For I will demand more of you now than before, since I have revealed my very self to you in my truth. Be careful never to leave the cell of self-knowledge, but in this cell guard and spend the treasure I have given you. This treasure is a teaching of truth founded on the living rock, the gentle Christ Jesus, clothed in a light that can discern darkness. Clothe yourself in this light, dearest daughter whom I so love, in truth.

167

N ow that soul had seen the truth and the excellence of obedience with the eye of her understanding, and had known it by the light of most holy faith; she had heard it with feeling and tasted it

---

2. S omits "If you travel. . . . Word's key."

with anguished longing in her will as she gazed into the divine majesty. So she gave him thanks, saying:

Thanks, thanks be to you, eternal Father, that you have not despised me, your handiwork, nor turned your face from me, nor made light of these desires of mine. You, Light, have disregarded my darksomeness; you, Life, have not considered that I am death; nor you, Doctor, considered these grave weaknesses of mine. You, eternal Purity, have disregarded my wretched filthiness; you who are infinite have overlooked the fact that I am finite, and you, Wisdom, the fact that I am foolishness.

For all these and so many other endless evils and sins of mine, your wisdom, your kindness, your mercy, your infinite goodness have not despised me. No, in your light you have given me light.[3] In your wisdom I have come to know the truth; in your mercy I have found your charity and affection for my neighbors. What has compelled you? Not my virtues, but only your charity.

Let this same love compel you to enlighten the eye of my understanding with the light of faith, so that I may know your truth, which you have revealed to me. Let my memory be great enough to hold your favors, and set my will ablaze in your charity's fire. Let that fire burst the seed of my body and bring forth blood; then with that blood, given for love of your blood, and with the key of obedience, let me unlock heaven's gate.

I heartily ask the same of you for every reasoning creature, all and each of them, and for the mystic body of holy Church. I acknowledge and do not deny that you loved me before I existed, and that you love me unspeakably much, as one gone mad over your creature.

O eternal Trinity! O Godhead! That Godhead, your divine nature, gave the price of your Son's blood its value. You, eternal Trinity, are a deep sea: The more I enter you, the more I discover, and the more I discover, the more I seek you. You are insatiable, you in whose depth the soul is sated yet remains always hungry for you, thirsty for you, eternal Trinity, longing to see you with the light in your light. Just as the deer longs for the fountain of living water, so does my soul long to escape from the prison of my darksome body and see you in truth. O how long will you hide your face from my eyes?[4]

---

3. Cf. Ps. 36:10.
4. Cf. Ps. 42:2–3.

O eternal Trinity, fire and abyss of charity, dissolve this very day the cloud of my body! I am driven to desire, in the knowledge of yourself that you have given me in your truth, to leave behind the weight of this body of mine and give my life for the glory and praise of your name. For by the light of understanding within your light I have tasted and seen your depth, eternal Trinity, and the beauty of your creation. Then, when I considered myself in you, I saw that I am your image. You have gifted me with power from yourself, eternal Father, and my understanding with your wisdom—such wisdom as is proper to your only-begotten Son; and the Holy Spirit, who proceeds from you and from your Son, has given me a will, and so I am able to love.

You, eternal Trinity, are the craftsman; and I your handiwork have come to know that you are in love with the beauty of what you have made, since you made of me a new creation in the blood of your Son.

O abyss! O eternal Godhead! O deep sea! What more could you have given me than the gift of your very self?

You are a fire always burning but never consuming; you are a fire consuming in your heat all the soul's selfish love; you are a fire lifting all chill and giving light. In your light you have made me know your truth: You are that light beyond all light who gives the mind's eye supernatural light in such fullness and perfection that you bring clarity even to the light of faith. In that faith I see that my soul has life, and in that light receives you who are Light.

In the light of faith I gain wisdom in the wisdom of the Word your Son; in the light of faith I am strong, constant, persevering; in the light of faith I have hope: It does not let me faint along the way. This light teaches me the way, and without this light I would be walking in the dark. This is why I asked you, eternal Father, to enlighten me with the light of most holy faith.

Truly this light is a sea, for it nourishes the soul in you, peaceful sea, eternal Trinity. Its water is not sluggish; so the soul is not afraid because she knows the truth. It distills, revealing hidden things, so that here, where the most abundant light of your faith abounds, the soul has, as it were, a guarantee[5] of what she believes. This water is a mirror in which you, eternal Trinity, grant me knowledge; for when I look

---

5. E: "a clarification."

into this mirror, holding it in the hand of love, it shows me myself, as your creation, in you, and you in me through the union you have brought about of the Godhead with our humanity.

This light shows you to me, and in this light I know you, highest and infinite Good: Good above every good, joyous Good, Good beyond measure and understanding! Beauty above all beauty; Wisdom above all wisdom—indeed you are wisdom itself! You who are the angels' food are given to humans with burning love. You, garment who cover all nakedness, pasture the starving within your sweetness, for you are sweet without trace of bitterness.

O eternal Trinity, when I received with the light of most holy faith your light that you gave me, I came to know therein the way of great perfection, made smooth for me by so many wonderful explanations. Thus I may serve you in the light, not in the dark; and I may be a mirror of a good and holy life; and I may rouse myself from my wretched life in which, always through my own fault, I have served you in darkness. I did not know your truth, and so I did not love it. Why did I not know you? Because I did not see you with the glorious light of most holy faith, since the cloud of selfish love darkened the eye of my understanding. Then with your light, eternal Trinity, you dispelled the darkness.

But who could reach to your height to thank you for so immeasurable a gift, for such generous favors, for the teaching of truth that you have given me? A special grace, this, beyond the common grace you give to other creatures. You willed to bend down to my need and that of others who might see themselves mirrored here.

You responded, Lord; you yourself have given and you yourself answered and satisfied me by flooding me with a gracious light, so that with that light I may return thanks to you.[6] Clothe, clothe me with yourself, eternal Truth, so that I may run the course of this mortal life in true obedience and in the light of most holy faith. With that light I sense my soul once again becoming drunk! Thanks be to God! Amen.[7]

---

6. There is a delightful play on words here that eludes translation: "flooding me with a light *di grazia*, so that with that light I may return *grazie* to you."

7. C closes with: "Here ends the book composed by the blessed virgin, the faithful spouse and servant of Jesus Christ, Catherine of Siena, dictated in ecstasy. She was clothed in the habit of Saint Dominic. Amen."

S closes with: "Here ends the book made and compiled by the most venerable virgin, the most faithful servant and spouse of Jesus Christ crucified, Catherine of Siena, of the habit of Saint Dominic, in the month of October, AD 1378."

SELECTED BIBLIOGRAPHY

Editions and Translations of the Dialogue

Gigli, Girolamo, ed. *L'opere di Santa Caterina da Siena*, vol. IV, *Il Dialogo*. Siena e Lucca, 1707–1721.

James, Dane, ed. *The Orcherde of Syon*. London: W. de Worde, 1519.

Thorold, Algar, trans. *The Dialogue of the Seraphic Virgin Catherine of Siena*. London: Kegan, Paul, Trench, Tuber, 1896.

Fiorilli, Matilde, ed. *Libro della divina dottrina volgarmente detto Dialogo della Divina Provvidenza: Nuovo edizione secondo un inedito codice senese*. Bari: Laterza & Figli, 1912.

Taurisano, Innocenzo, ed. *Dialogo della Divina Provvidenza*. Florence: Libreria Ed. Fiorentina, 1928.

Hurtaud, R. P. J., trans. *Le dialogue de Sainte Catherine de Sienne*. Paris: Lethellieux, 1931.

Hodgson, Phyllis, and Liegey, Gabriel M., eds. *The Orcherd of Syon*, vol. I: Text. The Early English Text Society, vol. 258, 1966. London: Oxford University Press, 1966.

Cavallini, Giuliana, ed. *Il Dialogo della Divina Provvidenza ovvero Libro della Divina Dottrina*. Rome: Edizioni Cateriniane, 1968.

Meattini, D. Umberto, ed. *Il Libro*. Rome: Edizioni Paoline, 1969.

Sources

Caffarini, Thomas Antonii de Senis. *Leggenda minore di S. Caterina da Siena (e lettere dei suoi discepoli)*. Edited by Francesco Grottanelli. Bologna: Presso Gaetano Romagnoli, 1868.

_____. *Libellus de Supplemento: Legende Prolixe Virginis Beate Catherine de Senis*. Edited by Giuliana Cavallini and Imelda Foralosso. Rome: Edizioni Cateriniane, 1974.

BIBLIOGRAPHY

Canigiani, Barduccio. *Il Transito di S. Caterina,* in *Lettere,* ed. Misciattelli VI, pp. 175–82.

Caterina da Siena. *Lettres de Sainte Catherine de Sienne.* Translated by E. Cartier. Paris: Librairie de Mme. Ve. Poussielgue-Rusand, 1858.

————. *Le lettere de S. Caterina da Siena, ridotte a miglior lezione, e in ordine nuovo disposte con note di Niccolò Tommaseo a cura di Piero Misciattelli.* Siena: Giuntini & Bentivoglio, 1913–1922.

————. *Selected Letters of Catherine Benincasa: Saint Catherine of Siena as Seen in Her Letters.* Translated and edited by Vida D. Scudder. New York: E. P. Dutton & Co., 1927.

————. *Epistolario di Santa Caterina da Siena,* vol. I. Edited by Eugenio Dupré-Theseider. *Fonti per la storia d'Italia, pubblicate dal R. Istituto Storico Italiano per il Medio Evo (Epistolari: Secolo XIV).* Rome: Sede dell'Istituto, 1940.

————. *Preghiere ed elevazioni.* 2nd ed. Edited by Innocenzo Taurisano. Rome: Ferrari, 1939.

Guidini, Cristofano. *Memorie di Ser Cristofano,* in *Fioretti di Santa Caterina da Siena.* 2nd ed. Edited by Innocenzo Taurisano. Rome: Ferrari, 1927.

Laurent, M. Hyacinta et al., eds. *Fontes vitae S. Catharinae Senensis historici.* [Of 22 proposed volumes, only 1, 4, 9, 10, 15, 20, and 21 ever appeared.] Siena: R. Università di Siena, Cattedra Cateriniana, 1936, etc.

Raimondo da Capua. [*Legenda major*] *S. Caterina da Siena.* Translated by Giuseppe Tinagli. Siena: Cantagalli, 1934.

————. *The Life of St. Catherine of Siena.* Translated by George Lamb. New York: P. J. Kenedy & Sons, 1960.

STUDIES

Anadol, Gabriella. "Le immagini del linguaggio cateriniano e le loro fonti: la chiave." *Rassegna di ascetica e mistica* 22 (1971): 243–254.

————. "Le immagini del linguaggio cateriniano e le lore fonti: la madre." *Rassegna di ascetica e mistica* 22 (1971): 337–343.

————. "Le immagini del linguaggio cateriniano e le loro fonti: la scala." *Rassegna di ascetica e mistica* 23 (1972): 332–343.

Ashley, Benedict. "Guide to Saint Catherine's Dialogue." *Cross and Crown* 29 (1977): 237–249.

Capecelatro, Alfonso. *Storia di S. Caterina da Siena e del papato del suo tempo.* Florence: Barbera, Bianchi, 1858.

BIBLIOGRAPHY

Cavallini, Giuliana. "La struttura del Dialogo cateriniano nella edizione francese del 1913 e in quella italiana del 1968." *Rassegna di ascetica e mistica* 21 (1970): 343–353.

Centi, Tito S. "L'Eucarestia nel pensiero e nella vita di S. Caterina da Siena." *Rassegna di ascetica e mistica* 21 (1970): 369–383.

Colosio, Innocenzo. "La infinità del desiderio umano secondo S. Caterina da Siena." *Rassegna di ascetica e mistica* 21 (1970): 355–368.

Devoto, Giacomo. *Itinerario stilistico.* ("S. Caterina da Siena," pp. 29–54) Florence: Felice le Monnier, 1975.

Dupré-Theseider, Eugenio. "La duplice esperienza di S. Caterina." *Rivista storica italiana* 62 (1950); 533–574.

————. "Sulla composizione del < < Dialogo > > di Santa Caterina da Siena." *Giornale storico della letteratura italiana* 117 (1941): 161–202.

D'Urso, Giacinto. *Il genio di Santa Caterina: Studi sulla sua dottrina e personalità.* Rome: Edizioni Cateriniane, 1971.

————. "Il pensiero di S. Caterina e le sue fonti." *Sapienza* 7 (1954): 335–388.

————. "Le più recenti ristampe del Dialogo." *Rassegna di ascetica e mistica* 21 (1970): 149–152.

Fawtier, Robert. "Cateriniana." *Mélanges d'archéologie et d'histoire* 34 (1914): 3–95.

Fawtier, Robert, and Canet, Louis. *La double expérience de Catherine Benincasa.* 6th ed. Paris: Librairie Gallimard, 1948.

Fawtier, Robert. *Sainte Catherine de Sienne: Essaie de critique des sources: II. Les oeuvres de Sainte Catherine de Sienne. Bibliotèque des Ecoles françaises d'Athène et de Rome,* vol. 135. Paris: De Boccard, 1930.

————. *Sainte Catherine de Sienne: Essaie de critique des sources: I. Sources hagiographiques. Bibliotèque des Écoles françaises d'Athène et de Rome,* vol. 121. Paris: De Boccard, 1921.

Fiorilli, Matilde. "Il Dialogo di Santa Caterina da Siena." *Rassegna nazionale* 176 (1910): 467–472.

Foster, Kenelm. "St. Catherine's Teaching on Christ." *Life of the Spirit* 16 (1962): 310–323.

Getto, Giovanni. "L'ispirazione di Caterina da Siena." *Letteratura religiosa del Trecento,* pp. 263–266. Florence: Sansoni, 1967.

————. *Saggio letterario su S. Caterina da Siena.* Florence: Sansoni, 1939.

Gigli, Girolamo. *Vocabolario cateriniano.* Siena: Vincenzo Pazzini Carli e Figli, 1797.

Grion, Alvaro. *Santa Caterina da Siena: dottrina e fonti.* Brescia: Morcelliana, 1953.

BIBLIOGRAPHY

Levasti, Arrigo. *Mistici del Duecento e del Trecento.* Milan, Rome: Rizzoli & Co., 1935, 1960.

Motzo, Bacchisio R. "Per un'edizione critica delle opere di S. Caterina da Siena." *Annali della Facoltà di Filosofia e Lettere della R. Università di Cagliari,* 1930–1931, pp. 111–141.

Oddasso-Cartotti, Adriana. "La dottrina di S. Tommaso d'Aquino insegnata e vissuta da S. Caterina da Siena." *Rassegna di ascetica e mistica* 25 (1974): 321–332.

Paris, Gerardo. "S. Caterina da Siena e S. Tommaso d'Aquino: conformità di dottrina." *Rivista di ascetica e mistica,* 1961, p. 522.

Taurisano, Innocenzo. "La vera Caterina da Siena e l'ultima opera di R. Fawtier." *Vita Cristiana* 18 (1949): 223–234.

Zanini, Lina. *Bibliografia analitica di S. Caterina da Siena, 1901–1950.* Rome: Edizioni Cateriniane, 1971.

BIOGRAPHIES

Drane, Augusta Theodosia. *The History of St. Catherine of Siena and Her Companions.* 4th ed. London: Longmans, Green and Co., 1915.

Gardner, Edmund G. *Saint Catherine of Siena: A study in the Religion, Literature and History of the Fourteenth Century in Italy.* London: E. P. Dent & Co., 1907.

Giordani, Igino. *Saint Catherine of Siena, Doctor of the Church.* Translated by Thomas J. Tobin. Boston: St. Paul Editions, 1975.

Jørgensen, Johannes. *Saint Catherine of Siena.* Translated by Ingeborg Lund. London: Longmans, Green, and Co., 1939.

Levasti, Arrigo. *My Servant, Catherine.* Translated by Dorothy M. White. Westminster: Newman Press, 1954.

Perrin, Joseph Marie. *Catherine of Siena.* Translated by Paul Barrett. Westminster: Newman Press, 1965.

INDEX FOR
PREFACE AND INTRODUCTION

Neri di Landoccio de' Pagliaresi, 19.
Niccolò di Tuldo, 5.

Obedience, 19.
Oddasso-Cartotti, 10.
The Orchard of Syon, 20.

Pagliaresi, Neri di Landoccio de', see under Neri.
Paris, 10.
Passavanti, 10.
Paul VI, 1.
Pisa, 5.
Processus of Venice, 2, 13, 14, 22.
Providence, 16, 18–19, 20.

Raymond of Capua, 1, 2, 4, 5, 6, 7, 8, 11, 12, 13, 14, 17, 18, 22.
Redemption, 17, 18.
Rocca d'Orcia, 6, 12.
Rome, 6, 7, 13.
Ryley, M.B., 9.

Sacraments, 18.
Salimbeni, Benedetta de', see under Benedetta.
Salvation, 5, 8, 17.

Schism, 7, 13.
Scriptures, 10, 11, 20, 22.
Siena, 5, 6, 7.
Soul, ascent of, 8; stages of, 17.
Stigmata, 5.
Suso, Henry, 1.

Tantucci, Giovanni, 11.
Tauler, John, 1.
Taurisano, 10.
Teresa of Avila, 1.
Thomas of Aquinas, 10.
Thorold, Algar, 20.
Trinity, 19.
Tommaso della Fonte, 2, 3, 11.
Tommaso Pietra, 11.
Truth, 8, 9, 12, 14, 16; of God, 9, 18.
Tuldo, Niccolò di, see under Niccolò.

Ubertino da Casale, 10.
Urban VI, 6–7.

Visions, 7.
Virtue, 8, 16, 19.

William of Flete, 2.
World, 16, 17, 18.
Word, 19.

INDEX TO
TEXT AND NOTES

love, 322, 364; persecution of, 218, 219, 220; power of, 138, 185, 208, 217, 220, 259, 279, 312, 333; reverence for, 216, 217, 236, 272; treasure of, 220; trust in, 260, 264, 267.
Body, as barrier, 91; of blessed, 84; of damned, 85, 86; glorified, 84, 85, 86; mortification of, 43, 186, 187, 189, 193, 345; and virtue, 105.
Breviary, 262.
Bridge, cf. also Christ; beneath, 71, 73, 93, 262, 362; climbing of, 110, 118, 145, 158, 159; Son as, 58, 59, 63–70, 76, 78, 90, 100–103, 105, 106, 122, 145, 159, 163, 262, 361; stairs of, 100, 101, 102, 107, 108, 109, 110, 112, 140, 141, 145, 158, 159, 181, 245, 361; travel on, 71, 78, 87, 91, 93, 112, 129, 137, 147; and virtue, 66; Word as, 58, 63, 66, 76, 90, 105, 285, 361.
Buonsignori, 318.

Cain, 79.
Catherine, *Letters*, 26, 27, 46, 146, 148, 194, 217, 224, 283, 298; *Supplementum*, 295.
Cavalca, Dominico, 241, 253, 292.
Cavallini, G., 40, 96, 204, 231, 242, 250, 256, 316, 318, 336.
Charity, bonds of, 83, 84, 219, 311; of Christ, 255; clothed in, 26, 190, 230, 355; and discernment, 42–44; divine, 33, 49, 57, 88, 108, 116, 118, 123, 138, 198, 199, 206, 221,

246, 292, 321, 322, 330, 347, 352; exercise of, 38, 311, 312; fire of, 112, 116, 123, 136, 138, 140, 152, 155, 157, 158, 171, 198, 225, 246, 254, 264, 266, 292, 294, 304, 319, 320, 322, 325, 332, 339, 347, 352, 360, 361, 364, 365; fruits of, 222, 229, 266; 346; and God, 45, 48, 50, 63, 112, 120, 123, 125, 129–136, 140, 141, 143, 146, 147, 150–152, 157–160, 164, 166, 171, 176, 179–182, 191, 209, 212, 213, 225, 246, 252, 268, 270–279, 284, 290–294, 301, 305, 339, 361, 364; and humility, 29, 40, 42, 63, 118, 252, 292, 328, 340; lacking, 34, 35, 55, 82, 88, 107, 132, 150, 218, 222, 227, 244, 247, 252, 266, 290, 291, 299, 304, 334, 344, 347; life of, 85, 89, 270; mutual, 38, 55, 176, 242, 311–313, 344, 350; and neighbor, 34, 36, 41, 44, 45, 107, 114, 116, 126–127, 131, 132, 137, 140–144, 152, 163, 164, 167, 170, 171, 179, 180, 192, 193, 198, 218, 223, 229, 239, 266, 269, 282, 290, 291, 297, 299, 304, 308, 311, 313, 334, 344; ordinary, 31, 106, 184, 193; and patience, 33, 39, 252, 340; perfection of, 302, 303, 312; power of, 30, 39, 44; and prayer, 127, 134; proving of, 39, 303; and virtue, 29, 35–38, 43, 88, 118, 141, 218, 251, 226, 328, 332, 336, 337, 346, 347; and works, 29.

Christ, and beatific vision, 146,
166; blood of, 122, 123, 125,
126, 138, 143, 147, 152, 169,
180, 210, 214, 233, 253–255,
264, 271, 279, 288, 295; body
of, 126, 137, 210, 253, 254, 258,
279, 294, 295; as bridge, 69,
122, 129, 132, 137, 147, 155,
158, 363; crucified, 25, 29, 69,
90, 108–110, 113, 119, 122, 123,
125, 129, 132, 134, 137, 141,
143–145, 147, 152, 153, 155,
158, 165, 169, 179, 180, 188,
189, 235, 239, 246, 279, 288,
295, 307–309, 366; death of,
120, 217; divinity of, 294;
following of, 25, 29, 35, 90,
110, 119, 189; as food, 255;
humanity of, 86, 254, 294; love
of, 255; and ministers, 215,
218, 254; name of, 25, 27; and
poverty, 321; resurrection of,
206; and suffering, 29, 279;
teachings of, 46, 69, 129, 132,
134, 137, 141, 145, 147, 152,
155, 179, 266; union with, 153,
154; vicar of, 215, 249, 328,
330.
Christian, 26, 36, 50, 54, 55, 60,
62, 74, 139, 142, 160, 172, 215,
220, 271.
1 Chronicles, 18:38, 28.
Church, cf. also Ministers; as
bride, 49, 50, 54, 160, 205, 219,
222, 223, 234, 235, 250, 256,
261, 271, 307, 362; and evil, 57,
249, 251, 262; harmed, 48, 250;
and light, 221, 222; mercy for,
275; mystic body of, 36, 47, 49,
50, 60, 62, 63, 69, 72, 123, 142,
143, 159, 176, 181, 189, 200,
204, 206, 209, 212, 214, 215,
217, 218, 222, 223, 225, 227,
230, 233, 234, 239, 274, 337,
339, 361, 364; Mystical Body
of, 36; needs of, 236, 248;
persecution of, 26, 27, 216,
220, 272, 361; pillars of, 340;
and prayer, 120, 159, 248, 272;
rebelling against, 26, 62, 216,
271; reform of, 26, 47, 49, 55,
204, 231, 256, 272, 276, 307,
362; and sacraments, 36, 60,
66, 72, 213, 214, 216, 219, 221,
222, 230, 232, 234, 235, 262,
293; and salvation, 228; and
State, 215; teaching of, 233;
and vows, 356; welfare of,
229.
Colosio, I., 170.
Colossians, 3:17, 127.
Commandments, 74, 96, 97,
106–111, 165, 176, 203, 217,
242, 251, 257, 278, 283, 309,
310, 319, 323, 327, 329, 330,
332–335, 355.
Compassion, 35, 38, 68, 82, 143,
144, 151, 159, 163, 190, 191,
193, 195, 197, 203, 228, 235,
238, 244, 263, 304, 305, 317,
321, 322, 343.
Confessors, 69, 71, 282, 311.
Conscience, 125; dog of,
257–263; fire of, 80; free, 351;
goading of, 131, 199, 216,
266–270, 294, 297, 352; holy,
135, 157, 265; judgment of, 88,
120, 135; peace of, 177, 225;
purity of, 136; roused, 30, 270;
troubled, 99, 233; wind of,

174, 175; weight of, 317, 318; worm of, 54, 73, 78–80, 86, 177, 217, 269, 333.

Consolation, 144; contempt for, 135, 136, 167, 188, 200, 201, 306; deprived of, 187, 193, 195, 196; from God, 47, 130–132, 145, 167, 177, 284, 323; love for, 127–136, 158, 162, 166, 187, 199–201, 303; testing of, 133, 198–200.

Constantine, 227.

Continence, 338, 341, 342, 345, 347, 349, 355, 356.

Contrition, 28–32, 45, 51, 60, 79, 93, 112, 124, 125, 130, 138, 152, 209, 254, 259, 272, 289, 298, 331, 361.

Copernicus, 206.

1 Corinthians, 1:30, 50; 2:9, 31, 68, 181, 326; 2:14, 287; 3:11, 66; 4:9–13, 225; 4:13, 143; 9:11, 213; 9:22, 228; 11:25–26, 212; 12:4–6, 37; 12:14–26, 311; 13:1–3, 29, 304.

2 Corinthians, 12:2, 25; 12:2–4, 152; 12:3, 158; 12:4, 326; 12:7, 78, 153, 305; 12:9, 149, 153; 12:9–10, 144.

Cortona, F. Simone de, 27.

Counsels, 96, 97, 106, 110, 111, 165, 309, 310, 319, 323, 327, 329, 334, 355.

Courage, 26, 33, 37, 39, 42, 44, 46, 58, 70, 90, 127, 142, 144, 150, 163, 178, 189, 225, 227, 289, 325, 359, 360.

Creation, 184; goodness of, 97, 98, 110, 288, 318; and love, 31, 49, 50, 55, 57, 84, 104, 152, 165, 171, 180, 205, 208, 220, 226, 273, 277, 278, 283, 284, 311; of man, 49–53, 58, 59, 71, 74, 114, 151, 152, 165, 191, 205, 208, 226, 273, 276, 281, 284, 287–290, 324, 363, 366; new-, 29, 53, 54, 180, 205; and providence, 277, 278, 288, 311, 362; of soul, 26, 42, 48, 84, 104, 180, 185, 261.

Creator, 28, 56, 125, 143, 167, 172, 179, 185, 202, 287, 289, 295, 300, 309, 322, 324, 331, 343, 360.

Cross, death on, 47, 52, 71, 76, 151, 156, 239, 252, 253, 278, 280, 289, 320, 327, 354; in life, 91, 129, 147, 307; of Son, 63, 64, 65, 71, 139, 146, 193, 201, 233, 245, 246, 247, 332; table of, 141, 144, 163, 177, 178, 189, 223, 229, 235, 239, 304, 332, 338.

Cruelty, 34, 35, 51, 72, 74, 80, 86, 213, 253, 259, 277, 289, 305, 312, 317, 343.

Daniel, 3:12–24, 358.

Dante, 51, 242, 254, 264.

Death, cf. also Sin; cause of, 300; conquered, 71, 214; desire for, 154, 322, 323; eternal, 77, 81, 97, 99, 105, 182, 285, 298, 316, 329, 349; freeing from 34, 50, 59, 65, 278, 289, 320; point of, 30, 33, 46, 47, 78, 79, 86, 88, 89, 126, 139, 143, 149, 227, 231, 256, 259–269, 273, 325, 328, 333, 339,347; power of, 175; of Son, 47, 52, 71, 72, 76, 151,

156, 201, 214, 217, 223, 239, 276, 278, 288, 307, 320; and tears, 162, 362; tree of, 42, 73, 74, 99, 171, 349; water of, 87, 89, 99, 106, 110.

Delusion, 94, 95, 98, 100–104, 110, 111, 124, 127–136, 159, 182, 183, 187, 196–202, 266, 284, 348, 349, 363.

Desire, flame of, 27, 48; fulfilled, 54, 84, 91, 92, 149, 153, 170, 199, 201, 204, 273, 274, 286, 294, 295, 325, 326, 332, 360, 361; for God, 83, 91, 92, 100, 108, 116, 149, 151, 170, 186, 273, 331, 332, 364; for God's honor, 25, 36–37, 40, 54, 108, 109, 189, 192, 195, 197, 200, 213, 223, 228, 247, 264, 275, 276, 306, 308; for grace, 44, 322; holy, 50, 57, 91, 97, 104, 136, 140, 141, 168, 170, 188, 190, 192, 194, 195, 203, 207, 235, 238, 279, 286, 293, 305, 308, 325, 326, 327, 338, 353; infinite, 28, 43, 170, 197; for neighbor, 34, 314; for perfection, 114; perverse, 300, 316; and sacrament, 207, 208, 209, 293, 294, 295, 296; for salvation of souls, 25, 37, 39, 40, 54, 84, 108, 109, 139, 140, 151, 152, 157, 189, 192,195, 197, 200, 203, 212, 213, 223, 228, 232, 234, 247, 264, 266, 275, 276, 304, 325, 353; of souls, 25–29, 32, 51, 52, 102–104, 108, 111, 123–126, 130, 133, 140, 151, 169, 170, 184, 293, 295, 303, 307–310,

332, 335, 353, 361, 364; and suffering, 29, 33, 37, 42, 45, 50, 54, 179, 304; table of, 188, 190, 192, 193, 195, 197, 338; vine of, 189.

Despair, 30, 79, 89, 228, 260, 267, 268, 269, 270.

Devil, 32, 34, 45, 52, 58, 60, 66, 76–80, 87, 88, 98–103, 106, 110, 122, 126, 133, 136, 142, 143, 146, 150, 152, 167, 168, 176, 187, 189, 192, 194, 196, 200, 210, 213, 217, 219, 220, 227, 228, 233, 235, 237, 241, 243–248, 250, 257, 260, 262, 264, 266, 267, 269, 272, 273, 278, 306, 309, 311, 312, 320, 330, 333, 344, 345, 347, 362.

Discernment, 343; and charity, 42, 43, 44; and faith, 92, 94; and judgment, 292; and justice, 265; lacking, 73, 76, 89, 131, 175, 199, 231, 234, 254, 266, 271, 281, 286; light of, 44, 45, 186; and love, 302; and penance, 40, 43, 44; and neighbor, 41, 190, 195; and self-knowledge, 41, 43; and understanding, 44, 156, 223; of visitations, 198, 199; and will, 343, 357.

Disciples, 68, 69, 77, 118, 123, 136, 156, 307, 309, 320, 345, 358.

Doctors, 69, 71, 282, 311.

Domenico, Monna Bartolomea di, 146.

Dominic, 264, 314, 337, 338, 339, 340.

leaving of, 46, 191; losing of, 80, 81, 95, 174, 196, 316; love for, 25, 29–34, 36, 38, 44, 46, 48, 50, 52, 54, 56, 57, 62, 83, 89, 92, 94, 96, 97, 100, 107, 109–116, 121, 123, 127–130, 134, 141, 150, 154, 155, 161, 165, 169, 177, 185, 186, 189, 190, 199, 202, 203, 212, 226, 227, 246, 251, 255, 258, 261, 263, 281, 291, 292, 297, 298, 302, 304, 306, 309, 317, 329–330, 338, 346, 354; love of, 25, 29, 31, 44, 46, 49–52, 55, 56, 61, 63, 75–77, 83, 85, 88, 93, 94, 108–116, 120, 121, 124, 125, 129–131, 164, 165, 175, 179, 184, 191, 195, 204–205, 220, 227, 231, 246, 247, 251, 273–275, 278, 279, 283–285, 297, 307, 325, 330, 335, 359, 361, 363, 364; became man, 50, 51, 53, 59, 72, 205, 320, 325; man in, 61, 67, 85, 106; mercy of, 27, 49–58, 63, 66, 71–76, 79, 84, 86, 87, 89, 101–104, 112, 118, 119, 124, 125, 139, 150, 151, 159–162, 164, 167, 175, 176, 182, 184, 190, 202, 204, 217, 220, 231, 238, 244, 255, 260, 267–273, 276, 286–288, 290, 292, 296, 298, 304, 313, 325, 343, 357, 361–364; mirror of, 48, 111; name of, 27, 30, 40, 42, 47, 49, 54, 57, 60, 75, 83, 105, 109, 110, 136, 141, 144, 149–152, 155, 163–165, 188–190, 195, 201, 203, 212, 218, 222, 231, 238, 246, 261, 265, 276, 290, 292, 300, 303,

306, 310, 316, 323, 338, 344, 365; offenses against, 27–30, 33, 35, 44, 46, 48, 51, 56, 57, 61, 68, 71, 79, 81, 87, 93, 101, 104, 112, 125, 131, 142, 147, 149, 151, 154, 162–164, 167, 179, 192, 210, 214, 216–218, 229, 233–236, 248, 241, 261, 267, 268, 274, 279, 287, 304, 306, 319, 334, 343, 361; offerings to, 28, 46, 47, 181, 191, 229, 238, 255, 265, 272; pardon of, 49, 56; pleasing of, 33, 36, 42, 43, 58, 95, 97, 110, 123, 125, 143, 169, 172, 178, 184, 187, 281, 310, 315, 324, 325, 331, 357, 358, 359; power of, 49, 61, 69, 70, 77, 78, 81, 84, 116, 119, 136, 206, 212, 222, 255, 278, 289, 296, 353; presence of, 56, 125–135, 146, 147, 163, 169, 181, 194, 195, 225, 262; promises of, 47, 71, 72, 204, 272, 274, 285, 327, 362, 363; reproofs of, 77–79, 81; seeking of, 113, 115, 116, 119; servants of, 25, 30–32, 39, 45–47, 54–62, 68, 77, 91, 92, 98, 100, 111, 113, 129, 132–134, 143, 146, 150, 151, 154, 157, 159, 160, 164, 169, 172, 173, 182, 184, 190–193, 196, 197, 201, 217, 218, 220, 238, 261, 272, 275, 276, 286, 290, 296–298, 307, 315–319, 336, 344, 359, 362; serving of, 65, 72, 113–115, 142, 155, 161, 167, 182–184, 187–189, 194, 235, 245, 280–284, 306, 317, 366; sight of, 25, 80, 83, 84, 90–92,

115–118, 149, 151, 154, 157,
210, 227, 259, 266, 306, 328,
333, 364; in soul, 36, 41, 42, 46,
75, 107, 108, 116, 168, 179, 211,
320, 366; as Sun, 206, 222, 239;
trust in, 38, 204, 226, 227, 267,
280, 285, 287, 289, 291, 293,
301, 314, 315, 317, 322; and
truth, 27–33, 37, 40, 44, 45,
47–49, 57–59, 63, 70, 71, 76–78,
86, 87, 92, 96, 97, 100, 103,
105–109, 115, 116, 121, 125,
130, 132, 133, 136, 138, 140,
143–145, 151, 152, 155, 158,
159, 163, 167, 169, 179,
188–192, 195–197, 200–204,
212, 214, 221–223, 225, 233,
235, 245, 248, 251, 252, 262,
264, 265, 270, 273, 275, 278,
280, 282, 283, 287, 289–291,
293, 303–305, 308–312, 319,
323, 326, 327, 329, 330, 334,
335, 337, 339, 342, 345, 346,
353, 354, 357, 359, 361;
unchangeable, 90, 91, 147;
union with, 25–28, 32, 42, 46,
51, 57, 59, 62, 64, 65, 93, 116,
137, 144–148, 152–155, 157,
158, 160–167, 179–181, 190,
191, 194, 202, 205, 222, 264,
295, 305, 306, 317, 323.
Gomorrah, 237, 238.
Gospels, 86, 181, 225, 233, 252,
280, 293, 308, 312, 328, 357.
Grace, and baptism, 52, 53, 60,
61, 62, 209, 279; and Christ,
280; fruit of, 30, 42, 63, 281;
gift of, 31, 51, 55, 186, 203,
208, 247, 264, 366; and God,
105, 109, 113, 135, 149, 175,

176, 182, 186, 202, 273; growth
of, 78, 122, 153, 165, 307; help
of, 329; infused, 155, 156, 339;
led to, 31; life of, 31, 37, 44, 46,
52, 54, 61, 65, 67, 73, 94, 95, 99,
172, 174, 179, 181, 185, 211,
221, 230, 285, 293, 327, 334,
349, 353; and light, 36, 57, 74,
156, 157, 166, 194, 208, 209,
221, 266, 267, 309, 332; lost,
33–34, 46, 51, 54, 61, 73, 74, 95,
99, 104, 107, 119, 138, 172, 173,
174, 175, 186, 217, 219,
220–221, 233, 254, 285, 287,
301, 306, 307, 308, 309, 334,
349; and love, 38, 277; and
new creation, 29; not taken
away, 113, 119, 145, 147, 154,
195, 287; and providence, 281;
received, 32, 40, 41, 135, 230,
235; renewed, 170; and
sacraments, 60, 208, 211, 215,
225, 230, 307; sign of, 328; and
sin, 78, 190, 308; and Son's
blood, 51, 138, 205, 264, 281,
287; source of, 94; and
suffering, 46, 93; and Word,
330.
Gregory, 135.
Gregory the Great, 64, 214, 222.
Gregory XI, 250.
Grion, A., 36.
Guilt, 27, 29, 32, 44, 46, 88, 89,
119, 124, 136, 194, 219, 224,
229, 233, 235, 248, 249, 255,
256, 272, 285, 297, 299, 338,
352, 356.

Heart, change of, 102; contrition
of, 29, 32, 79, 93, 139, 272, 289,

298, 331, 361; deceitful, 75;
desires of, 63, 274; hardness
of, 31, 32, 275 276; hatred in,
334; of Son, 138, 140, 246; and
tears, 161, 164, 166, 168, 170,
171, 174; weariness of, 297.

Heaven, 47, 58, 66, 67, 68, 69, 70,
75, 145, 152, 252, 277, 278, 282,
291, 328, 330, 331, 332, 334,
341, 344, 345, 346, 351, 355,
361, 363, 364.

Hebrews, 1:14, 229; 2:7–8, 317;
4:15, 305; 5:2–3, 305; 5:11–14,
132; 9:13–14, 32; 11:33–38, 179.

Hell, 68, 72, 79, 80, 88, 89, 91, 94,
98–100, 103, 125, 132, 158, 197,
247, 252, 268, 271, 291, 296,
301, 312, 318, 323, 347, 351.

Heresies, 339.

Holy Spirit, as Advocate, 70, 77;
coming of, 119, 120, 136, 156,
180; and fear, 119; fire of, 206,
227; gifts of, 35, 37, 129, 146,
251, 288, 289; and grace, 213,
221, 232, 244, 247, 248, 251;
light of, 293, 336; and love,
136, 227, 365; mercy of, 28, 31,
49, 69, 70, 116, 119, 152, 222,
227, 277, 289, 291, 294, 295,
297, 314; as mother, 292, 323;
and providence, 336; received,
152; and religious, 242, 340;
reproofs of, 77; and salvation,
335; as servant, 294, 296, 307,
314; as teacher, 69, 77; and
tears, 169, 171.

Hope, fulfilled, 292, 347; in
God, 27, 39, 48, 55, 101, 265,
280, 281, 290, 294, 306, 322,
342; lacking, 39, 79, 81, 88,
102, 175, 267, 284, 289, 294,
362; for mercy, 124, 162, 167,
267, 268, 325; of ministers,
226; in providence, 286; and
salvation, 49, 279; in self, 226,
227, 265, 267, 280, 281,
284–294, 301, 342; in Son's
blood, 79, 139, 264; tested, 38,
294; and time, 333; true, 319,
342.

Humbert, 338.

Humility, cf. also Charity; 37,
318; growth of, 130; and
ministers, 225, 226, 249, 252,
253, 265; and obedience, 329,
338, 341, 342, 353, 354, 360;
and patience, 40, 104, 135,
360; perseverence in, 120; and
prayer, 190; and pride, 53,
187; and self-knowledge, 29,
36, 41, 42, 113, 118, 124, 136,
168, 293, 301; testing of, 38,
305; true, 142, 167, 171, 178,
185, 194, 198, 222, 223, 225,
295, 296, 305, 308, 315, 319,
320, 328, 332, 344; and
visitations, 134, 200.

Hurtand, 283.

Isaiah, 1:9, 237; 5:1–4, 62; 9:3,
256; 11:5, 331; 13:19, 237;
29:13, 236, 269, 350; 42:3, 39;
43:1–5, 55, 53:7, 329; 53:12,
150; 55:1, 87; 56:7, 250; 56:10,
257; 66:24, 80, 269.

Italy, 250; city-states of, 26, 215.

Jacopo da Varagine, 292, 337.

James, 1:24, 48; 2:26, 94; 3:6, 300;
8:44, 273; 8:58, 273.

333; of Moses, 282, 288; New, 112, 156; Old, 112, 156; perfecting of, 157; perverse, 105, 182, 185, 192; and Word, 112.

Lawrence, 322.

Lazarus, 82, 323.

Leviticus, 19:18, 33.

Life, active, 126; bread of, 211, 295; contemplative of, 126; eternal, 31, 49, 56, 58, 59, 68, 76, 83, 89–95, 97, 100, 107, 112, 114, 151, 152, 155, 162, 172, 180, 182, 192, 214, 227, 264, 266, 284, 292, 301, 318, 323, 327, 328, 334, 346–348, 355, 356, 359, 363; example of, 41, 158, 204, 213, 225, 227, 229, 235, 236, 240, 245, 253, 265, 269, 274, 307; God as, 29, 42, 106, 107, 142, 176, 188, 192, 312, 322, 325, 346, 364; present, 68, 311, 333, 348, 351; and Son, 51, 52, 59, 65–67, 70, 85, 106, 122, 206, 221, 222, 285, 286, 289, 292, 293, 320, 329, 363; religious, 335–359, 363; states of, 110, 111, 115, 126, 355, 356; tears of, 162, 170; and virtue, 186; water of, 106, 107, 109.

Light, cf. also Faith, Grace, Knowledge; of baptism, 60, 61, 308; of discernment, 44, 45; divine, 323; God as, 184, 185, 213, 233, 284, 364, 365; of justice, 224, 225, 256, 274; lacking, 223, 224, 259, 286, 289, 290, 298, 324, 349, 351; of learning, 206, 223, 265, 267,

271, 337, 338, 339; and mercy, 72; and ministers, 208, 224, 225, 266, 274; natural, 156, 157, 281, 282, 293, 352; of obedience, 331, 350, 353; ordinary, 184, 186, 193; perfect, 187, 189, 193, 195, 292, 309, 319, 365; of reason, 76, 93, 96, 103, 104–105, 185, 226, 235, 248, 249, 262, 263, 281, 284, 309; and Son, 51, 66, 196, 211, 227, 285; in soul, 48, 57, 79, 180, 181, 293, 310, 322, 350, 354; and truth, 33, 155, 156, 196, 265, 273, 286; of understanding, 45, 108, 126; and virtue, 239, 264, 303; way of, 59, 66; and Word, 67, 206, 208.

Love, Cf. also Creation, God, Knowledge, Virtue; and affection, 25, 26, 28, 34, 36, 40, 46, 82, 83, 104, 113, 115, 116, 130, 135, 145, 151, 190, 198; debt of, 54, 56, 79, 97, 121, 165, 335; disordered, 44, 67, 73, 87, 90, 96, 97, 98, 99, 101, 102, 105, 109, 162, 168, 175, 218, 302, 306, 319, 322, 323; eternal, 49, 82, 83, 84; filial, 115, 118, 127, 135, 144; fire of, 57, 63, 273, 334, 342; of friendship, 115, 118, 127, 134, 135, 144; growth of, 33, 210, 306; imperfect, 113, 115, 121, 127, 128, 129, 134, 136, 140, 143, 145, 149, 153, 158, 161, 168, 243; infinite, 28, 42, 44, 138, 176; lacking, 94, 99, 241–242; mercenary, 115, 134,

386

135, 189, 306; mutual, 109,
110; and neighbor, 33, 34, 36,
37, 38, 44, 45, 54, 56, 74, 83, 85,
94, 96, 108, 109, 110, 113, 114,
121, 123, 131, 141, 158, 161,
164, 165, 176, 190, 191, 212,
247, 251, 265, 308, 309, 310,
319, 321, 330, 332, 334, 364;
ordered, 44, 168, 190, 302;
ordinary, 89, 97, 110, 116;
perfection of, 32, 97, 118, 131,
134–135, 136, 141, 143, 153,
161, 166, 168, 302, 303; and
providence, 298, 314; proving
of, 38, 46, 185, 201, 246, 255,
302; and sacrament, 211;
selfish, 30, 35, 43, 56, 62, 73,
75, 78, 79, 87, 89, 90, 94, 96,
100, 102, 103, 104, 107, 108,
110, 111, 113, 120, 134, 157,
162, 171, 173, 174, 175, 224,
234, 239, 247, 251, 252, 253,
254, 256, 258, 267, 281, 285,
292, 299, 306, 319, 327, 329,
333, 342, 343, 347, 348 349,
353, 365, 366; sensual, 70, 89,
93, 99, 134, 162, 171, 180, 251,
302; sign of, 46, 272; spiritual,
120, 121, 162, 302, 306; and
sufferings, 30, 33, 58, 99, 149,
306; tree of, 42, 73, 171;
unitive, 363; worthy of, 229,
230.
Luke, 1:38, 133; 3:9, 259; 4:4, 293;
4:23, 240; 5:4–8, 308; 5:27, 319;
5:31, 274; 6:38, 32, 226; 6:39,
225; 6:43–44, 176; 6:46, 280;
6:47–49, 321; 8:14, 102; 9:24,
131; 9:58, 321; 9:62, 46; 10:16,
217; 11:19, 275; 12:27, 116;
12:29–31, 291; 12:33, 345;
12:48, 53; 12:50, 151; 14:11,
252, 346; 16:13, 252, 280;
16:19–22, 323; 16:29–31, 282;
17:21, 76; 18:14, 252, 346;
18:16–17, 346; 18:28–30, 346;
18:25, 318; 19:12–27, 228;
19:41–44, 125; 19:46, 248, 250;
22:19–20, 255; 22:62, 118.

Man, becomes divine, 50, 53,
205; is called, 63, 72, 95, 106,
107, 109; corruption of, 51,
255; creation of, 49–53, 58, 59,
71, 74, 114, 151, 152, 165, 191,
205, 208, 226, 273, 276, 281,
284, 287–290, 324, 363, 366;
dignity of, 26, 49, 72, 74, 76,
205, 274, 277, 279, 313; freed,
53, 76, 235, 245, 282, 332; goal
of, 58, 100, 101, 108, 111, 150,
176, 191, 203, 277, 290, 323,
355; in God, 61, 67, 85, 106;
God became, 50, 51, 53, 59, 72,
205, 320, 325; good of, 52, 55,
58, 72, 83, 89, 114, 187, 281,
284, 289, 290, 317, 362; as
image of God, 49, 50, 53, 58,
114, 165, 205, 208, 273, 276,
277, 283, 288, 290, 324;
indebtedness of, 53, 54, 58, 59,
63, 113, 121; as pilgrim, 111,
123, 145, 150, 176, 186, 202,
212, 262, 279, 303, 318, 348;
recreation of, 53, 54, 71, 189,
205, 276, 279, 281, 365;
restored, 52, 245, 287;
salvation of, 102; selfishness
of, 55, 70; and sin, 49, 50, 52,
53, 55, 57, 58, 63; troubles of,

387

58, 59; in Word, 61, 85, 106.

Mark, 2:24, 319; 2:27, 98; 4:24,
226; 6:34, 232; 7:6, 236, 350;
8:35, 131; 9:43, 54; 9:43–48,
269; 9:48, 80; 10:25, 318;
10:28–30, 346; 11:17, 248, 250;
11:24, 33; 12:33, 33.

Martyrs, 69, 71, 138, 146, 156,
173, 223, 282, 311, 322, 339,
340.

Mary, 25, 27, 210, 283, 286, 315,
320, 337, 338.

Mass, 27, 210, 214, 223, 236, 259,
295.

Matthew, 319.

Matthew, 3:10, 259; 4:4, 293;
5:15, 69, 179; 5:17, 112, 107;
5:45, 291; 6:19–20, 345;
6:22–23, 92; 6:24, 252, 280;
6:25–34, 281; 6:28, 114;
6:31–33, 291; 6:33–34, 345;
6:34, 291; 7:1, 195; 7:2, 83, 226,
265; 7:6, 332; 7:7, 275; 7:7–11,
201; 7:13–14, 318; 7:15, 244;
7:16–18, 176; 7:21, 42; 7:21–23,
280; 7:24–29, 321; 8:20, 321;
8:22, 250; 9:9, 319; 9:12, 274;
9:36, 232; 10:8, 213, 247;
10:14–15, 346; 10:29, 114;
11:30, 68; 12:1, 320; 12:24, 76;
12:24–27, 258; 12:31–32, 79;
12:32, 268; 12:43–45, 100, 262;
13:44–46, 332; 15:8, 236, 269;
15:14, 225, 256; 16:16, 255;
16:19, 214; 16:25, 131; 18:3,
346; 18:15–17, 198; 18:20, 105,
107; 19:14, 346; 19:16–22, 97;
19:24, 318; 19:27–29, 346;
20:1–6, 60; 20:1–16, 357; 21:13,
248, 250; 22:1–14, 176;
22:37–40, 38, 165, 330; 23:2–3,
230; 23:3, 233; 23:4, 243; 23:12,
252, 346; 24:18, 143; 24:30, 81;
25:11–12, 280; 25:14–30, 32,
228, 269; 25:40, 34, 121; 25:41,
87; 25:42–46, 312; 25:45, 131;
26:27–28, 255; 26:74, 115;
26:75, 118; 27:40–42, 143.

Maurice, 358.

Meattini, 40.

Memory, 32, 49, 65, 73, 103, 104,
108, 113, 153, 180, 191, 221,
222, 244, 246, 257, 277, 299,
301, 310.

Mercy, cf. also God; deprived
of, 35; of Father 72, 85, 238,
275–277, 327; of Holy Spirit
28, 31, 49, 69, 70, 116, 119, 152,
222, 227, 277, 289, 291, 294,
295, 297, 314; hope in, 124,
162, 167, 267, 268, 325; refusal
of, 79, 89, 268; of Son, 66, 71,
85, 86, 276; trust in, 267, 268;
for world, 54, 55, 63, 71, 90,
151, 159, 160, 201, 255, 272,
275–277, 307, 361, 363.

Merit, 153, 346; and God, 48,
236; lacking, 99, 236; in this
life, 85, 306, 313; and love,
355, 356, 357; and obedience,
351, 355, 356, 357;
opportunity for, 305; and
patience, 93; and penance, 44.

Mind, darkened, 32, 239, 281;
enlightened, 108, 201, 211,
274, 283; eye of, 26, 59, 73, 88,
92, 108, 111, 113, 123, 135, 137,
152, 155, 158, 160, 161, 169,
188, 201, 202, 209, 211, 227,
239, 246, 253, 259, 264, 270,

Old Testament, 28, 279, 282, 288.

Papacy, 26, 159, 214, 215, 249.
Pardon, 30, 31, 49, 56.
The Passion, 66, 254.
Passion, selfish, 128, 130, 135,
  136, 202, 224, 291, 302, 340,
  348.
Patience, 29, 30, 33, 37–40, 42,
  46, 54, 93, 99, 101, 104, 128,
  135, 141, 143, 144, 150, 163,
  167, 175, 178, 179, 225, 227,
  239, 253, 254, 282, 283, 291,
  292, 303, 305, 307, 314,
  327–333, 342–345, 353–355;
  358, 360.
Paul, 29, 43, 44, 78, 121, 127, 142,
  149, 152, 153, 154, 172, 181,
  295, 305, 322, 325, 339.
Peace, 64, 65, 67, 87, 93, 106, 108,
  109, 120, 130–132, 141, 142,
  158, 163, 166, 178, 188, 189,
  203, 211, 263, 264, 275, 319,
  323, 332, 333, 342, 344, 350,
  357, 359, 360, 363.
Penance, 243, 335; bodily, 39, 43,
  97, 187, 263; desire for, 42,
  197; and discernment, 40, 43,
  44, 196; fear of, 350; judging
  of, 183; as means, 40, 42–44,
  196, 198; for sin, 125, 223, 228,
  231; table of, 196.
Perfection, cf. also Love; of
  God's children, 59;
  hindrances to, 40, 191, 194; of
  obedience, 334–360, 363; sin
  against, 187, 196; and Son's
  blood, 51; of soul, 44, 84, 104,
  114, 120, 124, 126, 130, 132,
  137, 140, 147, 152, 159, 161,

162, 167, 168, 177, 182,
  186–188, 192, 193, 195, 198,
  229, 263, 281, 297, 301, 303,
  305, 308, 309, 311, 313, 333,
  335–336, 355, 362; source of,
  111, 118; way of, 28–47, 48, 96,
  97, 110, 111, 184, 188, 193, 319,
  366.
Persecution, 26, 27, 32, 45, 47,
  71, 76, 107, 121, 135, 140–142,
  146, 162, 163, 167, 172, 178,
  189, 216, 217–220, 298, 355,
  361.
Perseverance, 101, 102, 105, 107,
  110, 113, 118, 120, 122, 123,
  125, 126, 130, 135, 136, 143,
  144, 150, 178, 181, 227, 275,
  304, 314, 321, 332, 335, 336,
  345, 353, 360, 365.
Peter, 115, 118, 123, 214, 215,
  221, 222, 307, 308, 309, 322,
  346.
1 Peter, 1:18–19, 247.
2 Peter, 2:22, 101, 164.
Peter of Verona, 339.
Philip, 117.
Philippians, 1:23, 154; 2:7, 329;
  2:8, 252; 3:8, 179; 3:19, 232,
  245, 298.
Pilate, 217.
Plague, 238.
Poverty, 315–325, 336–341, 345,
  347, 349, 350, 356.
Prayer, and action, 127; of
  blessed, 84; constant, 25, 32,
  46, 57, 97, 120, 122, 126, 127,
  136, 140, 150, 159, 169, 181,
  201, 203, 225, 229, 236, 263,
  272, 275, 298, 304, 308, 343,
  344, 353, 363; and desire, 32;

of Divine Office, 126, 131, 236, 245, 256, 259, 261, 269, 313, 322, 350; exercise of, 115, 122, 123, 131, 132, 134, 196, 301, 353; house of, 248, 250, 251; lacking, 342, 350; mental, 124, 125, 126, 127, 131, 344, 350; and neighbor, 34, 35, 37, 41, 127, 313; and servants, 30, 31, 194, 195, 204, 212, 238, 255, 297, 298, 363; for sinners, 71, 72, 142, 190, 203, 230, 231, 238, 298, 308; times of, 120, 122, 127, 131, 236, 245, 256, 259, 261, 359; vocal, 123, 124, 126, 127, 131, 344.

Pride, 35, 38, 41, 42, 50, 53, 56, 73–76, 78, 80, 86, 96, 104, 125, 151, 157, 173, 174, 185, 187, 213, 217, 219, 223, 231, 232, 239, 244, 249, 251–255, 256, 258–262; 267, 278, 284, 297, 312, 316, 327, 329–331, 333, 334, 338, 341, 342, 347, 349.

Prophecy, 116, 166, 282.

Proverbs, 8:17, 115; 16:12, 224; 26:12, 286; 26:27, 219; 28:26, 286.

Providence, 26, 55, 114, 136, 142, 169, 204, 212, 213, 225, 239, 265, 277–326, 333, 336, 338, 362.

Prudence, 37, 44, 45, 113, 119, 126, 133, 134, 199, 200, 278, 289, 294, 310, 321, 342.

Psalms, 8:6, 317; 17:15, 92; 36:10, 364; 42:2–3, 364; 49:12, 287; 62:12, 298; 104, 288; 105:15, 215, 272; 127:1, 226; 129:3, 66, 330; 145:13–14, 287.

Punishment, cf. also Sin; eternal, 32, 79, 95, 312, 333; fear of, 102, 113, 119, 156, 157, 161, 162, 167, 177; finite, 93; infinite, 93; in next life, 112; in this life, 112; of ministers, 215, 216, 217, 231, 233, 248, 249, 259, 262, 271, 272; pardoned, 30, 31; and prayers, 313; and Son, 50; worthy of, 29, 40.

Purgatory, 32, 89, 151, 313.

Raymond of Capua, 26, 27, 91, 203, 227, 283, 294, 295, 298; *Leg. Maj.*, 238, 283, 294, 295, 298, 315.

Redemption, 44, 53, 54, 138, 139, 246, 247, 284, 287, 308.

Reginald, 337, 338.

Repentance, 62, 75, 138, 152, 248, 249, 268.

Resurrection, 68, 82, 84, 85, 117, 148, 206, 307.

Revelation, to Catherine, 27, 55, 57, 91, 202, 210, 238, 270, 272, 286, 363; from God, 26, 27, 195, 202, 210, 238, 286, 363; of love, 274; and sin, 194, 195, 198.

Revelations, 1:5, 245, 276; 2:10, 107; 3:20, 275; 7:16–17, 92; 9:7, 10, 96; 13:8, 142; 21:6, 87.

Reverence, cf. also Ministers; 50, 81–82, 93, 187, 216, 220, 230, 283, 286, 292, 313.

Reward, cf. also Works; of chosen ones, 86; eternal, 311, 333, 359; God as, 264; for good, 68, 71, 93, 95, 144, 155,

172, 233, 259; hope for, 281;
joy in, 311, 312; and love, 357;
material, 95; of saints, 80,
147–148; and suffering, 30,
290; unworthy of, 29; for
virtue, 77, 92, 113, 176, 227,
231, 266, 270, 271, 298, 360.
Romans, 3:20, 288; 5:3, 46; 5:8,
120; 5:19, 280, 330; 6:15, 174;
6:19–21, 174; 7:23, 91, 105;
7:23–24, 149, 153; 8:26, 127,
169; 8:31, 227; 8:35, 153; 9:1,
265; 9:20–23, 276; 9:22–23, 283;
9:29, 237; 10:12, 290; 11:17–24,
62; 12:15, 164, 228; 12:17–21,
39; 12:19, 195; 13:8, 41; 15:3,
329.
Rome, 314.

Sacraments, cf. also Church,
Desire, Ministers; of the altar,
72, 145, 239; blessings of, 209;
of eucharist, 207, 208, 209,
210, 211, 254, 272, 362; food
of, 123, 244; and life, 293; and
light, 206, 207, 208, 209, 210,
239; power of, 211, 215, 217,
232, 234, 272 and providence,
307; and purity, 237;
reverence for, 244, 255; and
sin, 215, 230, 232, 234, 272.
Sacrifice, 28, 45–46, 52, 59, 155,
156, 223.
Saints, 78, 80, 83, 133, 142, 153,
176, 192, 242, 292, 310.
Salvation, cf. also Desire, Soul;
contrary to, 78; food of, 212;
help in, 226, 276, 287, 330;
hope in, 279; and obedience,
332; need for, 37, 51, 238, 280;

of neighbors, 37, 41, 44, 297,
304; and providence, 281, 283,
287, 292, 298, 301, 313, 324;
and sacraments, 213; seeking
of, 39; and world, 49, 57, 102.
Schism, 159.
Scripture, 39, 77, 155, 156, 157,
181, 215, 222, 233, 239, 249,
261, 266, 271, 321, 358.
Self, -centeredness, 231, 234,
240, 244, 269, 284, 286, 289,
311, 349, 353; -conceit, 75, 78,
80, 218, 219, 352; hatred
(contempt) for, 27, 40, 90,
118–120, 144, 158, 163, 167,
168, 186, 260, 263, 303, 307,
319, 324, 331, 334, 335, 340,
342, 344, 359; hope (trust) in,
226, 227, 265, 267, 280, 281,
284–289, 291–294, 303, 342;
-interest, 120, 121, 141, 161,
165, 200; -knowledge, 25,
27–30, 36, 40–44, 48, 49, 57, 63,
73, 80, 88, 90, 94, 113, 118–127,
133–136, 158, 162–168, 178,
185, 186, 194, 195, 198, 200,
219, 231, 254, 270, 275, 285,
293, 302, 303, 305, 307, 308,
320, 346, 350, 352, 359, 363;
reproof of, 79, 135, 196, 197;
rising above, 111, 120, 184,
238, 293, 342, 344.
Sensuality, condemned, 79, 185;
love for, 90; selfish, 29, 33, 34,
36, 39, 40, 43, 56, 73, 75, 79, 91,
94, 96–98, 101, 104, 118, 129,
135, 136, 141, 143, 166, 171,
172, 174, 178, 186, 189, 193,
212, 221, 223, 231, 232, 235,
247, 260, 262, 263, 266, 267,

363–365; body of, 101, 123,
126, 137, 145, 146, 158, 177,
206, 212, 213, 218, 221, 222,
225, 227, 229, 230, 235, 239,
245, 246, 258, 279, 320, 337,
353; divinity of, 65, 66, 81, 82,
123, 145, 146, 163, 205–210,
218, 230, 239, 254, 274;
following of, 61, 66, 67, 78, 90,
109, 116, 146, 188, 201, 206,
221, 223, 225, 235, 319, 320,
334, 346; as food, 72, 146, 212,
216; as gate, 83–84, 87; and
God, 61, 76, 82, 85, 116–118,
123, 135, 166, 206, 230, 252,
264; humanity of, 65, 66, 81,
82, 85, 117, 118, 123, 139, 145,
146, 163, 201, 205–210, 218,
239, 254, 274, 279; imitation
of, 163, 329; Incarnation of,
66, 207; as judge, 71, 81, 82, 85;
as Lamb, 71, 86, 89, 92, 138,
143, 146, 152, 156, 163, 169,
176, 179, 185, 188, 190, 205,
252, 257, 264, 312, 320, 328,
333–336, 348, 355; love for, 64,
100, 115, 188, 192, 196, 336;
love of, 29, 64–66, 75, 85, 116,
123, 138, 139, 188, 247, 284,
304, 320; as mediator, 50, 106,
108, 307; and mercy, 66, 71,
85, 86, 276; persecution of, 47,
76, 246; and redemption, 53,
54, 246, 247, 284, 287, 308;
resurrection of, 68, 82; return
of, 70, 71, 118, 119; sacrifice
of, 52, 59; and salvation, 59,
70, 151, 239; sent, 51, 52, 70,
117, 252, 253, 276, 278, 288;
and sin, 29, 50–52, 65, 188; as

sun, 206, 209, 212, 215, 229,
230, 271; teaching of, 69, 70,
77, 78, 105, 106, 109, 116, 122,
123, 136, 140, 143, 145, 159,
163, 167, 168, 188, 190, 192,
195–197, 200–201, 206, 221,
222, 225, 239, 250, 252, 262,
266, 289, 291, 303–305, 323,
329, 330, 332, 335, 355; and
Truth, 51, 65, 66, 67, 70, 75,
76, 78, 86, 87, 96, 97, 100, 103,
105, 106, 107, 109, 116, 118,
123, 132, 133, 136, 138, 140,
143, 155, 156, 159, 163, 167,
188, 190, 192, 195, 196, 197,
200, 201, 202, 212, 214, 221,
222, 223, 225, 233, 235, 245,
248, 250, 251, 252, 262, 264,
270, 275, 280, 285, 289, 290,
291, 293, 303, 304, 305, 308,
309, 310, 312, 319, 323, 326,
329, 330, 334, 335, 337, 339,
342, 345, 346, 354, 357, 361;
union with, 61, 116; as vine,
61, 62, 303; as Way, 66, 67, 70,
105, 270, 285, 304, 329.
Song of Songs, 8:7, 189.
Soul, cf. also Desire,
Enlightenment, Perfection;
and affections, 64, 65, 138,
337; ascent of, 64, 118, 119,
126, 135, 140, 162, 186, 296,
299, 301, 302, 307, 357; care of,
256, 258, 265, 293, 323; and
charity, 43, 147, 164, 252; as
city, 299, 301, 310, 321;
creation of, 26, 42, 48, 84, 104,
180, 185, 261; death of, 95, 98,
175, 301, 317, 350, 353;
deceived, 91, 98, 100, 110, 111,

129, 159, 187, 200, 202, 210, 211, 284, 285, 348, 349; dignity of, 48, 103, 104, 185, 186, 211, 261, 332; fishing for, 308–310; food of, 140, 141, 145, 146, 163, 177, 181, 190, 192, 195, 201, 211, 216, 235, 239, 244, 251, 279, 293, 294, 322, 351; goal of, 42, 101, 143, 151, 263, 270; God in, 36, 42, 46, 75, 107, 108, 116, 168, 179, 211, 320, 366; in God, 46, 211, 227, 266, 299, 325, 364–366; and grace, 98, 104, 108; harming of, 48, 171, 218, 227, 264, 266, 306, 332, 334, 335; as image of God, 26, 46, 48, 84, 103, 180, 185, 261, 365; imperfection of, 102, 114, 118–122, 124, 187, 200, 281, 297, 299, 301–303, 313, 335, 336, 362; joy of, 83–85, 92, 129, 132, 134, 144, 147, 155, 158, 163–168, 177, 182, 189, 190, 199, 200, 227, 264, 270, 279, 290, 292; light in, 48, 57, 79, 180, 181, 293, 310, 322, 350, 354; and love, 25, 30, 41, 43, 57, 61, 62, 64, 70, 82, 100, 103, 116, 125, 136, 137, 142, 148, 157, 162, 208, 265, 273, 294, 295, 310, 325, 351; needs of, 129, 130, 251, 322, 324, 336, 366; powers of, 60, 73, 105, 108, 109, 111, 113, 118, 137, 148, 158, 180, 181, 222, 246, 310, 361; purification of, 191, 304; salvation of, 25, 33, 39, 40, 57–60, 64, 70, 75, 77, 82–84, 108, 109, 127, 139–143, 151, 152, 155, 157, 159, 168,

175, 177, 178, 180–182, 187, 189, 192, 195, 197, 200–203, 212, 213, 216, 223, 228, 232, 234, 247, 258, 261, 264, 266, 269, 272, 275, 276, 293, 300, 304, 328, 335, 337, 343, 353; and sin, 64, 65, 75, 244, 257, 261, 262, 264, 271, 273, 285, 297, 300, 301, 341; spouse of, 45, 46, 94, 184; stages of, 111, 118, 119, 134, 141, 144, 147, 160, 162, 163, 180, 187, 194, 281, 296; state of, 140, 211, 362; suffering of, 28, 30, 99, 154, 164, 168, 192, 263, 302–306, 319, 322, 347; unworthiness of, 48, 129, 133, 134, 166, 187, 210, 232, 265, 293, 295, 303, 304; and virtue, 130, 141, 142, 144, 147, 159, 167, 229, 289.

Spirituality, and condemnation, 298; and perfection, 169; and poverty, 315–316, 318, 321; selfish, 115, 120, 121, 128, 130, 132, 162, 183, 200, 201, 362; and sensitivity, 211; stages of, 64, 105, 160, 161, 164, 166, 167, 170, 179, 187, 195, 281, 299, 362.

Stephen, 172, 322.

Suffering, cf. also Sin; acceptance of, 46, 58, 100, 137, 144, 146, 150, 154, 163, 187, 190, 263, 303; and atonement, 51, 52, 59, 81, 361; delivered from, 284; deserving of, 93, 187, 344; and desire, 29, 33, 37, 42, 45, 50, 54, 179, 304; escape from, 90, 91, 323, 348; fear of,

101, 111, 112, 114, 136, 142;
finite, 93, 138, 278, 361; fruits
of, 62, 139, 176, 187, 278, 304;
of hell, 79–82, 85–87, 91, 260,
268, 271; and life, 106, 176;
and love, 30, 33, 58, 99, 149,
306; permitted, 78, 93, 282; of
Son, 52, 81, 106, 138, 139, 143,
146, 152, 179, 180, 193, 214,
232, 246, 252, 253, 279, 304,
307, 320, 321, 329; of servants,
31, 45, 91, 98, 307, 362; source
of, 27, 98, 178, 263, 319, 323;
value of, 28, 29; of Word, 278.
Sylvester, 214, 222, 226.

Taurisano, 91, 283, 317, 339.
Tears, of death, 162, 362; and
fear, 161, 162; of fire, 161, 168,
169, 170, 171, 182; fruits of,
161, 169, 170, 178, 179, 182;
infinite, 170, 171, 176; kinds
of, 160, 161, 164, 166, 167, 170,
171, 179; sensual, 162, 163,
167; and sin, 161, 164, 165,
166, 171, 174, 182, 229, 230,
235, 255, 301; for sinners, 71,
297, 298; source of, 161, 166,
175, 362; stages of, 161, 165,
169, 171, 177, 178, 362.
Temperance, 37.
Temptation, 132, 142, 152, 162,
168, 189, 233, 260; allowed by
God, 87, 88, 93, 150.
1 Thessalonians, 4:3, 324.
Thomas of Aquinas, 155, 205,
210, 222, 339.
Time, and freedom to choose,
32, 60, 62, 115, 176, 260, 263,
333; lent, 104, 172, 217; selling

of, 74; use of, 111, 159, 264,
268; wasting of, 313.
1 Timothy, 6:10, 316.
2 Timothy, 4:8, 266.
Tobias, 13:1–5, 56.
Tommaso della Fonte, 91, 203,
296.
Trinity, 49, 149, 152, 153, 210,
278, 289, 295, 328, 364, 365,
366.
Truth, cf. also God, Knowledge,
Son; eternal, 28, 32, 44, 47, 57,
59, 63, 68, 144, 151, 158, 160,
169, 188, 202, 203, 366;
following of, 67, 90, 109;
First, 27, 48, 160, 163, 187;
light of, 33, 69, 70, 122; and
love, 33, 37, 43; seeking of, 25,
109; way of, 69, 70, 71, 87, 90,
103, 141, 142, 184, 185, 233,
333, 348.
Tuldo, Nicholas di, cf. under
Niccolò di Tuldo.

Understanding, 32, 49, 65, 73,
103, 108, 113, 153, 181, 299,
301, 310; and delusion, 94,
104; enlightened, 92, 287, 295,
364; eye of, 56, 57, 94, 104,
149, 156, 185, 191, 249, 363,
364; light of, 45, 108, 126, 180,
200, 201, 237, 263, 270, 365;
spiritual, 293; and will, 221.
Union, cf. also God; in God, 61,
69, 76, 77, 85, 106, 116, 117,
119, 135, 146, 152, 166, 206,
212, 218, 264, 295, 320, 365; in
love, 28, 29, 32, 37, 110, 115,
154, 163, 171, 181, 190, 362; of
natures, 46, 52, 53, 59, 69, 86,

and love, 108, 148, 154, 181;
ordered, 141; selfish, 42, 43,
78, 92, 122, 141, 158, 163, 178,
186–189, 193, 196–198, 203,
323, 335, 336, 340, 341, 342,
343, 353; sensual, 93, 178; of
servants, 91, 98, 100, 133, 137,
142, 151, 191, 221, 275; and
sin, 105, 113, 299, 301; and
suffering, 263; of Trinity, 49.

William of Flete, 190, 203.

Wisdom, of God, 287, 290, 313,
353, 364, 366; and ministers,
206, 226; of Son, 49, 68, 69,
119, 136, 201, 206, 211, 222,
227, 277, 289, 295, 365.

Wisdom, 5:18, 234; 10:6, 237.

Works (Actions), dead, 94, 99;
and endurance, 42; evil, 103,
173, 176; finite, 43, 197; fruits
of, 42, 58, 61, 86, 140, 286;
good, 95, 115, 128, 129, 142,
287, 304, 310; infinite, 42; of
penance, 42, 44; rewarded, 80,
115, 129, 144, 146, 155, 298,
322, 346; and salvation, 127,
300; of sin, 48; of virtue, 39,
43, 173, 310.

World, choosing of, 98;
delusions of, 285; judging of,
71, 82, 190; knowledge of,
30–31, 185; light to, 206, 209;
mercy to, 54, 55, 63, 71, 90,
151, 159, 160, 201, 255, 272,
275, 276, 277, 307, 361, 363;
needs of, 27, 37; and
persecution, 47, 55, 189;
pleasures of, 67, 89, 90, 96, 97,
98, 99, 104, 108, 141, 225, 232,
262, 267, 290, 291, 297, 299,

310, 323, 330, 334; redemption
of, 44; reproved, 69, 77, 81;
rule of, 73, 287; salvation of,
49, 57; scorn for, 45, 97, 142,
251, 260, 263, 291, 323, 330,
340; scorns God, 46; and
selfish love, 35–36, 56;
servants of, 100, 101; serving
of, 37, 235, 251, 280, 314; and
sin, 58, 238, 271; trust in, 290.

Word, blood of, 206, 208, 264,
316, 330, 359, 363; body of,
206, 361; as bridge, 58, 63, 66,
76, 90, 105, 285, 361; death of,
151, 188, 232, 289, 320, 327;
divinity of, 206; as example,
54; following of, 60, 62, 77, 92,
97, 116, 188, 291, 309, 337, 346;
as food, 67, 145, 206; as gate,
266, 276, 328, 330; and God,
61, 135, 152; and God's
goodness, 94, 279, 286;
humanity of, 117, 139, 206,
252, 310, 320; incarnate, 105,
130, 152, 188, 206, 278, 288,
289, 293, 359; as judge, 81; and
Law, 112, 156, 157; and man,
26, 50, 76, 105; man in, 61, 85;
as mediator, 106, 282;
obedience of, 156, 188, 252,
253, 278, 327, 330, 332, 333,
353, 354, 359; sent, 51, 52, 214,
253, 273, 274, 278, 288, 353,
361; sight of, 117; and sin, 218,
288; teaching of, 136, 152, 163,
168, 291, 293, 309, 354.

Zeboiim, 237.
Zechariah, 10–11, 232.
Zoar, 237.

398